Interdisciplinary Research in Jurisprudence and Constitutionalism

Edited by Stephan Kirste, Anne van Aaken, Michael Anderheiden, and Pasquale Policastro

AF847958

ARCHIV FÜR RECHTS- UND SOZIALPHILOSOPHIE

ARCHIVES FOR PHILOSOPHY OF LAW AND SOCIAL PHILOSOPHY

ARCHIVES DE PHILOSOPHIE DU DROIT ET DE PHILOSOPHIE SOCIALE

ARCHIVO DE FILOSOFÍA JURÍDICA Y SOCIAL

Herausgegeben von der Internationalen Vereinigung

für Rechts- und Sozialphilosophie (IVR)

Redaktion: Dr. Annette Brockmöller, LL. M.

Beiheft 127

Interdisciplinary Research in Jurisprudence and Constitutionalism

Edited by Stephan Kirste, Anne van Aaken,
Michael Anderheiden, and Pasquale Policastro

Franz Steiner Verlag

Nomos

Bibliografische Information der Deutschen Nationalbibliothek:
Die Deutsche Nationalbibliothek verzeichnet diese Publikation in der Deutschen Nationalbibliografie; detaillierte bibliografische Daten sind im Internet über <http://dnb.d-nb.de> abrufbar.

Dieses Werk einschließlich aller seiner Teile ist urheberrechtlich geschützt. Jede Verwertung außerhalb der engen Grenzen des Urheberrechtsgesetzes ist unzulässig und strafbar.
© Franz Steiner Verlag, Stuttgart 2012
Druck: Druckhaus Nomos, Sinzheim
Gedruckt auf säurefreiem, alterungsbeständigem Papier.
Printed in Germany.
Franz Steiner Verlag: ISBN 978-3-515-09941-7
Nomos Verlag: ISBN 978-3-8329-7183-0

Table of Contents

Introduction

For centuries scholars and students of law had no problem with law's interdisciplinary character: They accepted the artes liberales and theology, later philosophy, as a given precondition and part of their research subject. The implications of these fields of academia were part of legal argument; the methods of logic, topic, and rhetoric, as of theology were methods of law. Finally, Leibniz applied his mathesis universalis on the law. Even the gradual replacement of theology and the artes liberales by philosophy did not change the overall dependency of law on extralegal academic scholarship.

Things started to change when neither theology nor philosophy were regarded as the "leading" faculty anymore. When in the 18th century medicine changed its methods towards becoming a science, it emancipated itself the same moment from the methods and arguments of philosophy and theology. The same step became available to legal academics. The German name "Rechtswissenschaft" bears witness to the aspirations of lawyers working in the enlightenment's spirit. But even then many scholars of law stuck to philosophy and theology. Until the 1750s Samuel Pufendorf's magisterial "De iure naturae et gentium libri octo" (1672), remained the most successful textbook in law. And in the 1780s Immanuel Kant's treatise on legal philosophy was eagerly awaited by as many lawyers as friends of philosophy. The shift of natural law in the title from Gustav Hugo's "Naturrecht als eine Philosophie des positive Rechts" to Georg Wilhelm Friedrich Hegel's "Grundlinien der Philosophie des Rechts – Naturrecht und Staatswissenschaft im Grundrisse" marks more than a decrease of the importance of natural law; at the same time it signifies a separation of jurisprudence and philosophy and finally the emergence of positivism. Friedrich Carl von Savigny, although himself influenced by Kant, denied philosophy its influence on jurisprudence. Historicism became the precursor of positivism in the 19th century. Since Marx considered law to be part of a class-dependent superstructure of society, all disciplines analyzing the social basis were considered useful for analyzing the law as well. If law is defined by its goals, and the goals as serving some social interests – as in Jhering's concept of law – sociological methods and teleological interpretation were introduced into jurisprudence and hindered the separation of disciplines. When in 1844 Robert von Mohl started his interdisciplinary periodical "Zeitschrift für die Gesammte Staatswissenschaft" he wanted to fight this trend, include all sciences related to the state and "never let go economics" as far as they concerned the state.[1] On the long run, however, von Mohl was not suc-

1 Robert von Mohl: Vorwort. In: Zeitschrift für die Gesammte Staatswissenschaft 1 (1844), pp. 4 f.: "Es sind sämmtliche Staatswissenschaften, welche wir zu besprechen beabsichtigen. Somit Staatsrecht und Völkerrecht; politische Oekonomie in ihrem ganzen Umfange, Polizeiwissenschaft, Politik; Statistik und Staatengeschichte. Wir setzen uns dabei vor, einerseits die Erscheinungen des Lebens mit dem Blicke der Wissenschaft aufzufassen und zu beurtheilen; andererseits über die theoretischen Fragen aus den genannten Gebieten, so wie sie sich geltend machen oder wenn sie eine neue und nähere Erörterung verdienen, unsere Ansicht zu entwickeln … Dass wir die privatwirthschaftlichen Fächer nicht nach ihrem technischen Theile heranziehen, versteht sich. Nur in so ferne sie in das Staatsleben eingreifen, sei es durch Lieferung von Stoff zu staatswissenschaftlichen und polizeilichen Betrachtungen, sei es durch Forderungen, welche sie im Interesse ihrer Organisation an den Staat stellen, können sie in unserer Zeitschrift besprochen werden".

cessful. As early as 1876 Lorenz von Stein lamented, "We do not have a science of the state but only jurisprudence".[2] In the science of civil law, the historical school turned into the Pandectists, rather preparing a codification that later became the German civil code ("Bürgerliches Gesetzbuch") than unfolding the purity of the roman sources.

Purity instead was meant to be a feature of legal dogmatics themselves – at least in the eyes of Hans Kelsen's legal theory.[3] Methodological plurality became so overwhelming that H. Kelsen had enormous success in asking for a pure theory of law. Kelsen was not searching for a "theory of pure law", however. Neither did he believe in the separate content of law, independent from influences from the outside, and be it for the sake of argument. Accordingly, his approach supported the differentiation of the so-called basic disciplines of law for its investigation following a descriptive perspective as in the sociology of law, a historical perspective like in legal history etc. Nor did he believe in legal argument as a part of science: It remained impossible to translate legal evaluations into mathematical numbers and mere logic. Every such attempt of conceptual clarity and rigidity proved at best to be sterile and out of touch with reality. So, lawyers had to find their own way of argumentation, their own methodology, and their new place in academia.

After World War II a common move to re-idealization united lawyers across legal cultures: legal argument was again based on philosophical and theological grounds as the second renaissance of natural law in the 20th century proved, schools of history of law became as influential as those looking for a scientific approach to legal argument, sustained by, e.g., cybernetics. This development deeply questioned legal scholarly self-understanding, as Dieter Grimm, one of 1970s precursors of interdisciplinarity in law put it.[4] According to Grimm, it was the claim to social justice that called for an interdisciplinary approach of jurisprudence.[5] In the 1970s

2 Lorenz von Stein: Gegenwart und Zukunft der Rechts- und Staatswissenschaft Deutschlands. Stuttgart 1876, p. V: "Denn wer die deutsche Universität kennt, der muß mir zugeben, wir haben nun einmal keine Staatswissenschaft, wir haben an ihrer Stelle an unsern Universitäten nur eine Rechtswissenschaft. Formuliren und bestimmen Sie den Begriff beider wie Sie wollen, das Recht als Recht ist bei weitem die Hauptsache, ja die ausschließliche Sache der gesammten Berufsbildung für unser öffentliches Leben. Die Universität versteht von diesem öffentlichen Leben nur das, was sich als Recht formuliren, interpretiren, dociren läßt".

3 Hans Kelsen: Reine Rechtslehre. Studienausgabe der 1. Auflage von 1934. Hrsg. v. M. Jestaedt. Tübingen 2008, S. 15: "Wenn sie sich als eine 'reine' Lehre vom Recht bezeichnet, so darum, weil sie eine nur auf das Recht gerichtete Erkenntnis sicherstellen und weil sie aus dieser Erkenntnis alles ausscheiden möchte, was nicht zu dem exakt als Recht bestimmten Gegenstande gehört. Das heißt: Sie will die Rechtswissenschaft von allen ihr fremden Elementen befreien".

4 Dieter Grimm: Rechtswissenschaft und Nachbarwissenschaften. München 1973, p. 7: the debate with the neighbor disciplines would be "ein Ausdruck schwindender Selbstsicherheit der Rechtswissenschaft. Vor siebzig Jahren noch hätte sie die Frage [nach den Berührungspunkten mit den Nachbarwissenschaften, S. K.] als Angriff auf ihre Wissenschaftlichkeit zurückgewiesen. Wissenschaftliche Aussagen schienen nur dann möglich, wenn das Recht ausschließlich aus sich selbst verstanden wurde. Das methodische Bemühen richtete sich gerade darauf, die juristische Erkenntnis von allen fremden Einflüssen zu reinigen. Ethik, Politik, Wirtschaft gingen den 'Juristen als solchen' nichts an. Grammatik und Logik waren das einzig erlaubte Handwerkszeug. Der politisch-soziale Begründungszusammenhang, in dem das Recht steht, wurde für seine wissenschaftliche Behandlung bedeutungslos … Mit den Nachbarn verkehrte man nicht".

5 Grimm op. cit. p. 7: "Eine 'reine' Rechtslehre war freilich schon damals eine Täuschung … Das

everything was at offer, including now legal scholars consulting the arguments of psychology or the social sciences for their work. The Critical Legal Studies movement in the US was the American variation of this shift of paradigms in jurisprudence. In the 1980s the paradoxical situation can be observed that on the one hand interdisciplinarity appears to be a "repairing phenomena to overcome the epistemological disciplinarity"[6] postmodernism with its emphasis on contingency took hold in lawyers' circles as well.

It seems that under the conditions of functionally differentiated social systems and their respective sciences, interdisciplinarity – although it is considered to be necessary – has never received a convincing methodological and institutional foundation. It is time to ask where we stand today and elaborate these. The present volume contains surveys in this field and exemplary interdisciplinary studies, mainly in the area of constitution and economy. To this purpose a group of mainly younger scholars convened at the Krakow World Congress of the International Association of Legal Philosophy (IVR) in 2007 and met again in a larger setting at the "Centre for Interdisciplinary Studies" at Bielefeld/Germany (ZIF) in 2009. At Cracow the group met for a workshop entitled "Metatheory of Law: Import into and Export from Jurisprudence"; some of its members also came together with distinguished scholars for another special working group on "Constitutionalism Between Economic and Legal Theory: Factual and Theoretical Complexity in the Process of Globalization and European Integration". Both groups held special opening and final sessions together. In this reader the revised papers of the two groups are published together. The responsibility for the papers of the group working on the general subject of "Metatheory of law" was vested in Stephan Kirste and Michael Anderheiden, the management for the group working on "Constitutionalism Between Economic and Legal Theory: Factual and Theoretical Complexity in the Process of Globalization and European Integration" was taken care of by Anne van Aaken and Pasquale Policastro, who also held the responsibility of the respective parts of this volume.

The first part of this volume provides more general investigations in the possibilities, difficulties and limitations of interdisciplinary research using sociological, philosophical, historical and economic arguments. These methods are the topic *Sanne Taekema* and *Bart van Klink* ("Limits and Possibilities of Interdisciplinary Re-

Problem einer gerechten Sozialordnung läßt sich immer seltener unmittelbar durch Rechtsetzung lösen. Gerechtigkeit wird vielmehr zunehmend wirtschafts-, sozial- und bildungspolitisch vermittelt. Im selben Maß verliert das Recht seine Gerechtigkeitsunmittelbarkeit und nimmt instrumentellen Charakter an. Seine Steuerungsfunktion, die neben die alte Garantiefunktion tritt, kann es aber nur erfüllen, wenn es fähig ist, die Komplexität der zu steuernden Sachbereiche in sich aufzunehmen. Es partizipiert notwendig an der Verwissenschaftlichung der Welt insgesamt".

6 Mittelstraß, Jürgen: Interdisziplinarität – mehr als ein bloßes Ritual? in: Universitas 41 (1986), pp. 1052–1055, 1052: "Der Ruf nach Interdisziplinarität setzt voraus, daß die Grenzen der Disziplinen zu Erkenntnisgrenzen zu werden drohen und daß es ... so etwas wie die Einheit der Wissenschaft oder die Einheit der wissenschaftlichen Rationalität nicht mehr gibt. Im einen Fall ist Interdisziplinarität ein Reparaturphänomen zur Aufhebung erkenntnisbegrenzender Disziplinarität, im anderen Fall ein Kompensationsphänomen zur Wiedergutmachung gegenüber einer Idee, die etwa für Leibniz noch das Selbstverständliche war, für uns hingegen nur noch eine Erinnerung an unentwickelte wissenschaftliche Verhältnisse oder eine Utopie ist".

search into Law. A Comparison of Pragmatist and Positivist Views") deal with. As part of their broader investigation of interdisciplinary research in jurisprudence, they discuss the perspectives of a skeptical, positivist view vs. a more optimistic theory about the possibilities of knowledge-exchange between disciplines, presented by pragmatist thinkers such as Dewey and Putnam. In the end, they elaborate a dynamic model of interdisciplinarity. In his paper "Abstraction and Idealization as bases of Interdisciplinary Research Including Jurisprudence" *Michael Anderheiden* explores the possibility of long-term interdisciplinary research (LIR). Although it is generally seen as a promising endeavor it must be asked why it does not either produce a new discipline or if unsuccessful is terminated after short time. After consulting Luhmann on the issue the paper turns to mapping kinds of LIR and then to a philosophical answer to the question: For rational researchers it may be efficient to participate in LIR because it allows to give up some of the less important idealizations of one's own discipline, e.g. the law, in return for fresh insights and valuable hints from other disciplines. The arguments for this point will crucially rely on the difference between abstraction and idealization as proposed by O. O'Neill.

What forms a discipline and which mechanisms can transcend the walls of differences in language, method, professionalism, are questions *Stephan Kirste* asks in his article. On the basis of a distinction between epistemological and organizational interdisciplinarity he does not rely on abstract and "bridge building" concepts, but rather on different forms of institutionalized interdisciplinary discourse from frequent contacts during scientific conferences, research networks to building up new sub-disciplines such as the basic disciplines of law (legal history, philosophy of law, sociology of law).

Elucidation about the interdisciplinary communication between political sciences and jurisprudence is *Oliver Lembcke's* goal in his contribution ("Balancing Law and Politics – The Contribution of Political Theory"). Politicization of law and juridification of politics are matters that necessarily need an interdisciplinary investigation. In his view, political sciences can help jurisprudence in the critical reflexion of its normative foundations, the political impact on legislation and the ethical preconditions of legal decision making.

In her presentation *Vasiliki Christou* takes legal theory to give meaning to law as whole and as an integral system by filtering the information coming from other disciplines. By means of example she focuses on the insights that jurisprudence gets from philosophy of language. She points out that speech-act theory is of analytical importance to the interpreter of the free speech principle but due to its normative open-endedness is not in a position to dictate solutions to practical problems. Christou further shows that there is little gain in thinking of the legal sentence itself as a performative, because questions of rightness and morality are set aside and are replaced by an emphasis on the expressive function of law. In this way, thinking of a legal sentence as a performative one lays emphasis on a metaethical, instead of a substantive moral analysis of law.

Juliana Neuenschwander-Magalhães ("Law and Cinema: Knowing Law Through Art") reports interesting results of her research at the Federal University of Rio de Janeiro on the presentation of dictatorial regimes in the movies. Far from merely describing the concept of law in the plots of the respective films, on the basis of systems theory, she tries to substantiate the assumption that legal validity can also be determined by the structural coupling of law and cinema.

In his article "Collective Rights – A Case Study of Interdisciplinary Approach in Jurisprudence" *Miodrag Jovanović* exemplifies the shortfalls of Kelsen's Pure Theory of Law, analyzing norms that entitle minorities or other groups' rights. These norms cannot define the subject of the right, but have to presuppose it and accept the social definition of the groups themselves. Because of this structure, jurisprudence too cannot restrict itself to merely legal methods.

Though economic analysis of law applies concepts and categories of economics on law, the mere descriptive economic analysis of law does not ask to use efficiency as a normative principle in law. Still if the principle of efficiency is used in law questions arise as to how this principle is placed towards other legal principles, esp. justice and equity, and how it is used in law making and practice. *Klaus Mathis* gives some answers to these questions in his "Efficiency as a Normative Principle".

In his paper "Import, Export, and Multilateral Translation: Methodological Lessons from an Economic Analysis of Paternalism in Contract Law" *Péter Cserne* focuses on the conceptual and methodological background of an economic approach to paternalism in contract law. He takes up the different legal provisions of usury laws to serve consumer sovereignty in Europe and compares them to the many aspects of "paternalism" discussed primarily in economics. His in-depth discussion aims to serve as a case study to a more general problem: the role of inter- and multidisciplinary research in jurisprudence and legal studies in general.

The papers concentrating on Constitutionalism in the second part of this volume are unified by the question of how to analyze constitutionalism, especially in the process of Europeanization and Internationalization. The first two papers concentrate on challenges and methods of constitutionalism. *Anne van Aaken* takes a functional view on constitutionalism by using an old categorization of Hermann Kantorowicz for legal science. By clarifying the different methodological statements possible in law (normative statements in legal philosophy and policy, social science statements, and doctrinal statements), this permits to outline opening windows and connecting bridges between law and social science in the debate on constitutionalism and on international constitutionalism. Indeed, the use of common principles in the perspective of constitutionalism is deemed to be necessary but not sufficient. The search of the function of the legal institutions, related to the underlying problem structure, is an essential activity which ought to be performed to a growing extent especially to be international constitutionalists, in the attempt to concentrate on the values we aim to attain by means of law.

Pasquale Policastro outlines the possible connection between meta-theories of law and theories that he has been considering as complementary theories, and namely from one side constitutionalism and from the other side economic analysis. Interconnecting those theories permits to conceptually answer the question of the respondence of the economic system to the values of constitutionalism and vice versa. Under a poietic system of a dynamic constitution, considered by the author as a constitution which relies on the possibility to transform the rules concerning the influences of the political, social and economic processes, an open interpretation which also takes into account economic theory is possible. However, the results of the economic models may be used within the legal reasoning only after the transposition of the yielding of the economic models, within the terms of legal reasoning. For this reason it is essential to find adequate methods to match complementary theories with our object theories without leading to paradoxes. To this regard, the paradigms of constitutionalism, and more in general, the research of a hypertext to overarch between theories appear worth of a growing consideration.

The other papers focus on the process of Europeanization. *Markku Kiikeri* understands the European legal system as a legal-cultural system, elaborating a framework for future research. For him, in order to understand and explain the phenomenon of the European legal system, a "legal-cultural approach" and the theory of the European legal system needs to be taken seriously instead of the institutional, legal "order" and pragmatic point of view. By taking this approach he then asks, what were and are the basic legal philosophical and comparative approaches within the system and how the court thought and thinks now itself as a social actor as well as what would be the basic concepts to be considered and why. The approach to consciousness and to the intentionality of the activity of the European lawyer plays to this regard a paramount role in this cultural-spiritual integration, in which need and reality appear as a consequence of the seminal decisions of the European Court of Justice.

Jelena von Achenbach focuses on the democratic principle of the European Union and elaborates a methodological approach to develop a concept of a democratic supranational legislature by means of a critical and progressive analysis of the co-decision procedure. By looking at the democratic principle as a falsification standard for the setting-up of the organizational constitutional procedures and institutions of the European Union, she is also able to constructively criticize them.

Raffaele Lapenta, who takes the move from a criticism concerning the possibility to grant rights and freedoms outside the range of a formally defined constitution, concentrates on the right of defense in the framework of multilevel constitutionalism. After comparing several national constitutions finding stronger rights protection under those than under the European Treaties, including the European Union Charter of Fundamental Rights, he comes to the conclusion that multi-level protection of human rights may also weaken those very same rights. For this reason it seems that the standards of protection of specific fundamental rights, such as the rights to defense, granted in the national legal orders, ought to be seen as a baseline to be rendered more substantive by their protection at the European level.

Teresa Freixes and *Mercè Sales* analyze equality and discrimination under multilevel constitutionalism (Pernice). After outlining the main features of the concept, they illustrate the reality of the phenomenon of multilevel constitutionalism, by means of a practical case: equality in the multilevel system. They analyze the international, the European, the national as well as sub-national norms and case-law on the subject-matter (with a focus on Spain) and find that by this way of analysis, since norms and application differ, it is possible to apply the legal system that best protects the fundamental right concerned. This implies the necessity not only of a case-to-case analysis, but a clear attention to the different branches of law concerned by the cases in question.

Put together the articles provide for an overview of in-depth analysis in interdisciplinary research on law at large and constitutionalism taken as an example. The wide array of open questions, however, calls for continuation in some follow-up volumes.

Stephan Kirste, Anne van Aken, Michael Anderheiden, Pasquale Policastro

Part I

Import – Export: Interdisciplinary Approach to Law

Edited by
S. Kirste and *M. Anderheiden*

Bart van Klink / Sanne Taekema

Limits and Possibilities of Interdisciplinary Research into Law

A Comparison of Pragmatist and Positivist Views

Abstract:
In diesem Aufsatz werden die Möglichkeiten und Beschränkungen interdisziplinärer Forschung im Bereich der Rechtswissenschaft erörtert. Inwiefern ist die Rechtswissenschaft imstande, Konzepte und Ideen aus anderen wissenschaftlichen Disziplinen, wie der Soziologie, der Psychologie, der Philosophie, der Ökonomie und der Literaturwissenschaft, zu inkorporieren? Diese Frage wird anhand einer Konfrontation zweier entgegengestellter Positionen behandelt: die pragmatische Position (Dewey und Putnam), die von der Vergleichbarkeit und Vereinbarkeit von Theorien ausgeht, auf der einen Seite, und die positivistische Position (Kelsen und Luhmann), die die Grenzen der wechselseitigen Verständigung und Auswechslung betont, auf der anderen Seite. Im Anschluss an dieser Diskussion wird ein dynamisches Interdisziplinaritätsmodell präsentiert und werden Vor- und Nachteile der verschiedenen Typen der interdisziplinären Forschung diskutiert.

1 Facts and Values

To a growing extent, legal scholars seem to be dissatisfied with established disciplinary boundaries and turn to other disciplines, such as sociology (Cotterrell 2006), psychology (Wagenaar, Van Koppen & Crombag 1993), philosophy (Alexy 2003), economics (Posner 2007) and even literature studies (White 1985), for inspiration. In law faculties all over the world multidisciplinary and interdisciplinary research groups are operative, such as the Jurisprudence and Social Policy program at the University of California, Berkeley, or the Institute of Criminology at Cambridge University. In the hope of increasing their chances to acquire a grant, applicants nowadays try to cut a dash with promises of combining insights from many different sources (Vick 2004, 171). One may wonder who will undertake the important but time-consuming task of analyzing and classifying the existing body of legal norms in the future, when legal scholars are getting more and more reluctant to do so. However exciting these new research directions may appear, a fundamental question which deserves more attention is: What are the limits and possibilities of interdisciplinary research into law? Can concepts and methods from one discipline directly be transplanted into another discipline? What is lost and what is gained when insights from different origins are combined?

In this article, we want to explore what might make interdisciplinary research possible, on the one hand, and what makes it difficult or even impossible, on the other hand. Rather than pursuing these questions in the abstract, we investigate two theoretical positions that seem to offer radically different approaches to this question: pragmatism versus legal positivism. We have selected these approaches because they differ in particular on the issue whether facts and values can be separated or not, which seems to determine to a large extent – together with some other factors which will be mentioned below – their view on the limits and possibilities of interdisciplinary legal research. First, we will discuss the pragmatist theory, especially of John Dewey, which offers an optimistic view of combining different scientific disciplines (section 2). Rejecting a strict fact-value distinction, Dewey sees plenty of opportunities to combine insights from empirical and normative approaches. Secondly, we will discuss two positivist positions which both posit serious limitations on interdisciplinary legal research: to begin with, Kelsen's pure theory of law and, subsequently, Luhmann's system theory (section 3). Especially Hans Kelsen is skeptical about interdisciplinary legal research, because in his view no meaningful exchanges can be established between different types of disciplines. Whereas the sociology of law, in Kelsen's view, deals with law solely as an empirical phenomenon, that is as power, the science of law approaches law from a normative point of view as a body of norms that ought to be obeyed. Niklas Luhmann, in his earlier work particularly, takes a more moderate position. Finally, some of the major limits and possibilities of different types of legal research – ranging from strictly monodisciplinary to highly integrated interdisciplinary research – are discussed in the light of the foregoing discussion between pragmatism and positivism (section 4).

2 Possibilities of Interdisciplinary Research According to Pragmatism

Pragmatist philosophy is a good starting point for exploring the possibilities of interdisciplinary research for at least two reasons. First, pragmatism is generally suspicious of dichotomies, which also applies to the boundaries between disciplines. Second, pragmatism proposes a general scientific method which is meant to apply to all knowledge.

The classical pragmatism of William James and John Dewey is a theory that addresses questions of scientific truth and inquiry in the context of problem-solving in everyday experience (James 1975, 34–35; Dewey 1984, 178).

It[1] sees science as a mundane practice that is continuous with other activities people engage in. This view of science, to which we will return shortly, comes with a specific view of (scientific) reasoning in which strict separations or dichotomies are rejected: distinctions should only be made insofar as they are useful. Especially in Dewey's theory, the rejection of dichotomies is a central theme which is supported by a holistic view of the world as we experience it. Although it makes sense to distinguish categories such as for instance 'thinking' and 'doing' from each other, we should beware of turning such categories into separate entities: in reality they are connected in many ways and the categories are only relevant because and when they help us to reason more clearly. In the context of this paper, the most important separations to be rejected according to pragmatism are the separation between different types of science and the separation between fact and value.

In Dewey's work the continuity between inquiry in the natural sciences and inquiry in social and moral subjects is a major theme (1984, 201; 1988, 178). His belief that both physical science and moral 'science' would benefit immensely from the realization that knowledge of physical goods and knowledge of moral goods are interrelated, is his main drive for developing a theory of experimental inquiry in the

1 We will focus mainly on Dewey's theory because he has addressed the question of scientific disciplines more directly. In addition, we will present Putnam as a contemporary exponent of pragmatist thought.

normative realm. His theory can be described as an extension, a broadening, of the method of physical inquiry into a much wider field. This is true of law as well: what Dewey also calls "logical method" is equally applicable to mathematics, law, or even farming. Although Dewey acknowledges that there is a difference between science and practical reasoning in that scientific disciplines work in a narrowly delineated field and with specific methods and concepts, he believes that the same method can be applied in legal reasoning and judicial decision-making. He does not explicitly consider the differences between legal scholarship and the practice of law, but it is in the line of pragmatist thinking to see scholarship and practice on a continuum.

The pragmatist rejection of the fact-value separation is most forcefully defended by Hilary Putnam. In his formulation, the general claim is that knowledge of facts presumes knowledge of values and, vice versa, knowledge of values presumes knowledge of facts (1995, 14). Putnam's argument takes the form of a criticism of a non-cognitivist theory of ethics. According to non-cognitivists, we cannot know anything about values; values are a matter of commendation or preference which cannot be debated. According to Putnam, non-cognitivists are mistaken in their claim that evaluation of behavior as good or bad can be separated from factual judgments. There is no neat division between the factual characterization of behavior 'what you just did was rude' and evaluation of that behavior 'being rude is bad' (Putnam 2002, 36). Factual and value judgments go together, which can be most clearly shown by looking at criticism of a judgment. The typical way someone denies that his behavior was rude, for example, is by appealing to facts which change the judgment of the situation: "My behavior may have seemed rude, but I could not stop and talk to you because I was late for a meeting."

This thesis is based on the holistic ontology of classical pragmatism: the idea that we find ourselves in the middle of our own experience, in the middle of a world in which fact and value, natural and social factors, humans and other beings are not distinct nor neatly categorized (Dewey 1989, 352). If this experience of the world is taken as the starting point for ontology, the world appears as a whole: distinctions are made for special purposes but do not reflect ontological truths. Although we can in principle distinguish factual judgments from evaluative judgments, many of those judgments are mixed and there is not a clear separating line between the two categories. The examples Putnam uses to illustrate this point are so-called 'thick' moral concepts, such as cruelty or bravery, which are concepts giving a factual and an evaluative judgment at the same time (Putnam 2002, 38–39). To say that someone is cruel combines factual and evaluative elements in such a way they are interdependent, or in Putnam's terms, "entangled" (2002, 43).

The main underlying reason for making a sharp separation between facts and values is the common belief that values are merely subjective or emotive, and that therefore no true knowledge of values is possible. In the pragmatist view, this belief is false: there is no more a sharp separation between the subjective and the objective than there is between fact and value (or practice and theory for that matter). Although value judgments involve subjective appreciation by the individual, they are not merely that, and they may be subject to well-founded criticism. Such criticism is not simply another value judgment; most often, facts are invoked to underpin that criticism. Similarly, factual judgments can be accepted for reasons that are not factual themselves. This is most clear in the case of science: whether a fact is accepted as true is in part a matter of coherence and plausibility in the light of a theory and the clarity and simplicity of the explanation. These are all matters of evaluation.

The rejection of both separations, the one between scientific disciplines and the one between fact and value, is closely connected to the pragmatist view of scientific method. For pragmatists, the core of the scientific method is experimental: by testing hypotheses in experiments, a scientist can determine whether the hypotheses work and therefore hold them to be true. Scientific inquiry is thus regarded as an active process in which proposed solutions to problems are tested; it is also open-ended, because the truth of propositions is provisional and can be refuted by later experiences. Dewey proposes to apply the scientific model of inquiry to all problems, including moral problems (1988, 173). This implies that legal reasoning should also follow the scientific method: a case is a problem for which hypothetical solutions should be formulated and then tested by tracing their foreseeable consequences (Dewey 1998, 361).

The same holds for legal scholarship generally, extending beyond particular practical legal problems. Wherever a problem is perceived, whether practical or theoretical, that problem should be approached by inquiring into its conditions, i.e. how did it come about, and by considering the consequences of possible solutions. One of the questions that arise is to what extent legal solutions can be tested experimentally: does legal scholarship allow for testing in the same way as the natural sciences? Of course, there are limits to what we can test. Social and legal situations cannot be manipulated by a researcher as fully as natural ones can in a laboratory situation. However, there are other ways: small-scale social experiments are possible (as Dewey proved with his Chicago laboratory school in which he tried his pedagogical ideas), and more importantly, researchers can also go through this process imaginatively. By systematically thinking through the consequences of a solution, an experiment can be imitated in imagination. So, although there are small differences between natural and human sciences, they are nevertheless seen as capable of being investigated along the same lines.

In general, therefore, it seems we may conclude that pragmatist theory does not see the difference between disciplines as profound and sees interdisciplinary research as a perfectly normal way of approaching inquiry (without calling it 'interdisciplinary', a phrase which already draws attention to the difference between disciplines). This is slightly too quick, however. Although the experimental method of inquiry is to be applied generally, its starting point in problem-solving has a particularistic side to it as well. Dewey stresses that every problem has its own specific context, but that the relevance of this context is not clear automatically: it is a matter of selective interest (Dewey 1960, 101). Every researcher, consciously but more often unconsciously, makes choices by selecting some contextual elements as relevant and by ignoring others. This need for selection brings in the background of the researcher, including his disciplinary background, as an important determinant of what is seen as relevant and interesting. A person's disciplinary perspective is for numerous reasons, such as the theoretical and cultural traditions on which it draws (Dewey 1960, 99–100), the main lens through which a problem is analyzed.

This attention to context and the selective interest of a researcher in connection to his disciplinary perspective are starting points for an argument that pragmatist theory can make room for disciplines as a relevant category. On the general level of pragmatist philosophy, there is therefore no principled judgment for or against recognizing disciplines. On the one hand, they are a key factor in determining the perspective of a researcher; on the other hand, within all disciplines the general method of scientific inquiry is advocated. This means that pragmatism sees no real obstacles to practicing interdisciplinary research: although the traditions of a scientific discipline provide a specific focus and approach, researchers can overcome the boundaries of their discipline with a creative and critical attitude.[2] The differences between disciplines account for the different starting points of researchers, but as long as they are willing to apply the pragmatic method, they can distinguish between the relevant and the irrelevant aspects of the context of their inquiry and can combine the insights from different disciplines. Applying this to law, Dewey puts forward the idea that "law is through and through a social phenomenon; social in origin, in purpose or end, and in application" (1941, 76). Law should therefore be studied as a social activity in relation to other social activities.

We may conclude that pragmatism sees interdisciplinary research as desirable and is optimistic about the possibilities of doing research that crosses traditional boundaries. There are, however, a number of critical remarks that can be put to pragmatist theory, two of which we will mention briefly.[3] First, there is the matter of the general application of one, logical, method of inquiry to all fields of scholarship. Deweyan pragmatism assumes that all disciplines should work with a consequentialist, problem-oriented method. However, this method of inquiry is not necessarily the right method for legal scholarship in all its forms. From Dewey's perspective, seeing law as primarily a social phenomenon, it makes perfect sense, but there are other views of law which are equally legitimate that call for different methods. If we look at law as a field that is based on texts and arguments revolving around those texts, law has more in common with the methods of the humanities. Textual analysis, interpretation and argumentation instead of experimental testing of hypotheses are then the central methodology. Secondly, established practices of interdisciplinary research show that it is not so easy to be critical of your own perspective and to step outside the discourse of your discipline. In our view, the specific language and presuppositions of a discipline exert a larger influence than someone like Dewey acknowledges. As a researcher, you are educated and socialized in a particular practice, consciously and unconsciously internalizing its norms. Awareness of disciplinary differences does not automatically mean that you can also overcome those differences. Truly appreciating the work done in another discipline might require unlearning your own disciplinary perspective.

These are some critical remarks specifically addressed to pragmatism. For a more general critical view of interdisciplinary research, we now turn to positivism.

2 On the importance of the individual as a critical and creative interpreter of (legal) traditions in pragmatist theory, see Taekema (2006, 220 ff.).

3 An extended criticism of Dewey's position can be found in our paper 'A Dynamic Model of Interdisciplinarity. Limits and Possibilities of Interdisciplinary Research into Law', available at http://ssrn.com/abstract=1142847 (last checked on 1 May 2011).

3 Limits of Interdisciplinary Research According to Positivism

Whereas pragmatism highlights the possibilities of interdisciplinary research, positivist theories point to its limitations or even to its sheer impossibility. We will start with Kelsen's pure theory of law, because it offers one of the most radical and principled defenses of a monodisciplinary approach to law, and turn later to Luhmann's system theory that may provide a middle ground between the two extremes. Inspired by neo-Kantianism,[4] Hans Kelsen intends to construct a solid scientific foundation for the science of law in order to secure its position among other sciences, in particular the natural sciences. For that purpose, the question has to be answered what is typical or unique about the way the science of law understands its object and how it differs from other understandings. In his discussion with Eugen Ehrlich,[5] Kelsen (2003) argues that the phenomenon of law can be studied from two different perspectives. On the one hand, the law can be conceived of as a norm, that is, a rule that articulates a specific kind of 'ought' (*Sollen*): something *has* to be done or not be done. On the other hand, the law may be taken as a part of social reality, as a fact or an occurrence that takes place regularly. Here, the law takes the form of an 'is' (*Sein*) proposition with respect to human behavior: some action *is* done or not done on a regular basis. These two perspectives correspond with two different disciplines from which law can be studied: respectively, a *normative* science of law that determines deductively which rules are valid (*gelten*), and an *explanatory* sociology of law that establish inductively a certain regularity for which it tries to find a causal explanation. Thus, the science of law is a normative and deductive science of value, like ethics and logics, whereas the sociology of law, like other branches of sociology, is a science of reality, and conforms more generally to the methodological practices of the natural sciences. It is equally possible and legitimate to study law from both perspectives, but not at the same time. An object cannot be construed as something that is done or happens regularly and that ought to be done or happen simultaneously. Biology, as an explanatory science, may establish a causal link between two factual occurrences (e.g., between firing a gun and somebody's death), but is not capable of evaluating this link in terms of good/bad or legal/illegal. Conversely, ethics and the science of law, as normative sciences, may dismiss a certain action (e.g., killing someone by firing a gun) as bad, if it violates an ethical norm, or illegal, if it violates a legal norm; however, they are not able to explain this action.

According to Kelsen (2003, 5), combining perspectives from different disciplines would lead to a "methodological syncretism" and is, therefore, "inadmissible".[6] Moreover, if a certain phenomenon is approached from different disciplines it cannot, in his view, constitute one and the same object of knowledge (Kelsen 1962, 106–110). Because object and method of inquiry are correlated, different methods of inquiry necessarily generate different objects. Law can be studied either from a normative (e.g., legal) perspective or from an empirical (e.g., sociological) perspective, but these perspectives cannot be integrated into one single conception of the

4 On the relationship between Kelsen's pure theory of Law and neo-Kantianism, see Dreier (1990, pp. 56–90) and Pascher (1997, pp. 151–173).

5 On the Ehrlich-Kelsen debate, see Van Klink (2008).

6 All of the quotes from the works of Kelsen and Luhmann in this article are translated by us. For the sake of clarity, we have sometimes added the original German phrasing in italics.

object at hand. Otherwise, the unity of knowledge is threatened: it becomes possible to make contradictory claims about the same object. For instance, a legal norm may be considered valid from a legal perspective because its creation is authorized by a higher legal norm, as well as not valid from a sociological point of view, since it might not have any effect on real life (people do not actually comply with the norm). Law cannot be valid and not-valid at the same time, so apparently we are dealing with different senses of validity.

A less radical position is taken by Niklas Luhmann in *Ausdifferenzierung des Rechts* (1981). In this earlier work, he rejects the is/ought dichotomy on which Kelsen's pure theory of law is based. "Such a separation is impracticable for a sociology that has human action as its topic" (Luhmann 1981, 288–289). According to Luhmann (1981, 191), ever since the downfall of the natural-law doctrine, legal science has existed in "interdisciplinary isolation", separated from the social sciences. In his system theory he aims at re-establishing the connection between legal science and other disciplines. In his view, legal science should develop a "steering system that goes beyond legal dogmatics" (*überdogmatisches Steuerungssystem*) by which means it can secure its capability for interdisciplinary contacts (Luhmann 1981, 192). This "steering system" is provided by a general jurisprudence or legal theory that, in a short formula, reduces decision problems to system problems. The legal system is centered around decision: the legislature has to decide which general legal norms have to be issued, whereas the court has to decide on the right application of these legal norms in concrete cases. The science of law reflects on a more abstract and systematic level on the decisions made by legal authorities and unites them in a coherent system of legal norms. Therefore, Luhmann (1981, 283) characterizes the science of law as a "science of decision" (*entscheidungstheoretische Wissenschaft*). In relation to the juristic science of decision, legal theory plays an auxiliary role: by means of functional analysis, it identifies and clarifies existing problems in the various subsystems of society and gives suggestions how these problems can be solved with legal or other instruments. In this way, legal theory acts as a kind of portal through which insights from other disciplines are channeled to the science of law; it establishes "meaningful relations" that enable the "transfer of problem awareness, concepts and knowledge achievements" (Luhmann 1981, 193).

Consequently, in Luhmann's view, no fundamental distinction can be made between normative sciences, such as the science of law, on the one hand and empirical, reality-oriented sciences, such as sociology, on the other. Despite differences in methods and theoretical presumptions, legal science and sociology co-operate in the process of understanding and reducing complexity. This complexity results from the experience of contingency: in the modern era, reality is generally understood, not as a pre-given and fixed entity, but as something constantly changing and changeable. To make meaningful interaction possible in the face of contingency, expectations regarding experience and actions have to be generalized. This can be done, among other things, by means of norms. "Norms are a form of generalization in which the real can be perceived and endured as contingent" (Luhmann 1981, 213). Norms contribute to stabilizing expectations in social interactions. According to Luhmann, these expectations have a legal character only if they are generalized in temporal, objective and social terms. In a system governed by the rule of law, it is the primary task of the legislature to determine the content of the law and, thus, to reduce complexity. Generally speaking, the court has to take the legal norms promulgated by the legislature for granted and has to apply them to individual cases.[7]

In Luhmann's view, sociology may assist the legislature[8] in the process of norm creation and complexity reduction by providing a functional analysis of system problems. Because it is not restricted to the norms already issued, sociology has more freedom to explore alternatives within or outside the existing legal system. The functional method is a heuristic device or a method of clarification that does not result in a decision but may facilitate the decision process. As Luhmann (1981, 302–304) for instance shows, it follows from a functional analysis that financial compensation for erroneous administrative decisions can only be granted if there are no legal means for those concerned to prevent the damage. Without engaging itself in moral value judgments, sociology traces functional deficiencies in existing social systems and suggests possible solutions to overcome them. Whether this suggestion is turned into positive law, is up to the legislature to decide.

Given the complexity of today's world and the demand for information, sociology is a "necessary preparatory science for the science of law" that paves the way for juristic decisions (Luhmann 1981, 294–295). Although both disciplines are connected, they do not coincide. According to Luhmann (1981, 306), a clear distinction between system theories and decision theories still appears to be "unavoidable". System theories offer a functional analysis of problem constellations within systems, whereas juristic decision theories design and deploy hermeneutic-exegetical methods for the creation and application of legal norms. The relationship between both disciplines can best be described in terms of "separation *and* co-operation": functional analysis results in identifying problems that provide the input for "juristic decision programmes" which, subsequently, "concretizes" them in rightful decisions (Luhmann 1981, 307). As said earlier, legal theory is the locus in which these interdisciplinary contacts are established. By implication, it becomes a branch of general sociology.

Luhmann's system theory seems to offer an attractive middle position between two extremes: Dewey's integrative vision in which disciplines are mixed and mixed up in one unified whole on the one hand and Kelsen's rigorous separation of disciplines on the other. Against Dewey, Luhmann argues that there are limits to interdisciplinary research: every discipline has its own methods and theoretical presumptions, without which it would not be able to investigate anything. Therefore, a full integration of disciplines is never possible. Against Kelsen, he brings forward that meaningful connections between scientific disciplines are possible if one is willing to give up the categorical is/ought or fact/norm distinction. The key notion here is 'meaning' (*Sinn*; Luhmann 1981, 292) that functions as a hinge, both connecting and separating disciplines: system theories as well as decision theories seek to find a specific access to the world in order to understand and to come to grips with its complexity and contingency, but each has its own way of doing so, by functional

7 Only if the legal norm is not sufficiently clear, the court is allowed to take the aim or the function of the norm into account (Luhmann 1981, pp. 277–278).

8 According to Luhmann (1981, pp. 304–306), a sociological analysis is of limited use for the court's task, since it mainly has to apply existing legal norms (see also previous footnote).

analysis of problem complexes within social systems and by hermeneutic exegesis of previous understandings in authoritative texts respectively.

By presenting his sociological findings as likely candidates for adoption by the existing legal system and by prioritizing them over other candidates from other normative (religious, moral, or other) sources, Luhmann deliberately transgresses the boundaries of an empirical sociology and enters the realm of politics. His attempt to de-moralize sociology in fact constitutes a *re*-moralization of the discipline. The good/bad opposition of traditional morality is replaced by the only seemingly neutral, technological dichotomy between functional/non-functional. From a Kelsenian perspective, this position raises several questions. Firstly, how can normative claims are founded by means of sociology? How does one assess the functionality of social systems? Secondly, how can sociological findings be translated into normative-legal claims? In short: why should the law bother about a system's functionality? Thirdly, why are normative claims based on sociological research superior to claims from other normative sources? Why should functional considerations have to trump arguments based on, e.g., religion, morality or law?[9]

One way to save Luhmann's project and, at the same time, the potential for crossdisciplinary research it contains, is (i) to reject his reduction of legal theory to sociology and (ii) to recognize the autonomy legal science and legal practice have in addressing conflicting normative claims. That means that legal theory should offer a platform, without conflating disciplinary boundaries Dewey-wise, to many different disciplines that provide different descriptions and evaluations of law and legal practice, such as psychology, political philosophy, economics, rhetoric and ethics. Sociology has no monopoly on the production of both facts and norms. Moreover, it should be acknowledged that legal science and legal practice assess these concurring descriptions and evaluations according to their own, intersystemic standards, such as legal security and legality. As Luhmann (1981, 323) argues, "only insertable norms can become law". However, that limits the possibility of transplanting sociological findings into the law to a far greater extent than he seems willing to accept when he presents sociology as the preparatory science for the science of law. From a legal perspective, all non-legal norms are on an equal footing in their struggle for official recognition by legal authorities.

In his later work, in particular in *Recht der Gesellschaft* (1995), Luhmann abandons the privileged status he granted earlier to the sociology of law in the production of legal norms all together. Generally speaking, he develops a far more detached and skeptical view on the possibilities of interaction between the legal system and its environment [*Umwelt*]. He acknowledges that "structural couplings" between systems may occur, when "a system presupposes characteristics of its environment for a longer time and relies on them structurally" (Luhmann 1995, 441). However, structural couplings can only cause "irritations, surprises, disturbances" within a system (442). How a system deals with "irritations" caused by structural couplings, is determined by its own structures and the operations that are part of these structures. As a consequence, norms from outside the legal system (such as efficiency norms derived from the economic system) can never be transplanted into the exist-

9 An extended criticism of Luhmann's early position can be found in our paper mentioned in Fn. 3.

ing body of legal norms directly. Like any other system, a legal system can only be "irritated in its own values" (494). Norms – or any other input – from outside have a chance to enter the legal system, only if they can be connected to norms that are already included in that system; that is, if these 'foreign' norms are somehow familiar. Therefore, the possibilities of interdisciplinary exchange of ideas will be, by necessity, limited.

In his classification of scientific approaches to law, Luhmann reiterates the fact/norm opposition that he rejected earlier. He distinguishes between "self-descriptions" of the legal system on the one hand and "foreign descriptions" on the other (497). Self-descriptions of the legal system offered by the science of law and by legal theory have to understand law – predominantly or entirely – as a *normative* phenomenon: "it is not acceptable for the system to conceive of norms as something purely factual (like factual behavioral expectations)" (502). On the other hand, Luhmann states: "The external description can afford to restrict itself to the observation: that is the way it is" [*so ist es*] (529). Thus, the sociology of law and the science of law seem to inhibit different intellectual worlds: the ought-world versus the is-world respectively. By reinstating the fact/norm distinction, Luhmann is able to avoid most of the methodological questions that his earlier position encountered from a Kelsenian perspective. However, his detached view on interdisciplinary research makes it difficult to see how a meaningful exchange of concepts and methods between different scientific disciplines can ever take place. He does not deny that external and internal descriptions can influence each other: "The structure of social differentiation ... enables external descriptions to influence internal ones, and vice versa, because overarching communication remains possible as execution of society [*Vollzug der Gesellschaft*], even if boundaries between systems are drawn within society" (497). Though Luhmann in his later work[10] does not exclude the possibility of interdisciplinary research altogether, he mainly focuses on the problems of meaningful interactions between different systems caused by their relative closedness. The question remains under what conditions interdisciplinary research may be desirable or even unavoidable and how to deal with the methodological challenges it offers.

4 A Dynamic Model of Interdisciplinarity

Between the two extremes of Kelsen and Dewey, there is quite a broad range of middle ground. Luhmann (the earlier more than the later) is one of the theorists occupying this middle ground, but to his position a number of more and less extreme views may be added. On the basis of our assessment of Dewey, Kelsen and Luhmann we see a number of legitimate possibilities for viewing interdisciplinary research. The most important conclusion to draw from the different theories of these authors is that one's view of interdisciplinarity is determined first and foremost by one's general view of science. With an emphasis on scientific clarity and rigor, like Kelsen, disciplinary boundaries have a value in their own right, which is threatened by interdisciplinary research. With an emphasis on continuity between concepts and prob-

10 See also Luhmann (1991, in particular pp. 457–458).

lem-solving, like Dewey, disciplinary boundaries have value only insofar as they are useful in generating solutions. Therefore, fundamental choices and beliefs regarding concept-formation, the nature of truth, the status of distinctions, especially the fact-value distinction, and the tasks of scientific research, determine the place that interdisciplinarity can have. In our view, taking a particular approach to the nature of science is inevitable, a choice which entails the extent of interdisciplinary work that fits that particular perspective on scientific research.

Depending on the type of questions one wants to answer and one's own interests and capacities, one can decide either to stick to traditional monodisciplinary research, possibly with heuristical or more substantial input from another discipline, or to adopt a multidisciplinary or an interdisciplinary approach. However, every approach has its possibilities and limitations. In our concluding remarks, we will discuss briefly the main advantages of different kinds of research and the most important challenges or risks each of them faces. Our dynamic model of interdisciplinarity[11] consists of five different types of research: (i) traditional legal research, (ii) legal research that uses insights from other disciplines heuristically as a source of inspiration, (iii) legal research that uses other disciplines as supporting disciplines, (iv) multidisciplinary research into law in which two disciplines are on an equal footing and (v) interdisciplinary research into law that aims at an integration of disciplines.

(i) To begin with, monodisciplinary research into law consists in the collection, analysis and systematization of legal norms that are promulgated by the legislature and applied by the courts, in many cases together with an assessment thereof on the basis of legal or other (e.g., political, ethical, or sociological) standards. Traditionally, it has always been the task of the science of law to describe the content of the law in the past as well as in the present. Since the law changes continuously, there will always be enough work for this kind of monodisciplinary research. Different actors in society can profit from the knowledge accumulated by the science of law: from politicians who want to contest the legality of some draft or bill in Parliament to citizens who aim at getting their right before the court. According to Kelsen and other legal positivists, legal science should limit itself to a representation of the legal system as it is and to an assessment of its logical consistency, because otherwise it would lose its distinctive character and thereby its scientific *raison d'être*. In Kelsen's view, normative questions about what the law ought to be cannot be answered scientifically, but belong to the political sphere. However, legal scholars who are working within a natural law or interactionist framework reject a strict is/ought distinction and, therefore, consider evaluation to be an integral part of legal science. Scientifically speaking, a major advantage of a monodisciplinary approach that has been developed and refined over centuries is that a high level of harmonization in concepts and methods has been reached. Legal scholars have created a shared language to describe legal norms and hermeneutic tools to apply them to concrete cases. At the same time, when concepts and methods are more or less stabilized, there will be limited room for innovation. Innovation in the description and application of legal norms is not even considered to be an ideal to strive for within a traditional conception of legal science. Unlike literature studies, legal science is not

11 A more detailed description of our model can be found in our paper mentioned in Fn. 3.

interested in producing the most creative or original interpretation of authorative texts but in representing them in the most precise and accurate way. On the contrary, in order to protect the value of legal security, it is important that the legal system is presented as much as possible as a unified and univocal whole. A monodisciplinary approach to law, restricting itself to a representation and evaluation of the existing body of law on the basis of pre-established concepts and methods, *from a scientific point of view* may not seem very interesting or exciting – despite all its craftsmanship. It does not (and does not intend to) contribute in any significant way to the innovation of scientific thought.

(ii) More room for innovation is created when a legal scholar turns to another discipline in order to get inspiration. In this case, the source discipline is used as a heuristic device for generating new insights from which the target domain – the legal science – may profit. These new insights will be evaluated according to values and truth criteria internal to the science of law. For instance, philosophical theory may indicate that interpretation of legal texts is never a matter of sheer subsumption but always is a creative process. In order to make this insight acceptable to legal science, it has to justified in terms of its internal values, such as reasonableness or fairness. However, legal scholars who prioritize legal security over the fore-mentioned values will be inclined to reject this insight. Because external input is controlled by and mediated through internal standards, the heuristic approach has the same advantage as the monodisciplinary approach that it protects the unity of the concepts and methods used. An important weakness of the heuristic approach is, exactly because the external input has to be justified exclusively in internal terms, that the new insights are generated in a non-systematic, accidental and arbitrary way. Anything can be a source of inspiration to the science of law, not only other scientific disciplines but also novels, movies or long strolls along the sea. From the viewpoint of legal science it does not make a difference where the insights are taken from or how they are discovered, as long as they can be justified in legal terms; they have no argumentative force on their own.

(iii) If a legal scholar treats the source discipline not merely as inspiration but as a necessary contribution to the science of law, the transfer of insights may acquire a more systematic and less arbitrary character. That is only possible if one considers – against Kelsen – the task of legal science to be more than just the representation of the legal system and an assessment of its internal consistency; it should include also the development and improvement of the existing legal system. Otherwise, if legal scholars are seen solely as the bookkeepers of the law, there would be no need for external input. Suggestions for developing and improving the law may be taken from different sources. According to the early Luhmann, sociology constitutes a "necessary preparatory science for the science of law" that has to pave the way for juristic decisions. However, that raises the question, as discussed above, why one source discipline – in this case: sociology – is favored. Moreover, the problem is how to assess the quality of the external input. One has to be trained in two disciplines to be able to take a stand in debates that take place within these disciplines. If not, one has to rely on authoritive sources, but these may be contradictory. A final risk connected to the transfer of insights from one domain to the other is that the unity of concepts and methods used in the target domain is disturbed. For instance, what will happen when Luhmann's distinction between functional and non-functional or the economic distinction between efficient and inefficient is inserted into the legal discourse?

(iv) In multidisciplinary research all these risks are duplicated, because the transfer of insights is not one-way, as in the previous approach, but two-way: the disciplines involved are source and target domain at the same time. To be capable of doing this, a scholar has to be at home in both disciplines. If so, he does not have to rely on authorities but can assess himself the quality of the imported knowledge. The transplantation of foreign terminology into a scientific discourse may lead, as the later Luhmann (1991, 457) argued, to "understandable misunderstandings". Moreover, problems may arise when disciplines produce contradictory insights. From a sociological point of view a legal norm may seems invalid because it is not applied anymore, whereas from a legal perspective the act may still be considered valid law because it was created on the basis of a higher legal norm. In other words, how to secure coherence in knowledge claims in a multidisciplinary approach? At the same time, multidisciplinary research offers good opportunities of innovation in the target as well as in the source domain, if a fruitful interaction between the two can be established.

(v) Finally, an integrative approach offers the best opportunity for exchanging knowledge. Science is freed from artificial and arbitrary disciplinary boundaries. However, by transgressing boundaries, disciplines lose their distinct character and may become more and more identical. Moreover, in its effort to see everything from all sorts of perspectives at the same time, an integrative approach may end up in seeing nothing at all. Paradoxically, the more successful an integration of disciplines is, the more it resembles a monodisciplinary approach, with all its advantages and disadvantages.

Initially, we started from a dichotomy between an interdisciplinary or integrative approach to law, inspired by Dewey's pragmatist philosophy, and a monodisciplinary approach, advocated by Kelsen and other legal positivists. By distinguishing different types of legal research in our dynamic model of interdisciplinarity, we are in a position to make this opposition less rigid. On the one hand, a monodisciplinary approach to law does not by necessity exclude the possibility that legal science profits from insights from other disciplines, if only in a heuristic way. On the other hand, an interdisciplinary approach that is successful in integrating knowledge from different sources (like Luhmann's system theory) may at some point become a discipline in its own right. With Luhmann, we believe that a direct and 'full' access to reality is impossible. Our knowledge of the world is always mediated through some disciplinary perspective or other.[12] Whether one wants to stick to one perspective, that is the still dominant legal perspective as defended by positivism, or tries to transcend this perspective by confronting it with other (sociological, ethical, historical, economical, rhetorical etc.) perspectives is a matter of personal choice – a choice that will depend on a legal scholar's convictions on fundamental epistemological and ontological issues.

At the two extremes of our model of interdisciplinarity, there are two pitfalls that in our view need to be avoided: at the one end, the rigidity and closedness of a

12 For an elaborated description and defense of this constructivist position, see Arbib & Hesse (1986).

strict monodisciplinary approach and, at the other end, too much flexibility and openness that may result in an undifferentiated and undifferentiating fusion and confusion of perspectives. Between these extremes, meaningful exchanges between different disciplines are possible. However, these exchanges will not always be peaceful, since different disciplines will use concepts and methods differently, or may at first not recognize each other's methods, and so on. From these clashes, new insights may spring.

Literature

Alexy, Robert: Elemente einer juristischen Begründungslehre. Baden-Baden, 2003.

Arbib, Michael A. / Hesse, Mary B.: The Construction of Reality. Cambridge, 1986.

De Been, Wouter: Legal Realism Regained. Saving Realism from Critical Acclaim. Stanford, 2008.

Cotterrell, Roger B.M.: Law, Culture and Society. Legal Ideas in the Mirror of Social Theory. Ashgate, 2006.

Dewey, John: "My Philosophy of Law". In: My Philosophy of Law. Credos of Sixteen American Scholars. Boston, 1941, pp. 73–85.

Dewey, John: "Context and Thought". In: Richard J. Bernstein (ed.): On Experience, Nature and Freedom. Representative Selections. New York, 1960, pp. 88–110.

Dewey, John: The Quest for Certainty. In: Jo Ann Boydston (ed.), The Later Works, 1925–1953. Volume 4, Carbondale and Edwardsville, 1984.

Dewey, John: Reconstruction in Philosophy. In: Jo Ann Boydston (ed.): The Middle Works 1899–1924. Volume 12. Carbondale and Edwardsville, 1988.

Dewey, John: Experience and Nature. La Salle, 1989.

Dewey, John: "Logical Method and Law". In: Larry A. Hickman / Thomas M. Alexander (eds.): The Essential Dewey. Volume I. Bloomington, pp. 355–362, 1998.

Dreier, Horst: Rechtslehre, Staatssoziologie und Demokratietheorie bei Hans Kelsen. Baden-Baden, 1990.

James, William: Pragmatism and the Meaning of Truth. Cambridge, 1978.

Kelsen, Hans: Der soziologische und der juristische Staatsbegriff. Kritische Untersuchung des Verhältnisses vom Staat und Recht. Aalen, 1962.

Kelsen, Hans: The Pure Theory of Law (translation from the second [revised and enlarged] German edition by Max Knight). Berkeley, 1970.

Kelsen, Hans: "Eine Grundlegung der Rechtssoziologie". In: Hans Kelsen / Eugen Ehrlich, Rechtssoziologie und Rechtswissenschaft. Eine Kontroverse (1915/1917), Baden-Baden, 2003, pp. 3–54.

Klink, Bart van: "Can There Be Law Without the State? The Ehrlich-Kelsen Debate Revisited in a Globalizing Setting". In: Hanneke van Schooten / Jonathan Verschuuren (eds.), International Governance and Law. State Regulation and Non-State Law, Cheltenham, pp. 43–74.

Luhmann, Niklas: Ausdifferenzierung des Rechts. Beiträge zur Rechtssoziologie und Rechtstheorie. Frankfurt a. M., 1981.

Luhmann, Niklas: Die Wissenschaft der Gesellschaft. Frankfurt a. M., 1991.

Luhmann, Niklas: Das Recht der Gesellschaft. Frankfurt a. M., 1995.

Pascher, Manfred: Einführung in den Neukantianismus. Munich, 1997.

Posner, Richard A.: Economic Analysis of Law. Austin, 2007.

Putnam, Hilary: Pragmatism. An Open Question. Oxford, 1995.

Putnam, Hilary: The Collapse of the Fact / Value Dichotomy and Other Essays. Cambridge, 2002.

Taekema, Sanne: "The Appeal to Common Tradition. Its Progressive Potential". In: Paul van Seters (ed.): Communitarianism in Law and Society. Lanham, 2006, pp. 215–230.

Van der Burg, Wibren: "Essentially Ambiguous Concepts and the Fuller-Hart-Dworkin Debate". Available at http://ssrn.com/abstract=1009179 (last checked on 1 May 2011), 2007.

Vick, Douglas: "Interdisciplinarity and the Discipline of Law". Journal of Law and Society 31 (2004), pp. 163–193.

Wagenaar, Willem A. / Van Koppen, Peter J. / Crombag, Hans F.M.: Anchored Narratives. The Psychologicy of Criminal Evidence. Hemel Hempstead, 1993.

Michael Anderheiden

The Paradox of Interdisciplinary Research

Abstract:
Michael Anderheiden untersucht in seinem Beitrag die Möglichkeit langfristiger interdisziplinärer Zusammenarbeit. Obwohl solche Forschung weithin als vielversprechend angesehen wird, erscheint es doch nicht unwahrscheinlich, dass sie bei Erfolg in eigenen neuen Disziplinen aufgeht und bei Misserfolg nach relativ kurzer Zeit wieder eingestellt wird. Der Beitrag untersucht zunächst Luhmanns entsprechende Thesen und wendet sich dann einem Versuch zu, Formen langzeitiger interdisziplinärer Zusammenarbeit zu unterscheiden, um eine philosophische Antwort auf die Thematik vorzubereiten. Langfristige interdisziplinäre Zusammenarbeit mag, so seine abschließend für die Rechtswissenschaften untersuchte These, für Forschungen genau dann in Frage kommen, wenn sie den Gewinn neuer Einsichten aus anderen Disziplinen nur um den Preis der Aufgabe von Idealisierungen verspricht, die für die beteiligten Disziplinen von relativ geringer Bedeutung sind. Das Argument für diese These setzt die Unterscheidung von Abstraktionen und Idealisierungen voraus, wie O. O'Neill sie vorgeschlagen hat, und weiter die Bereitschaft der beteiligten Forscher, einige Idealisierungen als weniger wichtig anzusehen und aufzugeben.

Interdisciplinary research is currently "en vogue": It is endowed with personal, money, and research facilities; it is prominent in new academic journals and in the headlines of newspapers. Certainly one of the main attractions of interdisciplinary research is the promise of new insights, of fresh starts, of the advantages of looking at things from a new perspective, the promise of synergetic effects, of solutions to problems too puzzling for disciplines working on them on their own, let alone for a few researchers of a single discipline. Seen in a broader historical perspective, times of interdisciplinary research may well be advancing regularly, at a time when the disciplines of their own got into too many research impasses, after the (subsidizing) public gets impatient about unresolved scientific puzzles, and the research subjects of different disciplines are seen as the same, at least from a certain distance. After the establishment of interdisciplinary research, two ways of further advancements are obvious: One is the way back into the old disciplines, after a possible failure of interdisciplinary advancements or the insight into its short term advantages, for the time being. The other is the establishment of a new discipline, formed out of two or more of the older ones: biochemestry, mechatronics, biomedical ethics, and moral psychology bear witness of their ancestors already in their names. Others are offsprings of parent disciplines without name-taking: political science, geology, nanotechnology, to name but a few out of the last 200 years or so. Leaving them aside, the more difficult question is how interdisciplinary research is possible in the long run, that is: Is it possible and if so, how is it possible that some interdisciplinary research lasts for decades?

I will start to tackle this question by pointing out how Luhmann regards long-term interdisciplinary research (LIR) as impossible but at the same time at least in some instances as fruitful, thus treating LIR as a paradox. I will then briefly explore some kinds of LIR before I turn to a possible philosophical explanation of the paradoxical structure of LIR. The paper ends on an optimistic note about lawyers' role in LIR.

1 Autopoiesis or Interdisciplinary Research

The problem of interdisciplinary research for systems theory becomes obvious when we look at the idea of autopoietic systems.[1] According to standard systems theory, systems behave autopoietically that is they take on new information according to their own rules only. Thus, the legal system may include a reaction from the political system but only according to its own legalist terms, its own code. As long as this inclusion has not happened, the reactions of other systems are just noise to the system in question. Since every system behaves that way, interdisciplinary research is hard to imagine if disciplines are seen as systems. Of course, it may be possible that people as representatives of the different systems work together occasionally, but still everyone according to his own approach, every system according to its own terms and code, that is, according to the rules of autopoiesis.[2] On the other side it may be possible and even important to explore in more depth what is common to all disciplines. Again, this is research, however transgressing all disciplines, and based on a new paradigm specific for this way of research. In a way this transdisciplinary research is not interdisciplinary, but the attempt to initiate a new, single discipline.

Luhmann himself, however, did not share this view. For him, the whole "Wissenschaft" is but one system with its code. If we take this view seriously and to its end, disciplines within the system seem to be not only contingent and more or less spurious; they are not really an interesting or proper object of research.[3] Again, however, Luhmann stops short of this result and points out that systems may within themselves reproduce the difference between system and surrounding. Thereby, disciplines can be seen as systems within the "Wissenschaftssystem": All share the same code of truth-seeking, all work methodologically, based on theories and programs. But disciplines differ in their theories and methods, and thus are able to see the other disciplines as mere surrounding. To be sure "Wissenschaft" was never cut into slices named "disciplines"; rather disciplines can be seen as different ways to use the code of truth. So, at first sight, interdisciplinary research is possible to solve problems common to several disciplines, their overlap so to speak.

Still, one might argue, if disciplines behave like (autopoietic) systems, interdisciplinary research remains impossible. The different disciplines working on "a problem"[4] still work according to their respective methods and theories which in turn guide their interest in other disciplines. Besides transdiciplinary research there would be no interdisciplinary research proper. Yet Luhmann argues that disciplines share some features with systems but not all: only systems have a code, and they only follow the path of (stratificatory or) functional differentiation in that they solve specific problems of society. Disciplines, however, do not solve specific problems of the "Wissenschaftssystem" as such.[5] For them Luhmann introduces the term "segmentäre Differenzierung" ("segmentary differentiation"). What does this mean,

1 N. Luhmann: Wissenschaft als System. Frankfurt 1990, esp. pp. 457 ff.
2 op. cit., p. 457, the following on 459.
3 op. cit., p. 642.
4 Who is to determine that it is one and the same problem for all?
5 Again, with the exception of transdisciplinary research!?

and does it allow reconciling autopoiesis with the possibility of interdisciplinary research?

According to Luhmann the abstract problem that always triggers and then forces the creation of a new discipline is the combination of variety and redundancy, a problem typical of the "Wissenschaftssystem".[6] A broad variety of experience about subject matters including surprise findings contrasts with a slim margin of possible construction elements within the old discipline. Over time, the old discipline does not generate enough information to process the new information experience delivers. In this situation efficiency demands specialization, brought about, according to Luhmann, by an overall process within the old discipline to enhance its theoretical capability to dissolve and recombine its own elements, or more precisely: to make new use of its axioms.[7]

This story is at least underdetermined by Luhmann's own standards: The introduction of "segmentary differentiation" does not only look like an *ad hoc* closure of his theory, it leads us either to believe that the new disciplines are not autopoietic but generated by and dependent upon the old "mother" discipline, or to believe that there must be a gap, a leap, or a decisive element that separates the new discipline(s) from the old one. Such a decisive element to establish a new theory could be a new axiom. Its heuristic use may still keep the limits of the old discipline, but once the heuristics is abandoned by a certain part of research and researchers the new discipline might come into being. This at least might be an autopoietic story of the emergence of a new discipline. Still, whether or not enough research and researchers try to abandon the old heuristics is in part triggered by factors outside the "Wissenschaftssystem" with its code of truth: money, number of researchers, expert position in politics, and other elements from other systems come into play.[8]

More important here is the question whether or not the generation of new disciplines has significance on the possibility of interdisciplinary research. Luhmann himself allows not only for occasional interdisciplinary research and transdisciplinary research, but also for a third kind of interdisciplinary endeavor, temporary interdisciplinary research which in his view is only "problembezogen", oriented towards understanding and solving of a problem.[9] The difference between this temporary interdisciplinary research (TIR) and the occasional interdisciplinary research (OIR) seems at first to be limited to the factor time only. However, Luhmann himself compares the two also by pointing out TIR to be "more condensed". However, to me the decisive point is that TIR is planned interdisciplinary research, that there is a common description of "a problem" to be solved or at least treated by a collaboration of researchers of the different disciplines according to their respective methods and theories. But if this is so, TIR is clearly heteropoietic, brought about (and kept alive) by the resources of the disciplines involved. The project is over once the problem at hand is resolved. No new methods, techniques, and theory are involved. If this is the whole picture, TIR is a peripheral phenomenon of autopoietic disciplines.

6 op. cit., p. 451.
7 op. cit., p. 451.
8 op. cit., p. 454 f.
9 op. cit., at 458.

Yet there is a whole lot of TIR and LIR going on in the world, not all designed to be finished off after solving a problem. It is telling that Luhmann in his short discussion of TIR immediately turns to ridicule all "discourses" meant to establish TIR as a kind of ongoing or permanent, in any case long-term interdisciplinary process (LIR) which, he warns, might lead to encrustation of both, the old disciplines and the new (permanent or long standing) research group. Yet, encrustation on part of the interdisciplinary research group requires more than a mere addition of knowledge from the old disciplines (used for problem-solving). It assumes that something genuine and alien towards the old disciplines is in the making by such (long-term) interdisciplinary research groups that becomes sterile over time. What is the specific of the LIR-group?

Luhmann in his sometimes elusive and disparaging way of allusions points only to, but does not elaborate on, "achievements, mixture of languages, and success by cooperation".[10] Taken together LIR is, according to Luhmann, at once impossible and real, sometimes vaguely promising, but always in danger of encrustation. According to Luhmann, hence, the very idea of a freestanding LIR is paradoxical. In what follows I want to stress that this is not only a result of Luhmann's theoretical approach. For this I will point to different types of LIR by way of example and an explanation of its difficulties from the philosopher's perspective. My examples pertain to LIR; they all inaugurate in the 1970s at the latest and still continue as of today. Though I will not stress the example of legal research most of the approaches that follow are of immediate interest for lawyers and legal academic discussions, and most have already made their way into law.

2 Conditions of Interdisciplinary Research

2.1 Intrapersonal Interdisciplinary Research

"My study thus has cut across the traditional boundaries between the work of the philosopher, the historian, the philologist and the palaeographer", one now prominent member of the "Cambridge School of History" describes his approach in his seminal PhD-thesis.[11] He could have included the work of the legal historian, as he did in some of his later work. The "Cambridge School", though only vaguely united in its approach,[12] is one of the outstanding examples of research facilitated by interdisciplinary trained experts, working on related topics. Since its "inauguration" almost 50 years ago[13] the field of history, and especially of political and legal history, has profited from a growing number of people working "across the traditional boundaries". Their influence is enormous and, arguably, lasting. They provide therefore for a fine example of intrapersonal interdisciplinary research. And when and for

10 op. cit., at 459.

11 John Marenbon: From the Circle of Alcuin to the School of Auxerre. Cambridge 1981, reprint 2006, p. 8 f.

12 M. Mulsow and A. Mahler: "Einleitung", in: Die Cambridge School der politischen Ideengeschichte. Frankfurt 2010, S. 7–10.

13 Starting, arguably, with Peter Laslett's edition of John Locke: Two Treatises of Government, Cambridge 1960.

whom does it matter whether a single work of a single researcher is based in the last instance (whatever that may be) on the work of the philosopher or the historian of ideas or the philologist or the paleographer or the legal historian?

2.2 The Role of Institutional Design

The Cambridge School still forms one part of the history of ideas, and that is: of history. But research may lead to new disciplines. Institutional matters have been stressed as one factor for these new foundations. However, I doubt that they are decisive. Certainly, in some way or other, researchers of the hitherto different disciplines have to work together to establish a new, common discipline. But what kind of collaboration is necessary? Or at least: Are there common conditions for successful fusions of disciplines? On a regular basis, the old disciplines are not superfluous after the emergence of the new discipline. They exist side by side with their baby. Hence, it is not for the baby to erase all or most of the guiding questions and the research of the old disciplines, but only to set them aside in some areas. Some of the old questions are now tackled under the new heading, others within the old disciplinary boarders. A split between subjects of a hitherto united discipline has to be both possible and promising.

Certainly, this split can be merely institutional, but this is not the interesting case. Just because the computer laboratory moved across the street and is now responsible for all the university's units does not make it something else than the old computer laboratory, though working on more and more diverse demands. The interesting cases that make for new disciplines require more than just a new institutional design. They ask for changes in the subject matter of the disciplines.

2.3 Extension of Subject Matter

But by itself this change of subject matter is not enough, either, at least not initially, since there are cases which from the point of view of LIR seem at least in the beginning rather unspectacular and uninteresting. These are the cases when one discipline brings its whole research baggage into fields which have been neglected by them before. Thus in the 1960s and 70s economists following Gary Becker and others[14] started to investigate into e.g., family relations, discrimination (race, gender), crime, addictions. These fields are of course central to sociological, psychological and legal research and practice, and also to anthropology and cultural studies. But economists offered to describe family relations and the other subject matters in their own eco-

14 G. Becker: Human Capital: A Theoretical and Empirical Analysis, with Special Reference to Education Chicago 1964, may be seen as the starting point. – Another example though not as prominent in law's hallways are the different and interdisciplinary approaches to understand speech, see the very well known approach of "linguistic competence" of idealized speakers advanced by N. Chomsky et alt. versus the relatively little known "communicative competence" of speakers in concrete socio-linguistic settings advanced by D. Hymes et alt., see N. Chomsky: Syntactic Structures. Mouton, Den Haag 1957; D. Hymes: Foundations in Sociolinguistics: An Ethnographic Approach. Philadelphia 1974 (based on papers from the 1960s).

nomic language. Thereby they enriched the literature on families but did not merge with the other disciplines already working on this subject matter. All we had were economists working on families, crime, drugs, discrimination, etc., too. Thus, in the first 20 years or so, the economic approach to human behavior did not play a prominent role in the development of the other disciplines working on these topics.

Strategically it may have been of some importance that these economists offered a new concept: "human capital". Easy to grasp and to misunderstand, the concentration on this one term made the advancements of economists attractive to look into for academics of other disciplines even if only superficially. It enabled them to keep distance if this was required or desirable: Humans are/form no capital! The theory was in this way easy to dismiss and at the same time in about 1980 it was possible to pay some lip service to the changes in the political specter connected with the names of Thatcher and Reagan. However it is important to stress that I take the economics of social behavior movement in this initial phase not as an example for interdisciplinary research. But it generated LIR mainly caused by and heavily influenced from inside, that is from the scientific community itself.

Things started to change accordingly when the other disciplines took notice of the advanced economic problem descriptions and proposed solutions, many of them not altogether new. Still, the idea of efficiency as a basis for the description and normative solution of social developments and social problems was seen by many as repulsive. If it is possible to find an additional base for the own sociological, legal, psychological, etc. arguments in the mode of the economic approach to human behavior were welcome. However, if the contrary happened, and one's own research results in these disciplines were shattered by the economic approach in this field, it became commonplace to dismiss the basis of the economic argument as mere ideology and to lament about the "imperialism" of the economic doctrine.[15] This required thinking about the criterion of efficiency itself, its ideological underpinnings and shortages. In turn, economists could point to the shortcomings of the sociological, legal, or psychological bases, e.g., the ideas of classes, groups, cultural embeddings, the legal idea of a "person", or of rational behavior or the subconscious.

Strategies to answer the respective challenges may be chosen in defense of the old disciplines or in an attempt to come to a mutual understanding, thus providing for interdisciplinary research on the concepts of efficiency, rationality, biological vs. cultural conditions of human behavior, etc. This kind of interdisciplinary research leads to the (second) extension of the subject matter in each of the different disciplines. This extension can be grasped, I will propose, along the abstraction/idealization divide. The same holds true for the interpersonal LIR projects already mentioned and for a more practical approach necessitating LIR, the work of committees.

15 For the different perspectives see: I. Pies and M. Leschke (eds.): Gary Beckers ökonomischer Imperialismus. Tübingen 1998.

2.4 Committees

Often enough members of different disciplines are set up from third parties to solve together practical problems at hand and to redress these problems by a common proposal for a solution (which has to fulfill some further qualifications regarding time, money, and so on). Committees are a case at hand. In the case of troubled families or troubled neighborhoods of several such families committees are set up and stuffed with psychologists, psychiatrists, social workers, teachers, lawyers, economists, theologians, sociologists, cultural scientists specialized in the relevant ethnic groups, even architects and city planners, community activists and politicians.[16] Their task is to save this neighborhood from crime, drug trafficking, etc., and to come up with a plan to make it (again?) a good or at least a better place to live in. For the case of interdisciplinary research the interesting facts about these committees are the primacy of problem-solving capacities over basic research, including perhaps a trial and error-approach, and the re-introduction of the results of the solutions that worked and of those that did not work into the basic research in the different disciplines. Still, committee work commonly is not strictly bottom up, since the committee works on principles of the disciplines from all levels of abstraction, from the most basic to medium level principles to results of highly specialized experiments or cases.[17] They are interwoven somehow towards a common result for the sake of the committee's success. What is merely ephemeral or mundane in the single discipline may become central to a committee's finding, and vice versa. As a result, often enough terms take on new meanings, not only extensional but intentional as well.

This leads to the experience of those in the committee to see some of their view on the problems and of their guidelines for solutions followed through while other parts of their view completely neglected, without any valid explanation from the point of view of their own discipline why this part of the problem-solving capacity should be used and the other should be neglected.[18] Frustration of the love of one's own discipline becomes part of the business of work in committees. Seen from the outside control of the process is no longer with the different academic disciplines or one composed body of their representatives but with some outside body setting the agenda including time tables, corridors for solutions, accumulation of resources and personal, methods and places of investigation, and publication and use of results. At best, the outside body may represent society as a whole; at worst it may be some private organization looking not just for revenues but for the promotion of some

16 Other committees are set up to evaluate research proposals including research into the human body, or to find solutions for the treatment of difficult cases in hospitals, and so on. Obviously, they are stuffed according to the problems and the personal at hand. Still, their structure remains the same.

17 Thus mirroring the grounded-theory-approach, B.B. Glaser and A.L. Strauss: The Discovery of Grounded Theory: Strategies for Qualitative Research. New York 1967.

18 For what follows see: M. Carrier: "Erkenntnisgewinn und Nutzenmaximierung", in: P. Weingart, M. Carrier and W. Krohn (eds.): Nachrichten aus der Wissensgesellschaft. Weilerswist 2007, 93–110, and, in the same reader: P. Weingart: "Wissenschaft als Gegenstand politischer, wirtschaftlicher und ethischer Konflikte", pp. 229–233, and P. Weingart: "Unparteilichkeit und wirtschaftliche Interessen", pp. 234–246.

obscure and even morally questionable aims. How much money did, e.g., the tobacco industry spend to show that smoking does not enhance cancer even after the opposite could be seen as a given? How many committees and round tables did profit from this quest? And how many of their members did know about the donors and their aims? And how did this knowledge influence their substantial and methodological alignment?

But even if there is ample social control over these research processes the impact on research at large is substantial: Research becomes almost exclusively result-oriented. Research missing direct effects on public problems is at least in need of special justification. As a consequence, the epistemic role of scientific enterprises may dwindle whereas the usefulness of research becomes dominant. However, couched into non-academic setups, committees may lead participants from academia to caution regarding their results: These are seen as preliminary or provisional and in any case heavily contextualized, therefore without general relevance for seemingly equal phenomena. Academics may publish these results swiftly in order to be the first to explore a subject matter, with all further research only "in the making". In order to underline the usefulness of published results research processes are now implemented immediately, as long as special standards for implementation are not required by law. Still, this procedure requires an unbalanced use of the methods and contents of researchers' disciplines.

2.5 The Dangers of Academic Imperialism and Exploitation

To avoid the frustration of the love of one's own discipline, but also to keep one's vision of the own discipline unchanged, other researchers take a seemingly more cautious step into interdisciplinary research, if they leave their own discipline at all. They try to keep the process of interdisciplinary research under strict scrutiny according to their own standards, that is: They give up only as little as necessary and as unimportant as possible of their own research world, but try at the same time to make the most use possible of the questions, methods and results of all other disciplines. The result may become a kind of academic exploitation, as members of one discipline try to convince or to persuade members of other disciplines to accept their standards, or at least to use their standards without further knowledge of or interest in their implications. Since members of all disciplines are prone to the same timid thinking, interdisciplinary endeavors may well result in mutual exploitation without any common ground reached on equal footing. Even worse, it may lead to researchers' reassurance of the predominance of their own discipline over all others, and to jealously guarded "secrets" of the different disciplines. Thus, a benchmark of LIR is that researchers of the different disciplines have to give up something while working together with colleagues from other fields of knowledge but at the same time they have to keep in essence their academic background else they act no longer as experts for their field of knowledge.

To take law as an example: Lawyers and professors of law are frequently asked to participate in interdisciplinary research. They are also requested to cooperate with each other across borders and legal systems. In both cases they are required to represent their own legal system in an unfamiliar context. Within these endeavors lawyers are asked as lawyers, they are asked to make statements about the law. Members of Law Schools are often asked to bring the legal position into perspective: though still asked as experts in law, law professors are asked to participate in a common analytical enterprise which may well end in some kind of merger of hitherto different disciplines. Within this enterprise the law has to remain law, as much as economics remains economics, psychology, etc. Researchers of these different disciplines stick to their origins, none of them can fully adopt one of the others' methods. Yet they have to adopt some of these methods and results of other disciplines in order to participate in a common endeavor. The decisive question for the possibility of LIR, therefore, is what to keep and what to give up of one's own discipline. One possible answer makes use of the difference between abstraction and idealization to which I turn now.

3 Abstraction and Idealization

3.1 The Difference between Abstraction and Idealization

Both abstraction and idealization have in common that any argument has to start with some widely held and intuitively convincing starting points. They decisively differ however in that abstraction brackets predicates (and thereby reduces truth values) of a statement while idealization holds certain predicates to be true, sometimes against all evidence (and thereby adds truth values).[19] To provide for some examples: in legal and social science contexts theories might bracket information about sex, age, or political convictions. They might not matter for the purpose at hand or might open a whole lot of other problems. Idealizations are frequent, even in science; see the use of models[20] or of the perfect vacuum or of frictionless motions,[21] in economics the example of *homo oeconomicus* is striking. Although the difference between abstraction and idealization is conceptually clear, its application may be difficult. Sometimes the discussion may be restructured as a discussion whether or not a certain argument makes use of an abstraction or an idealization. Thus, John Rawls holds his "original position" to be a mere abstraction; critiques like Michael Sandel take it to be an idealization.[22] In some way, we will see, they both are right.

What are the advantages and disadvantages of abstraction? Logically, abstraction is a relatively safe method of argumentation, since it does not deny any predicates of the full picture, and brackets only some of them. So abstraction comes along without problematic additions and suppositions. This makes abstraction very promising as a method of argument in LIR. Still, abstraction remains dependent upon its starting point. These two characteristics may lead researchers to see abstractions as a safe method to incorporate one field of research into another (e.g., eco-

19 O. O'Neill: Towards Justice and Virtue: A constructive account of practical reasoning. Cambridge 1996, chap. 2.

20 Extensive discussion about the development in: S. de Chadarevian and N Hopwood (eds.): Models: The third dimension of Science. Stanford 2004.

21 O'Neill, o. c., p. 41.

22 For discussion of this example see O'Neill, op. cit., pp. 44 ff.

nomics or psychology into law and jurisprudence). However: abstractions may be of little use for problem-solving since they do not carry additional truth values with them and, hence, do (often?) not allow for additional truth values of the combined theories. And the very fact of combining the two fields of research by incorporating the abstraction of the argument of one discipline into the argument of another may well be or cause an idealization. In addition abstraction is not innocuous in itself if it separates what belongs together according to some other theoretical approaches (see below).

Idealizations in turn do carry additional truth values with them, as a consequence they allow for additional statements in a combined theory. These truth values are important within the frame of their original theory: Here they allow for many relevant statements. However: the additional truth values may be quite questionable, esp. without the frame of their original theory. And it remains an open question how useful and theoretically safe the idealization of the combination of theories itself will turn out to be. In any case there seems to be the additional disadvantage of idealizations for LIR that their use in theory may prove to be of less importance in practice: Idealization in the sciences of engineering aiming for explanation may be of little use for practical problems facing engineers who have to recommend action. Similarly, the ideas of idealized consumers in perfect markets let us learn something theoretically interesting about economic behavior. "But if as economic actors we assume that consumers and markets live up to these idealized fictions we will fail to adjust our action to actual circumstance, and may pay, or exact, a heavy price."[23] The same might hold for criminal theory relying on a certain view of man proposed by psychology, sociology, or philosophy to explain certain phenomena, and the criminal courts that have to decide the case at hand.

In short we might again face a paradox of interdisciplinary research, especially LIR: Abstraction is theoretically safe, but often enough content-irrelevant, idealization is content-relevant, but theoretically questionable. LIR therefore might become sterile, as Luhmann predicted, if it uses abstraction only. It might have a theoretically questionable status if it relies heavily on idealizations. In addition, if set up for recommendations and other practical purposes interdisciplinary boards and commissions face the problem of idealization exacting a heavy price on any solution they put forward. Here, idealization may be seen to put together what has to be kept separate or is seen as false from other points of view, including the point of recommendations and real life judgments. Taken together, LIR again seems to be a rather questionable enterprise.

3.2 The Common Problem of the Starting Point and its Influence

Still, the common starting point of reasoning may cause problems for the difference between abstractions and idealizations. All argument is based on some widely held and intuitively convincing assumptions.[24] These assumptions may in turn undermine the difference between abstraction and idealization. Though logically the dif-

23 O'Neill, op. cit., p. 41.

24 Of course, it makes a difference to whom an argument is addressed: Assumptions made by

ference between abstraction and idealization is strict, it is nevertheless content-dependent. This helps us to understand that the difference between abstraction and idealization is a useful analytical tool but by no means a decisive argument against the possibility of LIR.

Let me illustrate the content dependence of abstraction vs. idealization by giving an example: The different views of man may well play a decisive role in evaluating an argument in social science, law, philosophy, cultural science, etc., as abstraction or idealization. To illustrate this claim let us arrange the views of man into five groups: atomism, man as social animal, connectivism, man as organic whole, and collectivism, knowing, of course, that all thinking in -isms is in itself a heavy idealization.[25]

For atomism, only individuals count, each separated from the other. Social relations are without relevance for the importance of moral claims. Rational choice theory provides one example for atomism.

Theories relying on a view of man as social animal take the individual as a starting point, too, but include social relations to some degree in their evaluation of moral claims. Social relations are seen as revisable, individuals can freely choose between them. Still, these relations are significant for individuals at any given moment of time. This double character of social institutions (revisable and yet important to the individual at a time) allows for different points of view to be included in these theories: the point of view of spectator will emphasize the revisibilty of social relations while the point of view of participants in social interaction will put weight on the actual social relations that are. Most liberals like Rawls, Dworkin, and Alexy share this social animal view.

Connectivism takes individuals to be connected by a common bound, e.g., the bound of communication. Hence, man is thought of as an essentially social character. According to these views, to lose sight of the common bound leads theories to miss the social character of man. At the same token the social relations of man are reduced to or at least centered on the common bound. Luhmann at least in his later theory provides a case for connectivism, concentrating on communication.

Again, other theories see individuals as organic wholes, including their social relations. It is impossible to neglect some aspect of these social relations without changing some character of the individual as well. Michael Sandel in his critique of Rawls provides for a typical example of this line of thinking. Rawls aims to construct the original division as a device merely bracketing predicates about persons, thereby as a mere abstraction, and he is successful in this project from a social animal view of man. For Sandel the "original position" is an idealization which distorts the inherently social nature of man as embedded in specific social relations.

Finally, some theorists see man only as part of a larger collective entity, be it a class, a race, or a people. Marx is an obvious case in point for such collectivism.

Now, how do these bundles of theories evaluate the separation of man from its social embedding using the difference between abstraction and idealization? The answer may well be: The separation is an innocuous abstraction for atomists and

mathematicians for their like may be hard to understand and not at all intuitively clear to the lay-person.

25 I do not claim to be the first to use this arrangement, but have not found it anywhere else.

social animal views concentrating on the spectators view. For organics, the separation is an unacceptable idealization distorting the whole make-up of man. Depending on the content in the specific theories, the separation may be acceptable as idealization for connectivists or collectivists. As a result all theories relying on some view of man do not allow for a content-independent categorization of arguments into either abstraction or idealization. The answer is rather dependent upon the theory of man underlying the relevant research and so open to content-full discussion, it is not a mere question of logic.

This example shows how LIR is at once possible, relevant, and dubious at the same time. It is possible if researchers rely on abstraction according to their own substantial ideas. The same argument can, however, be seen as idealization from the point of view of other researchers, be it from the same discipline or other disciplines. What might look as a mere abstraction without any additional truth-value from the point of view of one theory can be seen as a meaningful (and perhaps hardly justifiable) idealization from other viewpoints. If researchers are more prone to give up on their own theory by way of abstraction (nothing is "wrong" with it), the very fact that the same move is seen as meaningful idealization by others may allow for LIR.

But does this not make LIR a rather dull enterprise in which everything relies upon the "mistake" of the others involved to see that their arguments are idealizations, containing even falsehoods? Seen from a bird's eye point of view this may be true. Yet, not every idealization is of equal relevance for a theory: To give up on minor points may be efficient if the promise to get something back in return (further knowledge and insight) seems to outweigh the losses. With abstractions this is arguably always the case in LIR. And even if the losses seem to outweigh the gains from some points of view it is only necessary that the gains are bigger from the point of view of the researcher involved in LIR. In the end, therefore, it is the pluralism of theories and approaches within the disciplines that allows for LIR.

Still some caution should be taken when participating in LIR: Participants in LIR should be aware of the difference between abstraction and idealization, and the problems of each of them. They should keep record for themselves and communicate among themselves and to the public at large whether they see a common assumption and an argument as an abstraction or an idealization from the point of view of their own theories, and most certainly they should point to the heuristic character of their results.

3.3 Implications for Lawyers

Law professors and legal practioners can easily participate in LIR. They are even used to idealizations and abstractions, if they only think about it. To provide for just one occurrence of these techniques let me rephrase H.L.A. Hart's famous "open texture of language problem": Hart's starting point is the observation that "(i)n all fields of experience, not only that of rules, there is a limit, inherent in the nature of language, to the guidance which general language can provide".[26] As much as lan-

26 H.L.A. Hart, The Concept of Law, Oxford 1960, p. 123.

guage is general, we know about plain cases that commonly fall under a given rule. But for these plain cases it is impossible to make sense of general language; general language would have no meaning.[27] In consequence for any given rule there are plain cases under any language. But often and even regularly there are not only plain cases but also hard cases in which it is not clear whether or not the rule applies. These cases are characterized by sharing some of the features of plain cases but not all of them.

The question therefore is, what the criteria are to determine whether or not to apply a rule to the hard cases. Standards of interpretation, like the reliance on the structure of a statute as a whole or of the will of the law-making body, may be of help in some cases but not in all. Anyway they may themselves be open to interpretation.[28] Deductive reasoning which starts with some "aim of the law" will not help in hard cases either: There may be several such aims leading to contradicting results, the origin of the "aims" may be highly questionable, arguments based on them often seem circular, and the aims are again open to interpretation. The decision in hard cases therefore seems to rely upon the discretion of the authorized person/body.

Still, it needs not to be irrational, and it might be possible to narrow the scope of discretion in hard cases. The promising way according to Hart is to bridge the gap between plain cases and hard cases by striving for a "general agreement in judgment" (typical for plain cases) in the hard cases. The decisive parameter for the decision in hard cases is the "resemblance" of the plain case: Is this resemblance legally relevant and is it sufficiently close?[29] However, whether these criteria are sufficient to decide a case is an open question due to the texture of language. Due to this dependence upon the use of language there exists an open texture of law.[30] Arguably, this is a particular instance of the general finding that no rule implies its application.[31]

More interesting in the context of LIR is whether all attempts to close the open texture of language have to be seen as idealizations. But this is not the case. If it is prohibited to ride a motorbike on a certain path we might well conclude that the prohibition also holds for quads and trikes. All we do to yield this result is to bracket our knowledge of the number of wheels of the different types of open motor vehicles. The argument thus is typical for an abstraction. Yet that we bracket this knowledge and no other knowledge (e.g.: about the emissions of noise of the machines) has again to be justified in view of the relevant statute. And this reason is hardly to obtain by mere logic; many will take this reasoning to be an idealization. Still as lawyers we can recognize the first reasoning ("bracket the number of wheels") as abstraction, and the second as idealization in need of further argument (based on the statute in question). Thus lawyers are quite frequently facing both kinds of argu-

27 op. cit., p. 124.
28 Hart, op. cit., p. 123.
29 Hart, op. cit., p. 124.
30 Hart, op. cit., p. 124.
31 Based on the argument of L. Carroll: "What the Tortoise said to Achill", Mind 4 (1895), pp. 278–280. For the general conclusion regarding rules cf. P. Winch: "The Idea of a Social Science and its Relation to Philosophy", London 1958, esp. pp. 53–57.

ment, and though they usually do not think about their difference they focus rightly on the further necessity to justify the idealization used.

In LIR-settings layers can make use of their daily experience in using abstractions and idealizations in order to further the argument in the right way, and to enhance the awareness for abstractions and idealizations within the group and towards the public addressed by their research. Lawyers may unite with others in a non-legal enterprise of LIR but still act as lawyers, and so it is with all other academics, respectively. This renders LIR at once possible and rational to pursue.

Literature

Becker, G. (1964): Human Capital: A Theoretical and Empirical Analysis, with Special Reference Education, Chicago.

Carrier, M. (2007): "Erkenntnisgewinn und Nutzenmaximierung", in: P. Weingart, M. Carrier and W. Krohn (eds.): Nachrichten aus der Wissensgesellschaft. Weilerswist, pp. 93–110.

Carroll, L. (1895): "What the Tortoise said to Achilles", Mind 4, pp. 278–280.

Chomsky, N. (1957): Syntactic Structures. Mouton, Den Haag.

de Chadarevian, S. and N. Hopwood (eds.; 2004): Models: The third dimension of Science. Stanford.

Glaser, B.B. and A.L. Strauss (1967): The Discovery of Grounded Theory: Strategies for Qualitative Research. New York.

Hart, H.L.A. (1960): The Concept of Law, Oxford.

Hymes, D. (1974): Foundations in Sociolinguistics: An Ethnographic Approach. Philadelphia.

Locke, J. (1960): Two Treatises of Government, Cambridge (ed. Peter Laslett).

Luhmann, N. (1990): Wissenschaft als System. Frankfurt.

Magen S. (2010): Review of: "Michael Anderheiden, Gemeinwohl in Deutschland, Europa und der Welt", in: RabelsZ 74 (2010), p. 222, at 224.

Marenbon, J. (2006): From the Circle of Alcuin to the School of Auxerre. Cambridge 1981, reprint 2006.

Mulsow, M. and A. Mahler (2010): "Einleitung", in: Die Cambridge School der politischen Ideengeschichte. Frankfurt, pp. 7–10.

O'Neill, O. (1996): Towards Justice and Virtue: A constructive account of practical reasoning. Cambridge.

Pies, I. and M. Leschke (eds., 1998): Gary Beckers ökonomischer Imperialismus. Tübingen.

Weingart, P. (2007): "Unparteilichkeit und wirtschaftliche Interessen", pp. 234–246.

Weingart, P. (2007): "Wissenschaft als Gegenstand politischer, wirtschaftlicher und ethischer Konflikte", pp. 229–233.

Winch, P. (1958): "The Idea of a Social Science and its Relation to Philosophy", London, esp. pp. 53–57.

Stephan Kirste

The Genuine Contribution of Jursiprudence to an Interdisciplinary Discourse

Abstract:
Wissenschaftliche Disziplinen werden durch Methoden, Sprache, Wissensbestände, Professionalisierung, Organisation und ihr spezifisches Verhalten zu Innovation geformt. Interdisziplinarität stellt dies nicht in Frage. Ein sinnvoller Ansatz zu ihrer Begründung unterscheidet zwischen einer begrifflichen bzw. erkenntnistheoretischen Interdisziplinarität, die auf hinreichend allgemeine und Brückenbegriffe baut. Demgegenüber versucht die organisatorische Interdisziplinarität entweder den wissenschaftlichen Austausch zwischen Disziplinen zu institutionalisieren oder bestehende wissenschaftliche Disziplinen zu differenzieren, indem Methoden und Perspektiven anderer Wissenschaften aufgegriffen und speziellen Einheiten zugewiesen werden. So kann sich etwa die Rechtswissenschaft in Rechtsdogmatik als Zentrum und die Grundlagenfächer als Peripherie organisatorisch differenzieren.

Interdisciplinary discourse in jurisprudence is necessary and precarious at the same time. It is necessary because the content of jurisprudence, the law, affects many other social systems. It is precarious, because its methods differ quite substantially from those of other sciences.

My paper will address both the dangers and the potentials of the participation of jurisprudence in an interdisciplinary discourse. To be able to outline some answers we have to look at the criteria that form a scientific discipline, first, have a look at the preconditions and forms of interdisciplinary discourse, second, and finally apply both on jurisprudence.

1 Disciplinarity

Disciplinarity forms a scientific discipline. The process of disciplining was most prominently investigated by Michel Foucault,[1] but has also been analyzed on the basis of other approaches.[2] The Latin term "discipline" has already had the meaning of knowledge on the one hand and education on the other hand. And indeed, not only the existing knowledge itself, but also an active attitude towards it seems to shape the characteristics of a discipline. Important factors for this formation process are a common knowledge, gained on the basis of a specific method, a more or less distinguished language, the professionalization of the development of this knowledge, and finally its organization in more or less densely integrated institutions.

1.1 Method

Scientific disciplines are not identified by their content but by their leading questions and their methods. The content may be the subject of different disciplines.

1 For the concept of "discipline" in Foucault with respect to law cf. Chian 2003, pp. 25 ff.
2 Shumway/Davidow 1991, S. 202 ff.

Law, for example, is being investigated as a tool to stabilize power in politics, as facilitating economic processes in economy, and so on. Accordingly, content cannot be the distinguishing feature of a certain discipline. Methods and the perspectives differ, however. If sociology deals with law, it observes it as a fact, how the legislator enacts it or the judge enforces it, as a communicative operation, as a means of submission etc. If theology deals with law, it may appear as a means of enforcing the will of God, or, on the contrary, it may be criticized for not being an expression of the eternal or the natural law. If philosophy investigates the law, it may reconstruct its rationality or justifies it on moral grounds. Each discipline concentrates on different aspects of the law and applies different methods to further its respective aim. If one likes to use spatial expressions it is appropriate to say that method demarcates the legitimate boundaries of a discipline[3]: If identified by its method, an investigation comes to its end where the method is of no help to analyze a subject. Hitherto, scholars of other disciplines either have to change their method or will have difficulties participating in this one.

Although this is generally quite agreed, one has to keep in mind one feature of law as an academic object: its artificial character. This particular quality is crucial to the fundamental distinction between natural sciences and cultural studies or humanities. This distinction is relevant not only for a certain method of understanding or explaining, but also for the relevance of method at all. Whereas in science the object is given without human influence, in the humanities knowledge is a precondition for the existence of an object. Works of culture are expressions of human spirit and knowledge. In law, this knowledge is in itself formed and trained by method and scientific effort. Thus, although it remains true in both the humanities and science that a discipline is identified by the perspective and the method chosen to investigate the object, the knowledge gained is not only the result of that process but also the beginning of the production and the continuation of a new object. As a consequence, the progress in the humanities, and especially in law, has a circular structure in which the scientific effort is directed at an object that in part has been produced by the same effort. – This distinction between science and the humanities is *idealtypisch*, however. Once using experiments, the two approximate each other. Through the order of the parameters of the experiment even an investigated aspect of nature becomes artificial and is thereby constructed.

Due to its artificial character law has other specific features: It is a norm or a set of norms, established by a normatively regulated procedure, and being enforced by a normatively empowered and limited professional staff.[4] Whereas works of culture in general can be formed by the individual intentions, craft, and will of the author; legislative acts, administrative acts, and jurisdiction have to follow certain procedures guaranteeing the rational character of the product. Under the rule of law principle – at least in the German understanding of "Rechtsstaatsprinzip" – legal action has to be free from arbitrariness, understandable and predictable by legal

3 It is inappropriate, however, to extend this thinking into a militarist mapping, stating that "boundary work" secures the frontiers against the intrusion of other disciplines (as in the works of Becher 1989, pp. 36 ff.): The disciplines, and those working in them, just cannot intrude, each other without giving up their own method, and that is, themselves – which in turn would be a strange way of fighting a war.

4 Kirste 2010, p. 86.

subjects in its content and enforcement. These rational criteria of law require again a certain systematic form and coherence which can only be achieved under the influence of jurisprudence. Not only the enactment of law is limited by rational criteria, however, also the interpretation, application and, finally, the enforcement of law has to meet rational standards. All these procedures follow methods that are also objects of scientific research.

Accordingly, the circular structure of the methodological investigation of the law and the influence of the knowledge gained in this way about the origins of law have several implications on jurisprudence as a discipline. Hence, legal methodology is not only relevant for the understanding of law, but also for its enactment and its application as well.

1.2 Language

It is a commonplace that jurisprudence uses a highly technical language.[5] Since law is a means of democratic control, and aims at steering people's action, it uses terms from ordinary language as well.[6] The systematic character of legal argumentation, however, soon transforms the meaning of these words into the specific terminology of a technical language.[7] Jurisprudence operates on the basis of this terminology, specifying it for the further needs of its discourse. As a result, legal language may be understandable for professional practitioners, but not for laymen – and not for colleagues from other disciplines. Both groups need a translation to understand the specific content of the legal terms. Therefore, it is quite obvious that language is another identifying factor of a discipline.

Different languages do not seem to be the major obstacle for interdisciplinary discourse, however.[8] They have less importance than the respective scholarly perspectives.[9]

1.3 Knowledge

Some scholars think that knowledge is strictly discipline-specific. Accordingly, Donald Davidson states: "I take it for granted that detailed knowledge of the neurophysiology of the brain will make a difference … to the study of such subjects as

5 Schwintowski 2003, p. 632 ff.

6 And should be comprehensible for everybody, Häberle 2004, pp. 155 f.

7 For the relations between everyday language and construction of reality by law, compare Felder 2005, pp. 133 ff., 163 f.; Simonnaes defines technical communication as: "Wahre Mitteilung kann nur unter 'Gleichgesinnten, Gleichdenkenden' stattfinden … das Decodieren sprachlicher Informationen kann nur gelingen, wenn ausreichendes Wissen beim Rezipienten bzw. Adressaten vorhanden ist … Sprache ist für das Recht unabdingbar, denn ohne Sprache ist das Recht nicht kommunizierbar." Furthermore, law has to be understandable.

8 Schwintowski 2005, pp. 379 f.

9 Gülich 2006, p. 10: "Für Verständigungsschwierigkeiten ist oft weniger die fremde Fachsprache der anderen Disziplin verantwortlich – nach unbekannten Termini kann man leicht fragen – als die Divergenz der Perspektiven und der Relevanzsetzungen, die die Beschäftigung mit den jeweiligen Gegenständen leiten."

perception, memory, dreaming and perhaps of inference. But it is one thing for developments in one field to affect changes in a related field, and another thing for knowledge gained in one area to constitute knowledge of another".[10] Accordingly, methods of a discipline seem to give knowledge a certain form, the walls of which cannot be surmounted by interdisciplinary discourse.

Specific knowledge plays an important role in legal theory as well as in its practice. Certain rules were never transformed into formal law but count as common heritage of legal wisdom or as general legal principles. Others develop over time, eventually elaborated and systematized by jurisprudence. All this knowledge works as a rationalizing and stabilizing canon that limits change. Thus, all innovations have to prove their usefulness not only with respect to legal practice, but also to these inherited criteria. Again, this knowledge does not only contain certain rules but also methods of applying the law, like the canon of interpretation.

For the elaboration and integration of knowledge various media, such as journals, play a key role.[11]

1.4 Professionalization

Although it is not a necessary condition, professionalization of a discipline seems to be an important factor for integration. Here, too, the forming of the object of the discipline may be a process that involves people who are not trained in the respective discipline, or at least have no academic degree.[12] In local history, for example, often hobby scientists dig out the treasures of local archives and estates, bring them together and exhibit them in town museums. But often this is not done on the basis of a well-elaborated method, rather led by chance and the enthusiasm about the subject as such. Their achievements may then be the objects of professional historians bringing them into a methodically elaborated order.

Turning to law, practitioners from courts, administrations, law firms or corporate lawyers participate in its production.[13] The more methodologically oriented this production is, the more relevant it becomes for evaluation by professional jurisprudence, and in some instances it may even cross the borders into an academic endeavor. Methodologically elaborated knowledge about law is not only produced in universities, but also in public ministries, big law firms, or in (higher) courts. Both the high degree of methodological training of practitioners and the dependence of the law on its methodological production may make the criteria of professionalization of legal academics a less important factor for the identification of the discipline.

Still, the sense for a consistent doctrinal system that values coherence of its propositions higher than its pragmatic use may rather be developed by academic

10 Davidson 1973, p. 247.

11 Goggin 1997, pp. 322 ff., 324: "Through their editorial policies and practices, they adjudicate the questions, the objects of study, the methods used and the discursive forms of a discipline."

12 Academic literature reflects this. In the beginning of their publication academic journals were read by a broad public. Later they were only subscribed by scholars of the respective field, Shumway/Messer-Davidow 1991, pp. 206 f.

13 Schmidt-Aßmann 1995, S. 2.

scholars than by practitioners. Research that has its starting point in everyday cases and questions with their problems solved by professionals in one way or another is different from academic research in which the scholar has the responsibility not only of providing a pragmatic solution but also of presenting a coherent and possibly innovative elucidation.[14] Furthermore, whereas the practitioner usually remains within the confinements of valid law, the academic is not bound by it. His research may result in solutions that never come into effect.

1.5 Organization

This may also explain why organization is less important for the forming of the discipline: There are forms of legal research inside and outside law schools or faculties. Organizing jurisprudence bears particular chances for forming a discipline, however. Aspects of rational choices as well as organizational culture contribute to these potentials.[15] In general the discursive community of a faculty, a professional school, or an academy,[16] leads to integration and also differentiation of a discipline. The colleagues are the experts in their fields, further distinguishing themselves from other experts within the faculty and from faculties of the same discipline in other parts of the world. The competition between faculties may be a mechanism for further specializing and elaborating specific knowledge. Organization also helps to keep up the inherited knowledge enshrined in libraries. It provides academics with opportunities for conversation, and usually gives them financial stability.[17] In some countries academic journals are attached to these organizations. Finally, they reproduce themselves by training their staff as successors.

Usually, faculties at least in part are sustained by subsidies that permit research not aimed at immediate profit but at long-term use, or that may even have no direct use at all but is necessary for the further development of the discipline.

Aspects of organizational culture[18] are certain categories of thought, vocabulary, codes of conduct, attitude towards "abstract" theoretical research, the balance of research and academic education, traditions and "profiles" of faculties. In part they are not discipline- but faculty-specific.[19] Although these factors don't comply with the idea of "University" – meaning also the universality of knowledge – they show the reality of highly specialized research universities. It becomes apparent, that organizational factors are of secondary importance for the forming of a discipline. This becomes also obvious in the examples Frost and Jean give in their study.[20] The

14 Kirste 2010, pp. 28 and 36 ff.
15 Frost/Jean 2003, pp. 120 ff.
16 Of special importance for the raise of sciences were the Royal Society and the Académie des Sciences.
17 Shumway/Messer-Davidow 1991, p. 207.
18 For organizational culture in general, cf. Scott 2001, pp. 37 ff.
19 Frost/Jean 2003, p. 120 and 145.
20 Frost/Jean 2003, p. 122: "For example, the pure sciences treat knowledge as quantitative and cumulative, the humanities and soft social sciences as reiterative and pluralist, the hard social sciences as functional and utilitarian, and the applied or technical disciplines as purposive and pragmatic. Thus, the humanities tend to be concerned with particulars or complication and

different ways in which sciences, humanities, hard and soft social sciences treat their respective knowledge rather originates in the different methods they apply to gain and preserve it.

Again, as much as professionalism in research is not a necessary condition for jurisprudence as a discipline, also its organization in faculties or law schools seems not to be decisive. One can find legal research in public offices, in the scientific departments of parliaments as well as in law firms. Here, too, the incentive for providing organizational structures for research in a surrounding primarily oriented towards practical issues contributes to the methodical character of the production and application of law.

This last aspect shows that Steven Toulmin did not take all relevant factors for the forming of an academic discipline into account, when he mentioned the continuity of problems and the development of its theoretical ideals and goals as the decisive factors.[21] Organization matters as well. But then again, it is not the sole forming factor of a discipline and not the most important one.[22]

1.6 Variation and Innovation

Another identifying factor of a discipline is its method of dealing with variation and innovation and the stabilization of its content. Apart from the fact that disciplines themselves are no a-temporal entities,[23] even the separation of humanities and sciences has developed and is still changing. If they are formed at a certain time, disciplines react differently to irritating influences.

The development or evolution of a discipline is no less stimulated by internal impulses – new ideas, new methods – than, and perhaps even more, by an external change of their subject. But here again, Toulmin and others underestimated the different structures of sciences and humanities. The weight of internal and external factors may shift between disciplines. The dynamic of the scientific object may have a different impact on the dynamic of the scientific research engaged with it. And again, in the humanities the drive of this development may be dependent upon dynamics in the respective discipline. When, for example, the idea of New Public Management was introduced to the field of administrative law as a new paradigm, many local administrations discovered the saving potentials of this new idea.[24] Panels consisting of scholars and practitioners were established to find ways to define and implement the ensuing forms of public steering. Furthermore, deficits in democratic legitimacy and other problems were subject to academic research. Again, this illustrates how the disciplinary circle in jurisprudence also affects its dynamics.[25] Because there is no clear cut difference between professional and academic jurispru-

interpretation, the pure or natural sciences with universals and simplification, and the applied or technical sciences with know-how and mastery."

21 Toulmin 1978, S. 185.

22 This neglects Fuller 1991, S. 302, stating: "In short, disciplines mark the point at which methods are institutionalized, or, so to speak, the word is made flesh."

23 Schleifer, pp. 441 ff.

24 Osborne/Gaebler: Reinventing Government.

25 Somek 2006, S. 14 f.

dence the impulses for change come from lawyers no less than from scholars. Also the selection and stabilization of these impulses derive from practice and the academic sphere alike. There is no strict delimitation of the two but rather a question of more or less influence. This is also expressed in commentaries, perhaps the most prominent tool for integrating new developments in practice into the scientific treatment of the law. Here, too, we find both short, more practically oriented commentaries and voluminous, more general ones.[26] In addition, the review of court decisions may serve a practical or theoretical purpose.

This enumeration does not include all factors. The characteristics mentioned above may not be all factors for the forming of an academic discipline. However, they belong to the most important ones.[27] All interdisciplinary approaches have to take these factors into account, because disregarding them would at the same time nullify or at least infringe upon the specific contribution these disciplines could provide for an interdisciplinary discourse.

2 Interdisciplinarity

2.1 What Does Interdisciplinarity Mean?

Julie Thompson Klein identifies six different meanings of the term "interdisciplinarity": (1) borrowing knowledge across disciplines; (2) engaging in collaborative problem-solving; (3) bridge-building between disciplines that remain discrete; (4) developing synthetic theories that operate across disciplines (e.g. general systems theory); (5) constituting new fields from overlapping areas of separate disciplines (e.g., legal psychology, criminology).[28] These aspects are not complete, however. Another form of interdisciplinarity can be seen when faculties differentiate and incorporate methods and goals from other disciplines, and institutionalize them in specialized chairs (6). This is the case with the so-called basic disciplines of law like legal history or legal sociology.

These distinctions combine epistemological and organizational aspects: Whereas (2), (5) and (6) concern organizational interdisciplinarity, the other forms relate to conceptual or epistemological questions of interdisciplinarity. Accordingly, one can speak of different levels of interdisciplinary research. If the method identifies a discipline than here too the conceptual aspects of interdisciplinarity are a precondition for the organizational ones. The understanding of basic concepts of another discipline is a precondition of interdisciplinary research, it is not sufficient to establish it, however.

26 Schmidt-Aßmann 1995, S. 2.
27 Others could be the rhetoric and the history of a discipline as a confirming factor, Fuller 1991, pp. 301 ff.; Shumway/Messer-Davidow 1991, pp. 221 f.
28 Klein 1990, pp. 11 ff.

Conceptual Interdisciplinarity			Organizational Interdisciplinarity		
Borrowing knowledge across disciplines	Bridge-building between disciplines that remain discrete	Developing synthetic theories that operate across disciplines	Engaging in collaborative problem solving	Constituting new fields from overlapping areas of separate disciplines	Differentiating disciplines by creating specialized institutes

Interdisciplinary research has many positive effects. It can lead, to stress out one point, to a broadening of the fundaments of one's disciplinary research.[29] On the basis of interdisciplinary discussions categories for the observation of the consequences of doctrinal findings for other areas of research and society can be observed.

2.2 Conditions of Interdisciplinarity

Similarly to other disciplines, the need for interdisciplinary research including the law does not originate from the form of jurisprudence, but from its content.[30] A multifaceted character of a subject may stimulate interdisciplinary research. From this starting point, you will not criticize the method of a participating discipline, but argue and learn from the perspective description of the content.[31] And indeed, looking at its content, law is embedded in other social norms, habits and other orientation for actions. It transforms these, however, by formal procedures into relatively stable and enforceable norms that provide guidelines and secure expectations. This very character relates law to other social systems and distinguishes it from them at once. This fact forms the basis for the necessity of interdisciplinary discourse of jurisprudence and other research areas, but it also limits the possibilities of such a discourse. – Another aspect underlines the particular need for interdisciplinarity in law: Discourses across the discipline's borders improve the capability to solve social problems.[32] Let us remember that jurisprudence is a practical science, meant to help settling conflicts of interest and to provide for principles to prevent them in the future. If it does not participate in interdisciplinary discussions, jurisprudence will lose the ability to serve its genuine goals.

Since academic disciplines are identified by their form – as shown above –, especially by their method, the question arises whether this form can be overcome for the sake of an adequate understanding of the scientific object.

29 Frost/Jean 2003, p. 132.
30 This may explain why the need for interdisciplinary research is especially prominent in applied sciences, which are built around a certain practical question.
31 Baldus 2005, S. 326.
32 Frost/Jean 2003, p. 120.

2.2.1 Conceptual Interdisciplinarity

Niklas Luhmann is of the opinion that an interdisciplinary discourse is possible if it is developed around general patterns like self-organization.[33] In this case, a similar mechanism could be discovered in different objects. If research is strictly oriented towards such a pattern or general concept the result, however, will be the emergence of a new discipline which takes the pattern as the leading perspective for new discoveries, including adequate methods for their investigation. This in itself would not be interdisciplinary, because the participating disciplines would yield themselves, and their methods, to this new perspective.

In their abstract generality, these concepts would have little significance in the different disciplines. General concepts, however, can be a way to start an interdisciplinary discourse, if they permit a re-specification or concretization in the participating disciplines. One classical example is based on the idea that mathematics by its formalization provides the semantics not only to produce rational knowledge in the sciences but in the humanities as well. The axioms and sentences of mathematics seem to provide sufficiently abstract concepts to be applicable in all languages. The point is not, whether this is true or false. The point is that the alignment of knowledge with mathematics seems not to be appropriate for all academic activities. Applying a mathematical method in humanities ignores that the phenomena produced here are expressions of individuality which loose this very characteristic if viewed under the generalizing criteria of *mathesis universalis* only. Accordingly, the critique is not that mathematics does not provide any understandable knowledge but that it does not entail an appropriate one. To criticize some knowledge as (in-) appropriate to its object, however, presupposes to have an understanding of the object as well as of the knowledge. This far the application of a seemingly strange concept taken from one discipline to another does not lead to a barrier of understanding but, at worst, to misunderstandings or to an inadequate use of terms – this again is something which can be debated between scholars using the concept. Examples of the "wrong" use of concepts could also be that all relevant events could be explained by "power" in politics and history as well, or "money" would be the basic concept for the explanation of events in economy, history, or law.

Let us take "human dignity" as an example. In a theological perspective it may be interesting to know that in a strictly legal understanding "human dignity" defines a right to have rights for every human being.[34] On the other hand, for a lawyer it may be helpful to know that the origin of the term in Christian theology comes from the idea of man being an image of god, which in turn is expressed by his liberty. Thus, he could translate or transform the term into law. In order to meet societal expectations in the use of this constitutional term it may also be useful to learn about the understanding of it in cultural studies as the ability and necessity of a human being to create oneself.[35] Unlike Luhmann's proposal here the general term is applied as a tool for translating or transforming knowledge from one discipline into the other. The concept serves as a measure for the different methods other disci-

33 Luhmann 1992, S. 457.

34 Enders 1997, S. 501 ff.

35 Pico della Mirandola 1990, pp. 5 f.; Oskar Kristeller; for an overview: Gröschner/Kirste/Lembcke 2008.

plines apply when dealing with a similar object. In this perspective the experience of difference allows for a more distinguished use of a term in one's own discipline.

Interdisciplinary discourse does not imply the mere adaptation of common concepts of one discipline by the other, or the development of sufficiently general concepts that overcome all differences in method and perspectives of different disciplines. Skeptics of interdisciplinarity are right that this approach would mean abandoning the disciplinary perspective and submit oneself under the possibly more fascinating foreign perspective.[36] Neither does interdisciplinarity mean the mere exchange of data which turn into information in the respective discipline. Taking such criticism into account, however, the question arises how the import or rather transformation of knowledge can be organized.

2.2.2 Organizational Interdisciplinarity

Niklas Luhmann suggests three forms of interdisciplinary discourse: First, occasional interdisciplinarity; second, temporary interdisciplinarity; and finally, transdisciplinarity. Occasional interdisciplinarity refers to the accidental confrontation with central terms of different disciplines. Informal communication about concepts of different disciplines may cause irritation. They may provoke new perspectives and new knowledge. They especially incite a sense of the consequences of one's research for other disciplines and social systems.[37] Temporary interdisciplinarity is a form of discourse that is meant to avoid encrustation of disciplines within the confines of inherited questions. They are institutionalized in temporally limited forms of cooperation. Such forms could be common seminars or conferences, which are gathered around a certain subject.[38] They attempt to integrate the different perspectives on the subject. Both forms do not lead to an institutional differentiation of the participating disciplines. They only share some of their temporal and intellectual resources. The import remains alien to the own discipline, and the import is left to the capacity of each participating scholar and his curiosity. The third form is the institutionalization of what was mentioned above: The forming of a new discipline around an innovative pattern. This institutionalization draws resources from existing disciplines shifting them into a new one. Since it leads to a new discipline the question remains how the knowledge of this new discipline can be transformed into the existing ones which may be interested in it.

Do these ways of institutionalization work better than a mere theoretical exchange? That might well be so. The reason may be that even academic communication has several modes, not all of them technical, although they contribute to the production of disciplinary knowledge. Analyzing scientific communication, Latour and Wolgar find four modes: The first consists in the exchange of facts. The second mode is characterized by nonverbal communication about methods. For a third level the theoretical elaboration of criteria for scientific communication is decisive.

36 Baldus 1995, S. 327.

37 Frost/Jean 2003, p. 131.

38 Frost/Jean 2003, pp. 124, report on a case study of the success of interdisciplinary seminars at a southeaster university in the US. They give an overview on the effects this interdisciplinary seminar had on the participants on p. 130.

Finally, for a fourth mode gossip around the experiment is typical.[39] Although this model may be coined on scientific experiments, it may show, more generally, the multifaceted structure of communications, which do not fully adhere to the strict confinements of the disciplinary method.

Beyond Luhmann's above-mentioned three forms of interdisciplinary research a fourth form of institutionalizing interdisciplinarity may be the (internal) differentiation of the participating disciplines. This is actually carried out when disciplines provide chairs for sub-disciplines that refer to others. In jurisprudence the basic disciplines of law – legal history, legal theory and philosophy, legal sociology – are examples for this move. These chairs work in an interdisciplinary manner, because first they apply methods of their referring disciplines to the main object of their respective field, and second they import knowledge from them into their own discipline. This, however, is not a "one to one" import, but a transformation of the "foreign" knowledge into the law under the leading question of jurisprudence.[40] They prepare the findings of other disciplines for the use of their own disciplinary argumentation. This gives their work a much more reliable and also concrete impact on the respective discipline. One can call this a differentiation of center and periphery. In the center one will find the leading perspective of a discipline – the normative perspective in jurisprudence, for example, – and its respective methods. Here, the purity of the discipline has its place. In the case of jurisprudence the well-known fields of legal activities would be this core.[41] In the periphery the system opens towards the knowledge of other disciplines, but only in so far as they are relevant and applicable to its own research. Scholars working at the periphery must be experts in their core discipline, but also capable of understanding the other approaches.

Subjects like the law which are on the one hand extremely formalized and on the other hand do affect the society in many fields, need an institutionalized form of interdisciplinarity in order to keep their specific capacities. The form adequate to these purposes is the differentiation of the discipline itself in center and periphery.

To sum up: conceptual interdisciplinarity is a necessary condition for interdisciplinary research. It has to be complemented by organizational interdisciplinarity to be successful. Organizational interdisciplinarity can have cooperative forms but also forms of differentiation. In jurisprudence the existence of the basic disciplines such as legal philosophy, legal history and legal sociology can be justified as organizational forms of interdisciplinarity, based on a differentiation of center – legal dogmatics – and periphery – basic disciplines.

39 Latour/Wolgar 1986, pp. 152 ff.; cf. also Schleifer 1997, pp. 446 f.

40 For the concept of transformation in jurisprudence cf. Kirste 2009, pp. 134 ff.

41 Kirste 2010, pp. 36 ff.

Literature

Baldus, Christian (2005): "Metasprache" und unhistorische Interdisziplinarität. In: Zeitschrift für Neuere Rechtsgeschichte (ZNR) 27 (2005), pp. 325–328.
Becher, Tony: Academic Tribes and Territories: Intellectual Enquiry and the Cultures of Disciplines. Milton Keynes, England 1989.
Davidson, Donald (1973): The Material Mind. In: Essays on Actions and Events, pp. 245–259, Oxford.
Enders, Christoph (1997): Die Menschenwürde in der Verfassungsordnung. Zur Dogmatik des Art. 1 GG. Tübingen.
Felder, Ekkehard (2005): Alltagsweltliche und juristische Wirklichkeitskonstitution im Modell der "Juristischen Textarbeit". Ein sprachhandlungstheoretischer Beitrag zur Kommunikation im Recht. In: Die Sprache des Rechts, Vol. 3: Recht vermitteln. Ed. by Kent D. Lerch. Berlin, pp. 133–169.
Frost, Susan H./Jean/Paul M.: Bridging the Disciplines (2003): Interdisciplinary Discourse and Faculty Scholarship. The Journal of Higher Education 74 (2003), pp. 119–149.
Fuller, Steve: Disciplinary Boundaries and the Rhetoric of the Social Sciences. In: Poetics Today, 12 (1991), pp. 301–325.
Giovanni Pico della Mirandola (1990): Über die Würde des Menschen / Oratio de hominis dignitate. Hamburg.
Goggin, Maureen Daly (1997): Composing a Discipline: The Role of Scholarly Journals in the Disciplinary Emergence of Rhetoric and Composition since 1950. In: Rhetoric Review 15 (1997), pp. 322–348.
Gülich, Elisabeth (2006): Das Alltagsgeschäft der Interdisziplinarität. In: Deutsche Sprache 2006, S. 6–17.
Häberle, Peter (2005): Das Verständnis des Rechts als Problem des Verfassungsstaates. In: Die Sprache des Rechts, Vol. 3: Recht verstehen. Hrsg. v. Kent D. Lerch. Berlin, pp. 155–169.
Joas, Hans/Kippenberg, Hans G. (Hrsg.): Interdisziplinarität als Lernprozeß. Erfahrungen mit einem handlungstheoretischen Forschungsprogramm. Göttingen, S. 7 ff.
Kirste, Stephan (2009): Recht als Transformation. In: Deutsche Rechtsphilosophie im 21. Jahrhundert. Ed. by W. Brugger, U. Neumann und S. Kirste (Autoren u. a.: R. Alexy, J. Habermas, O. Höffe, H. Hofmann, D. von der Pfordten, G. Teubner). Frankfurt/Main (Suhrkamp) 2008. (2. Aufl. 2009), pp. 134–156.
Kirste, Stephan (2010): Einführung in die Rechtsphilosophie. Darmstadt (in print).
Klein, Julie Thompson: Interdisciplinarity (1990): History, Theory, Practice. Detroit.
Latour, Bruno, Steve Woolgar (1986): Laboratory Life: The Construction of Scientific Facts. Princeton.
Luhmann, Niklas (1992): Die Wissenschaft der Gesellschaft. Frankfurt/Main.
Osborne, David/Gaebler, Ted (1992): Reinventing Government. How the Entrepreneurial Spirit is Transforming the Public Sector. Reading, Mass., 4th print.
Schleifer, Ronald (1997): Disciplinarity and Collaboration in the Sciences and Humanities. In: College English 59 (1997), pp. 438–452.
Schmidt-Aßmann, Eberhardt (1995): Zur Situation der rechtswissenschaftlichen Forschung. In: Juristenzeitung 1995, pp. 1–10.
Schwintowski, Hans-Peter (2005): Sprachwissenschaftliche Kriterien für das Transparenzgebot. Die Bedeutung interdisziplinären Arbeitens von Rechts- und Sprachwissenschaft. In: Die Sprache des Rechts, Vol. 3: Recht verstehen. Hrsg. v. Kent D. Lerch. Berlin, pp. 376–386.
Scott, Richard W. (2001): Institutions and Organizations. 2nd ed., Thousand Oaks.
Shumway, David R./ Messer-Davidow, Ellen (1991): Disciplinarity: An Introduction. In: Poetics Today 12 (1991), pp. 201–225.
Simmonaes, Ingrid (2005): Fachkommunikation im Recht unter Berücksichtigung der Mehrfachadressierung. In: Die Sprache des Rechts, Vol. 3: Recht vermitteln. Ed. by Kent D. Lerch. Berlin, pp. 377–397.
Toulmin, Stephen E. (1978): Kritik der kollektiven Vernunft. Frankfurt/Main.

Oliver W. Lembcke

Balancing Law and Politics

The Contribution of Political Theory

Abstract:
Die Leistungsfähigkeit des modernen Rechtssystems hängt entscheidend davon ab, ob es gelingt, die Prozesse der Entstehung und Veränderung von Normen nach eigenen (rechtlichen) Regeln durchzuführen. Diese Eigenständigkeit des Rechts setzt nicht nur Strategien der Immunisierung gegenüber Einflussnahmen seitens der Politik voraus, sondern ebenso ein vertieftes Verständnis für deren Eigenart und Funktionsweise. Auf dieser Grundlage beruht der interdisziplinäre Austausch zwischen Rechtswissenschaft und Politischer Theorie. Deren Dialog verfolgt das Ziel wechselseitiger Aufklärung, vor allem über die historischen und bis heute fortwirkenden Prozesse der Politisierung des Rechts sowie der Verrechtlichung der Politik, aus denen der Konstitutionalismus entstanden ist und mit ihm der für demokratische Verfassungsstaaten notwendige Verweisungszusammenhang zwischen Recht und Politik. In kritisch-konstruktiver Absicht kann die Politische Theorie gegenüber der Rechtswissenschaft dabei in drei Kontexten als Dialogpartner fungieren: im rechtsphilosophischen Kontext über die normativen Grundlagen einer freiheitlichen Ordnung; im rechtsdogmatischen Kontext, bezogen auf die politische Imprägnierung der Verfahren und Ergebnisse im Rahmen der Rechtssetzung; und im rechtspraktischen Kontext hinsichtlich der (Klugheits- Anforderungen gelingender Rechtsentscheidungen.

1 What's the Point?*

A good lawyer knows that there is no non-political law and no 'purely' legal decision – and that there should not be one. Modern law has been mixed with politics to such an extent that every significant legal norm has its own political history. Whoever works academically in a particular field of law will have to make use of the theories and methods of political science; he or she will otherwise not be able to follow the complex processes of decision-making under the circumstances of a pluralistic society: Every interest is someone's interest. This does not only hold true for the strongly politicized matters of public law, but also for the (reputedly non-political) matters of civil law. How, for example, should the growing trend towards consumer protection be explained, if not by the prevailing political and economic interests? In addition to the prominent role consumer law has gained in contract law today, it has been adjusted within the EU member states due to the politically desirable control by the EU.

Setting goals, seeking access, selecting instruments, or thinking about and dealing with consequences – all these activities are involved before, during, and after the legal decision-making. It is obvious that for these reasons law is (and always will be) oriented towards political power. The lawyer who gets involved in the political sphere is therefore well advised to know about the "real world" outside just as the legal academic is to keep up to date with the social science methodology.[1]

* This article is a revised and extended version of an earlier draft: see "Law and Political Theory: The Other Side of the Story" in Bart van Klink and Sanne Taekema (eds.): Law and Method. Interdisciplinary Research into Law, Tübingen 2011, pp. 153–174.

In doing so, however, one should not fail to notice that central legal concepts, principles and institutions have themselves been shaped by the political struggle for power. Political theory in particular can inform about this. As opposed to the history of law, it does not deal with the innovation and transformation within a field of law, for instance with the freedom of contract in civil law. It rather informs about the political function of such a principle: What protagonists have when and with what intention spoken out in favor of the freedom of contract? And of which relevance is this principle for the legitimacy of the prevailing political order? These are typical questions to which, in a historical perspective, the history of ideas tries to give answers. In a systematic perspective, a normative dimension arises: Political theory is concerned with political freedom. This is not only true with respect to the political arena, but also with reference to law. Each level of legal activity – the enactment, the enforcement, or the application of law – is under scrutiny of political theory: Do they (still) function in a way which preserves a free society? What challenges for the rule of law lie ahead? And what are the normative criteria to evaluate the dynamic changes that keep the engines of the political and the legal system running?

The importance of questions like the ones posed above is easy to assess, especially for lawyers: Most of the legal professions would look different, if they did not operate in a democratic society, but in an authoritarian or totalitarian regime. To be sure, in every political system jurisprudence takes part in the authoritative role of law, but it depends largely on the character of the political system, if and to what extent legal critique or legal research can actually find its place. In dialogue with political theory, jurisprudence will be able to look at itself in a mirror in order to discover how it contributes to the stability of a political order – and how it contributes to its legitimacy.

Law and politics are closely connected; to inform oneself about this special relationship, one will inevitably get involved with political theory. But what is political theory all about? Political theory is about the characteristics of politics. Originally invented by the Greeks, politics arises from the insight into the self-determination of human communities. According to Aristotle, the polis does not solely exist for the sake of life, it exist for the sake of good life.[2] Politics has always been concerned with developing and preserving the prerequisites to social existence under conditions of uncertainty. In the face of these complex practical challenges, political theory has established itself as a reflecting authority in two regards: Historically, it serves as an 'archive' in which the multifaceted forms of political systems are stored. Systematically, it represents an intellectual 'laboratory' in which the innumerable responses to the challenges of successful social coexistence are compared, evaluated and, if necessary, recombined in their components.

Differently from political philosophy, the emphasis of political theory is less on the *conditio humana* and its significance for human self-determination than on the processes of a society's political self-organization which takes place on three levels:

1 US Supreme Court Judge Louis Brandeis knew this a century ago, when he made copious use of social science data in his famous "Brandeis Brief", which led to victory in Muller v. Oregon, p. 208 U.S. 412 (1908).

2 Aristoteles, Pol. I 1253 a 30.

On the level of the structures and institutions which jointly form the constitution of a political order (*polity*); on the level of political acts where interests are imposed, conflicts resolved and compromises reached (*politics*); as well as on the level of political programs, their principles and goals (*policy*).

In modern societies, law plays a central part on all three levels of politics. At least since the great revolutions of the modern age, there is no political system without a legal constitution. The purpose of this article is to throw light on this observation from the perspective of political theory in two regards: In a historical perspective, the development of the symbiotic relationship between law and politics will be depicted; it distinguishes the modern era from previous times (sub 2.). In a systematic perspective, the normative implications of this symbiosis will be examined and the significance of a balanced relationship between law and politics within a liberal democracy will be pointed out (sub 3.). Subsequently, the second systematic section will illustrate the relevance of a constitutionalist theory balancing the relationship between law and politics on the several levels of the legal system (sub 4.). The concluding paragraphs of this essay summarize the essential structures of the relationship between law and politics and identify some recent challenges which could put the conciliation of the two realms into doubt. Against this background, once again the role of political theory for an interdisciplinary jurisprudence will be emphasized (sub 5.).

2 Politicization of Law, Juridification of Politics

Ancient and medieval systems are defined by a close connection between law, politics, religion and morality. Law of those times is firmly anchored in common conventions and customs. It is essentially based on the authority of a judge, often personified by the ruler himself, who legitimizes the law by means of his decisions. His perspective is always directed towards the past to which his verdict serves as a bridge of continuity – old law is good law.[3] The concept of justice changes with the "invention" of subjectivity during the Renaissance. The individual is conceived as a subject, who is responsible for his own development. It is no longer required by tradition which determines the individual life, but it is a task which is autonomously chosen and which every person is expected to fulfill. Yet, in addition to the joy one feels about being the creative sculptor, the 'plastes et fictor' (Pico della Mirandola) of one's own biography,[4] one is also concerned about the future which is now, in contrast to the mentality of the Middle Ages, conceived as open and uncertain. Therefore, guiding the future has come to be the main duty of law up to the present.

Caused by dramatic social upheavals, the processes which lead to an increased concentration on lawmaking accelerate during the 16th century. In general, law is still seen, as an expression of divine will, but as a result of religious division, the certainty about the content of this will begins to dwindle. This issue rather becomes the object of a dispute which irrevocably splits the Christians' unity and leads to the destruction of Europe during the Thirty Years' War. More and more, the idea pre-

3 Kern 1952, pp. 11–23.
4 Pico 1990, p. 6f.

vails – which had already been proclaimed by Bodin, Hobbes and others – that law alone cannot ensure peace. Peace also requires politics, more specifically, a sovereign power which holds the reins of law and justice in its own hand. Thus, law becomes an object of human creation – and an instrument of a constantly growing political will to create. This is the beginning of the politicization of law: From the mid-16th to the early 19th century, law increasingly serves to consolidate the peacekeeping system of the territorial state, to reduce privileges, to control jurisdiction and to centralize administrative structures. In the course of these developments, legislation continually increases in importance; as a consequence, the relationship between law and politics begins to shift. Law, formerly an expression of the concept of justice, becomes less important as a binding parameter for political orientation. Whatever remains of the concept of justice is turned into non-binding natural law, which does not endanger the legislative sovereignty of the ruler, nor its peacekeeping, system-securing effect.

With the rise of the bourgeoisie as a political power, the situation changes, as manifest in America's War of Independence (1775–1783) and in the French Revolution (1789–1799). The claim to power as a divine right is challenged just as vehemently as the state's unrestricted authority. Instead, all of a sudden, it is a "self-evident" truth "that all men are created equal [and] that they are endowed with certain unalienable rights".[5] The firm belief that society can rule itself for the greater public good is the common core of the different strands of liberalism. To the liberals, law becomes a guarantor of individual liberty – and that is to say of equal rights for everyone and not of privileges for the few. After all, it is the people, the citizens, whose cumulative effort forms the whole of society. Accordingly, the people must also be granted the right to political self-determination, as put forth by Abbé Sieyès in his famous pamphlet 'Qu'est-ce que le tiers État?' (1789). It has since been the legacy of the enlightenment era that political power can only be justified when its claim to power is democratically legitimized and legally limited. This is one element that contributed to the process of juridification of politics.

The other main element is the constant expansion of legislative activity in response to tremendous social transitions, for the most part caused by the Industrial Revolution. While the growing social demands intensify the political process by increasing the number of political decisions as well as their purview, an internal hierarchy is established within the European legal system. It differentiates between two principal levels of law: statutory law, which is enacted by the legislative power, and constitutional law, which is enacted by the constituent power. Constitutional law provides a regulatory framework for the establishment and purview of statutory law but is kept safe from a hasty interference of politics. The creation of a constitution itself differs fundamentally in its historic importance from the everyday passing of laws in a constitutional state. Most states store their own historical 'constitutional moment'[6] in their collective memory. Furthermore, amending the constitution requires in most countries a much more complicated and consensus-oriented process than changing laws. This internal hierarchy between constitutional law and statutory

5 This phrase is part of the opening of the Declaration of Independence written by Thomas Jefferson in 1776.

6 The concept refers to Ackerman 1989, pp. 476–478.

law enables a mutual dependence of politics and law.[7] It empowers the lawmaker to act politically swiftly and effectively, in order to change or adapt law according to his own ideas and to even create a completely new legal situation. Nevertheless, he must adhere to the constitutional requirements.

3 Symmetry or Asymmetry of Law and Politics?

The historical sketch above has illustrated the symbiotic relationship between law and politics. This interdependence shall now be brought into a systematic perspective dealing with the normative implications of this symbiosis. The central question of this section will deal with the nature of the relationship between law and politics: Should political power decide upon law and its normative quality alone? Should law, irrespective of politics, be determined solely according to its own rules? And which normative standards could lead to an interplay of law and politics that would be commensurate with the concept of a liberal political order? The answers to these questions are innumerable and preoccupy legal philosophy and legal theory of law as much as political theory.

For the purpose of simplification, three theoretical models are paradigmatically differentiated – decisionism (3.1), positivism (3.2) and constitutionalism (3.3) – here represented by the exponents Carl Schmitt, Hans Kelsen and Hermann Heller, respectively.[8] Compared to the two other models, Constitutionalism is less compelling in its theoretical orientation. It lacks the elegance of the other approaches which are more consistent by creating and pursuing the self-references of either law (positivism) or of power (decisionism). Constitutionalism rather endeavors to preserve a form of balance in the relationship between law and politics. Accordingly, it is the intention of every constitutionalist to avoid anything that could possibly jeopardize "progress in the consciousness of freedom" (Hegel) by preferring one side over the other. Viewed in a historical perspective, this practical concern has contributed a lot towards achieving stable constitutional orders of freedom wherever democracy and liberalism have been accepted as organizing political principles. On this account, the delineation of the three models will be concluded by a short outline of the modern variations of constitutionalism (3.4).

3.1 Decisionism

Carl Schmitt's distinction between the constitution and constitutional law is part of the remaining legacy of his constitutional theory. According to Schmitt, the constitution should not be seen as a sum of constitutional laws, but as an integrated whole; it is the expression of a nation's constituent power through which it takes a sovereign decision about its own existence, forming its particular identity ('we') and

7 Luhmann 1995, pp. 440–495.

8 For a more detailed discussion of this paradigmatic dispute about the relationship between law and politics see Dyzenhaus 2003, chap. 2–4.

separating itself from other forms of political identities ('them').[9] A people's fundamental decision on a form of political existence precedes the decision on a constitutional law as a system's normative foundation. This differentiation between the constitution as a political unity and the constitution as a legal concept distinctly illustrates the characteristic decisionism in Schmitt's thinking: Schmitt is convinced that the political system is not anticipated by constitutive moral principles or values but that it, normatively, represents a 'creatio ex nihilo,' a political order created out of nothing and for its own sake. Once established, it remains the criterion for the legitimacy of every legal norm and juridical decision. For him, the Weimar constitution serves as an example of an illegitimate norm, in his view conflicting sharply with the general constitution (and thus: decision) of the German people. Schmitt especially criticizes the basic rights and the division of power which he perceives as amounting to a constitutional restriction of the nations own political identity.

For Schmitt, this criticism is based on the incompatibility of liberalism (the civil rights and the separation of powers) and democracy (the self-determination of a people). He associates this with the difference between identity and representation as two different principles of decision-making:[10] While democracy is characterized by the identity between a government and those who are governed, other political systems like, for instance a monarchy, are based on political representation of the people, e.g., by the ruling king. A liberal democracy in the parliamentary variation of the Weimar Republic combines these two principles of self-determination and representation, which, according to Schmitt, has a weakening effect on democracy. In his opinion, this parliamentary system lacked the power to adequately articulate the political will of the people.

His analysis of the 'concrete constitutional situation' was forceful:[11] The contradictory economic and political interest groups will destroy the state's unity and thus render the government incapable of action – a condition which is against the intention of every reasonable constitution. In order to tame antagonistic forces, resist special interests and conciliate the conflicting parties, the guardian of the constitution must be a powerful political authority. For Schmitt, the only authority to come into question in that situation was the "dictatorship of the 'Reichspräsident'". Here, Schmitt's objections to a constitutional court are particularly revealing for the relationship between law and politics.[12]

The threat of a 'juridification' where "politics have nothing to gain, and justice has everything to lose",[13] serves as an argument for him against the role of the constitutional court as a guardian of the constitution. This view insinuates that the interpretation of a constitutional norm is no longer a judicial action, but a lawmaker's. In his eyes, every judicial verdict includes an element of pure decision which cannot solely be derived from the content of the norm. What, then, is so special about constitutional law? In Schmitt's opinion, it is the vague stipulations whose interpretation permits the court to become too independent. It is in danger of evolving from the guardian of the constitution into its 'master.' What is noticeable about this

9 References here and in the following are made to Schmitt 1928, chap. I.–II.
10 Schmitt 1928, chap. III.
11 Schmitt 1931, pp. 71–131.
12 Lembcke 2007, pp. 15–27.
13 Schmitt 1931, p. 35.

reasoning, though, is the change of attitude: Instead of helplessly observing political activities, the constitutional court suddenly seems to pave the way for the "judicial state."[14] On closer examination, it is thus less a supposed impotence that Schmitt warns about, but rather the accumulation of power in one legal institution: the constitutional court.

3.2 Positivism

For Kelsen, only the constitutional court can ensure the binding character of the constitution as the highest legal norm and, as such, maintain the constitution's precedence over all other norms.[15] Contrary to Schmitt, he is therefore not afraid of a strong constitutional court, provided that the constitution does not accommodate "vague key words" (e.g., justice, freedom, equity, morality). The safest way to counter the 'absolute power' of constitutional courts is for the constituent power to avoid the use of this "phraseology".[16] In Kelsen's view, the constitution is nothing but a system of norms which are determined by content; the guardian's function is limited to the enforcement of the constitution by examining the actions of other authorities and, if necessary, rescinding them as unconstitutional. In this sense, it is not a creative, but a 'negative' activity that the guardian of the constitution exercises – which is also why Kelsen describes him as a "negative lawmaker".[17] This depiction illustrates a similarity between jurisdiction and legislation: Legislation establishes general norms, while jurisdiction establishes individual norms. In both cases, the creation of law includes an element of decision-making and, as such, an element of exercising power.[18] This is where the necessary political character of every legal decision becomes apparent, including the decisions made by constitutional courts.

With regard to the constitutional courts, Kelsen bears a particular resemblance to Schmitt. Both believe that, in the end, decisions defy further rationalization. In Schmitt's opinion, this is an expression of power – and, at the same time, a sign of political involvement in a situation. According to Kelsen, Schmitt's argument is based on a fundamental mistake which lies in the separation of law and politics and in the traditional (but outdated) concept of the division of powers. In his opinion, a court decision always includes a decisionist moment. Every state organ 'enacts' legislation; the difference is to be found only in the degree of generality. In that way, the traditionally assigned functions in a state are abolished. Instead, a hierarchical order of state organs is established, in accordance with their proximity to the constitution as the state's highest judicial norm. Here, the superior norm serves as the standard for the legal interpretation or the enactment of norms at the respective lower levels.[19]

While Schmitt tries to separate the jurisdiction of the constitutional court from the political guardian function in the light of the separation of law and politics,

14 Schmitt 1922, p. 13.
15 Kelsen 1929, pp. 43 ff.
16 Kelsen 1929, pp. 24, 69 f.
17 Kelsen 1931, p. 28.
18 Kelsen 1931, pp. 15, 21 f.
19 Kelsen 1960, pp. 228–282.

Kelsen qualifies that distinction differently. For Kelsen, law is what has been established by authority. If the processes of legislative enactment have been formally correct, the result is law.[20] Seen from this point of view, the interpretation of law is reduced to the simple act of volition. The close scrutiny which precedes the decision loses its function and becomes arbitrary – just as with decisionism.

3.3 Constitutionalism

In the analysis of Kelsen and Schmitt, it is primarily Hermann Heller who defends the claims of constitutionalism against the objections of decisionism and positivism. His argument is especially valuable as a pattern of constitutional thinking, since Heller developed a decidedly democratic attitude towards the constitutional state and the relationship between law and politics. In his opinion, constitutionalism unites the principle of political self-determination and political equality, as every person or group has the capacity to independently recognize their own interests and represent them.[21] Both principles are mutually linked and adequately expressed in democratically enacted laws. For Heller, constitutionalism thus means enabling citizens to substantially participate in political life in a dual function within the democratic process of decision-making: as the political sovereign ('rulers') and as the obedient citizen ('ruled').[22]

The interaction of democratic political participation and civic rights – of democracy and liberalism – is especially important for Heller. In addition to the *limiting* function of the constitutional state, based on the restriction of state power, the organization of government authorities as well as the predictability of public actions, he emphasizes the *legitimizing* function which is closely connected to the democratic ideal of political participation. In a democratic state reciprocity, the delegation of political responsibility and feedback by consent or disagreement provide for symmetrical legal relationships between lawmakers and citizens.

In Heller's eyes, it is not enough to be primarily concerned with the reliability of expectations in legal relationships. This formal concept of constitutionalism ignores that every legal norm and every juridical decision represents a binding command to the obedient citizen. What really matters, according to Heller, is to meet these claims to power with rational justification to which the belief in legitimacy is always oriented (material concept of constitutionalism). The overall challenge for the political process is therefore to provide an adjustment of the general command to the individual circumstances during the legal process. The perpetual question about the standards of justification serves to abet the process of democratization by means of the general need for legitimacy.[23]

Just as law stipulates the process of individualizing a legal command from top down, it conversely stipulates the decision-making process from bottom up by which representatives are chosen and elected. In Heller's opinion, the legal determi-

20 Therefore, "every possible content can become law;" Kelsen 1960, p. 201.
21 Heller 1928a, p. 210.
22 Heller 1924, pp. 309, 331–333.
23 For more details see Dyzenhaus 2003, pp. 196 f.

nation of political power – in the dual perspective of 'bottom up' and 'top down' – is a decisive feature of constitutionalism. It comprises the election of representatives as well as their legal commitment in office. Moreover, it regulates the independence of officeholders and provides sanctions to guarantee democratic feedback.[24] For Heller, the legal relationship between representatives and those who are represented, which is founded on the political self-determination of a people, constitutes the difference between democracy and autocracy.

3.4 Modern Constitutionalism

The connection between liberalism (civil rights and individual liberties) and democracy (self-determination of the people) forms the core of modern constitutionalism. Older versions such as constitutional monarchy, no longer fulfill the requirements of political legitimacy.[25] Even if law and order reigned in those states, the possibilities of democratic legislation are limited. The idea of constitutionalism often remains only the pale shimmer of a guarantee for legal equality, together with some individual rights. Modern constitutionalism, however, is oriented toward Rousseau's concept of the general will (*volonté générale*) which refers to the interest of a people as an associated and integrated whole, opposed to a mere aggregated sum of individual self-interests (*volonté de tous*).[26] Yet, it is difficult – not only in practice but also in theory – to adequately determine the volonté générale and thus the balance in the fundamental relationship between the sovereignty of the people as a constituent power and the constitution as a legal framework of politics: How much deliberation does the ideal of the volonté générale demand from the democratic participants and processes? And how much decision-making by the majority can it tolerate?[27] Ideal-typically, three approaches can be distinguished in the present discussion.[28]

(1) In a liberal variation of constitutionalism, the basic rights and liberties of the individual – in the tradition of John Locke 'life, liberty and estate' – establish the essential foundation for every liberal political system. In that sense, they are of universal validity; and a large part of the liberal constitutional theory attempts to offer a convincing explanation for this claim on universality. Among the well-known and elaborated drafts is John Rawls' *Theory of Justice*. His theory allows a good examination of the precedence of law over politics in the process of constitutional development which is perceived as inevitable from the liberal perspective: Not the sovereign people but the moral principles of law and their consideration in developing the legal constitution determine the legitimacy of a political system. Rawls uses a thought experiment to justify such universal principles:[29] What constitutional principles would free and reasonable people choose in an original position, where they are adequately informed about the fundamental relationships of social and political

24 Heller 1928b, pp. 425–427.
25 Benhabib 1994.
26 Rousseau, Contrat social I/6, II/3–4.
27 Honig 2007.
28 Loughlin/Walker 2007, p. 6f.
29 Rawls 1971, chap. I/§§3–4, chap. III.

life, but where, under the veil of ignorance, they know nothing about their individual situation (i.e., about their social status, race, gender, etc.)? Rawls states that all of the participants would be able to agree on two basic principles of justice: (i) every person would have the same basic liberties, as far as they are compatible with the basic liberties of others; (ii) social and economic inequalities are permitted when they are either connected to an office or other positions which are attainable for everyone (fair equal opportunity) or when they are of benefit to those who are least advantaged (difference principle).[30]

(2) Rawls' demand for a universal concept of justice triggered criticism by communitarians. Michael J. Sandel, one of the early critics, pointed out that membership in concrete communities as well as the sharing of common moral concepts are necessary preconditions for enabling the individual to develop an opinion on principles of justice.[31] Placed in a political context, the result is a general precedence of public (and political) issues over private ones: Individual rights are subject to their compatibility with general welfare. And the constitution itself is primarily to be understood as an expression of political traditions, as the product of an organic development, behind which the action of establishing a constitution becomes secondary.

(3) Jürgen Habermas seeks a 'third' way between liberalism and communitarianism with his discourse theoretical reconstruction of the democratic constitutional state.[32] In his opinion, a liberal, rights-based limitation of political life threatens to cause negative effects on the political participation of citizens which will eventually lead to a division between state and society. But the communitarian, democracy-based primacy of the public is also disadvantageous, because it too easily relativizes individual rights in the name of the common good, leaving the citizen without any legal protection in the end. Consequently, Habermas advocates a symbiosis of private rights and public self-determination, a co-originality of the legal and democratic order, from which a productive tension emerges between the constitutional forces, on the one hand, and the people, on the other hand. In this approach, the people are still given a legitimizing and significant role as the democratic sovereign in the background, as long as the citizens' interests can be fed into the political system by means of deliberative processes.

4 Constituent Power, Law-making, and Legal Application

Regardless of the differences, all approaches to constitutionalism are understood as a reaction to a fundamental problem which has been illustrated by De Maistre: "The people are a sovereign who cannot exercise sovereignty."[33] If political self-determination is to succeed despite this lack of direct exercise of a people's sovereignty, political power must be legally restrained. According to the central insight of Thomas Hobbes, political government has to be bound by law and, thus legitimized,

30 Rawls 1971, chap. II/§ 11.
31 Sandel 1982, chap. II.
32 Habermas 1994, chap. III.
33 De Maistre 1965, p. 93.

become an 'authority'.[34] But the process of authorizing politics cannot be achieved by a single act. It is a dynamic process in which law and politics are related to each other on three levels: the constitutional level (4.1), the legislative level (4.2) and the level of application of law (4.3). On all three levels, political theory is assigned the task of observing and evaluating the relationship between law and politics.

4.1 The Normative Order of Politics

The differences between the several variations of modern constitutionalism depend largely on the way the people's sovereignty, as a foundation of the political system, is designed: Should the constitution be arranged in such a way 'as if' a people wisely had no other choice but to approve it? But how can this wisdom that is being referred to be justified? Or must there actually be some kind of consensus as a basis on which the constitution can legitimately develop? But what should be the source of that consensus? These are questions legal philosophy as well as political theory deal with. As for the last question, paradigmatically, two answers can be distinguished; one is the cultural, the other one the political concept of nation: The former is based on a common language, a shared understanding of history or a common educational ideal, for example, the "Germany of poets and thinkers." While in this concept the nation is seen as a pre-political entity, the concept of a political nation is the result of a foundational political action which, for example, in the case of France or the United States, was expressed in the revolutionary act of establishing a constitution. Against the background of this paradigmatic dichotomy, three areas for interdisciplinary research between political theory and legal philosophy (and legal theory) can be distinguished:

(i) Is the sovereignty of the people the embodiment of a normative entity, serving as an orientation for political action? Or does the sovereignty of the people characterize an historical subject which has implemented certain interests as generally binding? (ii) Closely connected to these questions are the questions regarding the status of the people: Is it a fictional or a factual bearer of sovereign political actions? Is it a real or just a potential participant? Or does it refer to the endpoint of the legal attribution of political actions? (iii) Finally: Does the identity of the political entity precede the establishment of the constitution, for example, as a community of values? Or does it only become a political community the moment the constitution takes effect?

The relevance of the theoretical reflection shall be clarified on the basis of the last aspect: Studies on political communities (nations, regions, etc.) display a clear tendency in the way the contingency of the creation and existence of those communities are illustrated. Common values or attitudes are not 'naturally' present. They only develop as mutual beliefs within the framework of a political process[35] and then receive their universally binding status through the law. That, of course, affects the way the constitution is perceived. Constitutions do not need to relate to previous political identities. They can, if necessary, create political identities them-

34 Hobbes, Lev. II/17.
35 Anderson 1991, chap. 1, 11.

selves. In that way, they do not just define boundaries and have a stabilizing effect but they also cross borders and have a dynamic effect. Thus, the evolutionary process of the constitution, its historical contingency comes into view – and, as such, the task of the political community to continue questioning the constitution about their own identity. An example for this is the project of European integration which will, in the foreseeable future, have difficulties finding a lasting answer to the question of Europe's real borders.

Towards such fundamental questions of political order, law's ability to act is as quickly exhausted as jurisprudence's ability to inform. Both are highly flexible when adjusting to modifications within the political system. However, the more these modifications concern the polity itself the clearer the political character of law emerges, as well as the prevailing socio-cultural conditions under which decisions are taken. In these cases, jurisprudence is well advised to seek the dialogue with political theory.

4.2 Lawmaking by Means of Law and Politics

The dialogue between jurisprudence and political theory should also be continued on the level of legislation. On this level, the focus of political theory is on the social function of law, consisting in the establishment and maintenance of public peace. To examine and delineate the function as well as the actual effects of law from the internal position of jurisprudence involves great difficulty. From the external perspective of political theory it is possible to observe how decisively law lightens the load of political communication which is frequently burdened with tough decisions, creating winners and losers. A legal framework legitimizes and limits political decisions and thus contributes to their acceptance. This fundamental connection can be characterized by four different relations to politics.

(1) *Law as the purpose of politics*: It is a part of the democratic self-conception that universally binding legal decisions are born in a pluralistic political struggle. Max Weber's definition of politics as the striving for power and the conservation of power emphasizes just this aspect. According to Weber, when it comes to politics, power means the chance to implement one's own will against the others' resistance.[36] But this enforcement of individual interests is always accompanied by a general desire that the orders are obeyed. The question about the motives of law abidance is an age-old topic from the history of ideas (e.g., Machiavelli, Hobbes), which has been adopted by the so-called 'compliance studies,' using the means of modern social sciences.[37] They tend to confirm the old concept that the permanence of a system of order depends on whether the appeal for justice by the specific political system is shared by the citizens of that system. In other words: Concepts of justice appear to be just as much a part of politics as the struggle for power. And specifically this aspect seems to make democratic systems less susceptible to crises

36 Weber 1988, pp. 506 f. (politics) and Weber 1980, p. 28 (power).

37 This approach plays a particularly important role in international relations; see the different contributions in Shelton (ed.) 2000.

than authoritarian regimes, provided they have completed their phase of implementation.[38]

(2) *Law as a product of politics*: The role of politics, however, does not limit itself to a service function with regard to law. Beyond that, it is supposed to provide the necessary means of adaptation to prevent a system which is considered fair from coming to a social standstill. The pretense of a modern political order goes beyond the mere preservation of the status quo: politics actively strives for reform and is only able to do so through law, i.e. in the form of juridification. Accordingly, law is an expression of the political will to create. In that way it becomes the object of the dispute – and a product which emerges from the 'struggle for justice.'[39]

The reference to political disputes which precede legislation and accompany it in the various institutional stages is capable of increasing the awareness of the complexity of political processes twofold: first, for those involved and their spheres of interest and different political styles (e.g., arguing vs. bargaining); second, for the political compromises underlying (more often than not) the legislation which cover the contradictory convictions of the political actors (even inside the coalition parties).[40]

(3) *Law as a framework for politics*: Another aspect characterizing the nature of politics can be seen in the negotiating processes which only partially take place within the institutionalized legal setting. Now and then, political arenas are created and recreated to suit the needs of those involved, while existing institutions lose their significance. In this sense, under the conditions of a modern party democracy, the parliament has forfeited its significance as the place of decision-making (e.g., by outsourcing political decision-making processes). These dynamics, however, do not leave any new legal room for politics. On the contrary, law shows itself to be a flexible companion by regulating not only membership but also the internal processes in statutes. No politics which are supposed to be implemented in a generally binding manner can refuse to accept the legal formalities. The legal constitution of political organizations benefits an internal outline of the decision-making process which Hannah Arendt grasped to be the facilitating factor for political actions (just as Hegel did before).[41] Law helps to stabilize the political space by enabling personal experiences, intentions, and achievements within its organization. First in this space which requires its own 'logic of appropriateness,'[42] politicians are more than just 'pure' lobbyists of whatever socio-economic interests. They have to be able to think and act politically. Intelligence and expertise can help, but they cannot replace the experience and the special ability to carry out a political struggle with other participants.

(4) *Law as a normative standard of politics*: Having differentiated between constitutional law and simple law (sub 2.) a functional division emerges between law and politics with advantages for both: A certain stability within the convertibility is es-

38 See, e.g., Hadenius/Teorell 2007, p. 153.

39 The locus classicus is Jhering 1872.

40 About the categories of policy analysis, that try to deal with the peculiarities of politics, see Stone 2002, pp. 17–34.

41 Arendt (1963, 150–152) turns against the traditional understanding of the division of powers in favor of the control of power.

42 March/Olson 2004, esp. 7–12.

sential for both the validity as well as the acceptance of law. Laws that do not adapt to living conditions become 'dead law.' But if law lacks permanence, it cannot ensure reliable expectations, which is one of law's most essential functions. Moreover, the relative stability of law serves to relieve politics, because the complex political processes of negotiating do not refer (directly) to the polity dimension, the institutional setting and guidelines of politics.[43] Hardly anything is more difficult to accomplish in politics than institutional reforms.[44] All the better, if the rules of the game are not re-invented every time. A familiar and accepted code of practice also makes it easier for the political opponents to accept their defeat. And the fundamental rights which are guaranteed by the constitution protect the defeated minority from a possible 'tyranny of the majority' which Alexis de Tocqueville so eloquently warned against.[45]

4.3 Prerequisites for Successful Legal Practice

Balancing law and politics is an essential aspect of the fundamental principles of a constitutional state, not only in the process of lawmaking but also in the application of the law. One striking feature of the Kelsen-Schmitt debate is the essential similarity between both positions in understanding the relationship of power, politics and the legal system (sub 3.2). For Schmitt as much as for Kelsen, decisions are expressions of (political) power. In this respect, they both recognize the political aspect of lawmaking. But unlike Schmitt, Kelsen acknowledges the discretionary powers as an element of the constitutional state's everyday practice[46] (and not as part of a state of emergency) – a challenge judges have to deal with in professional manner, which Kelsen calls a "code of ethics" based on the principle of neutrality.[47]

Kelsen's reference to the code of ethics illustrates that, in addition to the decisionist element of every law application, practical reasoning plays an important role for the deliberation and decision-making process. In order to gain access to practical rationality it is necessary to differentiate between two forms of decisionism. The first one results from the so-called "application aporia."[48] This impasse occurs, because law cannot apply itself but requires someone to apply it. For Kelsen and Schmitt, this instance emerges with the power of the decision-maker. But instead of immediately imputing the consequences of the aporia of application as a power problem to the vagueness of law, it would also allow an interpretation that emphasized, in a normative intention, the responsibility of practical reason to entrust interpretation and application to an institution (sub 4.1).

In this very act of justifying the creation of institutions lies a gain of rationality which can, however, be put at risk, if the aporia of application prematurely leads to eliminate the difference between law and politics. For this understanding of political

43 Immergut/Anderson 2008.
44 March/Olson 1996, p. 18.
45 Tocqueville 1835, I/2, chap. 7.
46 In Schmitt's view the uncontrolled power of norm application is a sign of the emerging state of the exception.
47 Kelsen 1931, p. 45.
48 Wieland 1989, p. 13.

decisionism can scarcely do justice to an ample description of the constitutional state and its institutions. Here, the actual power does not arise from a lack of control; it is not 'unauthorized' power. Instead, within a constitutional framework, political institutions derive their power from the creativity which they have to summon up in order to justify their constitutionally based claim to command. This again has consequences for the judicial doctrines of methodology which can only be briefly introduced here:

(i) Concepts like 'application' and 'subsumtion' are often accompanied by a non-political idea of law. In this case, law is only seen as the evolvement of logical concepts. But this point of view does not do justice to modern law. A democratic decision-making process requires not only the plurality of those involved and their diversity of interests; it also requires numerous compromises (sub 4.2.). Consequently, norms of such laws are certainly not an expression of pure logic, but the result of conflicting interests.

(ii) In order to make sense of these norms it is necessary to understand the lawmaker's intention: The 'applier' – especially in the case of a judge – must be familiar with the issues within a certain policy sector and should have comprehensive access to the political negotiation processes involved.

(iii) Due to the social function of law (public peace), the effects of the 'legal application' (especially on those actors involved in the policy process) should be observed. This kind of 'political' thinking can be seen in particular in upper courts which are usually informed about the possible consequences of their decisions prior to a verdict and thus take them into consideration.

The short introduction to the methodology of applying law illustrates that the relationship between law and politics does not only constitute a theoretical challenge. It also includes a very practical significance: Just as the citizen needs public spirit to be a citizen, the officeholder's understanding of his office decisively depends on his vision of the constitution and on his ability to grasp his specific duties in light of the constitution as an expression of the liberal system of order. Essentially, it is a person's wit which enhances his or her judgment, the understanding of a matter to the point of wisdom.[49] Wit is something you have to possess – without it even the most knowledgeable person remains a nerd, essentially a blockhead.

5 Challenges Ahead

One of the main purposes of this essay was to show that the achievement of modern rule of law has historically developed from the politicization of law and the juridification of politics. From this interrelation of law and politics, constitutionalism has evolved and lastingly left its mark on the concept of the democratic constitutional state. The history of political thought is capable of clarifying the relationship between law and politics without simplifying the concept of law by either omitting its necessary reference to politics – characteristic of positivism – or by allowing it to coincide with politics – characteristic of decisionism. Yet, the interrelation of law and politics should not be understood as the result of the unique act of establishing

49 Kant 1798, p. 516.

a constitution. In fact, it is a process of perpetually creating a balance in the channels of political institutions which requires a great extent of practical wisdom on the part of those involved when dealing with the particular logic and requirements of politics and law. That is why this process of balancing remains susceptible to faults in many regards, despite the routine elements stabilizing it. In closing, three of the major potential disruptive factors should at least be mentioned:

(1) An extensive juridification would deprive politics of its innovative potential. Political actions and decisions under the conditions of a modern representative democracy with political parties and interest groups cannot be limited to the 'administration of juridical judgments' in a Kantian Sense.[50] Majorities must be fought for, the power of opinion must be conquered, the masses must be mobilized; all of which cannot be achieved without compromises – even if they occur at the expense of the matter in question. In that sense, politics always thrives on the art of situational prudence which defies legal control. Political action always means acting for others – and being called to account for success as well as failure. In this sense, every politician is a 'politician of responsibility'.[51] But to measure political success, there are only very limited legal standards which apply; political responsibility barely intersects with legal responsibility. That is why it is rarely a legal question (or even a question of criminal law) whether a leading politician should step down or not. It is most often the result of public opinion that he is no longer 'acceptable.'

(2) The complaint about too little political free play as a result of the expanding juridification of every area of life is often heard. But it should not lead to the situation that the other extreme is overlooked: the so-called 'unlegislated areas.' What is meant are generally accepted areas where law can practically no longer be enforced, because the power of the state turns out to be no more than fiction. The examples are diverse: neighborhoods which are patrolled by private security companies ('gated communities'), municipal districts where the police no longer, or only sporadically, dare to enter ('slums'), the infiltration of administrative complexes by organized crime ('Mafia'), or of the entire state by terrorist organizations ('failing states').[52]

(3) The issue of unlegislated areas leads to the third problem: How can this bond between law and politics be legally secured? In the end, it cannot. For it is the state that has to control the actors exercising public power. It is the old question: Who will guard the guardians? The search for an appropriate constitutional guard, which has been carried out by political philosophy ever since Plato, is accompanied by the will to commit oneself. Plato's answer virtually anticipates a large part of the modern solution: Making a king out of a philosopher complies with the goal that the system of order should adhere to its own order as a matter of reason. The act of watching over the political commitment to law and order merges, in the end, with a self-commitment. We learn from Ulysses, the hero of Greek mythology, that this insight requires not only reason but also prudence. Aware of his own weakness, his inability to resist the songs of the sirens, he voluntarily lets himself be tied to the mast – thus enjoying the pleasure of their art without being harmed.[53]

50 Kant 1795, p. 229.
51 Weber 1988, p. 551.
52 A more radical picture of the problem of 'lawless' areas which aims at the normative aspect of law itself can be found with Agamben 1998, part III.
53 About the rationality of self-commitment see Elster 1979, esp. part II.

Law involves the "authorization to coerce," states Immanuel Kant in the preface to his Doctrine of Right (*Rechtslehre*).[54] This, however, is only the formal side of law. The metaphor of the self-commitment illustrates that law, as a part of the political order, is dependent on the legitimacy of this order. The coercion through which law can impose sanctions cannot replace the legal principles, which must be basically understandable to a reasonable person. Otherwise, legal principles would not give reasons for a legal decision, but would only disguise the (undeniable) fact that every law which is legislated and applied by the state is based on power. Power is the counterpart to law; they have jointly formed a unity ever since the beginnings of law. In this respect, there is some truth in the phrase: "might is right." By the same token, history as much as the intercultural comparison show that the immediacy of this unity is gradually replaced by an internal organization mediating the relationship between law and politics. The bond between might and right loses its character as a law of the jungle. The rule of the strongest is increasingly conveyed by institutions. In a democracy, for instance, it is transformed into the majority rule which is bound – via self-commitment – by the principles of the constitutional state, by civil rights, human rights, the rights of minorities, etc. This development is, in short, the success story of every political community that is based on freedom and social peace. It is the history of the institutionalization of law and politics. Politics does not only set generally binding norms, it also creates the institutions and rules of conduct, which alone give a legal culture its specific character.

Literature

Aristoteles (2005): Politics. With an english transl. by H. Rackham. Cambridge (Mass.).

Ackerman, Bruce (1989): Constitutional Politics/Constitutional Law. In: Yale Law Journal 99(3), pp. 453–547.

Agamben, Giorgio (1998): Homo sacer. Sovereign Power and Bare Life (transl. by Daniel Heller-Roazen). Stanford (Cal.).

Anderson, Benedict (1991): Imagined Communities. Reflections on the Origin and Spread of Nationalism. Rev. ed. London.

Arendt, Hannah (1963): On Revolution. London et al. 1991.

Benhabib, Seyla (1994): Deliberative Rationality and Models of Democratic Legitimacy. In: Constellations 1(1), pp. 25–53.

De Maistre, Joseph (1965): Study on Sovereignty. In: The Works of Joseph de Maistre. Ed. by Jack Lively. London, pp. 93–129.

Dyzenhaus, David (2003): Legality and Legitimacy. Carl Schmitt, Hans Kelsen and Hermann Heller in Weimar. Reprint. Oxford.

Elster, Jon (1979): Ulysses and the Sirenes: Studies in Rationality and Irrationality, Cambridge/New York.

Grimm, Dieter (1969): Recht und Politik. In: Juristische Schulung 9(11), pp. 501–510.

Habermas, Jürgen (1994): Faktizität und Geltung. Beiträge zur Diskurstheorie des Rechts und des demokratischen Rechtsstaats. 4th ed. Frankfurt a. M.

Hadenius, Axel/Jan Teorell (2007): Pathways from Authoritarianism. In: Journal of Democracy 18(1), pp. 143–157.

Heller, Hermann (1924): Politische Ideenkreise der Gegenwart. In: Gesammelte Schriften. Vol. 1. Ed. by Martin Drath et al. Leiden 1971, pp. 257–374.

54 Kant 1797, p. 338.

Heller, Hermann (1928a): Der Begriff des Gesetzes in der Reichsverfassung. In: Gesammelte Schriften. Vol. 2. Ed. by Martin Drath et al. Leiden 1971, pp. 203–242.

Heller, Hermann (1928b): Politische Demokratie und soziale Homogenität. In: Gesammelte Schriften. Vol. 2. Ed. by Martin Drath et al. Leiden 1971, pp. 421–433.

Hobbes, Thomas (1651): Leviathan or the Matter, Form and Power of a Commonwealth, Ecclesiastical and Civil. In: The English Works of Thomas Hobbes of Malmesbury. Vol. 3. Edited by Sir William Molesworth. Reprint: London 1839. Aalen 1962.

Honig, Bonny (2007): Between Decision and Deliberation: Political Paradox in Democratic Theory. In: American Political Science Review 101(1), pp. 1–17.

Immergut, Ellen/Karen M. Anderson (2008): Historical Institutionalism and West European Politics. In: West European Politics 31(1–2), pp. 345–369.

Jhering, Rudolf von (1872): Der Kampf um's Recht. 8th ed. Frankfurt a. M. 2003.

Kant, Immanuel (1795): Zum ewigen Frieden. In: Werke in zehn Bänden. Ed. by Wilhelm Weischedel. Vol. 9. Darmstadt 1983, pp. 193–251.

Kant, Immanuel (1797): Die Metaphysik der Sitten. In: Werke in zehn Bänden. Ed. by Wilhelm Weischedel. Vol. 7. Darmstadt 1983, pp. 303–634.

Kant, Immanuel (1798): Anthropologie in pragmatischer Hinsicht. In: Werke in zehn Bänden. Ed. by Wilhelm Weischedel. Vol. 10. Darmstadt 1983, pp. 397–690.

Kelsen, Hans (1929): Wesen und Entwicklung der Staatsgerichtsbarkeit In: Veröffentlichungen der Vereinigung der Deutschen Staatsrechtslehrer. Vol. 5, pp. 30–84.

Kelsen, Hans (1931): Wer soll Hüter der Verfassung sein? Berlin.

Kelsen, Hans (1960): Reine Rechtslehre. Einleitung in die rechtswissenschaftliche Problematik. Reprint of the 2nd ed. Wien 1992.

Kern, Fritz (1952): Recht und Verfassung im Mittelalter. Reprint. Darmstadt 1992.

Lembcke, Oliver W. (2007): Hüter der Verfassung. Eine institutionentheoretische Studie zur Autorität des Bundesverfassungsgerichts. Tübingen.

Loughlin, Martin/Neil Walker (2007): Introduction. In: Martin Loughlin/Neil Walker (eds.): The Paradox of Constitutionalism. Constituent Power and Constitutional Form. Oxford, pp. 1–8.

Luhmann, Niklas (1995): Das Recht der Gesellschaft. Frankfurt a. M.

March, James G./Johan P. Olson (1996): Institutional Perspectives on Political Institutions. In: Governance 9(3), pp. 247–264.

March, James G./Johan P. Olson (2004): Logic of Appropriateness (Working Paper No. 9). Oslo.

Pico della Mirondola, Giovanni (1990): Über die Würde des Menschen (Lat.-Dt.). Ed. by August Buck. Hamburg

Rawls, John (1971): A Theory of Justice. Cambridge (Mass.).

Rousseau, Jean-Jacques (1762): Du contrat social ou principes du droit politique. In: Œuvres complètes. Tome 3. Paris 1964, pp. 347–470.

Sandel, Michael J. (1982): Liberalism and the Limits of Justice. Cambridge (Mass.).

Schmitt, Carl (1922): Politische Theologie. Vier Kapitel zur Lehre von der Souveränität. 7th. ed. Berlin 1996.

Schmitt, Carl (1928): Verfassungslehre. 8th ed. Berlin 1993.

Schmitt, Carl (1931): Der Hüter der Verfassung. 4th ed. Berlin 1996.

Shelton, Dinah (ed.) (2000): Commitment and Compliance. The Role of Non-Binding Norms in the International Legal System. Oxford.

Stone, Deborah (2002): Policy Paradox. The Art of Political Decision Making. Rev. ed. New York/London.

Tocqueville, Alexis de (1835): De la démocratie en Amérique I. Paris 1981.

Weber, Max (1980): Wirtschaft und Gesellschaft. Grundriß der verstehenden Soziologie. Ed. by Johannes Winckelmann. 5th ed. Tübingen.

Weber, Max (1988): Gesammelte politische Schriften. Ed. by Johannes Winckelmann, 5th ed. Tübingen.

Wieland, Wolfgang (1989): Aporien der praktischen Vernunft. Frankfurt a. M.

Vasiliki Christou

Law, Performatives, and Normativity

Testing the Limits and Potential of Interdisciplinary Research*

Abstract:
Der Beitrag von Vasiliki Christou befasst sich mit dem Einfluss der „speech-act Theorie" und hier vor allem der Kategorie des Performativen auf die Auslegung des Rechts. Diese Kategorie ist von großer analytischer Bedeutung für das Verständnis der Grundrechtskollisionen, etwa im Fall freier Rede. Das wird exemplarisch am Fall der Drohungen gezeigt. Jedoch leisten die „performatives" keine normative Hilfe zur Lösung von Grundrechtskollisionen. Normative Aussagen kann dazu nur die Moraltheorie beitragen. Zwar besteht die Möglichkeit, Rechtsbefehle so zu verstehen, dass sie performativen Aussagen angenähert sind. Doch auch dann bleibt die Leistung der „performatives" auf normativer Ebene dürftig. Denn entscheidend ist im Konfliktfall nicht, ob eine Rechtsnorm eine Handlung billigt oder missbilligt, sondern ob die jeweilige Bewertung des Rechts ihren Ursprung in moralischer Erkenntnis oder moralischer Intuition hat. Zu dieser Frage können „performatives" aber nichts beisteuern.

1 Introductory Remarks

Being a very broad discipline, regulating a great part of social life, law is deemed to be an all-inclusive phenomenon and cursed to be dependent for its implementation on other disciplines. Social sciences for example have always offered substantial help to law interpreters. This is made particularly obvious, if one considers the principle of equality. The realization of this principle very much depends upon sociological analysis as regards the demarcation of disadvantaged groups and means of their effective integration. Psychological research may also prove of importance. In the Brown v. Board of Education opinion for example, the Supreme Court of the United States concluded that in the field of public education the doctrine "separate but equal" had no place, after consulting expert analysis regarding the psychological effects of segregation on black children, which is also thoroughly cited in Footnote 11 of the opinion.[1] The Federal Constitutional Court of Germany ruled that the imposition of state monopoly on oddest betting is not justified under the public interest of combating gambling and betting addiction, because – unlike play at slot and casino, for which it has been confirmed that they result in pathological addictive behavior – at present, all other forms of games of chance contribute markedly less to problematic and pathological gambling behavior.[2] Again, the federal constitutional judges consulted scientific reviews for public health to reach their decision.

* I would like to thank Dr. Steven Less, Member of the scientific staff of the Max Planck Institute for Comparative Public Law and International Law in Heidelberg, for copy-editing my English text.

1 Brown v. Board of Education, 347 U.S. 483, 494 (1954): "To separate [children] from others of similar age and qualifications solely because of their race generates a feeling of inferiority as to their status in the community that may affect their hearts and minds in a way unlikely ever to be undone."

2 BVerfG, 1 BvR 1054/01, opinion of 28.3.2006, par. 100.

The plurality of input in jurisprudence is justified, first by the fact that law implementation is dependent upon pragmatic presuppositions, and second, by the fact that the judge has no discretion, but is obliged to decide a case, even if that requires getting familiar with knowledge stemming from other disciplines. However, at this point a definitional issue regarding interdisciplinarity needs to be clarified. Starting from a positivist strand of a pure theory of law and of interpretation a greater part of judicial argumentation – especially in hard cases – involves an interdisciplinary method that needs to be accounted for. Most of all, the consideration of morals in legal interpretation is considered an interdisciplinary endeavor, and – what is more – an illegitimate one. A non-positivist moral theory of law sees the question of interdisciplinarity from a totally different angle. Moral argumentation is in this case already an integral part of legal theory. My perspective of the law discipline will be that of a discipline in need of a legal theory based on moral considerations of fairness on the one hand, consistency on the other hand.[3] To construct such a theory one may resort to readings of philosophy, ethics and generally to any normative reflection on persons and societies.

I find great comfort in supporting this view by referring to the 1798 essay of Immanuel Kant on "The Conflict of the Faculties". Kant, although supportive of the view that each science is a discipline in its own right, argues that reason functions as an ultimate value that transcends disciplinary vision.[4] Joe Moran's approach to interdisciplinarity also makes a very important point in this direction. For Moran, theory is undisciplined knowledge, and a theory, for example positivism, may be influential to different disciplines. It is a mode of thought used to question interpretations of the world that are taken for granted.[5] It is an instrument of constructive self-reflection in all kinds of disciplines.

In this presentation I will focus on the insight that jurisprudence gets from philosophy of language, and in particular from the performative uses of language.[6] *First*, I will present the main points of the so-called speech-act theory, and I shall try to illustrate by means of examples that speech act theory is of analytical importance to the interpreter of the free speech principle, but is not in a position to dictate solution to practical problems on a normative ground. This is what I shall call the normative open-endedness of the speech-act theory. *Second*, I will examine whether there is some gain in thinking of the legal sentence itself as a performative. This approach might offer a good account of emotions, imperatives or mental states of affairs to which legal sentences correspond, but is of no gain to legal theory, because questions of rightness and morality are set aside and are replaced by an emphasis on

3 I very much rely on Dworkin's approach and his idea of law as integrity, as supported in: Dworkin 1977, pp. 81–130; Dworkin 1986.
4 Kant 2005, for example p. 17 and p. 27.
5 Moran 2002, pp. 82–113.
6 I acknowledge the distinction emphasized by John R. Searle between the philosophy of language and linguistic philosophy. According to this distinction, "[l]inguistic philosophy consists in the attempt to solve philosophical problems by analyzing the meanings of the words, and by analyzing logical relations between words in natural languages", whereas "[t]he philosophy of language consists in the attempt to analyze certain general features of language such as meaning, reference, truth, verification, speech acts, and logical necessity." The philosophy of language is the subject-matter, whereas linguistic philosophy is the method. See Searle 1971, pp. 1–12, 1.

the expressive function of law. In this way, thinking of a legal sentence as a performative one lays emphasis on a metaethical, instead of a substantive moral analysis of law.

2 Performatives and analytical Gain

The relationship of law and language is evidently very close. Law is made typically by means of linguistic utterances and it is part of the task of the law interpreter to understand the meaning of words and communicate this meaning to others. Law is, like language, a means to coordinate the social life of people with different life plans, goals and ideas of the good. The question is, however, whether the philosophy of language has anything to say that is helpful in jurisprudential debates. I will try to illustrate by means of examples that performatives offer a sharpened awareness of the meaning of words and sharpen our perception of the phenomenon of expression. They are a gain on a cognitive level, but they are imperfect sentences implying no particular solution to practical problems.

Performatives and the speech-act theory have been introduced by J.L. Austin in his book "How to do things with words",[7] and John R. Searle gave the term "speech act" by further elaborations its technical sense.[8] Austin begins with the observation that speaking is simultaneously a way of acting.[9] This performative approach[10] to language is nevertheless not an original thought; it dates back to Wittgenstein's "Philosophical Investigations" (Philosophische Bemerkungen) that words are remembrances of experiences or even experiences themselves.[11] At another point in the "Philosophical Investigations", Wittgenstein refers to language as a form of action (Tätigkeit), and mentions that the idea of a language is the idea of a way of life (Lebensform). Wittgenstein also distinguished the meaning of a sentence from the communicative importance of the fact that the meaning is being expressed,[12] a distinction that to my mind roughly applies to the distinction between semantics and performatives.[13] Hart also pointed out, citing Wittgenstein and Austin, that people

7 Austin 1989.

8 See Searle 1994.

9 It should be noted that Austin initially made a performative-constative distinction, which amounted to a distinction between utterances, which are sayings (constatives) and utterances, which are doings of some other kind. Latter he revised this distinction and claimed that constatives were speech acts as well; so they were also included in the category of performatives. See Austin 1971, pp. 13–22. To this turn in Austin's theory see also John Lyons 1995, p. 238; Searle (Fn. 6), p. 7.

10 Hart points out that lawyers use the term "operative" (instead of performative) to refer to language used not just to describe certain things, but to bring about certain changes. See Hart 1983, p. 276.

11 Wittgenstein 1933, in: The Wittgenstein Archive, http://www.hit.uib.no/wab/sample/vw115-ad.htm#92, Item 115 Verso Page 33.

12 See von Savigny 1998, pp. 7–39.

13 John R. Searle distinguished between a typical question of semantics, which is "How do the meanings of the elements of a sentence determine the meaning of the whole sentence?" and the question "What are the different kinds of speech acts that the speakers perform when they utter expressions?", which is typical to the performative uses of language. He identifies these two strands in contemporary work in the philosophy of language, and points out that "The mean-

use language to do things other than making statements and that this insight might be important for jurisprudence.[14] Hart also views law as a performative, as an imperative, an order. He writes: "If, following Austin, we call such a supreme and independent person or body of persons the sovereign, the laws of any country will be the general orders backed by threats which are issued either by the sovereign or subordinates in obedience to the sovereign."[15]

Austin distinguishes among three categories of speech acts: the locutionary, the illocutionary, and the perlocutionary acts.[16] A locutionary act refers to the act of a speaker saying something to a hearer in a given context. It is more than just the utterance of a sentence, because it appeals not only to the sounds made or to the words used, but rather to the propositional content and the semantic meaning of the utterance.[17] Through the illocutionary act the speaker already does something *in* saying something. This is the case of an order, a command, a promise, a statement of admiration or of defamation. Through the perlocutionary act the speaker affects the hearer in a certain way *by* saying something. Here we can consider the case of a leaflet urging employees to go on strike.

Habermas largely builds on this tripartite categorization by Austin to lay down his own theory of communicative action. He explains the troubling distinction between illocutionary and perlocutionary acts in a very illuminating way.[18] According to Habermas, the act-component of a speech act is in the case of illocutions an element internal, inherent in language, an intralinguistic element.[19] The act element is constituent to the very act of communicative action.[20] On the other hand, in the case of perlocutionary speech acts the act-element is external to expression; it is the result of expression in the outside world. Therefore, this result is mediated by the free will of the hearer and is not totally controlled by the speaker. A perlocutionary speech act is not a self-executing act, like an illocutionary speech act; it is strategic action, an action, whose end (telos) is not just the communicative effect.[21]

ing of a sentence does not in all cases uniquely determine what speech act is performed in a given utterance of that sentence, for a speaker may mean more than what he actually says." He concludes that the two approaches to investigation are complementary to each other. See Searle (Fn. 8), pp. 18–19.

14 Hart (Fn. 10), p. 275.

15 See Hart 1994, p. 25.

16 Austin (Fn. 7), pp. 94–108. Sometimes other kinds of speech acts are also introduced, for example "master speech acts", which are speech acts intended to control other speech acts. See Fotion 1971, p. 232.

17 Solum 1988, pp. 54, 89.

18 I consider Habermas's account of the distinction between illocution and perlocution to be the closest one to Austin's analysis, and simultaneously very optimizing of Austin's analysis. Austin also throws emphasis on the effects as the distinctive element between illocution and perlocution. He considers the effects to be characteristic of the perlocutionary act, and suggests that we must distinguish "I ordered him and he obeyed" from "I got him to obey". He points out: "The general implication of the latter is that other additional means were employed to produce this consequence as ascribable to me." See Austin (Fn. 7), pp. 109, 117–118.

19 Habermas 1995, p. 389.

20 Habermas, op. cit. See also Boer 1974, p. 169.

21 Habermas, (Fn. 19), pp. 389–390.

One of the main points of Austin's speech act theory was to criticize the way legal theory had been ignorant of the illocutionary dimension of speech.[22] Indeed, an awareness of the illocutionary effect of speech reveals the shortsightedness of the so-called no-cost or low-cost minimalism,[23] a strand of thought claiming that the harm inflicted by expression is either nil or minimal. A conception of no-cost or low-cost minimalism has long allowed a very strong protection of free speech in the United States, going back to a dubious, ontological dualism between body and mind, material and spiritual spheres that are to be treated totally differently.[24] Speech as an illocutionary act can harm other people actually, even materially. I shall use the example of true threats and incitement to imminent lawless action to illustrate my point, as well the great analytical gain resulting from the distinction between illocutionary and perlocutionary acts.

In the American legal system, true threats and incitement are considered to be two categories of unprotected speech under the scope of the First Amendment. For a long time judicial opinions and constitutional theorists have failed to distinguish between these two categories of unprotected speech, and have very often regarded them as identical.[25] An opinion of the Supreme Court of 1969,[26] dealt with the conviction of a student, who announced during a demonstration against the Vietnam War: "If they ever make me carry a rifle the first man I want to get in my sights is L.B.J." It was not clear from the language of the Court whether the expression was examined as a threat against the President or as an incitement towards the public to hurt the President. To my mind, the distinction between illocutionary and perlocutionary acts can shed new light to the understanding of these speech categories and describe the different kind of wrong they represent. True threats are illocutionary acts of expressive conduct, because their wrong is fulfilled and the damage is done already by uttering the expression. The speaker threatens the listener that A (something harmful) will happen to her, if she does not do B (something undesired to her). It does not matter whether the speaker has the intent or the actual ability to carry out her threat. What counts is the serious intention of the speaker to terrify the listener in a way that the listener will be forced to fulfill the speaker's demand and to act against her own wishes. A threat is an assault on the free will of the hearer, which is already committed by the utterance of the threatening words. Speech-act theory can to this extent be useful in pointing out that a threat already exists not just in an assertion of fact and value, but in a "situation-altering"[27] utterance. However, speech act theory cannot answer the question of the rightness or wrongness, the goodness or the badness of the actual change resulting from the speech-act. This is the task of a moral theory integrated into law. To say that a threat is bad, being an assault on the free will of the hearer, presupposes that we recognize and value the principle of autonomy as part of our legal system.

22 Austin (Fn. 7), p. 100.

23 To the tendency to regard the harm of speech as minimal, see Cohen 1993, pp. 207, 210, 217–222 (in a critical perspective).

24 Brison 1998, p. 39; Bracken 1994, p. 5.

25 Thoroughly to that point Christou 2007, pp. 303–317.

26 Watts v. U.S., 394 U.S. 705 (1969).

27 Greenawalt 1989, p. 58.

On the other hand, incitement to imminent violence is a perlocutionary speech act and strategic action, because the speaker aims at persuading the hearer to do something wrong. The effect of speech is dependent upon the free will of the listener and in this way it is not internal to the act of expression. This is why it is often said that incitement can be punished only when the speaker precisely describes the lawless act and has a double intent. Namely, the speaker must seriously want to persuade the hearer to commit the lawless act and intend that the lawless act be committed.[28] It is because the effect of language is in this case extralinguistic, that law demands a very clear causation between expression and crime committed. In other words, as Jeremy Martin points out, "Incitement cases are distinguished from threat cases in that the harm resulting from the former does not come from the expression itself, but rather, from whatever actions potentially follow the expression. Threats, on the other hand, are harmful because of the effect of the actual words used."[29] The key difference between threats and incitement is that the evil to be averted in an incitement case is the "actual violence" itself, whereas the evil to be prevented in a threat case is the "actual fear".[30]

3 Normative Open-endedness and Speech-act Theory

The awareness of the illocutionary force of speech sharpens our perception of the condition-altering power of a threat, but speech act theory, as already mentioned, does not provide us with the tools to morally evaluate and classify the change caused in the real world by speech. Concerning this point, I would like to make the normative open-endedness of speech act theory more explicit. There is a variety of ways to translate the premises of the performatives into normative language, none of which is necessarily preferred by the theory of language itself. Some writers point to people's use of language to do things other than making statements to diminish the so-called speech-act distinction as a way of understanding the free speech principle. In the American legal system the speech-act distinction has served as a guide to an absolutist understanding of the First Amendment. According to this understanding, speech is almost absolutely protected from state interventions, whereas actions are proscribable under lower standards of scrutiny.

Feminist theories and critical race theories emphasize two points: *First*, that all speech is a form of action; so no talismanic protection of speech (under the First Amendment) can be morally justified.[31] However, as it is wrong to turn the descriptive, and for a long time intuitively very attractive assertion, that speech is something totally different than action, into a normative prescription, one that ascribes full protection to speech, it is equally wrong to affirm normative claims to the reverse ontological assertion, namely that all action is speech. We run the risk of turning a possible ontological fallacy into a metaphysical one. Besides, the way the

28 Zer-Ilan 1997, pp. 2697, 2700.
29 Martin 2000, pp. 751, 790.
30 Scott Hammack 2002, pp. 65, 66–67.
31 See for example Brison 2004, p. 261; Particularly to the case of pornography see MacKinnon 1993. To the case of racist speech see Williams 1987, 127; Matsuda 1989, p. 2320; Matsuda 1995, p. 87.

words "speech" and "action" are used within the performatives is different from the legal use of the same terms. Performatives appeal to the more or less common, everyday meaning of speech and action, whereas in the legal system we have to get used to talking even about the non-speech categories of speech, meaning expressive conduct, which is not covered by the free speech principle and is no speech in the constitutional sense of the word. *What is regarded as speech and non-speech is again guided by considerations about right and wrong, instead of considerations about action and non-action in some descriptive, empiricist sense.* The constitutional-legal boundaries of speech and action are the product of a normative balance of rights and liberties. So we may even use the analytical insight, offered by the performatives, and still maintain a normative speech-act distinction as a manifestation of a line already drawn by some moral considerations.[32] Speech infringing the rights of others, such as threats, blackmail and fraud, involves illocutionary speech-acts and is no protected speech legally speaking, even though threats and blackmail are made of linguistic utterances. Speech altering of a situation, such as the phrase "I do", when asked before the Church or the Mayor at a marital ceremony, is an illocutionary speech act and yet legally protected speech. Lastly, the assertion that all speech is conduct, taken as a normative sentence, conflicts with a deep-rooted conception of free speech as a fundamental right.

Second, some critical race theorists claim that all action is simultaneously speech, in the sense that doing something is a way of expressing oneself. Charles Lawrence III, for example, views the Brown opinion of the Supreme Court that brought an end to racial school segregation in the United States, as a speech case, that rightly restricts the free speech rights of the segregators. According to Charles Lawrence "If segregation's primary goal is to convey the message of white supremacy, then Brown's declaration that segregation is unconstitutional amounts to a regulation of the message of white supremacy. Properly understood, Brown and its progeny require that the systematic group defamation of segregation be disestablished."[33] In the same direction Kenneth Clark sees Plessy and the Dred Scott opinions that affirmed racial segregation in United States, as an act of defamation against black people.[34]

To my mind, this example illustrates quite clearly why it is not fit to transfer categories of linguistics into legal interpretation without reflection upon a coherent legal theory giving some consistent meaning to the legal order as a whole. The sentence "all action is speech" taken normatively fails to take into consideration the distinctiveness of the principle of equality in the constitutional order. As much as we can all agree that each action has an expressive content and that segregation defames black people, we are intuitively urged to say that segregation is more than defamation. Segregation is not just an act of showing contempt; it is a policy of denying certain people their equal, participatory rights and privileges in society. The strong legal tradition of the principle of equality as a distinct principle from that of free speech and the moral weight ascribed to equality hinder us in turning a clever,

32 Compare Nimmer 1968, pp. 935, 937. He describes the speech-act distinction as "no more than a metaphorical device for rationalizing a line already drawn".

33 Charles R. Lawrence III 1990, pp. 431, 441.

34 Kenneth Clark, in: Monroe H. Freedman/Freedman (Fn. 31), pp. 3, 5.

descriptive observation, that all action is actually speech, into a normative premise. The premises of speech act theory do not simultaneously gain normativity when used by the law interpreter as an analytical instrument of the expression phenomenon, just because they are valid in the linguistic field of studies. From my perspective, speech-theory elements must be filtered through a normative theory, in this case a theory combining free speech and equality as fundamental principles that sets the standards for deciding speech cases.

I would like to refer to one more example in which the performatives fail to give some normative premise but they leave behind a very useful, descriptive account of the various aspects of human behavior, a multi-dimensional analysis of expressive activity. This is the case of pornography. I will use some points made by *Rae Langton* in one of her articles.[35] According to Langton, pornography has certain obvious perlocutionary effects, which she summarizes as follows: "[Pornography] can affect attitudes and behavior, making its hearers more likely to view women as inferior, more disposed to accept rape myths, more likely to view rape victims as deserving of their treatment, and more likely to say that they themselves would rape, if they could get away with it."[36] However, the perlocutionary effects of pornography are to some writers not an argument to the penalization of pornography, because the danger posed by pornography is too abstract. Furthermore – this argument goes on –, no clear, direct causality between pornography and its perlocutionary effects can be reconstructed with any sort of certainty.[37]

This is why Langton turns to the illocutionary effects of pornography. As already mentioned the awareness of the illocutionary dimension of language, long neglected by legal theory, has been considered as one of the highlights of the speech-act theory. According to Langton, pornography as an illocutionary act actually conveys to women the message that they are inferior; it orders them to stay away from social engagement and public dialogue. In this way, pornography encroaches on their speech rights both as locutionary and as illocutionary acts, and silences women. The silencing argument[38] is multi-faceted. *First*, there are two locutionary ways in which a woman may be hindered from expressing herself: an abstract way and a rather more concrete one. Abstractly speaking, a woman may not be eager to express herself in public discourse due to the inferiority stereotype reproduced by pornography. Concretely speaking, a woman may not respond to sexist speech addressed to her individually because of fear or some sense of humiliation. *Second*, pornography may restrict the capability of a woman to make successful illocutionary statements. There is the perlocutionary frustration case[39] which occurs when a woman makes a statement, is perfectly understood by the hearers, but then her voice is outnumbered. It is like shouting in a crowded street, where everybody listens, but nobody pays attention or gives a second thought to what they hear. There is also the

35 Langton 1993, p. 293. See also Hornsby/Langton 1998, p. 21.

36 Langton (Fn. 35), p. 310.

37 This view starts from the perspective of a strong theory of free speech as a fundamental right, not to be balanced against conceptions of the common good. See predominantly Dworkin 1986, p. 359; Dworkin 1984, p. 153; Dworkin 1991, p. 100; See also Collier 2001, p. 203.

38 Langton (Fn. 35), p. 297. In favor of the silencing argument as an argument for the regulation of pornographic and racist speech Fiss 1996, p. 21; Fiss 1986, p. 1405.

39 Langton (Fn. 35), p. 315.

case of the illocutionary disablement,[40] in which a woman expresses herself, but her speech act fails on an illocutionary level, because the message is totally misunderstood due to stereotypes that mediate between the speaker and the hearer. Langton names the example of a woman saying "no" to a rapist and of him not taking this locutionary act seriously.[41]

These observations are very interesting and useful for analyzing expressive conduct and grasping its various dimensions. But no prescriptive sentence flows directly from them. Whether to protect a woman, in fact anybody from being directly or indirectly hindered from speaking, from illocutionary disablement or from the possibility that her voice might be outnumbered, are questions that speech-act theory cannot alone satisfactorily answer. Of course, the act of saying that somebody's interests are hurt in this or the other way already implies – for a reasonable person – that something has to be done against it. Therefore, an intuitive urge to take some moral action comes into play. In this way, an is-statement already implicates an ought-statement. Still, how can we choose between different ought-statements that may be considered? What are the criteria for choosing between the statements "You ought to do A" and "You ought to do B"?

A considered answer to this question is the task of a legal theory, which has to clarify *first* whether the state protects only negative liberty or positive liberty as well. I take negative liberty to be liberty from intervention while exercising one's freedoms and positive liberty as the actual capacity and capability to exercise one's freedoms, which might be hindered not only by intervention, but by lack of support and pragmatic accommodation.[42] *Second*, it has to be clear, whether in a system of positive liberty, the accommodation of the various interests in enhancing capacities and capabilities takes place through coercive measures (like penal law) or economic protection policy or cultural protection policy etc. One has to consider the whole system of liberties that might be disrupted by protecting some of its aspects. Speech-act theories offer an intuitively deducted hint of the need for taking a moral action that has to be further dealt with by the law interpreter in view of a legal theory.

4 Thinking of Legal Sentences as Speech Acts?

I shall now try to reverse the question: Instead of asking whether thinking of expression as a speech-act may bring something to jurisprudential debate, I shall pose the question whether thinking of the legal sentence as a speech act might be of some use. It is quite obvious that legal sentences order or urge people to do or not to do something: they may express emotions, approval or disapproval of certain forms of life. Words in legal documents are all operative words; they are used performatively and instrumentally. Even law itself may generate a state of affairs that does not exist in some naturalistic way, as is the case with legal fiction or the legal personality of associations. The issue is whether legal interpretation or legal theory gains some-

40 Langton (Fn. 35), p. 321.

41 Langton (Fn. 35), pp. 321, 325.

42 I take this definition of positive liberty as capacity or capability from Sen's and Nussbaum's "capability approach" to human rights. See mainly Sen 1984, pp. 313–314; Sen 2004, p. 315; Nussbaum 1997, p. 273.

thing by stressing the performative nature of law beyond the acknowledgement that law effects reality in a very real and practical way.

Thinking of law as a performative can certainly be particularly useful for political sciences and for public communication theories. Law is the reliable and authentic way for authorities to get their messages across to the people. It is essential for democratic dialogue and the principle of publicity that the right message is conveyed. Legislation supporting pregnant women financially and securing their employment rights, for example, may be interpreted as disapproving a life without children or as preferring a family life. It may also be interpreted as a value neutral legislation, namely as a legislation that neither approves nor disapproves traditional family, but is simply interested in promoting new life, either out of considerations of economic policy or simply in order to give a chance to potential or new autonomous agents. How legislation may be understood and interpreted has to do with the way a law justifies itself in public debate and with the social circumstances themselves.

Even the form of government may define how the action or non-action of the legislator may be understood. For example, absence of regulation of certain categories of expression that do not inflict harm to others, but could be considered as intrinsically wrong or flawed or moralistic grounds,[43] may be interpreted as: a) a way of approving this kind of expression,[44] b) as a way of tolerating it, in order to show respect to individual autonomous agents, or c) as indifference towards this expression. In this case, I think the whole system of government may affect the way we think about legislative silence. In a form of government fostering ethical, substantive pluralism, and moral paternalism legislative silence may mean the validation of the forms of life not prohibited. In a form of government guided by the principle of neutrality, legislative silence is more likely to be understood as a form of indifference. To put it in a nutshell, law has expressive[45] and pedagogic importance and democracy cannot function properly, if the legislator and the public are somewhere lost in interpretation not only of the meaning of words, but also of motives.

However, as Timothy Endicott also points out in his essay on "Law and Language",[46] thinking of law as a speech act cannot offer new insight or replace legal theory. Austin's theory, by focusing on the varieties of approving or disapproving actions that people perform, inevitably leaves out of the picture the question of what is good or bad. This "linguistic turn" in ethical philosophy gives priority to the concern with what we say and the preoccupation on what we say.[47] However, such a preoccupation with legal sentences as linguistic utterances implies a skeptical approach to the validity or truth of moral sentences embedded within legal sentences. It allows one to avoid considering whether it is legitimate that law does this or that by focusing only on whether law does this or that, and is inclined to emotivism and

43 See the thorough analysis of Feinberg 1985, and Feinberg 1988.

44 This is the opinion of Raz 1994, pp. 1, 9–10: "[P]ublic portrayal and expressions of forms of life validate the styles of life portrayed, and [...] censoring expression normally expresses authoritative condemnation not merely of the views or opinions censored but of the whole style of life of which they are part."

45 See Sunstein 1996, p. 2021.

46 Endicott 2004, pp. 935–967, 963.

47 See Williams 2006, pp. 120–131. See also Rorty (ed.) 1967.

non-cognitivism. An emotivist, denying that moral sentences correspond to any moral properties, treats moral sentences as expressions of emotions, of approval or disapproval. The emotive element may be action-initiating,[48] as already discussed in the case of pornography, but thinking of legal sentences as performatives alone restricts law to rhetoric and fails to account for whether the emotions or other mental state of affairs expressed are responses to moral principles. Moral argumentation gives way to a non-conclusive process of identifying the content of an utterance with emotions and other mental state of affairs that are not at the least justified as ethical or rational as a response to some intuitive knowledge of the good.

5 Conclusion

Interdisciplinary research, as a form of interaction and dialogue between two or more disciplines, is very often necessary for the law interpreter, because law bases itself upon a variety of pragmatic presuppositions in need of clarification by other disciplines, such as medicine, environmental sciences, social psychology etc. Normative patterns of moral behavior can be used in order to construct a coherent legal theory providing a unifying umbrella, which covers the entire legal system. In this way legal theory helps constitute the law itself. Legal theory, giving meaning to law as whole and as an integral system, filters the information coming from other disciplines.

I have used the example of linguistics and, more particularly, of performatives to illustrate that the premises of the speech-act theory can be of great analytical gain and can shed light on the different dimensions of the complex phenomenon of expression. Thinking of law as a performative emphasizes the attentiveness of legal sentences to emotions, expressions of approval or disapproval, desires, and mental states of affairs in general. Such a preoccupation with legal sentences is inclined to a non-cognitivist, emotivist reading of law. The results of performatives remain open-ended from a normative point of view. It is the task of reasoned, moral argumentation to examine, whether expressions of approval or disapproval in legal sentences are motivated by moral intuition or moral knowledge acquired through practical thinking and to discern the alternatives for action.

Literature

Austin, John L. (1989): How To Do Things With Words (The Williams James Lectures Delivered at Harvard University in 1955), 2nd edition, Oxford/New York.

Austin, John L. (1971): Performative-Constative, in: The Philosophy of Language, ed. by John R. Searle, Oxford, p. 13.

Blackburn, Simon (1993): Essays in Quasi-Realism, New York.

Blackburn, Simon (1998): Rulling Passions: A Theory of Practical Reasoning, 1st edition, Oxford.

Boer, Steven E. (1974): Speech Acts and Constitutive Rules, The Journal of Philosophy 71, p. 169.

48 Expressivism also suggests that the attitudes, expressed through moral sentences, urge to some kind of action. But expressivism, especially in the form introduced by Simon Blackburn, sees this urging to action as a practical one and may make value judgments of linguistic utterances. See Blackburn 1993; Blackburn 1998.

Bracken, Harry (1994): Freedom of Speech. Words Are not Deeds, Westport, Conn./London.

Brison, Susan (1998): Speech, Harm, and the Mind-Body Problem in First Amendment Jurisprudence, Legal Theory 4, p. 39.

Brison, Susan (2004): Speech and Other Acts. A Reply to Charles W. Collier "Hate Speech and the Mind-Body Problem: A Critic of Postmodern Censorship Theory", Legal Theory 10 (2004), p. 261.

Christou, Vasiliki E. (2007): Die Hassrede in der verfassungsrechtlichen Diskussion. Ein Beitrag im Lichte des deutschen, des U.S.-amerikanischen und des griechischen Rechts (Beiträge zum ausländischen und vergleichenden öffentlichen Recht, Band 24), Baden-Baden.

Clark, Kenneth (1995): Group Defamation and the Oppression of Black Americans, in: Defamation and Freedom of Speech. The Relationship Between Language and Violence ed by. Monroe H. Freedman/Eric M. Freedman, Westport, Conn./London, p. 3.

Cohen, Joshua (1993): Freedom of Expression, Phil. & Pub. Aff. 22 (1993), p. 207.

Collier, Charles W. (2001): Hate Speech and the Mind-Body Problem. A Critique of Postmodern Censorship Theory, Legal Theory 7 (2001), p. 203.

Dworkin, Ronald (1986) Do We Have a Right to Pornography?, in: Dworkin, A Matter of Principle, Oxford, 1986, p. 359.

Dworkin, Ronald (1986): Law's Empire, 2nd edition, London.

Dworkin, Ronald (1984): Rights as Trumps, in: Theories of Rights ed. by Jeremy Waldron, Oxford, 1984, p. 153.

Dworkin, Ronald (1977): Taking Rights Seriously, London.

Dworkin, Ronald (1991): Two Concepts of Liberty, in: Isaiah Berlin. A Celebration, ed. by Edna and Avishai Margalit, Chicago, 1991, p. 100.

Fiss, Owen (1986): Free Speech and Social Structure, Iowa L. Rev. 71 (1986), p. 1405.

Fiss, Owen (1996): The Irony of Free Speech, Cambridge, Mass./London, p. 21.

Endicott, Timothy A.O. (2004): Law and Language, in: The Oxford Handbook of Jurisprudence and Philosophy of Law ed. by Jules Coleman/Scott Shapiro, Oxford, 2004, p. 935.

Feinberg, Joel (1985): The Moral Limits of Criminal Law, vol. II: Offense to Others, New York/Oxford.

Feinberg, Joel (1988): The Moral Limits of Criminal Law, vol. III: Harmless Wrongdoing, New York/Oxford.

Fotion, N. (1971): Master Speech Acts, The Philosophical Quarterly 21 (1971), p. 232.

Greenawalt, Kent (1989): Speech, Crime, and the Uses of Language, New York/Oxford, 1989.

Habermas, Jürgen (1995): Theorie des kommunikativen Handelns (Band I: Handlungsrationalität und gesellschaftliche Rationalisierung), 1st Edition, Frankfurt am Main.

Hammack, Scott (2002) The Internet Loophole: Why Threatening Speech Online Requires a Modification of the Courts' Approach to True Threats and Incitement, Columbia Journal of Law and Social Problems 36 (2002), p. 65.

Hart, H.L.A. (1983): Essays in Jurisprudence and Philosophy, Oxford.

Hart, H.L.A. (1994): The Concept of Law, 2nd edition with a postscript, Oxford.

Hornsby, Jennifer/Rae Langton (1998): Free Speech and Illocution, Legal Theory 4 (1998), p. 21.

Kant, Immanuel (2005): Der Streit der Fakultäten, Hamburg.

Langton, Rae (1993): Speech Acts and Unspeakable Acts, Phil. & Publ. Aff. 22 (1993), p. 293.

Lawrence III, Charles R. (1990): If He Hollers Let Him Go: Regulating Racist Speech on Campus, Duke L. J., p. 431.

Lyons, John (1995): Linguistic Semantics. An Introduction, 1st edition, London/New York.

MacKinnon, Catharine A. (1993): Only Words, Cambridge, Mass.

Martin, Jeremy C. (2000): Deconstructing "Constructive Threats": Classification and Analysis of Threatening Speech After Watts and Planned Parenthood, St. Mary's L.J. 31, p. 751.

Matsuda, Mari J. (1995): Outsider Jurisprudence. Toward a Victim's Analysis of Racial Hate Messages, in: Defamation and Freedom of Speech. The Relationship Between Language and Violence ed by. Monroe H. Freedman/Eric M. Freedman, Westport, Conn./London, p. 87.

–, Public Response to Racist Speech (1989): Considering the Victim's Story, Mich. L. Rev. 87, p. 2320.

Moran, Joe (2002): Interdisciplinarity, London/New York.

Nimmer, B. (1968): The Right to Speak from Times to Time: First Amendment Theory Applied to Libel and Misapplied to Privacy, Cal. L. Rev. 56 (1968), p. 935.

Nussbaum, Martha (1997): Capabilities and Human Rights, Fordham L. Rev. 66, p. 273.
Raz, Joseph, (1994): Free Expression and Personal Identification, in: Free Expression. Essays in Law and Philosophy ed. by W.J. Waluchow, Oxford, p. 1.
Rorty, Richard (ed.) (1967): The Linguistic Turn, Chicago.
Savigny, Eike von (1998): Sprachspiele und Lebensformen: Woher kommt die Bedeutung?, in: Philosophische Untersuchungen ed. by Eike von Savigny, Berlin, p. 7.
Searle, John R. (1971): Introduction, in: The Philosophy of Language ed. by John Searle, Oxford, p. 1.
Searle, John R. (1994): Speech Acts. An Essay in the Philosophy of Language, 18th edition, London/New York (first published in 1969).
Sen, Amartya (2004): Elements of a Theory of Human Rights, Phil. & Publ. Aff. 32 (2004), p. 315.
Sen, Amartya (1984): Resources, Values and Development, Oxford: Basil Blackwell.
Solum, Lawrence (1988): Freedom of Communicative Action: A Theory of the First Amendment Freedom of Speech, Northwestern U. L. Rev. 83 (1988), p. 54.
Sunstein, Cass R. (1996): On the Expressive Function of Law, U. Pa. L. Rev. 144 (1996), p. 2021.
Williams, Bernard (2006): The Linguistic Turn, in: Williams, Ethics and the Limits of Philosophy, London/New York (First published by Fontana Press in 1985), p. 120.
Williams, Patricia (1987): Spirit-Murdering the Messenger: The Discourse of Fingerpointing as the Law's Response to Racism, U. Miami L. Rev. 42, p. 127.
Wittgenstein, Ludwig (1933): Philosophische Bemerkungen, in: The Wittgenstein Archive, http://www.hit.uib.no/wab/sample/vw115-ad.htm#92.
Zer-Ilan, Avital T. (1997): Case Note, The First Amendment and Murder Manuals, Yale L. J. 106, p. 2697.

Juliana Neuenschwander-Magalhães

Law and Cinema

Knowing Law through Art

Abstract:
Ähnlich wie im Bereich der Forschung über Recht und Literatur hat sich die Forschung im Fachgebiet Recht und Kino [in den letzten Jahren] zu einer Untersuchung der Idee des Kinos als Recht entwickelt. Beginnend mit einer an der Universidade Federal do Rio de Janeiro durchgeführten Forschung über die Art und Weise, wie das Recht im Zusammenhang von diktatorischen politischen Systemen im Kino dargestellt wird, habe ich die Hypothese aufgestellt, dass das Recht durch die Kinosprache nicht nur dargestellt, sondern vielmehr konstituiert wird. Die Forschung hat darüber hinaus auf weitere Anknüpfungspunkte zwischen dem Recht und der Kunst im Allgemeinen hingewiesen, ohne sich dabei auf die Darstellungs- und Fiktionsbegriffe beschränkt zu haben. Von konstruktivistischen sowie systemischen Annahmen ausgehend, bin ich zum Schluss gekommen, dass sich die Rechtsgeltung auch im Bereich der strukturellen Kopplungen zwischen das Rechtssystem und Kunst bestimmen lässt.

The axis of Law and Cinema may suggest different approaches. Even though it might sound as a new subject matter, at least since the 1980's studies have been developed in this field, especially in Canada, Israel and the United States. In Brazil, the research group "Law and Cinema" was created in 2005 at the Universidade Federal do Rio de Janeiro (UFRJ). This group was formed from the project "Law and Cinema: representations of law under dictatorship in cinema", financed by CNPq, the Brazilian National Council of Technological and Scientific Development, and coordinated by myself and by Dr. Rainer Maria Kiesow, Professor at the Goethe University of Frankfurt and researcher at the Max Planck Institute for European Legal History.

1 Representation of Law in Cinema

As observed in Law and Literature studies, which have been gradually developed towards an approach known as Law as Literature, a shift in the Law and Film perspective could point towards a Law as Film approach. The Law and Film concept would include both, the observation of the representation of law in cinema – the analysis of legal films – and the pedagogical role these films could play on legal studies, substituting the legal texts as well as the traditional teaching methods.

The idea underneath perspectives of this type is that cinema represents law and, by these representations, getting to know law could be possible. This assertion may be acknowledged in David Black's book *Law in Film: Resonance and Representation* in which the relationship between Law and Cinema is explained in terms of "representation of an important cultural practice by the significant means of another form of cultural practice".[1]

1 Black 1999, p. 2.

Nevertheless, to which extent does "representing" mean "knowing"? This is a question that is linked to the meaning of analogy and to the evident distinction between representation and the object being represented. In the Theory of Knowledge, according to Niklas Luhmann, the idea of representation only makes sense assuming the existence of some kind of isomorphism between facts in the exterior world and scientific knowledge. As Edgard Morin said, the "projected 'image' in the exterior world completely identifies itself with the world, in other words, totally identifies the world to itself".[2] An isomorphism of this type would imply assuming the meaning of scientific knowledge as a mere tautology. This tautology, justified as the objective vision "des choses réelles", may also be described as a paradox: "everything goes on as if the reality that we know was at the same time ours and foreign, totally familiar and totally unknown".[3]

Therefore, it is hard to conceive that law might be knowable just by observing a film – since cinema would provide representations of law, not law itself. So the research on law representations under dictatorship has led to the current problem in understanding the representation idea as a cognitive model. Observing fascist representations in cinema as a form of the stabilization political-legal order has contributed on our way towards that problem. The function of cinema as an artistic expression and as a mass communication medium could be observed on a much broader scale than as a mere notion of representation and cognition.

2 Propaganda Films

From the analysis of classical political propaganda films, like Leni Riefenstahl's Triumph des Willens (1934), we have pursued to observe how cinema – by both documentary or fiction – has been used to glorify or for doctrine. In Marc Ferro's words, "since the rulers of a society comprehended the possibilities that cinema might represent, they tried to appropriate in order to have it under their service".[4]

In the 20th century, fascist regimes used cinema not only as a means of mass communication, but also as a means of constituting masses. According to Hannah Arendt, a typical phenomenon of the 20th century occurred mainly after capitalist breakdowns, like those observed in the 1920's in Weimar Republic and during the civil war in post-revolutionary Russia: the masses. They are composed by atomized individuals united by a common loss, willing to devote their loyalty to a nihilist movement full of hate towards all existing institutions. Consequently, we may affirm that the primordial function conferred to cinema in the National Socialist regime towards the massification of its propaganda aimed firstly, to keep collective imaginary indefinitely away from reality; and secondly, to replace reality itself with a forged official reality, in an effort to keep collectivity in the above mentioned state of pathologic trance to assure unconditional adhesion to the movement.

According to Niklas Luhmann's remarks in *The Reality of the Mass Media* – in the production and reproduction of reality that takes place within the operations taken

2 Morin 1986, pp. 206 ff.
3 Luhmann 1996, p. 228.
4 Ferro 1992.

in the mass media system – we consider that totalitarian propaganda aims at much more than keeping the masses away from reality. Its objective would be to replace reality with another one, adequate to the aims of the movement, generated by the propaganda machine.

Thus, law is also subject to totalitarianism. The function of a totalitarian norm is to support the totalitarian state and repression against citizens. As Adam Podgorecki pointed out, the totalitarian "Grundnorm" is the will of dominant elites or leaders, which compromises both integrity and validity of legal systems under fascism. In Podgorecki's perfect and precise definition, "totalitarian law is a social technique that includes perverted modes of legal validity [...], and a dark instrument of social engineering that is based on an irrational 'dead end' 'legitimacy'".[5] In Orson Welles' film *The Trial* (1962), which is based on Franz Kafka's homonym book, this obscure and irrational social engineering is narratively reproduced by exploring light and shadow contrast, empty spaces' amplitude and labyrinthic architecture uniting the court to the judges' portraitist studio.

3 Movies and Society

These early conclusions on the relationship between law and fascism as observed in movies have allowed the Law and Cinema research group to advance in its hypothesis by focusing on a constructivist view of knowledge instead of following traditional notions of representation and cognition. This hypothesis considers that in spite of political attempts – which sometimes have led to the constitution of masses resulting in the alienation of individuals – no politician will ever be able to void the constructive potential of filmic narrative (communication). In this direction, Marc Ferro has pointed that despite efforts made by different politically oriented regimes towards transforming cinema into a subservient tool, it has kept its independence, offering autonomous views of reality acting as a form of counterpower.[6] This is due to the fact that cinema, as will, does not constitute a social reality – only communication produces communication.

This way, our problem has become trying to comprehend the process of reality construction from filmic narrative, heading towards a constructivist epistemology. In a first approach of a constructivist thesis, the comprehension process of cultural meanings is seen as a subject's process constructing these meanings. This is a circularity that refers what is known to what is, in fact, constructed during the knowledge process. This first approach puts the subject, as a craftsman's construction, in the middle of the circle. When discussing a filmic comprehension process, authors who adopt this subjective and constructivist view, consider a cinematographic narrative to be based on the audience's active role in the construction of the meaning of the film.[7]

There is, however, one more modality of constructivism that may be qualified as "radical". "Radical" is what this form of constructivism is called, in a sense already

5 Podgorecki 1996, p. 13.
6 Ferro 1992, p. 14.
7 Bordwell 1987.

used by Niklas Luhmann, because here we assumed that science "works constructing a world",[8] but also in a sense given by Anthony Giddens, since this perspective is an alternative to many traditional formularizations on the possible connections between science and art, law and art, law and cinema. According to this radical point of view, law is not only represented, but also constituted by means of art diffusion. In this sense, knowing forms of filmic expressions of law and means knowing law itself.

Based on the premise of constructivism by Niklas Luhmann, our Research Group assumed the point of view that, in modern society, law and art constitute functionally differentiated social systems. Functional differentiation is, at the same time, condition and consequence of the modern society. In the functionally differentiated society reality is a product of social system activities, not something objectively given.

4 Differentiation between Law and Art

Law is constructed by the legal/illegal (Recht/Unrecht) distinction. Art, in its turn, constructs its own reality by applying the difference between reality/fiction. The function of art is to establish in the world its own reality about the world. By using the distinction between reality and fiction, art turns imagined reality into a form of dealing with reality, in other words, in a way of affirming, denying and criticizing reality. The function of law is the stabilization of normative expectations, treating them as reality.

The progressive differentiation between law and art may be acknowledged by observing a fictional conceptual path. According to Ernst Kantorowicz, fiction was originally a legal concept. Until Renaissance, art was seen as an imitation of nature. Later, this Aristotelian concept was reproduced in Justinian's Digesto, and by Middle Age it was used to justify why it was not allowed for a person to be adopted by someone younger than him or her: "because adoption imitates nature and it would be monstrous a son older than their parents". Law, considered by that time as art, mirrored itself in the example given by imitation. Even though, by imitation, the adoptive father could not be younger than his adopted child, only by fiction this could eventually happen. In this perspective, law functions as a legal fiction: someone could be considered as a relative of someone older than him or her but with no blood connections. At this point, Kantorowicz makes reference to a lesson by BALDO – that in his turn reminds Bartolo: "fiction imitates nature and for this reason fiction can play a role when just the truth may do the same".[9] In the words of Petrarca, fiction can be understood as the "function of the poet", which must "disclose and glorify the truth of things hidden in a cloud of fiction". Fiction is "created" by juristic "art".

Later, with Legal Positivism, legal fictions assumed the form of truths, of objective meanings, while Art remained in the fictional field. At this point, the boundaries of functional differentiation had already been established: on the one hand

8 Luhmann 1996, p. 77.
9 Kantorowicz 2004.

there was law, with its function of stabilizing normative expectations; on the other hand there was art, with its function of producing, in the world, a *representation* of the world. Legal Positivism, rejecting the fictional and inventive aspect of law, also banishes the possibility of criticism from legal knowledge. The idea which states that law imagines society was put aside, since law reconstructs the world from the distinction between the legal and the non-legal.

The Jurisprudence has abandoned imagination and criticism in an attempt to construct truths about law. This is a consequence of functional differentiation itself and of the fact that, in modern times, the problem of truth has also become a specific function of a social system: Science. From an objectivist view of science, truth as a scientific value has been seen as an adequacy to reality. Here, there is a problem: how would it be possible to talk about truth in a world composed not just by one, but by many realities contemporaneously constructed by different social systems? Evidently, as Luhmann says, it is not just science system that guarantees society to achieve the real.[10] All social systems simultaneously work towards that goal.

Here, there is another question. Mass media have played a more active role in constructing social reality. As the above mentioned systems, mass media also produce and reproduce knowledge of the world, and as a result produce and reproduce reality. Nowadays, the means of mass communication go beyond social systems. If these systems use them in order to accomplish their functions, those means certainly are places for an adequate production of the reality of social systems.

5 Movies as Sources

This becomes more evident to the extent that, by observing the dynamic of contemporaneous sociability, it is possible to consider this phenomenon as predominantly orientated by image criteria, images that "talk" about images, images indefinitely reproduced, images that are reality and constitute reality.[11] This way, one may talk about a global semantics formed by images – and no longer just by texts – a global scale phenomenon impacting on many different social systems. Science, Religion, Education, Economy, Politics, all of these social systems construct their senses and meanings under the aegis of that semantics. Therefore, it makes sense to talk about a more and more imagetic sociability, constituted and constituting communications by using images.

It is impossible not to consider the impact of images on law – one of the social subsystems that, coupled with other systems, constitutes itself and constitutes the most inclusive social system, which is society. It is also undeniable that in contemporary societies, "telling the law" and "doing justice" are recurring themes. This recurrence seems to express a growing judicialization of social life.[12] and may easily be checked by the observation of those means of communication audience – especially imagetic ones, but not exclusively – in society's different segments.

10 Luhmann 1996, p. 97.
11 Baudrillard 1991; Sodré 2006.
12 Garapon 1996.

Cinema, television broadcasting, newspapers, radio programs, the Internet, all media, with more or less intensity and competence, always make reference to legal questions. In the specific case of imagetic media, films and documentaries with law and order topics are largely offered and consumed. Cinematographic and television images are important instruments to ensure the "telling the law/doing justice" actions for which the legal system is responsible. However, these images could be blamed for the legal field erosion, replacing it with different ones, showing no indication of who should be in charge of the possible meanings law can have.

Such a paradox, observable within the legal system, occurs from communication friction between the legal system and the media. The first one chooses information offered by media images (that build meanings of "reality", "fiction", surpassing and reversing those meanings), as does the second one selecting information given by the legal system ("telling the law/doing justice"). Such operation provides legitimacy to the legal system, reinforcing its peculiarities, even though some of the legal field specialists consider it an undesirable interference for the differentiation and autonomic dynamics of the legal system that should be confronted.[13] In fact, it is a possible menace to the differentiation of law, once the legal/illegal code could be corroded or weakened by the media appeals. On the other hand, the reality built by the media could also be a manner of stabilizing the normative expectations. In a way, it's possible to say that the media produces law. Except, in reality, it's always law that produces law; after all, legal communication always requires legal communication, in a communication network.

Cinema as a social communication medium allows what the theory of systems calls structural coupling between Law and Art. Evidently, in the face of this coupling, the meanings of film fictions are certainly not the same in coincident for the Law and Art system. In this case, it's our interest to explore the hostility between Art and Law, and more specifically between Cinema and Law. By using images and sounds, movies are manifesting modern society's paradoxes. As Luis Alberto Warat says, motion pictures disseminate the knowledge of many different ways of life in the world at the same time it devastates such differences in ways of life and distinct traditions.[14] The idea of structural coupling also makes it possible to understand how movies can be a form of normative production, beyond any idea of representation. Movies with reference to legal matters contribute to what Pierre Bourdieu called "symbolic efficiency". This concept translates the fact that the efficiency of law "is exercised beyond the circles of those who are converted in anticipation", in other words, ahead of the knowledge of those to whom knowledge is assumed. "It is known that it's part of the symbolic efficiency not being able to exercise itself without the complicity – more correct as more unconscious, and even more subtly extorted – from those who support it. A legitimate speech form by excellence, law may only exercise its specific efficiency while it obtains the recognition or, while it remains unknown the greater or smaller part of arbitrary that is in the origin of its functioning".[15]

13 Bourdieu 2005, pp. 211–212.
14 Warat 2011, p. 536.
15 Bourdieu 2005, p. 243.

The legal value is also built in the structural coupling's territory. Cinema is a source of information which has to be studied. Paraphrasing LUHMANN, we may say that movies are sources, as legal texts are, not information. They must be read, meaning they must be legalized. Only interpretation produces information.[16]

Literature

Asimow, M.; Shannon, M.: Law and Popular Culture. New York, 2004.
Baehr, Peter; Richter, Melvin: Dictatorship in History and Theory. Cambridge, 2004
Baudrillard, Jean: Simulacros e Simulação. Lisboa, 1991.
Black, David A. (1999): Law in Film. Resonance and Representation. Illinois University Press.
Bordwell, David (1987): Narration in the fiction film. Madison, Wis.
Bourdieu, Pierre (1991): Langage et Pouvoir Symbolique. Paris.
Bourdieu, Pierre (2005): O Poder Simbólico. 8ed, Rio de Janeiro.
Chase, Anthony (2002): Movies on Trial. The Legal System on the Silver Screen. New York.
Denvir, John (org) (1996): Legal Reelism. Movies as Legal Texts. Illinois University Press.
De Giorgi, Raffaele (2006): Direito, Tempo e Memória. São Paulo.
Deleuze, G; Guattari, F. (1975): Kafka. Pour une Littérature Mineure. Paris.
Deleuze, Gilles (2005): A Imagem-Tempo. Cinema 2. Trad. Eloisa de Araújo. São Paulo.
Derrida, Jacques et al. (1985): La Faculté de Juger. Paris.
Derrida, Jacque (2005): Force de Loi. Le Fondement Mytique de l'Autorité. Paris.
Dworkin, Ronald (1999): O Império do Direito. São Paulo.
Dworkin, Ronald (2005): Uma Questão de Princípio. São Paulo.
Ferro, Marc (1992): Cinema e história. Rio de Janeiro.
Garapon, Antoine (1996): A Ilusão da Democracia Direta in: O Juiz e a Democracia. O Guardião das Promessas. Rio de Janeiro, 1996, cap. III, pp. 75–96.
Kantorowicz, Ernst (2004): La Souveraineté de l'Artiste in: Mourir pour la Patrie. 2ed., Paris.
Kiesow, Rainer Maria (2005): Il Silenzo delle Leggi. Palestra proferida no 1° Seminário "Cinema e Direito: Representações do Direito em 'O Processo' de Kafka/Welles", realizado na Faculdade Nacional de Direito da Universidade Federal do Rio de Janeiro (inédito).
Lacerda, Gabriel (2007): O Direito no Cinema. Rio de Janeiro.
Luhmann, Niklas (1983): Sociologia do Direito. Rio de Janeiro, 2 v.
Luhmann, Niklas (1990): Sociedad y Sistema: la Ambición de la Teoria. Barcelona/Buenos Aires/México.
Luhmann, Niklas (1995): Social Systems. Stanford University Press.
Luhmann, Niklas (1996): La Ciência de la Sociedad. Trad. Javier Torres Nafarrate. Mexico, DF.
Luhmann, Niklas (2005): A Realidade dos Meios de Comunicação. Trad. Ciro Marcondes Filho. São Paulo.
Morin, Edgar (1986): La Méthode. La connaissance de la connaissance. Paris.
Podgorecki, Olgiati (1996): Totalitarian and Post-totalitarian Law. Dartmouth Publishing Company.
Sodré, Muniz (2006): Antropológica do Espelho. Uma Teoria da Comunicação Linear e em Rede. 2ed, Petrópolis.
Warat, L.A.; Cunha, R.M.C. (1977): da. Ensino e Saber Jurídico. Rio de Janeiro.
Warat, Luis Alberto (2000): A Ciência Jurídica e seus dois maridos. 2ed. Santa Cruz do Sul (RS).
Warat, Luis Alberto (2004): Territórios Desconhecidos: a Procura Surrealista pelos Lugares do Abandono do Sentido e da Reconstrução da Subjetividade. Florianópolis.

16 De Giorgio 2006, p. 66.

Miodrag A. Jovanović

Collective Rights

A Case Study of Interdisciplinary Approach in Jurisprudence

Abstract:
Der dominante methodologische Ansatz der gegenwärtigen Rechtswissenschaft ist eine Form von Rechtspositivismus, der von der Idee ausgeht, dass diese Disziplin im methodologischen Sinne ausgeprägt sein soll. Trotz der wesentlichen Unterschiedlichkeit zwischen Herbert Harts ‚analytischer Jurisprudenz' und Hans Kelsens ‚Reine Rechtslehre', ist gemeinsamer Nenner der beiden Schulen die Ablehnung der Auswertungsmethoden. Die Reine Rechtslehre ist sogar noch enger, weil sie auch die soziologischen Methoden aus der Rechtsforschung fernhält. In diesem Aufsatz bemühe ich mich darum zu beweisen, dass die rechtstheoretische Konzeptualisierung der ‚kollektiven Rechte' – als ein neuer rechtstheoretischer Begriff – auf der methodologischen Grundlage der Reinen Rechtslehre kaum möglich ist. Insbesondere zeige ich, dass Kelsens Hilfskonzept der ‚zentralen Zurechnung' (später ‚Zuschreibung') nicht angemessen ist, wenn sie an eine Rechtsnorm, die kollektive Rechte bestimmt, angelegt wird. Bei Normen über kollektive Rechte kann das individuelle Mitglied der Gruppe die Rechte ausüben, vorausgesetzt dass es seine Mitgliedschaft beweisen kann. Diese Mitgliedschaft ist aber eine soziologische, prä-rechtliche Kategorie, insofern die Gruppe „objektiv", unabhängig vom Gesetzgeber existiert. In einer solchen Situation kann man nicht mit Kelsens Konzeption das Subjekt-Element dieser Rechtsnorm festlegen. Deshalb kann eine Rechtstheorie der kollektiven Rechte keine Reine Rechtslehre Kelsens sein. Das heißt, dass eine solche Theorie in ihrer Forschung nicht nur die juristische (normative), sondern auch die philosophische und soziologische Methode verwenden muss.

1 Introduction

In his 1983 voluminous treatise on the international law of human rights, Sieghart designates one chapter to the topic of collective rights. There he notes that, unlike rights of individuals, those which the international order assign to 'peoples', as collective entities, suffer from several conceptual indeterminacies. The most serious one concerns criteria for defining who should count as a 'people' and who should be recognized as belonging to it. In that respect, he finds it highly ironical that these issues were equally bothering for both the Nazi state, in its attempt to define all those not belonging to Aryan race as legal outcasts, and the Israeli state, in its effort to provide preferential treatment to Jews under *The Law of the Return.*[1]

As for the former case, in September 1935, the German government passed the notorious Nürnberg Race Laws. The first one of them, *The Reich Citizenship Law* (*Reichsbürgergesetz*) granted the German citizenship only to a person "who is of German or kindred blood and who, through his conduct, shows that he is both desirous and fit to serve the German people and Reich faithfully." (Art. 2) The Jews and other non-Germans were reclassified as aliens and denied the German citizenship. The second one, *The Law for the Protection of German Blood* (*Gesetz zum Schutze des deutschen Blutes*), proclaimed on the same day, forbade marriages and even sexual relations between the Germans and the Jews. Since these laws had not cleared up the major

1 Paul Sieghart, The International Law of Human Rights, Oxford 1983, p. 367, Fn. 1.

issue who was to be counted as a 'full Jew', the Nazis then issued, in November 1935, *The First Regulation to Reich Citizenship Law* (*Erste Verordnung zum Reichsbürgergesetz*). The category of 'full Jew' was ascribed to a person with at least three Jewish grandparents. Those with less were designated as *Mischlinge* (the Germans of mixed race) of two degrees: the first degree – with two Jewish grandparents; the second degree – with one Jewish grandparent.[2]

As for the latter country, the first major case of the so-called 'who is a Jew?' debate concerned Oswald Rufeisen, also known as Brother Daniel, who was born to a Jewish family living in Poland. During the Nazi occupation, in order to save his life, he had hidden in a monastery and afterwards decided to convert to Catholicism. After the war, he became a monk. In the 1950s, Rufeisen submitted an application for the Israeli citizenship, basing it on the provisions of *The Law of Return*. However, the Israeli government denied his request, on the grounds that he had converted to Christianity. Rufeisen then appealed the case to the Supreme Court of Israel, and in 1962, the Court upheld the government's decision. Its reasoning was that all Jews converting to another religion shall lose their preferential access to the Israeli citizenship.[3] After the *Shalit* case,[4] the Israeli legislature decided to amend the law as to include the legal definition of Jew. According to that amendment, Jew is defined as "a person who was born of a Jewish mother or has become converted to Judaism." Nevertheless, the manner of conversion was not defined in details, and this imprecision has led to further contentious court challenges, since Orthodox Judaism has different standards for conversion from Reform or Conservative Judaism.[5]

To say that for all those defending some sort of collective rights the aforementioned examples, and especially the first one, represent a major challenge would be an understatement. Yet, I proceed exactly from these 'hard cases' in an attempt to demonstrate that if legal orders can be said to occasionally designate collective entities, such as national, linguistic or religious groups, as legal subjects, then it is up to jurisprudence to provide legal-theoretical grounding for this concept. In what follows I will argue that this approach of legal theory should necessarily be interdisciplinary one, insofar as it should lean not only on the normative method, but also

2 English version of these laws is available in, Jeremy Noakes/Geoffrey Pridham, Documents on Nazism 1919–1945, New York 1974, pp. 463–467.

3 Rufeisen vs Minister of Interior (1962) 16 PD 2428

4 Shalit vs Minister of Interior (1968) 23 PD II 477 Benjamin Shalit, an Israeli Jewish naval officer, married a Scottish woman abroad and returned with her to Israel. Their two children, as native-born Israelis, automatically became Israeli citizens. However, when parents attempted to register them as Jews under the 'nationality' designation, while leaving the 'religion' category blank, the Ministry of Interior refused them. Shalit went to the Supreme Court, which narrowly ruled by 5–4 in his favor. However, the court's decision was primarily based on technical grounds, and being aware of the possible reaction to this decision, the court emphasized that "it is in fact a mistake to think that the matter under consideration requires us to determine who is a Jew."

5 One author argues that "[t]he problem is insoluble on the religious level … It is a fact that Reform Judaism does not recognize the divinely binding force of the totality of Rabbinic law. Hence, conversions to Reform Judaism lack a substantial requirement of Orthodox law. Moreover, they raise, in the eyes of Orthodoxy, the mentioned fundamental problem of unnecessarily causing a person's ultimate failure by imposing upon him religious duties which he will violate in the future." Izhak Englard, "Law and Religion in Israel", The American Journal of Comparative Law 35 (1987), 1, p. 195.

on methods of other disciplines, such as philosophy, sociology, or cultural anthropology.

2 Interdisciplinarity in Legal Theory (Jurisprudence)

The legal theory that most forcefully tries to expel all non-normative methods from legal research is Kelsen's Pure Theory of Law (*Reine Rechtslehre*).[6] In his own words: "It is called 'pure' because it seeks to preclude from the cognition of positive law all elements foreign thereto." That is, "the specific science of law, the discipline usually called jurisprudence, must be distinguished from the philosophy of justice, on the one hand, and from sociology, or cognition of social reality, on the other."[7] The 'purity' of legal theory is equated, thus, precisely with the absence of 'mixture' of different scientific methods as applied in the field of law.[8]

Kelsen's methodological orientation stems from a more basic posture of a strand of the neo-Kantian philosophy that makes a sharp distinction between what 'is' (*Sein*) and what 'ought to be' (*Sollen*). These two worlds, which are divided by "an unbridgeable gap",[9] generate the respective distinction between the *normative* and *explicative* sciences.[10] Jurisprudence falls in the former category, not in the sense that it itself is "a law-setting authority" (*rechtsetzenden Gewalt*), but because its object is the world of norms – *Sollen*.[11] However, in order to stay objective, that is scientific,[12] jurisprudence's only task is to clarify and explicate positive legal norms.[13] This, in

6 Kelsen's Pure Theory of Law has gone through several modifications in the course of time, but leading scholars of Kelsen's work disagree about the characterization and duration of exact phases. Thus, Heidemann speaks of the four phases: 'constructivist', 'transcendental' (or 'neo-kantian'), 'realistic', and 'analytico-linguistic'. In addition, he emphasizes "the radical break" in Kelsen's theory that comes with the 'realistic' phase. (Carsten Heidemann, Die Norm als Tatsache – Zur Normentheorie Hans Kelsens, Baden-Baden: Nomos 1997) On the other hand, Paulson tries to demonstrate that there is no such thing as "radical break", but only two sub-periods (neo-kantian and hybrid) of the integrated 'classical' phase of Kelsen's theory, which stands in-between its 'constructivist' and 'skeptical' phases. (Cf. comparison of periodization in, Stanley L. Paulson, "Four Phases in Hans Kelsen's Legal Theory? Reflections on Periodization", Oxford Journal of Legal Studies 18 [1998], 2, p. 161) In this paper, I am mainly concentrated on arguments from this 'classical' phase of Kelsen's Pure Theory of Law (1922–1960), which does not exclude relevant references from other phases as well.

7 Hans Kelsen, "The Pure Theory of Law and Analytical Jurisprudence", Harvard Law Review 55 (1941–42), 1, p. 44.

8 Cf. Stanley L. Paulson, "Konstruktivismus, Methodendualismus und Zurechnung im Frühwerk Hans Kelsens", Archiv des öffentliches Rechts 124 (1999), p. 638.

9 Hans Kelsen, Hauptprobleme der Staatsrechtslehre, Tübingen 1911, p. 8.

10 Hans Kelsen, Grenzen zwischen juristischer und soziologischer Methode, Tübingen 1911, p. 10.

11 As Kelsen emphasizes, "It is of the greatest importance clearly to distinguish between legal norms which comprise the object of jurisprudence and the statements of jurisprudence describing that object." Kelsen (Fn. 7), p. 51.

12 "Science is the product of cognition expressed in sentence describing an object; cognition is directed at truth; it can not constitute moral or political values." Hans Kelsen, Politics, Ethics, Religion and Law, in: Faktoren der politischen Entscheidung – Festgabe für Ernst Fraenkel zum 65. Geburtstag, hg. v. Gerhard A. Ritter/Gilbert Ziebura, Berlin 1963, p. 6.

13 Kelsen (Fn. 10), pp. 13, 15.

turn, means that legal theory should be "an analysis free of all ethico-political value judgments."[14]

In comparison to Kelsen's endeavor, it seems that the contemporary methodological debate within the Anglo-American jurisprudence, which nowadays dominates the global discourse in legal theory, revolves around more modest philosophical aspirations.[15] The boundaries of this methodological debate are largely set by Hart's influential book *The Concept of Law*, the subsequent criticisms, raised primarily by Ronald Dworkin, and Hart's *Postscript*, which thirty-two years after the first edition of his book tries to recapitulate the main points of the debate and to defend the key tenets of his version of legal positivism. As stated explicitly by Hart, the aim of his book "was to provide a theory of what law is which is both general and descriptive." This theory is *general* insofar as "it is not tied to any particular system of legal culture",[16] and it is *descriptive* insofar as "it is morally neutral and has no justificatory aims".[17] In contrast, Dworkin's conception of legal theory (jurisprudence) is concerned with "a particular legal culture" – in his case, Anglo-American law – and unlike Hart's theory, it is both evaluative and justificatory. Dworkin dismisses general and descriptive legal theory as useless, since only those theories that are "interpretative of a particular stage of a historically developing practice" can be considered useful.[18]

In holding so, Dworkin targets both of the thesis that are commonly associated with the contemporary Anglo-American legal positivism – *The Social Thesis* and *The Separation Thesis*. The former thesis asserts that law is a social phenomenon and that the source of legal validity is to be found in social facts, more precisely, certain social conventions, such as an act of legislation or a judicial decision. The latter thesis asserts that there is a conceptual separation between law and morals, that is, between what the law is and what the law ought to be.[19] Dworkin, on the contrary, holds that to determine what the law is in particular cases inevitably depends on moral-politi-

14 Hans Kelsen, Introduction to the Problems of Legal Theory (translation of the first edition of the Reine Rechtslehre, by B.L. Paulson and S.L. Paulson), Oxford 1992, p. 53.

15 This should not be taken as automatically devaluing the Anglo-American legal theory, since it is largely concerned with the concept of law as a social practice.

16 Herbert Hart, The Concept of Law (2nd ed.), With a Postscript edited by Penelope A. Bulloch and Joseph Raz, Oxford 1994, p. 239.

17 op. cit., p. 240; According to Hart's own words, one of the points that he wanted to discuss with Kelsen on a meeting held in November 1961 at the Berkley Law School, was Kelsen's expression "Rules of law in a descriptive sense." What puzzled Hart was exactly Kelsen's methodological claim that while explicating and analyzing the existing law, the Pure Theory of Law still falls within the category of "normative sciences". However, in the subsequently published paper that summarizes their discussion, Hart grasped more fully into Kelsen's methodological apparatus. Hence, he eventually states: "I do not think his terminology of rule and ought 'in a descriptive sense' happy, but I do think he was wise to reject the alternative I proffered." Herbert Hart, "Kelsen Visited", UCLA Law Review 10 (1963), pp. 716–717.

18 Ronald Dworkin, Law's Empire, Cambridge, MA 1986, p. 102.

19 Anglo-American legal theorists are separated in the two camps – exclusivists and inclusivists. While the former hold that 'it is necessarily the case that there is no connection between law and morality', the latter claim that 'it is not necessarily the case that there is a connection between law and morality.' Leslie Green, Legal Positivism, Stanford Encyclopedia of Philosophy, Spring 2007 Edition, at http://plato.stanford.edu/archives/spr2007/entries/legal-positivism.

cal considerations about what the law ought to be. Therefore, evaluative judgments partly determine what the law is.[20]

The other attacks on *The Separation Thesis* come from a modern version of the natural-law theory.[21] John Finnis, for instance, acknowledges Hart's effort to construct a legal theory around an 'internal', participants-oriented point of view, but suggests that the participants should not be perceived as unconditionally accepting the legal system as given. Instead, legal theory should proceed from the participant who is following the law *because* the law imposes presumptive moral obligations of obedience and who is capable of judging correctly on these subtle moral issues.[22] For Finnis, "A natural law theory is nothing other than a theory of good reasons for choice (and action)", whereas these reasons "will instantiate and express human nature precisely because they participate in and realize human goods."[23] Accordingly, unlike classical natural-law theorists, Finnis does not fundamentally challenge *The Social Thesis*, according to which immorality of the law does not affect its legal validity,[24] but he challenges the claim that legal theory can in any meaningful sense be non-evaluative.[25]

At the same time, separate methodological frontlines are opened within the community of legal positivists as well. For instance, there is an ongoing dispute of whether Hart's assertion that his legal theory is descriptive does necessarily excludes every instance of evaluation from it. Julie Dickson, for example, argues that this is not the case, since statements from Hart's *Postscript* should be put in a proper context of rebutting key points of Dworkin's theory of law. Consequently, Hart wishes not to distance himself from 'evaluative' jurisprudence *per se*, but only from the one advanced by Dworkin.[26] In contrast to that author's view, the 'evaluative-but-not-morally-evaluative' legal theory, according to Dickson, would be the one that operates with "'purely methatheoretical' value judgments – judgments about which data to focus on and how to order and arrange materials for explanation in order for one's theory to exhibit such general theoretical virtues as simplicity, clarity, consistency, and comprehensiveness".[27]

20 Andrei Marmor, The Nature of Law, in: Stanford Encyclopedia of Philosophy, Spring 2007 Edition, at http://plato.stanford.edu/archives/spr2007/entries/lawphil-nature/

21 One prominent representative of that school is Fuller, whose theory is also known as 'procedural natural law theory'. See, Lon L. Fuller, The Morality of Law, New Haven and London 1964; Lon L. Fuller, The Law in Quest of Itself, Boston 1966. Lon L. Fuller, Anatomy of the Law, New York 1969.

22 John Finnis, Natural Law and Natural Rights, Oxford 1980, pp. 9–15.

23 John Finnis, "Natural Law and Legal Reasoning", Cleveland State Law Review 38 (1990), 1, 1, p. 2; Finnis holds that there are seven "basic human goods".

24 Yet, he argues that, though not invalid in legal sense of the word, such laws are in moral aspect defect and, hence, do not provide good reasons for action. Finnis (Fn. 22), pp. 359–361; This Finnis' position has led many commentators to conclude that on the matter of validity of law the hatchets has been buried between the contemporary Anglo-American legal positivism and natural-law theory. Cf. Brian Bix, "On the Dividing Line Between Natural Law Theory and Legal Positivism", Notre Dame Law Review 75 (2000), 5, p. 1624.

25 See, John Finnis, "On Hart's Ways: Law As Reason and As Fact", The American Journal of Jurisprudence 52 (2007), 1, pp. 25–53.

26 Julie Dickson, "Methodology in Jurisprudence: A Critical Survey", Legal Theory 10 (2004), p. 120.

27 op. cit., p. 125. Dickson says that this kind of view of legal theory is also advanced by Jules

To sum up: What in methodological terms contemporary Anglo-American legal positivists share with Kelsen is the thesis that legal theory should be "an analysis free of all ethico-political value judgments." However, when it comes to the endorsement of methods of social sciences in legal research, it is *prima faciae* clear that Kelsen's Pure Theory of Law is far more stringent than its Anglo-American counterparts. Accordingly, for the sake of defending the interdisciplinary approach in jurisprudence, *Reine Rechtslehre* seems to be more appropriate adversary than, for instance, Hart's theory, which he tends to describe as "descriptive sociology".[28] Having said this, if I succeed in showing that Kelsen's approach is on its own merits inadequate in dealing with certain rights that I consider collective, then I will assume that the case is being made for an interdisciplinary approach into this subject matter.[29]

3 Kelsen's Concept of 'Imputation'

One of the main preoccupations of the Pure Theory of Law is to eliminate the "ideologically" motivated dualism of objective law, on the one side, and subjective right and legal subject, on the other side.[30] In that respect, Kelsen argues that "there is a subjective right (*qua* legal right) only in so far as the objective law is at the disposal of a concrete subject."[31] The same applies to legal subject, or as it is commonly referred to – 'person', which is "simply a personifying expression for the unity of a bundle of legal obligations and legal rights, that is, the unity of a complex of norms."[32] In order to fully demystify what he holds to be "an artificial aid" and "a heuristic concept" of legal cognition, Kelsen introduces the concept of 'imputation'. In the first edition of his book *Reine Rechtslehre* (1934), Kelsen speaks of the two forms of 'imputation' – 'central' (*zentrale Zurechnung*) and 'peripheral' (*periphere Zurechnung*). The first one, the one described above, is an auxiliary tool of legal thinking, which helps us avoiding *anthropomorphism* in legal theory. The second one is "a formal relational category" of the Pure Theory of Law,[33] and it differs from the 'central imputation' insofar as here, "a material fact is connected not to the unity of the system but to another material fact within the system, that is … two material

Coleman, Andrei Marmor and Wil Waluchow. op. cit., p. 123.

28 Hart (Fn. 16).

29 Since any legal theory of collective rights can only be a segment of a more general legal theory, this would have obvious methodological implications for the discipline as a whole.

30 The ideological function of this separation is, in Kelsen's opinion, in that "the subjective right, which really means private property, is a category transcending the objective law, it is an institution putting unavoidable constraints on the shaping of the content of the legal system … Since property has always been a part of individual liberty, of autonomous personality … [a] system that does not recognize the human being as a free personality in this sense, a system that does not guarantee subjective rights, should not be considered a legal system at all." Kelsen (Fn. 14), pp. 40–41.

31 op. cit., p. 44.

32 op. cit., p. 47.

33 Carsten Heidemann, Der Begriff der Zurechnung bei Hans Kelsen, in: Hans Kelsen – Staatrechtslehrer und Rechtstheoretiker des 20. Jahrhunderts, hg. v. Stanley L. Paulson/Michael Stolleis, Tübingen 2005, p. 32.

facts are linked together in the reconstructed legal norm."[34] Paulson says that "[t]he ordering principle of peripheral imputation, governing the extra-linguistic connection of elements, can be given expression with the legal 'ought'."[35] In Kelsen's own words, the principle of 'peripheral imputation' "has, in the rules of law, a function analogous to that which the principle of causality has in the natural laws by which natural science describes nature."[36]

In the second edition of *Reine Rechtslehre* (1960), Kelsen comes to the conclusion that the proposed terminology was "unsatisfactory" and that it led to "misunderstandings". Therefore, instead of '*zentrale Zurechnung*', he uses the term '*Zuschreibung*'.[37] On the other hand, the concept '*Zurechnung*' refers now only to what was previously discussed as 'peripheral imputation', as applied on 'general' and 'individual' legal norms.[38] For the purpose of this study, I will be predominantly focused on '*zentrale Zurechnung*', that is '*Zuschreibung*', and when used without an adjective, the word 'imputation' shall denote this concept solely.

When referring to 'physical person', this concept implies that "the 'physical' person is the common point of imputation for the material facts of human behavior that are normatively regulated as obligations and rights."[39] As for 'legal person', alike its 'physical' counterpart, it "has no natural, real existence." Therefore, again, what might be spoken of as 'real' is "simply the human behavior that is governed by norms", with the difference that in this case "obligations are imposed on, and rights are granted to, individual human beings indirectly, that is, mediated by the legal subsystem."[40] Hence, saying colloquially, that legal person, such as a corporation, is a bearer of right or obligation cannot reverse the fact that in the end it is some human being that has that right or obligation. Consequently, "[a]ll acts of the legal person are acts of human beings, human acts that are imputed to the fictitious subject that one imagines the unity of a legal subsystem or comprehensive legal system to be."[41] In that respect, the legal person of state represents this "comprehensive legal system" and as such, it is "the end point" of imputation.[42]

34 Kelsen (Fn. 14), p. 51.

35 Stanley L. Paulson, "Hans Kelsen's Doctrine of Imputation", Ratio Juris 14 (2001), 1, p. 60.

36 Hans Kelsen, "Causality and Imputation", Ethics 60 (1950), 1, pp. 1–2. Consequently, whereas "[t]he principle of causality states: If there is A, there is (or will be) B. The principle of imputation states: If there is A, there ought to be B." (op. cit., p. 6)

37 Hans Kelsen, Reine Rechtslehre – Mit einem Anhang: Das Problem der Gerechtigkeit, (2. Aufl.), Wien 1960, p. 154, Fn. 1.

38 For a critical stance with respect to its application on general norms, see, e.g., Joachim Hruschka, Die Zurechnungslehre Kelsens im Vergleich mit der Zurechungslehre Kants, in: Hans Kelsen – Staatrechtslehrer und Rechtstheoretiker des 20. Jahrhunderts, hg. v. S. Paulson/M. Stolleis, Tübingen 2005, p. 6.

39 Kelsen (Fn. 14), p. 48.

40 op. cit., p. 49.

41 op. cit., p. 50.

42 Kelsen argues that there is one special feature of legal person's rights and obligations, insofar as "[t]hese human beings 'have' these obligations and rights not in the usual way – that is, individually – but collectively." More precisely, this "collective character of the right expresses itself, inter alia, in the fact that the exercise of the right proceeds not by way of every individual member, but by way of an organ designated by the subsystem." However, this peculiarity does not change the essential nature of the held right or obligation. op. cit., p. 50.

In the second edition of his *Reine Rechtslehre*, Kelsen further develops this explanation by emphasizing the significance of the concept of 'organ's function' (*Organfunktion*).[43] This is a "primary" and "fundamental concept", since it helps us in defining those acts that can be imputed to a legal person.[44] Namely, an individual is organ of a legal person (*Gemeinschaft*) insofar as he/she undertakes acts that are imputable to the legal person, and an act is imputable to the legal person when it is as such determined by the constituting legal order of that legal person.[45]

Finally, Kelsen argues that "two elements can be distinguished in the human behavior that is the content of the legal norm, and thus of the obligation and right." The first one is "a personal (subjective) element", while the second one is "a material (objective) element". That is, the complete legal norm determines both "the subject of the act or forbearance, and the act or forbearance itself – *who* does or forbears from doing, and *what* is done or forborne." In cases of legal norms that regulate rights and obligations of 'legal persons' it is common that the legal norm contains only the objective element, while leaving the norm of a legal subsystem (e.g. statute of corporation) to determine the missing subjective element.[46]

4 'Imputing' Rights to Collective Entities?

Let us now test this methodological apparatus of *Reine Rechtslehre* on several positive legal norms of international and domestic law, which resemble those from the beginning of the article, insofar as they seem to address, directly or indirectly, certain collective entities. For instance, Article 14(1) of the International Labor Organization's *Convention concerning Indigenous and Tribal Peoples in Independent Countries* states: "The rights of ownership and possession of the peoples concerned over the lands they traditionally occupy shall be recognized."[47] Article 13 of the Council of Europe's *Framework Convention for the Protection of National Minorities* goes as follows: "Within the framework of their education systems, the Parties shall recognize that persons belonging to a national minority have the right to set up and to manage

43 Kelsen essentially tries to put to an end very lively 19th century scholarly debate in Germany about the legal subjectivity of legal persons, by giving Savigny's "theory of fiction" a new life (Cf. Paulson (Fn. 8), p. 650) In this debate, which was largely influenced by Savigny's teaching, the dissenting voice was coming from Otto von Gierke. He argued that for legal theory the question of the nature of human groupings (Verbände) was not only the "prior", but also the "core" one. In addition, he held that the 19th century legal theory "cracked" on the issue to which "reality" entities, such as state, church, community, or association, belonged, since it claimed that these human groupings were mere "fictions" and artificial creations of legal order. Otto Gierke, Das Wesen der menschlichen Verbände, Rede bei Antritt des Rektorats gehalten in der Aula der Königlichen Friedrich-Wilhelms-Universität, 15. Oktober 1902, pp. 5, 6.

44 Renzikowski is of the opinion that the concepts such as Organschaft or Stellvertretung (representation) are "for Kelsen prime examples of the imputation." Joachim Renzikowski, Der Begriff der "Zurechnung" in der Reinen Rechtslehre Hans Kelsens, in: Neukantianismus und Rechtsphilosophie, hg. v. Robert Alexy et al., Baden-Baden 2002, p. 266.

45 Kelsen (Fn. 37), p. 155.

46 Kelsen (Fn. 14), pp. 49–50.

47 Convention concerning Indigenous and Tribal Peoples in Independent Countries (ILO No. 169), 72 ILO Official Bull. 59, entered into force 5 September 1991

their own private educational and training establishments."[48] The United Kingdom's *Motor-Cycle Crash Helmets (Religious Exemption) Act 1976* provides that a requirement of wearing motor-cycle helmets, imposed by regulations in section 32 of the *Road Traffic Act 1972*, "shall not apply to any follower of the Sikh religion while he is wearing a turban."[49] Article 19 of the *Special Statute for Region Trentino-Alto Adige/Südtirol* provides, *inter alia*: "The Italian, German and Ladin linguistic groups shall be represented in the Provincial Schools Council and the Provincial Disciplinary Council for Teachers. Teachers' representatives in the Provincial Schools Council shall be elected by the teaching personnel in proportion to the number of teachers in the respective linguistic groups."[50]

In the aforementioned examples, it seems that the *objective* element is rather clear. Namely, legal norms regulate respectively: the right of ownership and possession of traditionally occupied lands; the right to set up and manage private educational and training establishments; the right not to wear motor-cycle helmet, while driving with a turban; and, the right of proportional representation in the relevant school bodies. In Kelsen's terminology, all these rights would actually be 'points of imputation' for certain number of acts and forbearances.

What about the *subjective* element? From the exact wording of these legal norms, one can say that the *who*-element is defined in the following way: in the first case, the norm refers to "the peoples concerned", that is, tribal and indigenous peoples; in the second case, it refers to "persons belonging to a national minority"; in the third case, it refers to "any follower of the Sikh religion"; and, in the fourth case, it refers to the "teaching personnel" and "teaching representatives" of "the Italian, German and Ladin linguistic groups".

As for the first norm, it is supplemented with the provisions from Article 1(1) of the same document, which state several objective criteria for defining tribal and indigenous peoples.[51] However, the second paragraph of the same article says that "[s]elf-identification as indigenous or tribal shall be regarded as a fundamental criterion for determining the groups to which the provisions of this Convention apply." This approach led in practice to the proliferation of claims for the status of 'indigenousness', even though many of them might be reasonably challenged.[52] As for the second norm, the Council of Europe's *Framework Convention* does not con-

48 Council of Europe – ETS No. 157 – Framework Convention for the Protection of National Minorities, entered into force 1 February 1998.

49 Motor-Cycle Crash Helmets (Religious Exemption) Act 1976

50 Special Statute for Region Trentino-Alto Adige/Südtirol, English version available at, http://www.consiglio-bz.org/downloads/Statuto_E.pdf

51 Tribal peoples in independent countries are those "whose social, cultural and economic conditions distinguish them from other sections of the national community, and whose status is regulated wholly or partially by their own customs or traditions or by special laws or regulations." On the other hand, indigenous peoples are regarded as such "on account of their descent from the populations which inhabited the country, or a geographical region to which the country belongs, at the time of conquest or colonization or the establishment of present State boundaries and who, irrespective of their legal status, retain some or all of their own social, economic, cultural and political institutions."

52 See, e.g., Jeff J. Corntassel/Tomas Hopkins Primeau, "Indigenous 'Sovereignty' and International Law: Revised Strategies for Pursuing 'Self-Determination'", Human Rights Quarterly 17 (1995), 2, pp. 349 ff.

tain definition of 'national minority', nor does any international treaty instrument for that matter. The most cited definition of minority is provided in the report of the UN Special Rapporteur Francesco Capotorti,[53] but in practice, again, it is far from clear which groups qualify for this status. The separate difficulty concerns determining individual membership in a national minority group. The third norm might seem to be clear about the subjective element, when addressing "any follower of the Sikh religion", but it is questionable whether the traditional visible signs of this religion, such as a beard and a turban, would be in each concrete case sufficient for one person to qualify for the stated legal exemption. Finally, the fourth norm says that representatives in school bodies shall be selected from teaching personnel of the three enumerated linguistic groups, but it is unclear, for instance, whether a teacher whose mother-tongue happens to be other (say, French) than the one in which he instructs (say, Italian) can also qualify for the status of a representative of the respective linguistic group.

Note that in all the examples, there exists no legal norm of a subsystem that might serve as the 'point of imputation' for determining the concrete *who*-element.[54] At the same time, the above stated norms might at first glance seem precise enough in defining themselves the subjective element, but the fact is that whenever doubts are raised as to their applicability in a concrete case, the endpoint of reference would not be the norm itself but *the prior social recognition of the group membership*. As pointed by Kis, this is exactly what differentiates collective rights from the somewhat similar category of jointly exercised rights of associated individuals.[55] Namely, "their subjects do not come into being by way of association but are simply given ... for members and non-members alike, by the signs used and identified, by mutual recognition paid by members to each other, and by regard of outsiders." What is ad-

53 "A group, numerically inferior to the rest of the population of a State, in a non-dominant position, whose members – being nationals of the State – possess ethnic, religious or linguistic characteristics differing from those of the rest of the population and show, if only implicitly, a sense of solidarity, directed towards preserving their culture, traditions, religion or language." Francesco Capotorti, Study on the Rights of Persons Belonging to Ethnic, Religious and Linguistic Minorities, UN Doc. E/CN.4/Sub.2/384, at 96.

54 In that respect, one should apparently differentiate between numerous legal statuses, such as being a 'student', 'tax payer', 'worker' etc., which are authoritatively defined by legal norms, and collective entities of the aforementioned sort. In the former case, we speak of "a category of persons, understood to mean all those people who fit a particular description, such as being under twenty-one or having red hair", while in the latter case, we speak of "group proper, understood to mean a set of people who by their shared characteristics think of themselves as forming a distinct group." David Miller, "Group Rights, Human Rights and Citizenship", European Journal of Philosophy 10 (2002), 2, p. 178.

55 Hence, the way one right is exercised cannot be considered as the decisive criterion for defining it as a collective right. Just as there are individual rights which can be exercised only in group – such as the right to association, assembly or strike – so there are also collective rights that can be exercised only individually – such as the right of a member of a linguistic group to have her identity card written according to the linguistic rules of her own mother tongue. See, Miodrag A. Jovanović, "Recognizing Minority Identities Through Collective Rights", Human Rights Quarterly 27 (2005), 2, pp. 640–642; Cf. Allen Buchanan, Liberalism and Group Rights, in: In Harm's Way – Essays in Honour of Joel Feinberg, hg. v. Jules L. Coleman/Allen Buchanan, Cambridge 1994, pp. 1–15.

ditionally needed for these collective entities to become right-bearers is that state recognizes them as such.[56]

The aforementioned demonstrates that collective rights can obviously not be explicated with Kelsen's methodological apparatus. However, this is not the only problem with his concept of 'imputation'. Constructed in such a way, this methodological tool proved to be generally deficient in explicating the concept of legal subject. In the first edition of *Reine Rechtslehre*, this concept implies that only obligations-fulfilling and rights-exercising 'person' can be a point of 'central imputation', insofar as acting differently from the behavior required by a legal norm means committing a delict, and this is a material fact that triggers another material fact – coercive act of sanction – and these two can be linked together in the reconstructed legal norm only be means of 'peripheral imputation'. Unlike this latter concept, which is constitutive for a norm-oriented theory of law, such as Kelsen's one, 'central imputation', in Heidemann's opinion, can be considered as meaningful only in the process of norm-implementation, where a relevant authority perform 'central imputation' when deciding that the taken act is as such determined by a particular complex of norms.[57]

In the second edition of the *Reine Rechtslehre*, problems are getting even bigger, inasmuch as Kelsen now argues that, "in a broader sense", legal system or sub-system give also individuals "authorization" (*Ermächtigung*) to commit delicts. Namely, in trying to explain the fact that legal persons are commonly held liable for wrongdoings taken by their organs,[58] Kelsen comes to the conclusion that legal capacity to fulfill obligations cannot be separated from the corresponding capacity to commit delict. Since only an individual, whose acts are as 'organ's functions' determined by the legal sub-system of a legal person, can perform acts that are 'imputable' to that legal person, Kelsen argues that just as he is manifestly authorized to exercise rights and fulfill obligations, it could also be said that he is "indirectly" authorized not to fulfill obligations. Consequently, just as lawful acts of the organ are imputed to the legal person, so would also his unlawful acts.[59]

By emphasizing that this 'imputation' of delict to legal person is "only possible, not necessary",[60] Kelsen does not succeed in avoiding the further confusion surrounding the concepts of *Zurechnung* and *Zuschreibung*.[61] It turns out, in Heide-

56 Janos Kis, "Beyond the Nation State", Social Research 63 (1996), 1, p. 221; This actually implies that even in the case of the aforementioned norm that provides for the self-identification of indigenous and tribal peoples, which might serve as the normative "point of imputation" for the subjective element, it is rather the prior social recognition of the entire community of indigenous peoples that would decisively determine whether one group qualifies for that status.

57 Heidemann (Fn. 33), pp. 22–23.

58 In the first edition, he only hints this line of reasoning by saying that liability "emerges as a particular type of obligation." Kelsen (Fn. 14), p. 43.

59 Kelsen (Fn. 37), p. 186.

60 op. cit., p. 186.

61 Heidemann points to other problems as well. When speaking about the concept of 'representation' (Stellvertretung), Kelsen implies that acts of one individual would be 'imputed' to another individual, which is, in Heidemann's opinion, hardly "compatible" with his emphasis on the relationship between 'imputation' and the concept of 'person'. As for the legal person of state, as the "endpoint" of all 'imputation', Heidemann argues that this reasoning leads to "an absurd outcome, that ultimately every legally relevant act must be imputed to state." Heidemann

mann's opinion, that 'imputation' is a mere expression for the allocation of certain acts to certain persons, without clear *criteria* according to which this allocation is taken. Hence, this author concludes that a plausible explanation of concepts, such as subjective right and legal subject, are not possible within the Pure Theory of Law, understood as "a formal theory of necessary preconditions of legal knowledge".[62] Since the initial impetus for avoiding *anthropomorphism* stems from Kelsen's rigorous methodological dualism and his intention to purify jurisprudence from all non-normative methods, I assume that it was demonstrated that an inquiry into the topic of the mentioned *criteria* for defining legal subjectivity and subjective rights could be undertaken only with the helping hand of other methods as well.

As already indicated elsewhere,[63] this firstly implies a prior *axiological* investigation, because legal research has to deal with the preceding issue of justification of collective rights.[64] This step amounts to a philosophical elucidation of the so-called 'value-of-groups question', which pertains to "the value of the existence of certain groups and the importance of protecting these groups against forces which might weaken or destroy them, perhaps even to the extent of outweighing certain rights of individuals (either within the group or outside it)."[65] In the next step, legal theory has to address the issue of what it takes a collective entity to be legally conceptualized as a separate type of right-holders, different from physical and juristic persons. That inquiry implies abandoning the so-called "legal omnipotence" argument, according to which legal authorities have power to vest rights in whatever entities they like, which, thus, makes also possible to speak of collective rights whenever happen to be that certain collective entities are in legal documents singled out as right-bearers. Instead, this demanding task of legal theory has to be accomplished with the strong methodological support of sociology, and even cultural anthropology. Only using the methods from these disciplines, legal scholars can address the problems of group membership, which can be fluid and uncertain; of defining the boundaries of collective right-holders in a non-arbitrary and non-coercive way; of manipulation or coercive imposition of collective identities, etc.[66] Without solving these problems, legal theory wouldn't be able to provide a basic explication of the concept that is employed in various valid international and domestic legal instruments.

(Fn. 33), pp. 31, 32; At the same time, Renzikowski notes that Kelsen is not consequential in using the concept Zuschreibung in the second edition of the Reine Rechtslehre. Renzikowski (Fn. 44), p. 255.

62 Heidemann (Fn. 33), p. 32.

63 Jovanović (Fn. 55), pp. 630–637.

64 Galenkamp rightly argues that "the question of the justification of collective rights is not an empirical, but a normative one. It does not concern the question whether these rights 'exist'", but rather "whether they should exist." Marlies Galenkamp, "Collective Rights: Much Ado About Nothing?", Netherlands Quarterly for Human Rights 9 (1991), 3, p. 293.

65 Michael Hartney, "Some Confusions Concerning Collective Rights", Canadian Journal of Law and Jurisprudence 4 (1991), 2, p. 294.

66 This will be the topic of a separate paper to be presented at the conference 'Interdisziplinarität in den Rechtswissenschaft', Zentrum für Interdisziplinäre Forschung, Bielefeld, 15.–17. April 2009.

5 A Concluding Note

As pointed out at the beginning of this paper, any pleading for an interdisciplinary approach to the subject matter of collective rights cannot leave the entire jurisprudence unaffected by this methodological proposal. If methodological influxes from other disciplines are indeed indispensable for legal theoretical grounding of such fundamental concepts as legal subject and subjective right, then, I believe, this is a conclusive indication that jurisprudence in general must, at least, reject the hypostazation of the priority of the normative method. Yet, to say anything further on this topic, apart from this modest concluding remark, would be to go far beyond the intended scope of this paper.

Literature

Bix, Brian (2000): 'On the Dividing Line Between Natural Law Theory and Legal Positivism' (2000) 75 Notre Dame Law Review 5, pp. 1613–1624.

Buchanan, Allen (1994): 'Liberalism and Group Rights', in Jules L. Coleman and Allen Buchanan (eds.), In Harm's Way – Essays in Honour of Joel Feinberg, Cambridge, pp. 1–15.

Capotorti, Francesco: Study on the Rights of Persons Belonging to Ethnic, Religious and Linguistic Minorities, UN Doc. E/CN.4/Sub.2/384

Corntassel, Jeff J. and *Tomas Hopkins Primeau*, 'Indigenous "Sovereignty" and International Law: Revised Strategies for Pursuing "Self-Determination"' (1995) 17 Human Rights Quarterly 2, pp. 343–365.

Dickson, Julie, 'Methodology in Jurisprudence: A Critical Survey' (2004) 10 Legal Theory 3, pp. 117–156.

Dworkin, Ronald (1986): Law's Empire, Cambridge, Mass.

Englard, Izhak (1987): 'Law and Religion in Israel' 35 The American Journal of Comparative Law 1, pp. 185–208.

Finnis, John (1980): Natural Law and Natural Rights (Oxford).

Finnis, John (1990): 'Natural Law and Legal Reasoning', 38 Cleveland State Law Review 1, pp. 1–14.

Finnis, John (2007): 'On Hart's Ways: Law As Reason and As Fact' 52 The American Journal of Jurisprudence 1, pp. 25–53.

Fuller, Lon L. (1964): The Morality of Law (New Haven and London).

Fuller, Lon L. (1966): The Law in Quest of Itself (Boston).

Fuller, Lon L. (1969): Anatomy of the Law (New York)

Galenkamp, Marlies (1991): 'Collective Rights: Much Ado About Nothing?' 9 Netherlands Quarterly for Human Rights 3, pp. 291–307.

Gierke, Otto, Das Wesen der menschlichen Verbände, Rede bei Antritt des Rektorats gehalten in der Aula der Königlichen Friedrich-Wilhelms-Universität, 15. Oktober 1902.

Green, Leslie, 'Legal Positivism', in Edward N. Zalta (ed.), The Stanford Encyclopedia of Philosophy (Spring 2007 Edition), at
http://plato.stanford.edu/archives/spr2007/entries/legal-positivism/

Hart, Herbert, 'Kelsen Visited' (1963) 10 UCLA Law Review 4, pp. 709–728.

Hart, Herbert (1994): The Concept of Law (2. ed.) (With a Postscript edited by Penelope A. Bulloch and Joseph Raz), Oxford.

Hartney, Michael (1991): 'Some Confusions Concerning Collective Rights' 4 Canadian Journal of Law and Jurisprudence 2, pp. 292–314.

Heidemann, Carsten (1997): Die Norm als Tatsache – Zur Normentheorie Hans Kelsens (Baden-Baden).

Heidemann, Carsten, 'Der Begriff der Zurechnung bei Hans Kelsen', in Stanley L. Paulson and Michael Stolleis (eds.), Hans Kelsen – Staatrechtslehrer und Rechtstheoretiker des 20. Jahrhunderts (Tübingen, 2005), pp. 17–34.

Hruschka, Joachim, 'Die Zurechnungslehre Kelsens im Vergleich mit der Zurechungslehre Kants', in Paulson and Stolleis (eds.) Hans Kelsen – Staatrechtslehrer und Rechtstheoretiker des 20. Jahrhunderts, pp. 2–16.
Jovanović, Miodrag A. (2005): 'Recognizing Minority Identities Through Collective Rights' 27 Human Rights Quarterly 2, pp. 625–651.
Kelsen, Hans (1911): Grenzen zwischen juristischer und soziologischer Methode (Tübingen).
Kelsen, Hans (1911): Hauptprobleme der Staatsrechtslehre (Tübingen).
Kelsen, Hans (1941): 'The Pure Theory of Law and Analytical Jurisprudence' 55 Harvard Law Review 1, pp. 44–70.
Kelsen, Hans (1943): 'Collective and Individual Responsibility in International Law with Particular Regard to the Punishment of War Criminals' 31 California Law Review 5, pp. 530–571.
Kelsen, Hans (1949): General Theory of Law and State (Cambridge, Mass.).
Kelsen, Hans (1950): 'Causality and Imputation' 60 Ethics 1, pp. 1–11.
Kelsen, Hans, Reine Rechtslehre – Mit einem Anhang: Das Problem der Gerechtigkeit (2. ed.) Wien.
Kelsen, Hans, 'Politics, Ethics, Religion and Law', in Gerhard A. Ritter and Gilbert Ziebura (eds.), Faktoren der politischen Entscheidung – Festgabe für Ernst Fraenkel zum 65. Geburtstag (Berlin, 1963), pp. 3–10.
Kelsen, Hans, 'Naturrechtslehre und Rechtspositivismus', in Friedrich Koja (ed.), Hans Kelsen oder Die Reinheit der Rechtslehre (Wien, 1988), pp. 231–247.
Kelsen, Hans (1992): Introduction to the Problems of Legal Theory (translation of the first edition of the Reine Rechtslehre, by B.L. Paulson and S.L. Paulson) (Oxford)
Kis, Janos (1996): 'Beyond the Nation State' 63 Social Research 1, pp. 191–245.
Marmor, Andrei, 'The Nature of Law', in Edward N. Zalta (ed.), The Stanford Encyclopedia of Philosophy (Spring 2007 Edition), at http://plato.stanford.edu/archives/spr2007/entries/lawphil-nature/
Miller, David (2002): 'Group Rights, Human Rights and Citizenship' 10 European Journal of Philosophy 2, pp. 178–195.
Noakes, Jeremy and Pridham, Geoffrey (1974): Documents on Nazism 1919–1945, New York.
Paulson, Stanley L. (1998): 'Four Phases in Hans Kelsen's Legal Theory? Reflections on Periodization' 18 Oxford Journal of Legal Studies 1, pp. 153–166.
Paulson, Stanley L. (1999): 'Konstruktivismus, Methodendualismus und Zurechnung im Frühwerk Hans Kelsens' 124 Archiv des öffentliches Rechts, pp. 631–657.
Paulson, Stanley L. (2001): 'Hans Kelsen's Doctrine of Imputation' 14 Ratio Juris 1, pp. 47–63.
Renzikowski, Joachim, 'Der Begriff der "Zurechnung" in der Reinen Rechtslehre Hans Kelsens', in Robert Alexy et al. (eds.), Neukantianismus und Rechtsphilosophie (Baden-Baden, 2002), pp. 253–282.
Sieghart, Paul (1983): The International Law of Human Rights, Oxford.

Klaus Mathis

Efficiency as a Normative Principle

Abstract:
Die Ökonomische Analyse des Rechts stellt den interessanten Versuch dar, die Konzepte und Denkweisen der modernen Wirtschaftstheorie auf rechtliche Probleme anzuwenden. Es ist dabei zu beachten, dass die positive ökonomische Analyse von der normativen Forderung, wonach das Rechtssystem gemäß dem Effizienzprinzip ausgestaltet werden soll, klar zu unterscheiden ist. Diese Forderung bedarf nämlich einer Begründung, welche die ökonomische Theorie selber nicht zu liefern vermag. Doch selbst wenn man Effizienz als ein zentrales Prinzip anerkennt, stellt sich die Frage, wie es sich zu anderen Zielen verhält und wie es in der Rechtsetzung und Rechtsanwendung umgesetzt werden kann.

Dieser Aufsatz beginnt mit der Darstellung und Diskussion von Richard A. Posners Versuch, das Effizienzziel im Recht zu legitimieren (2). Im Anschluss daran wird das Verhältnis von Effizienz und Verteilungsgerechtigkeit ganz allgemein beleuchtet (3), um dann im Speziellen auf den Vorschlag, insbesondere das Privatrecht habe sich ausschließlich am Effizienzziel zu orientieren, näher einzugehen (4). Der letzte Abschnitt widmet sich der umstrittenen Frage, wie ökonomische Analysemethoden in kontinentaleuropäischen Rechtssystemen mit kodifiziertem Recht als hilfreiches und ergänzendes Instrument Anwendung finden können (5).

1 Introduction

Economic analysis of law is an interesting attempt to apply the concepts and reasoning methods of economic theory to legal problems. One important consideration is that the positive economic analysis must clearly be separated from the normative claim which holds that a legal system ought to be defined in conformity with the efficiency principle. This claim requires a justification which economic theory in itself cannot provide. And even if it is accepted that efficiency should be a guiding principle, there is still the question of how it relates to other goals and how it can be implemented in legislation and in adjudication.

This essay starts by introducing and discussing Richard A. Posner's attempt to legitimize the efficiency goal in law (2). It goes on to offer a very general explanation of the relationship between efficiency and distributive justice (3), including a more detailed analysis of the proposition that – particularly in private law – efficiency should be pursued as the sole and exclusive goal (4). The final part is dedicated to the challenging question of how economic analysis methods might be incorporated as a helpful, supplementary instrument in continental European codified law systems (5).[1]

1 For a fuller discussion of these questions see Klaus Mathis, Efficiency Instead of Justice? Searching for the Philosophical Foundations of the Economic Analysis of Law, New York 2009; German edition: Effizienz statt Gerechtigkeit? Auf der Suche nach den philosophischen Grundlagen der Ökonomischen Analyse des Rechts, 3rd edn., Berlin 2009.

2 The Concept of Wealth Maximization

In his essay "Utilitarianism, Economics, and Legal Theory" (1979) Posner outlines his concept of *wealth maximization* as an ethical principle. He thereby intends to disassociate himself from concepts of utilitarianism:

> "The important question is whether utilitarianism and economics are really the same thing. I believe they are not and, further, that the economic norm I shall call 'wealth maximization' provides a firmer basis for a normative theory of law than does utilitarianism."[2]

Wealth maximization means that a transaction, or some other change in the use or the ownership of resources, is advantageous if it increases social wealth. In relation to the law, Posner suggests that where transaction costs are prohibitive, i.e. where a voluntary bargaining solution cannot be reached because the costs associated with the exchange of services are too high, the market – the outcome of voluntary transactions – should be simulated *by means of state compulsion*:

> "This approach attempts to reconstruct the likely terms of a market transaction in circumstances where instead a forced exchange took place – to mimic or simulate the market, in other words."[3]

The idea is curiously simple yet, at the same time, paradoxical: making use of state compulsion, the model of voluntary transactions in competitive markets should be imposed, by analogy, on legal decisions. Should private arrangements fail to ensure efficiency because transaction costs are prohibitively high, the state will dispense justice in line with the goal of efficiency and *mimic the market.*

The "wealth" of a society, according to Posner, is the sum of all tangible and intangible goods, which are valued in monetary terms as follows: either according to willingness to pay, i.e. the maximum price that a potential buyer is willing to pay for a good, or – in the event that someone already owns the good – according to the minimum price which would have to be offered to induce the potential seller to sell:[4]

> "Wealth is the value in dollars or dollar equivalents [...] of everything in society. It is measured by what people are willing to pay for something, or if they already own it, what they demand in money to give it up. The only kind of preference that counts in a system of wealth maximization is thus one that is backed up by money – in other words, that is registered in a market."[5]

Utilitarianism has to value all kinds of antisocial behavior, because even feelings such as envy or sadism are a common source of pleasure (the problem of the "utility monster"). In contrast, wealth maximization is based on the mutual benefit of exchange transactions. The individual – however egoistic he may be – cannot increase his own advantage without benefiting others in the process. Even incredibly egoistic individuals cannot avoid generating more wealth for society than they obtain themselves, Posner claims, that because productive work produces a consumer surplus for others, whereas idleness does not.[6] Contrary to utilitarianism, which focuses on consumption, wealth maximization stresses people's productive abilities. That focus

2 Posner 1979, p. 103.
3 Posner 1998, p. 16.
4 Cf. Posner 1987, p. 15.
5 Posner 1979, p. 119.
6 Posner 1979, p. 132.

derives from Posner's claim that desires only count provided that there is a *willingness to pay*. Indeed, wealth maximization means generating a maximum of consumer and producer surplus (see figure 1).

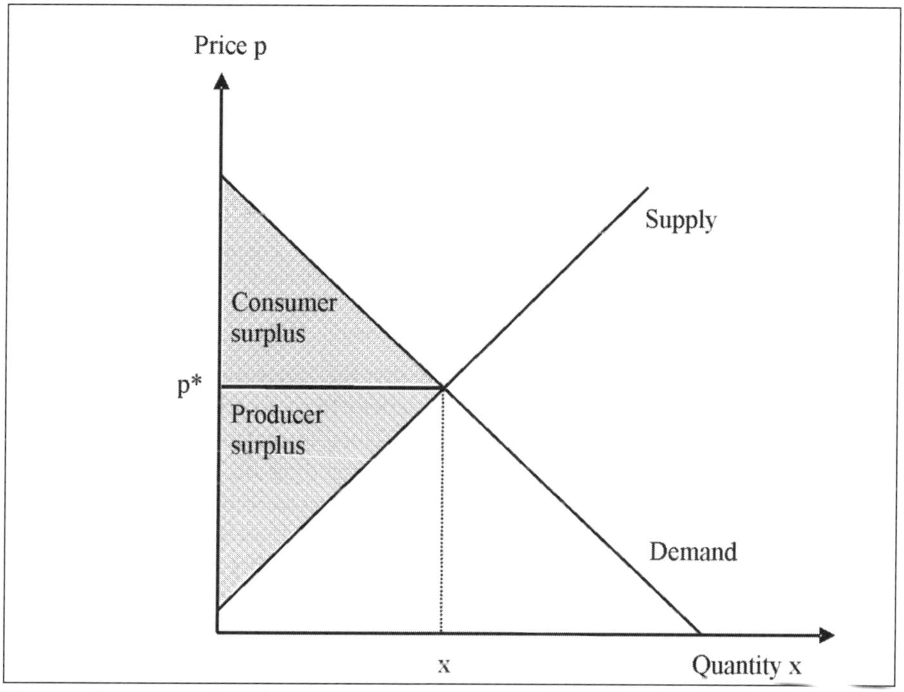

Figure 1: Consumer and producer surplus

The idea of wealth maximization is closely associated with the Kaldor-Hicks efficiency criterion according to which *a change is an improvement if the gainers value their gains more highly than the losers their losses.*[7] *Thus, the Kaldor-Hicks test does not require any actual but merely a hypothetical* payment of compensation. The winners must only be capable of compensating the losers; actual compensation is not necessary. Note that this is in contrast to Pareto efficiency, where only a change which puts at least one member of society in a better position without making somebody else worse off is a Pareto improvement.

At the beginning of the 1980s Posner tries to bolster his ethic of wealth maximization by justifying it in the light of the *consensus theory*. In introducing the concept of ex ante compensation he constructs a hypothetical consensus that supplements the Kaldor-Hicks criterion.[8] Its advantage over the Pareto criterion is that its application is not limited to cases which make nobody worse off. The Pareto criterion can claim not only to be compatible with utilitarianism – because a Pareto-superior change always increases social utility – but also to respect the autonomy of individuals (a "Kantian" or "libertarian" requirement, according to Posner) since it relies

7 Baumol 1972, p. 402.
8 Posner 1981, pp. 92ff.

on their voluntary consent.[9] In contrast, to satisfy the Kaldor-Hicks criterion, a measure need not necessarily increase social utility nor respect the autonomy of the individual because the consent of the losers is not required. Posner subsequently forms a view of wealth maximization as a theory which is compatible with both utilitarianism and with Kantian positions:

> "Wealth maximization as an ethical norm gives weight both to utility, though less heavily than utilitarianism does, and to consent, though perhaps less heavily than Kant himself would have done."[10]

However, the coercive character of the Kaldor-Hicks rule could pose a problem. Yet Posner believes that principle to be consensual once ex ante compensation is taken into account, and so finds his concept entirely compatible with these theories:[11]

> "I want to defend the Kaldor-Hicks or wealth-maximization approach, not by reference to Pareto superiority as such or its utilitarian premise, but by reference to the idea of consent that [...] provides an alternative basis to utilitarianism for the Pareto criterion. The notion of consent used here is what economists call ex ante compensation."[12]

Ex ante compensation works on the principle that the "price is paid" for the consent of the potential losers, so that they too can benefit from an advantage that accrues to all under the wealth maximization system. Thus, on balance they too, end up better off *ex ante* (but not necessarily *ex post*, depending on the specific circumstances). Posner explains the principle with reference to various examples. Firstly he compares consent to wealth maximization with the purchase of a lottery ticket. Anyone who buys a ticket implicitly agrees to the eventuality of a loss. Posner understands ex ante compensation in the following terms: if, for example, an entrepreneur loses money due to tough competition, he has been compensated for it ex ante, because the expected value of the entrepreneur's income must have contained a premium for risk to cover the risk of losses resulting from competition. Another example: assuming that property prices in a district fell because a large firm moved away. The owners of neighboring properties – who had to anticipate this relocation – had received compensation ex ante in the form of a lower purchase price for their properties; the probability of the firm's move away was already accounted for in this reduced price.[13]

Posner's favorite example of ex ante compensation, however, is liability for road accidents. Here he works on the assumption that negligence is more efficient than strict liability, i.e. the total of insurance premiums paid by potential injurers and victims would be lower under a negligence system than a strict liability system. Posner concludes that a negligence system is advantageous for all, because all would benefit from an overall reduction in insurance premiums. The benefit of lower premiums would be ex ante compensation which would, on average, outweigh any disadvantages of basing liability on negligence. This does not imply that a negligence system would make everyone better off *ex post* in any given case; but that issue

9 Posner 1980, pp. 489 f.
10 Posner 1981, p. 98.
11 Posner 1987, p. 21.
12 Posner 1980, pp. 491 f.
13 Posner 1981, p. 94.

is irrelevant under the concept of ex ante compensation.[14] Finally, Posner is not completely rigid on the matter of consent. Unanimity is not an absolute requirement:

> "[O]nly a fanatic would insist that unanimity be required to legitimize a social institution such as the negligence system."[15]

By the mid-1980s he began to relativize his positions, henceforth paving the way for a transition towards what he calls *pragmatism*, a position which he has advocated since the 1990s. He sees efficiency as an important legal principle, but not necessarily the only one. Nonetheless he still stresses the importance of the empirical relation between free markets and human welfare. In this sense efficiency is a means to maximize human welfare.[16] Unfortunately, all of these attempts to legitimize the efficiency goal are unpersuasive:

1 – The attempt to conceive wealth maximization as an alternative to utilitarianism in the sense that it preserves the good utilitarian elements and eliminates its worse characteristics, must be considered as a failure. In fact, Posner has achieved quite the opposite of what he intended to do: *wealth maximization eliminates the good characteristics of utilitarianism and preserves its weaknesses.* Although wealth maximization restrains the "utility monster" by imposing the constraint of willingness to pay, this in turn does not solve the problem of inalienable rights. In the end, the "utility monster" is just replaced by the "wealth monster". Wealth maximization is thus a blighted version of classical utilitarianism, and not the fundamentally new ethical concept which Posner originally took it for.

2 – The consensus theoretical underpinning of wealth maximization is even less persuasive. *The Kaldor-Hicks criterion is not consensual, because there are always losers, and they will not consent.* Not all members of a society can count on benefiting from a system of wealth maximization in the long run. By relativizing the consensus principle – not requiring everyone's but most people's consent – Posner parts company with consensus theory. By definition, consensus means unanimity: anything less is not a consensus at all.

3 – With regard to his pragmatic argumentation, Posner is to a certain extent less open to attack. Although his overall position is of little persuasive force, *his suggestion to strive for the efficiency goal instrumentally, as a means of pursuing other social goals, seems to be highly plausible.* With more resources, more goals can be achieved. It is a truism that a larger cake can be cut into larger slices. But that is far from guaranteeing that distribution will be just by whatever definition one chooses.

Utilitarianism can be commended for its orientation to human needs and its equal treatment of every person, rich or poor. Under a system of wealth maximization, this is different: the utility of the rich is privileged. Moreover, the same objection must be raised to wealth maximization as to utilitarianism: *the individual as such is not taken seriously*, a flaw which is brought into particular focus by the question of *basic rights* and the problem of *distributive justice.*

14 Posner 1981, p. 95.
15 Posner 1981, p. 97.
16 Posner 1990, pp. 382 ff. See also his later writings, esp. Posner 2003.

3 Distributive Justice and Efficiency

Economists generally describe the relationship between justice and efficiency as a trade-off. For instance, in Arthur M. Okun's book "Equality and Efficiency: The Big Tradeoff" (1975), the antagonism between efficiency and distributive justice is characterized as the greatest socio-economic goal conflict of all:

> "[The] tradeoff [...] between equality and efficiency [...] is, in my view, our biggest socioeconomic tradeoff, and it plagues us in dozens of dimensions of social policy. We can't have our cake of market efficiency and share it equally."[17]

The goal conflict arises, he says, because redistribution is often bound up with efficiency losses. To illustrate this problem, Okun uses the image of the "leaky bucket": a bucket is used to scoop water from a full container and pour it into another container which is empty. But because this bucket leaks, some water is lost on the way from one container to the other.[18] Okun goes on to list various factors which cause such leakage losses:

1 – Redistribution entails *administrative costs*. The state must employ officials to collect taxes and hand out the money to claimants. Private individuals also face administrative costs, from form-filling to lawyers' fees in the event of legal disputes. These aspects absorb resources which could otherwise be deployed productively.[19]

2 – Redistribution can have a negative effect on *work incentives*, both for taxpayers and for recipients.[20] For recipients of social transfers, there is little incentive to work if earnings from employment are penalized by deducting the full amount from the social transfer. In any case, higher income taxes lower the effective rate of post-tax pay for all working people. This presumably reduces the incentive to work. However, the opposite effect can also occur: households may increase their working hours to make up for higher taxes, in order to maintain their household income at a constant level (tax recovery). This second effect occurs primarily among high earners and in families in which both parents are not working full-time.

3 – It is also possible for redistribution to have a negative effect on *saving and investment*.[21] Since poorer people normally have a higher rate of consumption than the wealthy, the fear is that less will be saved or invested, which holds back growth in the national economy. The counter-argument is that as consumer expenditure rises, the self-financing of business firms improves thanks to higher profits. The reserves built up by firms can thus compensate for the decline in savings by households.

4 – Okun also fears that people's *values* could be negatively affected by redistribution, and anti-productive tendencies could detract from their attitude to work. Furthermore the population's sense of self-reliance could be weakened.[22] The counter-argument is that major income disparities in a society can foster far more de-

17 Okun 1975, p. 2. Okun uses the term "equality" which is geared towards distributive justice. Other authors more commonly use the term "equity", and less frequently "fairness" or "justice".
18 Okun 1975, pp. 91 ff.
19 Okun 1975, p. 96.
20 Okun 1975, pp. 96 ff.
21 Okun 1975, p. 98.
22 Okun 1975, p. 100.

structive tendencies. Both poverty and extreme wealth may lead to decadence and decay. Moreover, large income disparities weaken a society's cohesion.

The trade-off between justice and efficiency is often represented by means of a *transformation curve* (see figure 2).[23] This transformation curve represents all the possible combinations of justice and efficiency. The negative slope means that more justice is associated with less efficiency, and vice versa. The concave line of the curve expresses that with growing concentration on one of the two goals, sacrifices increasingly have to be made in respect of the other goal.

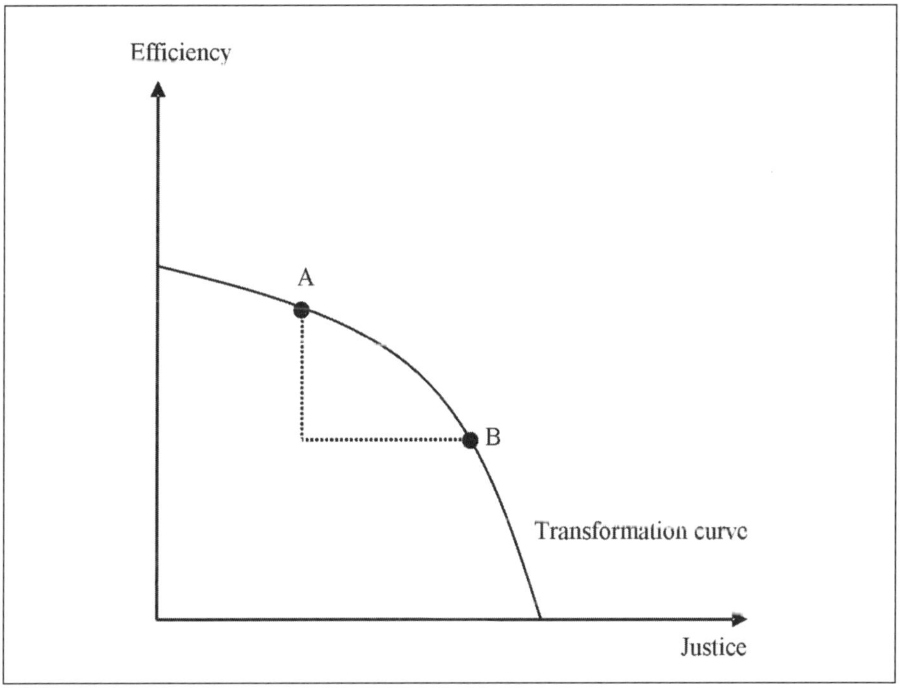

Figure 2: Trade-off between justice and efficiency

In order to establish the limits of redistribution according to this concept, there are two aspects to consider:[24]

1 – On the one hand, there is an empirical question to clarify: what *actual trade-off* can be observed in a society between just income distribution and the efficiency of the economy (cf. the line of the transformation curve).

2 – On the other hand, it is necessary to resolve the problem of *value competition* between efficiency and distributive justice. That is, society has to decide what mixture of justice and efficiency it wants (i.e. the choice of the optimal point on the curve).

Okun leaves the empirical question of what line the transformation curve takes in individual countries open; it has not been answered conclusively to this day. It is

23 See e.g. Stiglitz 1989, p. 60.
24 Hagel 1993, p. 266.

undeniable that redistribution entails administrative costs. Meanwhile the other arguments raised by Okun are very speculative, and the relevant research findings are contradictory, so they do not yield substantiated results.[25]

In a democracy, the second question is answered in the course of the democratic process. The taxation system, the social security system, the education sector and the public services all play a central role in redistribution. One particular approach to equalizing income distribution is to manipulate the initial endowment with resources, i.e. to equalize people's starting opportunities. An individual's initial endowment is heavily dependent on the parents' incomes and assets. Here corrective interventions could be made by means of *inheritance taxes*. On the other hand, starting opportunities can also be equalized by means of an *education system* which is accessible to all, either free of charge or at least on an affordable basis.[26]

It must also be borne in mind that the relation between efficiency and distributive justice need not always be a trade-off; on the contrary, in many areas there is a positive correlation:

1 – An education system geared towards equalizing starting opportunities increases the number of highly skilled workers, and these can make a major contribution to value creation.

2 – Socio-politically motivated integration programs for the unemployed foster their reintegration into the labor market.

3 – Socio-political measures are fundamentally integrative in their effects and are thus a means of counteracting crime. This not only gives the population more security, but also reduces the costs of prosecution and law enforcement.

4 – Societies with less *inequality of income distribution generally have* greater social and political stability. This makes such countries more attractive to investors.

These considerations show that the trade-off concept only highlights one aspect and is thus one-dimensional. There is no monocausal connection between efficiency and distributive justice. In point of fact, there are multiple interdependencies between the two goals, and while they conflict in some respects, in many other ways they actually stand in a harmonious or at least a neutral relationship to one another.[27]

4 Efficiency as an Exclusive Goal?

Several authors argue in favor of the efficiency goal as the exclusive guiding principle, at least in private law. Thus, for example, Posner proposed that *the civil courts should be committed to the efficiency principle, whilst the public sector could concern itself with distributive justice.*[28] So a modern legal system would have to be subdivided into two sections: the first, which would regulate the private exchange of goods and services, should be guided by the efficiency goal. The second, dealing with tax and social law,

25 See e.g. Alesina/Rodrik 1994, pp. 465 ff.; Persson/Tabellini 1994, pp. 600 ff.

26 From this perspective, both the raising of university tuition fees and the abolition of inheritance taxes are to be decisively rejected.

27 Cf. Lukes 1996, p. 37.

28 Posner 1990, p. 388.

should counterbalance this by pursuing the goal of distributive justice.[29] In simplified terms: private law would have to prioritize the efficiency criterion, and public law would have to prioritize the principle of justice. Kaplow and Shavell share Posner's view:

> "[R]edistribution through legal rules offers no advantage over redistribution through the income tax system and typically is less efficient."[30]

In their book "Fairness versus Welfare" (2002) Kaplow and Shavell even assert that giving independent consideration to principles of justice (especially corrective justice) in assessing legal rules – specifically within liability and contract law[31] – reduces welfare, and in certain instances actually makes everyone worse off:

> "Under welfare economics [...] the analyst would not take into account factors that do not bear on individuals' well-being, notably, whether liability under the negligence rule is required by corrective justice or other notions of fairness that some would accord independent significance."[32]

They go on to try and prove this point using various constructed examples, and with apparent success. But there is a problem with this approach: in the context of their utilitarian analytical framework[33] the statement that taking account of non-utilitarian principles of justice reduces welfare compared with a policy based solely on social welfare is bound to be right. However, it would still be necessary to justify why a utilitarian ethic should be preferred over a deontological ethic. That would require adopting a meta-ethical position. The idea that, from a (preference-) utilitarian perspective of utilitarianism, deontological or mixed conceptions must be superior should come as no surprise. It is an utter *tautology* as Kaplow and Shavell frankly admit:

> "[I]t is true that it is virtually a tautology to assert that fairness-based evaluation entails some sort of reduction in individuals' well-being, for notions of fairness are principles of evaluation that give weight to factors unrelated to individuals' well-being."[34]

The two authors emphasize that they are only averse to the independent consideration of principles of justice; whereas if they were integrated into the utility function of individuals as matters of preference ("tastes for fairness") and thus made a contribution to the welfare of society, it would be unproblematic:

> "We further note a particular source of well-being [...], namely, the possibility that individuals have a taste for notions of fairness, just as they may have a taste for art, nature, or fine wine."[35]

This would overcome the conflict between a utilitarian conception and principles of justice. Nevertheless, as a solution to the problem, it is dubious: it is dangerous to leave principles of justice to the taste, and hence the discretionary whim, of indi-

29 Schäfer/Ott 2000, p. 31.
30 Kaplow/Shavell 1994, p. 667.
31 See Kaplow/Shavell 2002, pp. 85 ff. and 155 ff.
32 Kaplow/Shavell 2002, p. 17.
33 They themselves talk about "welfare economics" and the consideration of "well-being", explicitly distancing their utilitarian viewpoint from wealth maximization. Kaplow/Shavell (2002), pp. 5 and 35 ff. Even so, they continue to treat wealth as a proxy variable for social welfare. Kaplow/Shavell 2002, p. 37.
34 Kaplow/Shavell 2002, p. 58; a similar statement is found on page 7.
35 Kaplow/Shavell 2002, p. 21.

viduals' for it is uncertain whether they are sufficiently weighted in a utilitarian calculus to warrant any observance. *Principles of justice are in danger of sinking in the morass of the social "good" unless they are accorded some weight in their own right, as a corrective.*

Although the concept put forward by Kaplow and Shavell fails to convince, their analysis does bring to light one or two useful insights. They conclude, for example, that any welfare loss that could arise as a consequence of taking principles of justice into account should be made transparent:

> "[B]ecause notions of fairness sometimes result in a reduction of individuals' well-being – and in certain cases lead to a reduction in everyone's well-being – when they are given weight as independent evaluative principles, the manner in which a notion of fairness sacrifices welfare should be identified clearly so that it will be possible to appreciate what is at stake in adopting the principle."[36]

This demand certainly merits approval: what it calls for is a legislative impact assessment regime (ex ante or prospective analysis) that determines what effects future laws will have,[37] as well as an evaluation of the effects of existing laws (ex post or retrospective analysis). However, Kaplow and Shavell provide no criteria for weighing up fairness and welfare – and their concept has no need of them, because fairness comes into the equation, at best, as a subjective preference in the utility function. Yet it remains equally unclear how these individual utility functions should be aggregated into a societal utility function. Nor do they resolve the known methodological problems of utilitarianism regarding the intrapersonal and interpersonal comparison of utility.[38]

Polinsky considers redistribution measures in contract law – e.g. via stricter seller's liability – to be ineffective, because the expected costs of liability would be shifted onto the consumer via the product price.[39] Conversely, according to Polinsky, redistribution via non-contractual liability law would be a fundamental possibility, since involuntary transactions do not normally offer cost-shifting opportunities.[40] In spite of this, he too prefers redistribution via the tax and transfer system, because it is not only cheaper but can also be effected with much greater precision:

> "[R]edistribution through the government's tax and transfer system may be cheaper and is likely to be more precise. In other words, the potential conflict between efficiency and equity when income redistribution is costly should be considered in the design of the government's tax and transfer system, but not generally in the choice of legal rules."[41]

For Coleman, on the other hand, it is the concept of *corrective justice* that best explains the relationship between the violator and the injured party.[42] But instead of taking its orientation from corrective justice, which is predicated on the bilateral

36 Kaplow/Shavell 2002, p. 471.
37 See for example the relevant arguments on Regulatory Impact Analysis in Switzerland in section 5 below.
38 On the whole subject, see also Coleman 2003, pp. 1511 ff., esp. pp. 1514 ff. and pp. 1538 ff.
39 Polinsky 1989, p. 123.
40 Polinsky 1989, p. 124.
41 Polinsky 1989, p. 10.
42 Similar arguments are found in Weinrib 1995; Zipursky 1998, pp. 1 ff.; and Stone 1996, pp. 235 ff. On the same theme, also see Coleman 1991/92, pp. 349 ff.; and Perry 1991/92, pp. 381 ff.

nature of the legal relationship, economic analysis of law pursues a social goal, that of promoting efficiency.[43] In this light, according to Coleman, properties of tort law which are obvious and intuitively transparent – like bilateralism and corrective justice – suddenly appear inexplicable and obscure.[44]

Therefore he leveled the criticism (known as the *bilateralism critique*) that economic analysis of law is incapable of explaining the normative relationship between the injured party and the injurer: it relies on ex ante analysis of hypothetical cases of damage from the viewpoint of cost and risk minimization, whereas in reality a court has to give an ex post ruling on real damages cases involving two concrete parties, who stand in a normative relationship with one another based on the case at issue:[45]

> "The problem that confronts economic analysis, or any entirely forward-looking theory of tort law, is that it seems to ignore the point that litigants are brought together in a case because one alleges that the other has harmed her in a way she had no right to do. Litigants do not come to court in order to provide the judge with an opportunity to pursue or refine his vision of optimal risk reduction policy."[46]

Indeed, it is difficult to conceive of liability law as oriented exclusively towards the efficiency goal, ignoring the bilateral nature of the relationship between injurer and victim. In future, it will continue to be the primary objective of liability law to achieve corrective justice. This does not preclude the attempt, as a secondary objective, to bear social costs in mind and take them into account when defining liability rules, beginning perhaps with the type of liability rule to choose: both strict liability and negligence are based on the idea of corrective justice, but negligence may be fundamentally superior to strict liability in terms of efficiency. The goal of any economic analysis of law must be to shed light on the effects of different regulations without demolishing the fundamental structures of liability law, like the bilateral nature of the relationship between injurer and victim, in the process.

The bilateralism critique of the economic analysis of liability law can equally be leveled against the economic analysis of contract law. If efficiency is elevated to the target criterion in law, it is argued, there would be no explanation for the *"privity rule"* that a contract only confers rights and obligations upon the contracting parties:

> "[E]ven if courts were capable of engaging in this kind of reasoning, doing so would ignore the fundamental bilateral interactional framework of contractual interactions because courts have to introduce considerations that are *not* related to the parties to the contract."[47]

Indeed, it is hard to conceive of the social goal of efficiency alone, entirely removed from the reciprocal relationship between the concrete parties to the contract, as the definitive criterion in contract law. Even so, there is nevertheless scope for taking efficiency aspects into consideration – e.g. in determining whether expectation dam-

43 Bound up with this, according to Coleman, is the unassailable belief in the state as the engine of social change. Coleman 2005, p. 344.

44 Coleman 2001, p. 21.

45 Coleman 2001, pp. 16 ff.

46 Coleman 2001, p. 17.

47 Hevia 2007, p. 113.

ages or just reliance damages are due –, without necessarily compromising the bilateral structure of the contractual relationship.

Consequently, the demand that private law should exclusively pursue the goal of efficiency and public law the goal of justice must be rejected. *It is rather the role of the legislator, and the courts in their turn, to strike a subtle balance between conflicting principles in all areas of the law.* Moreover, the discussion should not be confined merely to the two goals of justice and efficiency, but should also be extended to other goals such as legal certainty or human dignity.[48] In every case a multitude of legal policy goals exist which could step forward to compete with the efficiency goal in particular instances.[49]

5 Regulatory Impact Analysis

The final question to be considered is how economic analysis methods might be incorporated as a helpful, supplementary instrument in codified law systems. In legislation, at least, this can be done with relative ease by means of *Regulatory Impact Analysis* (RIA), an instrument for assessing the economic impacts of laws. One of the main instruments used is cost-benefit analysis. In the United States, cost-benefit analyses have long been standard practice in relation to major new regulations. Since 1995, the OECD has recommended that its member countries should carry out Regulatory Impact Analysis as part of the legislative process. Also, in the wake of the *Mandelkern Report* (2001), the European Union passed a plan to simplify and improve the regulatory framework. This imposes impact analysis for the most important legislative proposals.[50]

Since the year 2000, Switzerland has had its own instrument of Regulatory Impact Analysis at the Confederation level which is geared towards the recommendations of the OECD.[51] Its constitutional basis is given in Art. 170 of the Swiss Federal Constitution, according to which the Federal Assembly has to ensure scrutiny of the effectiveness of Federal Government measures.[52] The specific statutory hook for prospective analysis of draft legislation is found in Art. 141 (2g) of the Parliament Act. Under this provision, the notices to draft bills proposed by the Swiss Federal Council (Swiss Government) must include statements on the legislation's anticipated impacts on the economy, society and the environment, insofar as substantial comments on these aspects can be made. According to the decree and guidelines of the Swiss Federal Council of September 15, 1999, all legislation must now be subjected to an economic impact analysis before it is enacted. The analysis should include scrutiny of the following five points: *(1) Necessity and possibility of state action; (2) Impacts on individual social groups; (3) Impacts on the whole economy; (4) Alternative regulations; and (5) Expediency in enforcement.*

The strength of *cost-benefit analysis* is that it attempts a comprehensive evaluation of the economic impacts of a measure or a project. But attention should also be

48 Cf. Eidenmüller 1998, p. 273.
49 Eidenmüller 1998, p. 316.
50 On impact orientation in law, see e.g. Weigel 2003, pp. 194 ff.; and van Aaken 2003, pp. 146 ff.
51 See OECD, Regulatory Impact Analysis: Best Practices in OECD Countries (1997).
52 On the general situation in Switzerland, also see Mader 2003, pp. 100 ff.

given to this method's weaknesses: the insistence on monetization means that a financial value must be attached to all impacts, even those for which no market prices are available. Whilst it is relatively easy to evaluate costs in monetary terms, benefits must often be assessed using ad hoc reference data and rough approximations. These uncertainties produce valuations with rather broad scope for interpretation, which can cast doubt on the meaningfulness of the results. Moreover, future costs and benefits must be discounted to a reference point in time.[53] Here the choice of the discount rate has significant implications for the result.[54] A further point to bear in mind is that in a cost-benefit analysis, essentially it makes no difference which social groups are the beneficiaries of a legal regulation and who will have to bear the likely costs. Indeed, it is sufficient if society's balance sheet of all discounted costs and benefits is positive. Hence, in the terminology of welfare economics, only *Kaldor-Hicks efficiency* is required.[55] It would therefore be a desirable objective for all legal regulations to be analyzed with regard to their *impact on income distribution*, to enable political decision-makers to form a rounded overall judgment.

Less problematic than the normatively-laden efficiency criteria of welfare economics are the analysis methods of positive economics. At the very least, these methods are useful in the analysis of the impact of laws while taking into account the *incentives* they exert on the economic subjects. Even purely qualitative consideration can prove very useful in this regard. Such a review should be made the minimum standard for absolutely all legislation – not just at central government level, but also at subordinate levels of the state.

Under common law, it is principally the role of the courts to bring economic rationality into judgments. Under a codified law system, however, this is only possible within very narrow confines due to considerations of legitimization, given the principle of separation of powers and the legality principle. *Unless legitimized by the legislature, any recognition of economics-based argumentation strategies within the judicial process should be viewed with caution.*[56] Instead, the legislator can explicitly instruct the administration and the courts to give due regard to efficiency as a legal principle.[57] In doing so, however, care must be taken not to overload the relevant enforcement authorities with the associated information procurement and processing work.[58]

53 On this issue, see Klaus Mathis, Discounting the Future? (2011).

54 On the problems of cost-benefit analyses in general, see Lave 1996, pp. 104 ff.; for the specific problem of valuing human life, see Balz Hammer, Valuing the Invaluable (2011).

55 See section 2 supra.

56 See esp. Eidenmüller 1998, pp. 414 ff.; for criticism, also Janson 2004, p. 152. On the economic analysis of court rulings, nevertheless, see Kötz/Schäfer (2003).

57 Swiss federal judge Hansjörg Seiler and Laurent Bieri take the view that in Switzerland, application of the "Hand Rule" in liability law would already be a fundamental possibility de lege lata. See Seiler 2007, pp. 140 ff.; and Bieri 2007, pp. 289 ff.

58 For a more detailed discussion of these problems see Klaus Mathis, Consequentialism in Law (2011), and Péter Cserne, Consequence-based Arguments in Legal Reasoning: A Jurisprudential Preface to *Law and Economics* (2011).

Literature

Alesina, Alberto/Rodrik, Dani (1994): "Distributive Politics and Economic Growth", Quarterly Journal of Economics 109 (1994), pp. 465–490.

Baumol, William J. (1972): Economic Theory and Operations Analysis, 3rd ed., London, 1972.

Bieri, Laurent (2007): "La faute au sens de l'article 41 CO – Plaidoyer pour une reconnaissance explicite de la 'règle de hand'", Schweizerische Juristen-Zeitung 103 (2007), pp. 289–296.

Coleman, Jules L. (1991/92): "Tort Law and the Demands of Corrective Justice", Indiana Law Journal 67 (1991/92), pp. 349–380.

Coleman, Jules L. (2001): The Practice of Principles: In Defence of a Pragmatist Approach to Legal Theory, Oxford.

Coleman, Jules L. (2003): "The Grounds of Welfare", The Yale Law Journal 112 (2003), pp. 1511–1543.

Coleman, Jules L. (2005): "The Costs of The Costs of Accidents", Maryland Law Review 64 (2005), pp. 337–354.

Cserne, Péter (2011): Consequence-based Arguments in Legal Reasoning: A Jurisprudential Preface to Law and Economics, in: Efficiency, Sustainability, and Justice to Future Generations, ed. by Klaus Mathis, New York.

Eidenmüller, Horst (1998): Effizienz als Rechtsprinzip: Möglichkeiten und Grenzen der ökonomischen Analyse des Rechts, 2nd ed., Tübingen.

Hagel, Joachim (1993): Effizienz und Gerechtigkeit: Ein Beitrag zur Diskussion der ethischen Aspekte in der neoklassischen Wohlfahrtstheorie, Baden-Baden.

Hammer, Balz (2011): Valuing the Invaluable? Valuation of Human Life in Cost-Efficiency Assessments of Regulatory Interventions, in: Efficiency, Sustainability, and Justice to Future Generations, ed. by Klaus Mathis, New York, pp. 211–235.

Hevia, Martin (2007): "Kronman on Contract Law and Distributive Justice", Journal of Contract Law 23 (2007), pp. 105–119.

Janson, Gunnar (2004): Ökonomische Theorie im Recht: Anwendbarkeit und Erkenntniswert im allgemeinen und am Beispiel des Arbeitsrechts, Berlin.

Kaplow, Louis/Shavell, Steven (1994): "Why the Legal System is less efficient than the Income Tax in Redistributing Income", The Journal of Legal Studies 23 (1994), pp. 667–681.

Kaplow, Louis/Shavell, Steven (2002): Fairness versus Welfare, Cambridge.

Kötz, Hein/Schäfer, Hans-Bernd (2003): Judex oeconomicus: 12 höchstrichterliche Entscheidungen kommentiert aus ökonomischer Sicht, Tübingen.

Lave, Lester B. (1996): Benefit-Cost Analysis – Do the Benefits Exceed the Costs?, in: Risks, Costs and Lives Saved – Getting Better Results from Regulation, ed. by Robert W. Hahn, New York, 1996, pp. 104–134.

Lukes, Steven (1996): On Trade-Offs between Values, in: Ethics, Rationality and Economic Behaviour, ed. by Francesco Farina et al., Oxford, 1996, pp. 36–49.

Mader, Luzius (2003): Zum aktuellen Stand der Gesetzesfolgenabschätzung in der Schweiz, in: Wirkungsforschung zum Recht IV: Möglichkeiten einer Institutionalisierung der Wirkungskontrolle von Gesetzen, ed. by Ulrich Karpen/Hagen Hof, Baden-Baden, 2003, pp. 96–110.

Mathis, Klaus (2009): Efficiency Instead of Justice? Searching for the Philosophical Foundations of the Economic Analysis of Law, New York: 2009 (German edition: Effizienz statt Gerechtigkeit? Auf der Suche nach den philosophischen Grundlagen der Ökonomischen Analyse des Rechts, 3rd ed., Berlin).

Mathis, Klaus (2011): Discounting the Future?, in: Efficiency, Sustainability, and Justice to Future Generations, ed. by Klaus Mathis, New York, pp. 165–180.

Mathis, Klaus (2011): Consequentialism in Law, in: Efficiency, Sustainability, and Justice to Future Generations, ed. by Klaus Mathis, New York, pp. 3–29.

OECD (1997): Regulatory Impact Analysis: Best Practices in OECD Countries, Paris, 1997.

Okun, Arthur M. (1975): Equality and Efficiency – The Big Tradeoff, Washington.

Perry, Stephen R. (1991/92): "Comment on Coleman: Corrective Justice", Indiana Law Journal 67 (1991/92), pp. 381–410.

Persson, Torsten/Tabellini, Guido (1994): "Is Inequality Harmful for Growth?", American Economic Review 84 (1994), pp. 600–621.

Polinsky, Mitchell A. (1989): An Introduction to Law and Economics, 2nd ed., Boston.
Posner, Richard A. (1979): "Utilitarianism, Economics, and Legal Theory", The Journal of Legal Studies 8 (1979), pp. 103–140.
Posner, Richard A. (1980): "The Ethical and Political Basis of the Efficiency Norm in Common Law Adjudication", Hofstra Law Review 8 (1980), pp. 487–507.
Posner, Richard A. (1981): The Economics of Justice, Harvard.
Posner, Richard A. (1987): "The Justice of Economics", Economia delle scelte pubbliche 1 (1987), pp. 15–25.
Posner, Richard A. (1990): The Problems of Jurisprudence, Cambridge, 1990, pp. 382 ff.
Posner, Richard A. (1998): Economic Analysis of Law, 5th ed., New York.
Posner, Richard A. (2003): Law, Pragmatism, and Democracy, Cambridge.
Seiler, Hansjörg (2007): "Wie viel Sicherheit wollen wir? Sicherheitsmassnahmen zwischen Kostenwirksamkeit und Recht", ZBJV 143 (2007), pp. 140–150.
Schäfer, Hans-Bernd/Ott, Claus (2000): Lehrbuch der ökonomischen Analyse des Zivilrechts, 3rd ed., Berlin.
Stiglitz, Joseph E. (1989): Finanzwissenschaft, Munich and Vienna.
Stone, Martin (1996): "On the Idea of Private Law", Canadian Journal of Law and Jurisprudence 9 (1996), pp. 235–277.
van Aaken, Anne (2003): "Rational Choice" in der Rechtswissenschaft: Zum Stellenwert der ökonomischen Theorie im Recht, Baden-Baden.
Weigel, Wolfgang (2003): Rechtsökonomik, Munich.
Weinrib, Ernest J. (1995): The Idea of Private Law, Cambridge.
Zipursky, Benjamin (1998): "Rights, Wrongs, and Recourse in the Law of Torts", Vanderbilt Law Review 51 (1998), pp. 1–100.

Péter Cserne*

Import, Export, and Multilateral Translation

Methodological Lessons from an Economic Analysis of Paternalism in Contract Law

Abstract:
Als Fallstudie zu den Möglichkeiten und Grenzen der inter-/multidisziplinären rechtswissenschaftlichen Forschung werden im Aufsatz die begrifflichen, methodologischen und normativen Grundlagen einer ökonomischen Analyse von Paternalismus im Vertragsrecht analysiert. Nachdem die Fragestellungen rund um den Begriff und die Rechtfertigung von staatlichen Einschränkungen der individuellen Entscheidungsfreiheit im philosophischen Diskurs skizziert werden, wird analysiert, ob die gegenwärtig üblichen Methoden der ökonomischen Analyse geeignet sind, um die Problematik, die der Paternalismus mit sich bringt, adäquat herauszustellen. Ich stelle dar, wie Ökonomen ihre analytischen Instrumente verfeinern und das Konzept des Paternalismus uminterpretieren, um es in ihr eigenes theoretisches Konzept einzupassen. Dabei argumentiere ich, dass die ökonomische Analyse als sozialwissenschaftlicher Ansatz in rechtspolitischen Debatten über paternalistische Eingriffe relevant ist. Sie soll aber sowohl ihre normativen Grundannahmen überdenken als auch sich mehr auf systematische empirische Forschung, insbesondere auf die Ergebnisse der psychologischen Forschung über menschliches Urteils- und Entscheidungsverhalten, verlassen. Die Interaktion zwischen Rechtspolitik, Rechtsphilosophie, theoretischen und empirischen Sozialwissenschaften kann am besten als multilaterale Übersetzung verstanden werden. Formell rationales Recht setzt aber Grenzen für den Import nichtjuristischen Argumenten in die juristische Argumentationspraxis.

In this paper I discuss the conceptual and methodological background of an economic approach to paternalism in contract law. This should serve as a case study to a more general problem: the role of inter- and multidisciplinary research in jurisprudence and legal studies in general.

1 Motives and Methods of Analyzing Legal Paternalism

In recent years, contract regulation and legal paternalism have raised interest within both American legal academia and European private law scholarship. There are several reasons for this: the practical ones are related to the revision of the consumer *aquis* and the ongoing discussion regarding the pros and cons of the harmonization of contract law in the European Union. Understandably, this subject induces eager interest, both academic and practical. This interest is nurtured by some theoretical considerations as well. First, contract regulation and paternalism draw attention to the philosophical and methodological difficulties involved in the justification of the limitations on freedom of contract. Second, they demonstrate that empirical findings on human behavior may lead, in many cases, to conclusions, especially

* This paper is an extended version of my presentation in the Special workshop "Import and export" at the XXIIIth IVR world congress (Kraków, 4 August 2007) and is based on my PhD thesis submitted at Hamburg University, Faculty of Law (Cserne 2008). I am grateful to the organizers of the workshop, Michael Anderheiden and Stephan Kirste for the invitation; to the participants for valuable suggestions.

policy recommendations, that are significantly different from the outcomes of traditional economic arguments.

More specifically, in the law and economics literature, the question has been raised as to whether the traditional anti-paternalist view of mainstream economics based on "consumer sovereignty" remains valid if (at least) one contracting party is imperfectly rational or not fully informed. Furthermore, as some of these imperfections of judgment and choice behavior characterize humans generally, legislators and regulators with the task of setting a legal framework for contracting, or judges and juries involved in individual contract disputes, are not necessarily immune to these biases either. Thus the question should be raised whether the traditional anti-paternalistic stance of law and economics has to be modified, or even replaced, by anti-antipaternalism: a limited and critical version of paternalism.[1]

In order to give a flavor of the complexity of the problems concerning paternalism in contract law, let me give an example here. Usury laws have a very long history, and not only in the Christian world.[2] Laws limiting the interest rate for credits have been in force in many legal systems; they are not uncommon in today's Europe either. For instance, in France the maximum interest rate is regulated in the *Code de la consommation* in a detailed manner.[3] In England, usury has been traditionally prohibited by both statutes and judicial decisions. In Germany, judges regulate usury with reference to § 138 I of the BGB (*Bürgerliches Gesetzbuch*).[4]

By prohibiting usurious contracts, the law does not allow people to grant and take on credits on very harsh or unbalanced terms. To be sure, financial contracts are also heavily regulated in other ways. For instance, the purpose of modern consumer credit regulation is to provide consumers with all the information necessary to allow for a rational decision.

With regard to this kind of regulation one could ask the following question: if consumers are aware of the conditions of the credit contract and the relevant market is workably competitive, how can any substantive limit such as a cap on the interest rates be justified? In other words, if usury laws are unnecessary for controlling the circumstances surrounding the contracting situation (this job is done by rules on fraud, duress, and information disclosure) they do not altogether seem necessary. Eventually, such laws could be defended by paternalism, redistributive arguments, substantive fairness, or with reference to widely shared moral principles; but how compatible are they with another widely held principle, freedom of contract?

A related issue is that usury laws can be counter-productive. By prohibiting credit contracts with interest rates above a given limit, the law makes it impossible for certain consumers to legally access credit, as their default risk, and thus the interest rate, is so high that in a competitive credit market there is no (private) bank

1 "[B]ounded rationality pushes toward a sort of anti-antipaternalism – a skepticism about antipaternalism, but not an affirmative defense of paternalism." Jolls – Sunstein – Thaler 2000, p. 46. See also Trout 2005.

2 Cf. Baldwin 1959. For instance, according to an ancient Hindu rule called damdupat, interest in excess of the principal cannot be recovered. A similar rule was also codified in the Usurious Loans Act 1918 in India, see http://punjabrevenue.nic.in/usurios_loan_act.htm.

3 For the English text of the relevant regulation see http://195.83.177.9/code/liste.phtml?lang=uk&c=30&r=1503.

4 For a historical and comparative overview of usury laws see Menyhárd 2004, pp. 33–47.

prepared to lend them at or below the legally fixed maximum rate. Consequently, some potentially mutually beneficial transactions do not take place, and those whom the law wanted to protect are possibly made worse off. Usury laws make "it more difficult for poor people to borrow, thus harming them ex ante though benefiting some of them ex post."[5]

Another question that arises concerns the way usury laws actually work in practice. In a recent article, Hynes and Posner give an overview of usury laws in force in the different states of the U.S.[6] Some state laws are very restrictive, others more lenient. As the authors also demonstrate, there are many ways to make these restrictions ineffective through contractual arrangements. At least in the United States, strict usury laws are hardly relevant in practice.

It is interesting to note that some legal systems seem to have found ways to deal with the problem of poor (high-risk) debtors mentioned above. In South Africa, the Supreme Court "has decided that micro-lenders operate under exemptions to the Usury Act which give them the freedom to charge unrestricted interest on loans under R 10000 (EUR 1400). The interest rates for such credits are often higher than 50 per cent per year, and sometimes even higher."[7] This South-African example seems to reflect the court's understanding that there is a group of, probably low-income, people who need a special regime. In this market segment, credit is only viable at a relatively high interest rate, because of the high average default risk of the borrowers as a group. Thus this ruling of the Supreme Court is probably efficient, i.e. mutually beneficial from an *ex ante* perspective. It makes it possible for borrowers of smaller amounts to take credit legally. *Given their current set of opportunities* it serves the interest of the low-income group as well.

Not surprisingly, when consumer credit is more easily available, there is more credit outstanding and more cases of over indebtedness. As psychological studies confirm, people are not rational in taking credits: they fall prey to cognitive and emotional biases which make their decisions erroneous, even measured on the scale of their own interest. Currently there is intensive discussion about the possible causes of, and policy responses to, consumer over indebtedness throughout the world.[8] The potential policy responses can be preventive ones working *ex ante*, including the provision of adequate information, cooling-off periods and other procedural limits. Meanwhile, other measures may help to get out of indebtedness *ex post*. There are many promising initiatives which give assistance to consumers not only financially but by providing information about rational management of personal finances. For instance, NGOs work on designing and distributing easily accessible information, like brochures with simple rules of thumb and vivid illustrations about how to notice the threat, and then fight the danger of over indebtedness. As we will see later, this is an instance of what is called "debasing through law", a regulatory idea suggested in behavioral law and economics.

5 Posner 1998, p. 129.
6 For a recent critical summary of the economic arguments and the legal rules of the US, see Hynes – Posner 2002.
7 Personal communication from Prof. Hans-Bernd Schäfer (Hamburg). For a detailed analysis see Meagher 2005.
8 See, e.g. http://www.responsible-credit.net/.

As a sort of indirect paternalism, another way of intervening is to regulate the behavior of the lenders. Starting from the 1970s, the many "Fairness in Lending Acts" in the U.S. have basically mandated that the true costs of credit should be communicated to the consumer. As I will argue below, while these information provision rules are not unnecessary, unfortunately, they seem insufficient. Typically, they do not help when consumers take credits knowingly but irresponsibly. One of the current regulative ideas which are supposed to address this problem, parallel to helping borrowers, is promoted under the label of "responsive lending". The term refers to voluntarily assumed norms of ethical and responsive business. Indeed, it resonates with some jurisprudential arguments which seek to include the principle of "transactional care"[9] into contract law in order to counteract exploitation.

"Responsive lending" and "transactional care" are terms with strong moral undertones. What could be the theoretical and normative background of these ideas? Why am I my brother's keeper? Such ideas can have different philosophical roots and justifications. Arguments in favor of paternalism by a better informed (endowed) fellow citizen, or transactional partner (and not the state) are in part based on the idea that not only legal norms matter: rather, social norms do, and should, regulate which business practices are considered fair and socially acceptable.

As the 2007 subprime mortgage financial crisis indicates, irresponsible lending (in a wider sense) may also have serious macroeconomic effects. Even a non-paternalistic state may have reasons for intervention in certain circumstances. These widespread economic consequences also indicate that the impact of credit contracts definitely goes beyond the competencies and capacities of contract law and the judicial system.

In sum, the example of the regulation of credit contracts between formally equal but economically diverse parties suggests four general ideas.

(1) Throughout history, policymakers have regulated such transactions using various justifications.

(2) In modern legal systems, a wide variety of legal instruments are used for paternalistic purposes, which can be compared with regards to their effectiveness.

(3) Economic theory can illuminate these issues.

(4) As these contracts are embedded in a social context, understanding this contextual richness requires going beyond the standard economic approach.

2 Regulatory Doctrines in Contract Law

To be sure, these ideas are not completely new. For judges solving contract disputes, their policing role in regards to labor, consumer and other standard-form contracts has become increasingly apparent since the early 20th century. Since then, there have been several types of cases where modern legal regimes have set limits upon the general principle of freedom of contract. In fact, many contract law rules do not aim at enforcing the parties' intentions, be they actual or hypothetical. Illegality, public policy and numerous other doctrines, along with the mandatory rules of labor law, tenancy and consumer protection set such limits too, for the right or wrong

9 Bigwood 2004.

reasons. These doctrines are argued for in the literature in a number of different ways: third-party effects (externalities), redistribution, fairness, moralism, and paternalism are amongst the reasons.

Following Cooter and Ulen,[10] I give here an overview of some regulatory doctrines of contract law. The main purpose is to identify the links between the reasons for setting limits to contractual freedom, and the typical rules that serve these reasons.

Legal doctrine	**Fact triggering legal doctrine (problem)**	**Incentive (solution)**	**Legal solution**
Incompetence	Incompetent person makes promise	Protect incompetents at least cost	Interpret contract in incompetent's best interest / No enforcement
Duress	Promisee threatens to destroy	Deter threats	No enforcement of coerced promises
Necessity	Promisee threatens not to rescue	Reward rescue	Beneficiary pays cost of rescue plus reward
Impossibility	Contingency prevents performance	Encourage precaution and risk-spreading	Liability for the least-cost risk-bearer
Frustration of purpose	Contingency destroys purpose of performance	Encourage precaution and risk-spreading	Liability for the least-cost risk-bearer
Mutual mistake about facts	Buyer and seller make same mistake about facts	Encourage precaution and risk-spreading	Liability for the least-cost risk-bearer
Mutual mistake about identity	Buyer and seller have different object in mind	Prevent involuntary exchange	Unwind contract
Unilateral mistake	Buyer or seller mistaken about facts	Unite knowledge and control; encourage discovery	Enforce contract
Duty to disclose	Promisee harms by withholding information	Induce supply of true information	Liability for harm
Fraud	Promisee supplies false information knowingly	Deter supply of false information	No enforcement of contract and liability for harm
Adhesion contracts	Cartel uses standard forms to promote collusion	Destabilize cartels	Deny enforcement to contracts of cartels
Procedural unconscionability	Consumer ignorant of critical terms in retailer's contract	Create incentive to communicate meaning of contract terms	Deny enforcement unless bargaining process communicates crucial information

Although based on American law, the information in this table can also be generalized to other legal systems. The economic reasons for intervention are essentially

10 Cooter – Ulen 2004, p. 294 (Table 7.5).

twofold: contracting failures and market failures. Contracting failures or problems with individual rationality are either cases of bounded rationality which is addressed by the doctrine of incapacity; or of constrained choice which is addressed as coercion, duress, necessity, or impossibility. Market failures can be explained by three types of transaction costs and addressed in contract law accordingly. First, they can be externalities which lead to the unenforceability of contracts which derogate public policy or violate a statutory duty. Second, failures deriving from imperfect information are addressed as fraud, failure to disclose, frustration of purpose, or mutual mistake. A third type is structural or situational monopoly which leads to the lack of competition, which is addressed by doctrines such as necessity, unconscionability, and lesion.[11] How is this categorization relevant for the discussion of paternalism?

Paternalism relates primarily to contracting failures. One can speak of paternalistic intervention mainly: (1) in the case of systematic cognitive failures or insufficient cognitive capacities; (2) when there is insufficient or asymmetric information; and (3) when there are insufficient outside opportunities, due to the circumstances of necessity or, situational or structural, monopoly.

The fact that the number of regulatory contract law doctrines in the table above is larger than the number of problems might suggest that economic theory cannot fully capture the problems the various doctrines are intended to solve. Contract regimes follow a number of goals besides correcting market failures. On the other hand, there are contract law doctrines that at first glance look paternalistic, as well as a number of legal instruments which, in modern legal systems typically serve paternalistic purposes. Regulators have a wide set of instruments at their disposal: formation defenses; mandatory rules and default rules; procedural (formal) requirements (formalities, cooling-off periods, information disclosure); substantive rules; rules of interpretation (construction).

Contract law is not the only, or the best, policy instrument in the service of paternalism, however. Economic theory suggests that some market failures should be addressed primarily through public-law-type regulation, rather than in private law. Trebilcock argues for a "relative institutional division of labor" among regulatory techniques. He suggests that the "law of contracts will be principally concerned with autonomy issues in evaluating claims of coercion, antitrust and regulatory law [with] issues of consumer welfare, and the social welfare system [with] issues of distributive justice".[12] When we look at this carefully argued proposal by Trebilcock, it does not even mention paternalism. Is it possible to analyze or explain away paternalism in an extended law and economics approach?

I think that paternalism should indeed be considered a residual category. If we can find a (possibly implicit) reason for intervention in terms of a market failure or some third party effect, we should give priority to these, and not attribute the regulation to paternalistic purposes. Still, this strategy is mainly pragmatic and I intend to apply it only to the domain of contract law. Social burden arguments are not always relevant in terms of common moral intuitions. Similarly, there are legal areas like criminal law or medical law where market failures and externalities, if relevant

11 Cooter – Ulen 2004, p. 267.
12 Trebilcock 1993, p. 101.

at all, count only as rather weak arguments. But we should not go ahead too fast. First, the concept and justifiability of paternalism should be clarified.

3 Paternalism in Moral and Political Philosophy

Without going into terminological controversies, I give a rough definition of paternalism, simply indicating how I use the term in this paper. There are three conditions for an act to be paternalistic. The paternalist (1) interferes with the subject's liberty, (2) acts primarily out of benevolence toward the subject (i.e., his goal is to protect or promote the interests, good or welfare of the subject), and (3) acts without the consent of the subject.

If we follow this definition, paternalism has both justifiable and unjustifiable cases (forms). These cases differ with regards to their justifiability, legitimacy, or reasonableness, etc. According to the definition, paternalism implies doing something against the freedom of the subject without his consent. Under any theory which attaches value to freedom of choice, this lack of concern for the subject's consent needs justification. Actually, paternalism provides such a *reason*: it refers to the protection or promotion of the interests (welfare or good) of the subject.

As to the justification of paternalism, the philosophical discussion is centered around three values: freedom (autonomy); welfare (interests); and benevolence. These refer to three conflicting philosophical positions: deontological, consequentialist, and perfectionist. Under the deontological (autonomy-based) view, freedom of choice is valuable because of the value of autonomy. Under the consequentialist (welfarist) view, freedom of choice is the instrument through which preferences are fulfilled. In some perfectionist (Aristotelian) views, making choices is part of being human. Looking at the extensive philosophical literature on the topic, it seems difficult to decide between the standpoints without discussing such far-reaching questions as the nature of the good, and the meaning of free will. The justification of paternalism is a complicated case where autonomy and welfare concerns should be balanced. In some sense, the conflict between these two values is at the core of paternalism. The divergent implications of the two basic values eventually force the philosopher to choose. But, if Dan Brock is right, at the level of theories there can be convergence.[13] We are not forced to choose between different theories in discussing the justification of every case of paternalistic intervention. One way to avoid taking sides in far-reaching metaphysical debates is suggested by John Rawls' ideas about 'public reason' and 'overlapping consensus.'[14] In this spirit, I will use arguments that can be, at a medium level of abstraction, acceptable, or at least reasonable from several comprehensive perspectives. Speaking about legal issues of more practical concern, the idea of searching for an overlapping consensus seems quite attractive and plausible. Even such a prominent figure of the law and economics movement as Richard Posner once argued for this idea as one possible basis for the general acceptance of the minimization of social costs as the objective of tort (ac-

13 Brock 1988, p. 565.

14 See Rawls 1993. To be sure, in Rawls' view overlapping consensus is not simply a compromise reached by softening or mixing irreconcilable views.

cident) law.[15] As I have argued in detail elsewhere,[16] regarding the justifiability of paternalism in the limited domain of contract law, one can find an overlapping consensus among these normative conceptions. By comparing some representative versions of these philosophical perspectives, the practical conclusions drawn from the different philosophical positions turn out to be surprisingly similar.

In contrast to *philosophical* discussions, *pragmatic* arguments draw attention to the side-effects and the unintended or counter-intentional consequences of paternalistic interventions. The intervention may be more costly or harmful than beneficial, either (1) for the paternalized subject (e.g. due to the double bind effect), (2) for third parties (e.g. due to the over-inclusiveness of the legal rule), (3) or for the general public (e.g. due to implementation costs). In regards to the unintended consequences, overly protective regulation always runs the danger that certain transactions become unprofitable and lead to the collapse of the market, or at least the segment which was the object of protection. To put it in another way, paternalism may be problematic in these cases not only because it is costly for others, but also because it might backfire, i.e. make worse off the very group of persons it is intended to protect.

4 Paternalism in Economic Analysis

In this section I discuss the methodological tools economic theories offer for analyzing paternalism. I also refer to the empirical findings in psychological research on human decision making and choice behavior which are possibly relevant for paternalism.

The traditional economic approach to freedom of contract and paternalism is a non-reflexive mixture of liberalism and utilitarianism. As such, it is ill-equipped to handle the problems which arise when these two principles collide. The potential conflict between welfare-maximization and autonomy draws attention to the non-welfarist dimension of the problem of paternalism. When this dimension is *not* taken into account, the whole problem of paternalism is reducible to a more or less sophisticated exercise in welfare-maximization. Within a strictly welfarist perspective, if the regulator knows better, he should decide in every case in the agent's place. In terms of the preceding section, the constraints to paternalism can only be pragmatic. In contrast, autonomy provides a principled constraint. As we will see, economists also take this constraint into account, at least implicitly.

In another dimension, contemporary economics has often been criticized on the basis that it accepts existing preferences as given. As the critique goes, economic theory does not offer "ethical criteria for disqualifying morally offensive, self-destructive, or irrational preferences as unworthy of recognition." If, to the contrary, it acknowledges some exceptions, as it usually does (e.g. in case of minors or mentally incompetent persons) then "some theory of paternalism is required, the contours of which are not readily suggested by the private ordering paradigm itself."[17] Being

15 Posner 1995, p. 505.
16 Cserne 2008.
17 Trebilcock 1993, p. 21.

reluctant to criticize or "launder" preferences or rethink their model of individual choice as a combination of information (beliefs) and preferences, economists use an "eliminative redefinition" strategy in order to fit paternalism in the neoclassical models.

The economic literature on paternalism[18] strives to justify instances of reasonable, seemingly paternalistic regulations in several ways which, for the sake of simplicity, can be put into four categories: market failures, merit goods, non-standard preferences and non-welfarist objectives.

The first approach sticks with consumer sovereignty and revealed preferences. Paternalism is redefined or "explained away" by showing that the policy in question serves to prevent externalities or other market failures. This strategy of eliminative redefinition does not question consumer sovereignty; arguably, this is the natural way to treat the substantive problem in economics. Indeed, at first glance it is relatively easy to incorporate paternalism in mainstream economic analysis: we just have to identify specific transaction costs and/or informational imperfections and asymmetries which lead to a market failure. In this way not only the case *for* freedom of contract, but many of its limits can be explained in relatively narrow economic terms, by neither relaxing the rationality assumptions nor recurring to fairness arguments.[19] In fact, the biggest "advantage" of this approach is that the conflict between welfare and autonomy does not come to surface.

The second approach clearly and almost openly faces this conflict and solves it in favor of welfare. In the 1950s Richard Musgrave introduced two new, closely related concepts in the theory of public finance: merit wants and merit goods.[20] These concepts serve to formalize the welfarist idea of paternalism with regard to certain publicly provided or publicly subsidized goods. In the case of merit wants or goods, the welfare function that the policymaker has to maximize on behalf of the individuals is formally modeled in a way which is different from the way the individuals themselves (are modeled to) perceive and reveal their preferences. In other words, "consumer sovereignty" is openly questioned and abandoned in favor of a supra-individual assessment as to how much one should receive and consume of certain "merit goods". Choice is driven not by revealed preferences but by merit wants. In the case of merit goods, individual choice is overridden in the name of what a particular (political) community considers worthwhile for individuals to do (consume).[21]

The third category of redefinitions comprises those more or less sophisticated models of preference-formation and decision-making which introduce specific *ad hoc* assumptions about the preference structure of individuals. Examples include choice models based on path-dependent preferences, dynamic inconsistency or the multiple self. The methodological goal here is to analyze certain conflicts between autonomy and welfare with a minimal deviation from mainstream economic theory (rational choice theory). When economists analyze market behavior, they not only implicitly rely on a standard of voluntariness but also explicitly on a standard of rationality. According to rational choice theory, weakness of will, "sour grapes"

18 E.g. Burrows 1993 1995 1998; Saint-Paul 2004; Zamir 1998.
19 Mitchell 2002, cf. Hermalin – Katz – Craswell 2006: §2.
20 For a useful introduction see the still very illuminating summary article by Head 1966.
21 Musgrave 1987.

mechanisms etc. are irrational behavioral patterns. This view implies that the preferences of real-world individuals should be measured on a normative scale. The actual or revealed preference structure of individuals is compared to an ideal or rational preference structure of an abstract model construct, the rational decision-maker. Irrationality in this sense may justify intervention. One's preferences are to be respected if they truly and consistently reflect one's desires. But this is not always the case. The rational self can be in conflict with other features of the very same person or in other terms with different selves. These models re-conceptualize paternalism as a multiple-self problem or even as an 'intra-personal externality' or 'internality' problem. In other words, paternalism is justified when and to the extent that the limitation of freedom of choice is instrumental to the defense of the 'true self' of the subject against one's weakness of will or judgment errors. Eventually, these limitations may even increase the subject's rationality and/or autonomy.

Finally, there are such heterodox economic approaches that criticize mainstream economic theory for the reduction of every normative instance to preferences over outcomes and suggest this simplistic view be remedied. By stressing the difference between what one desires and what one has reason to value Amartya Sen belongs within this category. This distinction would move economic analysis in a perfectionist direction. Other economists (or the same ones in other writings) highlight the need for including freedom of choice in economic models.[22] These lines of research can be extremely helpful for an economic analysis of the non-welfarist dimension of paternalism. Originating from Amartya Sen's seminal article on the impossibility of a Paretian liberal,[23] there is now an emerging branch of literature in social choice theory which searches methods and modeling techniques for the incorporation of the dimension of freedom of choice into formal economic (social choice) models. The intuition behind this line of research is that the extent of opportunities, i.e. the number and diversity of alternatives open to an individual might be valuable in and of itself. The freedom to choose among alternatives might have some value independent of the intrinsic value of these alternatives.[24] In regards to paternalism however, this line of research has no clear and direct policy implications.

From the discussion of economic analysis of paternalism so far it has become clear that the mainstream economic approach has to face two problems. First, it remains controversial from a normative point of view whether the function of law can be reduced to the maximization of individual preferences. Second, there remains a methodological difficulty: the growing amount of evidence on biases and other irrational behavior calling the scientific fruitfulness of *ad hoc* modeling of bounded rationality into question. To put it differently: in cases where people systematically make suboptimal choices, paternalistic intervention may be justified. To determine the appropriate scope and technique of intervention, systematic empirical research on bounded rationality is necessary. However, the justification of interventions cannot be based simply on revealed individual preferences as the ultimate normative benchmark, because the concept of preference has also become questionable. Em-

22 See, e.g. Sugden 1998, Van Hees 2002, Sen 2002.
23 Sen 1970.
24 Cf. Van Hees 2004, Sugden 1998.

pirical research is crucial in order to answer questions about the best possible way to design legal rules, be they paternalistic or otherwise, and in the discussion of the reasons for paternalism. This implies the relevance of psychological research for law and economics, which, in fact has recently become a widely accepted branch of the discipline called, somewhat misleadingly, behavioral law and economics. Thus, whether legal policy needs empirical foundations is not a real question.[25] The question is rather, what will, and should, these foundations look like? In recent decades there has been a large volume of ongoing empirical research in this direction, both by psychologists and economists.[26] It has been shown in thorough and extensive empirical studies that human behavior systematically deviates from the precepts of expected utility theory and rational choice theory in general.

Human decision-making, choice and judgment reaching behavior are often characterized by loss aversion, the endowment effect and framing effects. Furthermore, people commit judgment errors when assessing probabilities. By using mental shortcuts called heuristics (availability, representativeness etc.) their judgments might become biased and vulnerable to manipulation – self-serving bias, hindsight bias, over-optimism, unstable risk-assessment being the most well-known examples.

For instance, several hundreds of studies raised fundamental doubts about the assumptions regarding preferences in economic theory. The framing effect shows that in many situations the concept of preference itself is indeterminate. In a descriptive psychological sense, the assumption that preferences are autonomous and stable is false. Several other features and mechanisms of human judgment and choice have been also described which contradict the assumptions in neoclassical economics (rational choice theory). Cognitive limits and emotional biases are ubiquitous. These should be, and have been, theoretically explained and modeled within neuro-sciences and cognitive psychology. It is important to note that in terms of these sciences, the issue is not one of biases and anomalies but the understanding of the very way human minds work.

The question to be raised is this: how should law and economics (being interested in how *law* works) react to these insights? Is it possible to build a competing (and possibly superior) version of legal theory based on the analysis of these psychological phenomena? There are many obvious difficulties impeding such an endeavor. On the whole, however, the objections usually raised against behavioral law and economics are either not convincing or not decisive in dismissing it as a line of research.[27]

As to the policy implications of psychological research, it is clear that empirical findings alone cannot justify legal intervention. The normative implications (and policy conclusions) are not straightforward. Psychological insights suggest that the justifiability of paternalism is an "uncertain case" – outright anti-paternalism should not be replaced by uncritical paternalism.[28] In short, there are strong arguments both for and against paternalism. The behavioral findings may lead, in certain cir-

25 On empirical research in contract law scholarship see Korobkin 2002.

26 For overview with further references see Sunstein 2000, Englerth 2004, Camerer et al. 2004, Korobkin – Ulen 2000.

27 In Cserne 2008, I discuss six objections against behavioural law and economics and the possible answers (counter-arguments), loosely based on Rachlinski 2006.

28 Rachlinski 2003, Blumenthal 2007.

cumstances, to normative conclusions (policy recommendations) that are significantly different from those arising from the traditional anti-paternalism of mainstream economics. The consequences for normative analysis, however, are not simply the uncritical endorsement of paternalism. Some researchers speak about anti-anti-paternalism in this respect.

The *prima facie* arguments for paternalism seem obvious: when law can promote the interests of humans by reducing their biases, increasing their autonomy, it should. But why should the law *not* always intervene despite systematic irrationality? Besides the well-known pragmatic antipaternalist arguments (discussed above), there are numerous specific psychological arguments for not intervening in people's choices which can complement traditional skepticism toward governmental regulation.

First, they refer to the fact that biases are highly context-dependent. We simply do not know enough about the biases to suggest a general remedy. Second, what are called "biases" in the light (or shadow) of rational choice theory are in fact (in terms of psychology) components embedded in a complex decision-making mechanism. In this complex cognitive and emotional system, there are several interactions between these mechanisms. It is possible that one bias may temper another. When such interactions are neglected, debiasing might make the overall result worse than the initial situation.

Third, learning effects can be at work. In a dynamic perspective, regulation may lead to the inhibition of learning and negatively affect rational and autonomous choice in the future. This provides a dynamic or developmental argument against paternalism.[29] This dynamic effect, already stressed by J.S. Mill, has been now convincingly demonstrated in empirical studies.[30] In my view, it provides a reason why the law should deliberately deviate from a "psychologically adequate" view of man. Arguably, if rational autonomous choice is accepted as a normative ideal, especially for contracts, then the law should counterfactually slightly "overshoot" with its assumptions concerning both of them. This should be done in order not to simply map and thus stabilize biases but to leave space for learning and development.[31]

Fourth, since biases are so varied and complex it is often the case that individuals themselves are in the best position to cope with their own irrational tendencies and deficiencies. In fact, this is what happens when people hire experts, use self-binding techniques etc. Law should encourage, or at least not neglect these mechanisms.

5 New Regulative Ideas

In arguing for protective rules, legal commentators often refer to empirical data about the vulnerability of consumers to biases and manipulation. The psychologi-

29 Feinberg 1986, p. 24: "If adults are treated as children, they will in time come to be like children. Deprived of the right to choose for themselves, they will soon lose the power of rational judgment and decision. Even children, after a certain point, had better not be 'treated as children,' else they will never acquire the outlook and capability of responsive adults."

30 See Klick-Mitchell 2006.

31 Eidenmüller 2005.

cal, pragmatic, economic and philosophical arguments, and counter-arguments, discussed in the previous section should make supporters of legal paternalism cautious. An uncritical, across-the-board support of paternalism is unwarranted. Recently, law and economics scholars have suggested a number of more or less sophisticated approaches to take into account both the behavioral insights and some of the counter-arguments. I briefly recall here three regulatory ideas: asymmetric paternalism, libertarian paternalism, and debiasing through law.

5.1 "Asymmetric Paternalism"

"A policy is asymmetrically paternalistic if it creates large benefits for those people who are boundedly rational while imposing little or no harm on those who are fully rational."[32] More concretely, it is argued that legal interference with private choices is justified (in a firm/consumers setting) if:

$$(p * B) - [(1 - p) * C] - I + d\prod > 0,$$

where B denotes the net benefits to boundedly rational agents, C is the net costs to rational agents, I stands for the implementation costs, $d\prod$ denotes the change in firms' profits, and p is the fraction of consumers who are boundedly rational (all other consumers are supposed to be fully rational).[33]

The economists and psychologists who argue for 'asymmetric' paternalism on a welfarist basis also compare real-world agents with the fully rational individual as assumed in orthodox economic models. They go on to say that bounded rationality is something which can be justifiably regulated in a way similar to externalities. Here one has, first, to suppose the existence of a true 'inner self', characterized by such desires and beliefs which are normatively undisputed, or accepted as rational. Second, one has to explain the behavior of real world individuals as cases where their inner self falls prey to certain anomalies. As I mentioned above, one of the problems with this approach is that it is not clear which features of the empirical self should be respected and protected.

Asymmetric paternalism is a purely consequentialist argument. As such, it is open to criticisms for not taking autonomy seriously. Read in a different way, this formula only illustrates the structure of the problem of legal paternalism. It does not serve to measure and quantify these variables, but to highlight who are the beneficiaries, and who are the cost bearers of a paternalistic intervention. These costs and benefits can be more precisely assessed in specific contexts.

5.2 "Libertarian Paternalism"

While "asymmetric paternalism" suggests policies that protect boundedly rational individuals while not (significantly) burdening others who do not need protection, "libertarian paternalism" draws attention to the different methods and techniques of this protection. More precisely, "libertarian paternalism" suggests policies that re-

32 Camerer et al. 2003, p. 1219.
33 Camerer et al. 2003, p. 1219.

spect the autonomy of boundedly rational people to the extent possible, but nevertheless helps them to avoid making bad choices.[34] It advocates paternalistic interventions mainly in the form of default rules and "menus." As we will see, contract law is the legal area *par excellence* where even non-mandatory rules can improve the welfare of the parties.

5.3 "Debiasing through Law"

Still another regulatory ideal, suggested by Christine Jolls and Cass Sunstein is more ambitious.[35] Instead of searching for legal rules which are adaptive to judgment and decision errors, it aims to reduce the occurrence of boundedly rational behavior at the first place. In addition, the novelty of this view is to suggest debiasing be achieved by exploiting (or at least relying on) bounded rationality itself. As already mentioned, psychologists have found several instances where biases interact, and more specifically, offset each other. In these cases, an intervention aimed at the reduction of only one of the biases can actually worsen the overall result. Now, the interaction between compensating biases may be deliberately designed and used by policymakers as well. Jolls and Sunstein illustrate, with examples from various legal areas, how legislators can make use of the presence of one psychological mechanism (e.g. the availability heuristic) in order to counteract the self-detrimental effects of another (e.g. over-optimism). One of their examples is consumer safety law.[36]

It is a well-established fact that consumers are asymmetrically uninformed about the safety features of most of the products they purchase. Mandatory disclosure requirements are a wide-spread legislative response to this kind of informational asymmetry, both in the United States and in Europe.[37] In principle, this is a preferable way of intervention, as information provision respects individual choice. In practice, disclosure does not necessarily work well. One reason for this is that people do not process the information in a rational way. Not only do they deviate from Bayesian theory. Even if their understanding (estimations) of the general risk probabilities is correct in a statistical sense, they are overly optimistic about the occurrence of safety risks in their own specific case. In the psychological literature this is called over-optimism bias. The idea of debiasing through law is to remedy this bias by making use of another, the availability heuristic. By using vivid and personified examples, the tendency towards underestimation of personal risks can be compensated. If people are confronted by a story about a recent real-life case of harm caused by a defective product, they become more aware or even overly aware of the risks involved.

To be sure, this rudimentary idea of debiasing through law should be refined in many ways before making actual use of it in information regulation. Even if the psychological argument is sound, a traditional legal scholar would definitely have a

34 Thaler – Sunstein 2003, Sunstein – Thaler 2003. For a restatement of their view see Thaler – Sunstein 2006.

35 Jolls – Sunstein 2006.

36 Jolls – Sunstein 2006, p. 215.

37 See e.g. Grundmann – Kerber – Weatherhill 2001.

large number of doctrinal and systemic arguments as to why the idea cannot be easily put in legal form.[38]

This brings us back to the core questions of this workshop: how, and to what extent can philosophical, economic, and psychological arguments be "imported" in legal discourses? Before answering this question directly, I should say a bit more about the methodological premises (assumptions, commitments) of the extended law and economics approach I am arguing for. Elaborating on these issues in the following section will hopefully provide some more general methodological lessons as well.

6 Methodological Lessons

In my view, in order to assess the problems of paternalism in contract law properly, an empirically based policy-oriented view is both fruitful and necessary. More generally, legal scholarship should take into account not only practical philosophy, but insights from both economic theory and empirical research as well.

6.1 Economists Learning from Law?

Specifically and succinctly, lawyers can, and should, learn from both economics and psychology. Or is it the other way around? Interestingly, Robert Cooter and Thomas Ulen, two eminent law and economics scholars suggest that this learning should *also* work the other way around. Economists should learn from law, most notably contract law. In the introductory chapter of what is probably the most popular textbook on the subject, they write: "*Economists frequently extol the virtues of voluntary exchange, but economics does not have a detailed account of what it means for an exchange to be voluntary.* [...]*[C]ontract law has a complex well-articulated theory of volition. If economists will listen to what the law has to teach them, they will find their models being drawn closer to reality.*"[39]

Although these sentences have been reprinted in the book several times since 1988, they seem to have elicited little formal comment. Nevertheless, their claim is far from trivial. In this statement Cooter and Ulen argue for a kind of import; if not from jurisprudence, at least from the law. In my view, even if this gesture of two economists towards lawyers is to be appreciated, it cannot be taken at face value. The "theory of volition" of contract law, well-articulated as it may be, is not well-founded theoretically.[40] In the law, this generally seems to be the case. Legal rules and doctrines doubtlessly often reflect practical rationality and offer at the level of folk psychology an intuitively appealing shortcut to endless philosophical debates. For instance, in many legal systems there is a close-to-ordinary-language or doctrinal-technical legal meaning to concepts like voluntariness, intent, or causation – the

38 Cf. Aaken 2006.

39 Cooter – Ulen 2004, p. 11.

40 Another problem is that, important overlaps notwithstanding, there are as many "theories of volition" as national (as well as infra- and supranational) contract laws.

former interpretation typically characterizes the Common law, the latter Continental legal rules. These legal concepts usually half-knowingly reflect philosophical or scientific standpoints of earlier ages[41] or just express some folk-psychological notions. For the everyday working of law as a practical enterprise these naive or common sense theories are fully satisfactory, at least in the so called 'easy cases'. But what the law says about voluntariness, causation etc. can be called a "theory" only in this "practical" sense.[42]

A further difficulty is that this "legal world view" is not of much help in policy design. It is impossible, for instance, to answer from a purely legal perspective how the legally required degree of voluntariness of contract formation, or the criteria for the judicial control of standard form contracts *should* be reasonably regulated. If we want to understand and/or criticize the rationale behind legal rules, then what law regulates in this or that way has to be analyzed and evaluated from an outside perspective, i.e. from a not strictly *legal* point of view.

6.2 Interdisciplinarity

Regarding the proper methods and scope of such a non-doctrinal analysis of legal issues, many methodological questions can be raised. Here, mention will only be made of a couple of points which help elucidate the methodological stance taken in this work.[43]

The reason why legal policy should be informed by empirical and theoretical research on human decision making and judgment is mainly instrumental. This information makes it possible to systematically predict the consequences of legal rules, and their alteration. Here, both economic and psychological insights are highly relevant.[44]

In modern societies law is often conceived of as a means to various policy ends. On the other hand, it is also understood as a system of institutional actions performed in the name of 'the law'. To the extent that legal discourse is formally rational, it has some autonomy that does not allow for the direct codification or application of any normative philosophy or the results of empirical research *in* law or *as* law.[45] In this sense, 'the law' is a specialized practical activity rather than a political or academic, i.e. scientific, or philosophical discussion.

41 "[T]he metaphysics of the Stone Age" (Hart – Honoré 1985, p. 2). These authors do not share the critique implied by the term.

42 For a classical analysis of causation from an "ordinary language philosophy" perspective see Hart – Honoré 1985. The rather innocent quote by Cooter and Ulen raises important jurisprudential and philosophical questions. The relations between folk psychology, legal epistemology and scientific knowledge are a fascinating research topic but it is beyond the scope of this work.

43 These questions are discussed extensively in the German-speaking law and economics literature. See e.g. Behrens 1986, Eidenmüller 1995, Aaken 2003.

44 This does not imply that law should have a "psychologically adequate" view of man. As I have mentioned above, there can be reasons for the law to deliberately deviate from such a "psychologically adequate" view.

45 On legal formalism see Kennedy 1973, 1976. Theorists like Luhmann and Teubner represent some version of this idea.

An important implication of this is that 'the law' as a practice cannot be suspended until the best theoretical solutions are found. Since time constraints are strict, resources, including expertise, are limited, and experimentation is exceptional, pragmatism and simple rules are used and needed.[46] In legislation and, to an even larger extent in adjudication, the use of external knowledge is limited by both systemic and practical considerations.

As to the incorporation of interdisciplinary knowledge in the theoretical understanding or analysis of law, these practical limits are irrelevant. On the other hand, whether the findings of (behavioral) economics are as relevant for jurisprudence proper, as for legal policy, is not straightforward. Much depends on the self-understanding (definition, purpose, methods) of legal scholarship itself.[47]

In this respect, I can only note a few points here. Economic, psychological, sociological etc. analyses *of* law are legitimate theoretical approaches. They provide insights to law from an external point of view. While such analyses do not *replace* doctrinal argumentation which has important separate functions to fulfill in a complex modern legal system, they interact with it in a number of ways. For the purposes of this paper one of these ways is especially relevant: economics, psychology, philosophy help scholars who criticize and improve legal rules and doctrines through policy recommendations.[48]

As I have argued, various factors place limits upon the *direct* usefulness of philosophy, economics and psychology in the development of legal policy and in jurisprudence. It is important to note however, that the proper role of economic and other non-legal insights in adjudication, or legal decision-making in general, cannot be determined generally: rather, it depends on a number of characteristics of legal decision-making (linked to various issues like discretion, expertise and legitimacy). Particular legal cultures (Continental, common law, and non-Western), national legal systems, or even legal areas (private law, administrative law, and criminal law) differ crucially along these dimensions. An important sub-question in this context concerns the role of consequentialist reasoning, especially that of economic analysis in legal decision-making.[49]

In various legal systems and in different legal areas, this role is considered to be different. As noted above, law as a practical institution needs, and has, some autonomy. One should avoid "the jurisprudential naïveté about the ultimate connection, if any, between […] economic analysis and the sort of argument that might be acceptable to courts."[50] This idea suggests that the direct impact of economic analysis on adjudication depends on the *canon of arguments* considered legitimate or ac-

46 There are various normative legal theories arguing for "simple rules", see e.g. Epstein 2006.

47 As Peter Behrens convincingly argues, the methodological self-understanding of "legal science" (Rechtswissenschaft) and economics has a crucial impact on the possible ways of their cooperation and the perspectives of interdisciplinary research on law and the economy (Behrens 1986, pp. 6–30).

48 Roughly, this is the way Hans Albert conceives of jurisprudence. See e.g. Albert 1972 1986 1992 1993.

49 On the role of consequentialist arguments in adjudication see e.g. Wälde 1979, Deckert 1995, Cane 2000. For two opposing views on the role of efficiency arguments in (German) law see Eidenmüller 1995: part IV, Kötz – Schäfer 2003: vi–viii.

50 Craswell 1993, p. 293.

ceptable within a particular legal system or legal area.[51] This reasoning applies to contracts and torts in common law as well. As Richard Craswell argued, "it is appropriate to regard each economic analysis as being limited by the preface" which makes clear that the particular efficiency arguments of the analysis should be considered by judges *to the extent prudential arguments are relevant*.[52] In brief, economic analysis is relevant in adjudication if and when prudential arguments in general are relevant.

To be sure, policy arguments are not necessarily addressed to judges. In other, non-judicial arenas other "canons of acceptable arguments" operate. As I argue below, for the issue of paternalism in contract law, the arena of legal policy is of primary relevance. Concerning the role of economic analysis in legal policy, it may be said it is both *vindicated* and *limited* by the following meta-criterion. "[E]conomic analysis can claim that its reasons justify outcomes because of the role the principle of efficiency plays in the overall set of institutions sanctioned by the normative political theory justifying political authority."[53]

To sum it up, while interdisciplinarity does not imply that lawyers should become economists, psychologists or philosophers, they should nevertheless rely both on a transparent normative theory about the goals to be achieved through law, and on empirical research about, and a theory of, human behavior facilitated and regulated by law. In the complex interrelations of empirical research, theoretical models and philosophical questions, multilateral translation and learning seem not only fruitful but necessary. In my particular subject, the need for "multilateral translation" is almost obvious, for a simple reason. Paternalism is a *philosophical* concept which is used in the analysis of *legal* problems with the tools of *economics*.

6.3 The Policy Perspective

Roughly speaking, one can distinguish three different discourses in which arguments from law and economics can be relevant. It can be conceived as a (consequentialist) normative legal philosophy; as an explanatory theory of law (rational choice theory applied to law); and as a set of propositions for legal reform (legal policy).

In the first branch, what I mean by law and economics as legal philosophy is a normative analysis dealing mainly with questions regarding the justifiability of adopting efficiency as the main guiding principle of law.[54] In the second, explanatory branch, law and economics seeks either to explain how law influences human behavior by changing incentives (law as *explanans*), or to analyze legal, and possibly non-legal, rules as the outcome of interactions between rational individuals (law as *explanandum*). The emergence and change of legal rules and doctrines are the subject matter of "positive political economy" or public choice theory. Finally, by law and

51 On the "canon of acceptable arguments" see Honoré 1973, pp. 64–66.
52 Craswell 1993, pp. 292–293.
53 Kraus 2006, p. 15.
54 For book-length arguments for efficiency in this respect see Posner 1981, Kaplow – Shavell 2002. For discussion and criticism see the still informative collection of articles in Symposium 1980, especially Kornhauser 1980.

economics as legal policy it is meant: a more or less coherent system of proposals for reforming legal rules in order to fulfill certain given or hypothetical normative criteria, among which efficiency has primary importance.

As with categorizations usually, this one is useful if it helps systematize our arguments. Thus the main research questions addressed by the paper can be grouped into three categories which correspond to the three levels of economic analysis.

(1) Conceptual and normative questions. What does paternalism mean? Is it justified to limit someone's freedom in order to promote his interests? If so, in which cases, to what extent, and by whom? Why and to what extent do we need freedom of contract? What are legitimate reasons for interfering with contracts?

(2) Empirical questions. Do people generally, and in given contexts, choose rationally? Do they evaluate risks correctly? How do they process the information available to them? How do individuals (consumers) and legal entities (firms) react to different regulations? What are the side-effects and possible non-intended consequences of contract regulation?

(3) Policy questions. Assuming sub-optimal contracts may occur, should the law interfere with contractual agreements in which one party was not fully informed, or not fully rational? If so, which instruments would be most applicable to achieve this? What are the legal, political and other institutions or mechanisms most suitable in any given case?

Obviously, the questions raised on each of these levels are linked to each other. Most importantly, the third level of analysis relies on both the first and the second level. As legal policy refers to a more or less coherent system of proposals for reforming or interpreting legal rules, the basic idea behind such proposals is that the law should fulfill certain, either hypothetically or tacitly accepted, normative criteria. In the law and economics literature, Pareto or, more often, Kaldor-Hicks, efficiency is the most important of these criteria.[55] In this work, the analysis is based on arguments regarding the justification of certain instances of paternalism, and some empirical facts or hypotheses concerning the effects of freedom of choice and legal intervention. These are combined in order to contribute to a legal policy discourse regarding the possible legal means for achieving certain normative goals in an effective way.

6.4 Extending Standard Methods

In the quote above Cooter and Ulen also suggest, rightly, that sometimes legal problems draw attention to highly important questions, to which standard economic analysis does not offer any well-developed answer. Arguably, the meaning and value of freedom of choice and the arguments for or against paternalism are such ques-

55 A social arrangement (the allocation of resources) is Pareto-efficient if reallocation can make nobody better off without making somebody worse off than in the status quo. When it is possible to make at least one person better off without making anybody worse off, we speak about a Pareto improvement. In contrast, a change is called potential Pareto improvement if the winners' gains from the change are higher than the losses of the losers, so that the former are capable to compensate the latter. Such changes are also called Kaldor-Hicks improvement. For technically precise definitions and refinements see Zerbe 2001.

tions. This observation raises the methodological question, whether and how the traditional economic arguments against paternalism and for freedom of contract should be reassessed in light of recent empirical and theoretical studies. If Cooter and Ulen are right, then law and economics scholars should be open to insights coming from elsewhere. While the methodological starting point of policy-oriented legal research should be rational choice theory, as applied in the law and economics literature, limitations, corrections and extensions to this approach should be taken into account.[56]

As we have seen, the standard law and economics literature usually rejects paternalism as a bad reason for limiting freedom of contract. This view is neither, however, strongly nor coherently argued. First, it largely fails to take into account relevant empirical facts about contracting behavior. Second, it generally uses a strange mixture of liberal and utilitarian (welfarist) arguments without reflecting about their relationship. As I have illustrated, the tools recently developed within two branches of economic theory can contribute to an approach to paternalism which is simultaneously more coherent and richer in nuances than the traditional law and economics perspective. By reconsidering standard economic arguments and confronting them with psychological, philosophical and jurisprudential considerations, I suggest enriching and modifying the traditional law and economics arguments about paternalism in two main ways. The first way is to incorporate the empirical findings of behavioral decision theory which offer a more realistic view of the situations susceptible for paternalistic intervention. The second is to take into account insights from the analysis of freedom of choice in social choice theory concerning the possibility to include the non-welfarist dimension of the subject in economic analysis.

Instead of discussing the benefits and methodological difficulties of incorporating these ideas, methods and results in legal scholarship *in abstracto*, these questions should be dealt with in the context of specific issues. Here I merely note that these methodological extensions have consequences for all three levels or types of legal discourse. On the level of normative political and legal philosophy the problem of autonomy makes economic theories on freedom of choice and a non-instrumental analysis of opportunities relevant. On the level of explanatory social science the empirical results and theoretical constructs of psychology come into play. Furthermore, the level of legal policy should rely on the two other levels, and finally, in order to avoid *naïveté* or the accusation of being dictatorial, it has to take into account the politico-institutional framework within which the legal policymaking of a modern democracy operates.[57]

56 On rational choice theory in law and economics see Ulen 2000.

57 Cf. how James Gordley concludes his paper on paternalism in contract law: "This Essay may have disappointed the reader because it does not attempt to prove which particular voluntary agreements the state should prohibit, require, encourage, discourage, or fund. If those issues were subject to proof, academics should rule the world. In our society, such decisions must be left to the prudence of the citizens, to that of leaders whom one hopes are prudently elected, and subject to constitutional constraints that one hopes are prudently imposed. That is what one might expect in a representative democracy." (Gordley 2007, p. 1772) While I do not fundamentally disagree with this, being at an earlier stage in my career I allow myself to be somewhat more trustful in academics and the role of proofs.

Literature

Aaken, Anne van (2003): Rational-Choice in der Rechtswissenschaft Zum Stellenwert der ökonomischen Theorie im Recht. Baden-Baden.

Aaken, Anne van (2006): 'Begrenzte Rationalität und Paternalismus: Rationalitätssteigerung durch rechtliche Verfahren?' in Paternalismus und Recht In memoriam Angela Augustin (1968–2004), Hrsg. Michael Anderheiden – Peter Bürkli – Hans Michael Heinig – Stephan Kirste – Kurt Seelmann. Tübingen, pp. 109–144.

Albert, Hans (1972): 'Erkenntnis und Recht. Die Jurisprudenz im Lichte des Kritizismus' in Rechtstheorie Grundlagenwissenschaft der Rechtswissenschaft, Hrsg. Hans Albert – Niklas Luhmann – Werner Maihofer – Ota Weinberger. Düsseldorf, pp. 80–96 [Jahrbuch für Rechtssoziologie und Rechtstheorie Bd. 2].

Albert, Hans (1986): 'Law as an Instrument of Rational Practice' in Contract and Organization Legal Analysis in the Light of Economic and Social Theory, ed. Terence Daintith – Günther Teubner. Berlin – New York, pp. 25–51.

Albert, Hans (1992): 'Zur Kritik der reiner Jurisprudenz. Recht und Rechtswissenschaft in der Sicht des kritischen Rationalismus' in Demokratie und Rationalität, Hrsg. Ota Weinberger – Michael W. Fischer. Wien, pp. 343–357 [Internationales Jahrbuch für Rechtsphilosophie und Gesetzgebung].

Albert, Hans (1993): Rechtswissenschaft als Realwissenschaft Das Recht als soziale Tatsache und die Aufgabe der Jurisprudenz. Baden-Baden [Würzburger Vorträge zur Rechtsphilosophie, Rechtstheorie und Rechtssoziologie, Heft 15].

Baldwin, John W. (1959): 'The Medieval Theories of Just Price: Romanists, Canonists, and Theologians in the Twelfth and Thirteenth Centuries' Transactions of the American Philosophical Society, New Series vol. 49 pt. 4.

Behrens, Peter (1986): Grundlagen einer ökonomischen Theorie des Rechts. Tübingen

Bigwood, Rick (2004): Exploitative Contracts. Oxford – New York.

Blumenthal, Jeremy A. (2007): 'Emotional Paternalism' Florida State University Law Review 35, pp. 1–72.

Brock, Dan W. (1988): 'Paternalism and Autonomy' Ethics 98, pp. 550–565.

Burrows, Paul (1993): 'Patronising Paternalism' Oxford Economic Papers 45, pp. 542–572.

Burrows, Paul (1995): 'Analysing Legal Paternalism' International Review of Law and Economics 15, pp. 489–508.

Burrows, Paul (1998): 'Legal Paternalism and Efficiency' in The New Palgrave Dictionary of Economics and the Law, ed. Peter Newman. London – New York, vol. 2, pp. 539–542.

Camerer, Colin et al. (2003): 'Regulation for Conservatives: Behavioral Economics and the Case for »Asymmetric Paternalism«' University of Pennsylvania Law Review 151, pp. 1211–1254.

Camerer, Colin F. – George Loewenstein – Matthew Rabin (eds.) (2004): Advances in Behavioral Economics. Princeton.

Cane, Peter (2000): 'Consequences in Judicial Reasoning' in Oxford Essays in Jurisprudence (Fourth Series), ed. Jeremy Horder. Oxford, pp. 41–59.

Craswell, Richard (1993): 'Default Rules, Efficiency, and Prudence' Southern California Interdisciplinary Law Journal 3, pp. 289–302.

Cserne, Péter (2008): Freedom of Choice and Paternalism in Contract law: Prospects and Limits of an Economic Approach PhD Thesis Submitted at the University of Hamburg, Faculty of Law.

Deckert, Martina Renate (1995): Folgenorientierung in der Rechtsanwendung. Munich.

Eidenmüller, Horst (1995): Effizienz als Rechtsprinzip Möglichkeiten und Grenzen der ökonomischen Analyse des Rechts. Tübingen.

Eidenmüller, Horst (2005): 'Der homo oeconomicus und das Schuldrecht. Herausforderungen durch Behavioural Law and Economics' in Juristische Grundlagenforschung – Tagung der Deutschen Sektion der Internationalen Vereinigung für Rechts- und Sozialphilosophie (IVR) vom 23. bis 25. September 2004 in Kiel, Hrsg. Robert Alexy. Stuttgart, pp. 13–28.

Englerth, Markus (2004): Behavioral Law and Economics – eine kritische Einführung. Preprints of the Max Planck Institute for Research on Collective Goods, Bonn 2004/11, online: http://www.mpp-rdg.mpg.de/pdf_dat/2004_11online.pdf

Epstein, Richard A. (2006): 'The Optimal Complexity of Legal Rules' in Heuristics and the Law, ed. Gerd Gigerenzer – Christoph Engel. Boston, pp. 141–157.
Feinberg, Joel (1986): Harm to Self. Oxford.
Gordley, James (2007): 'Morality and Contract: The Question of Paternalism' William and Mary Law Review 48, pp. 1733–1772.
Grundmann, Stefan – Wolfgang Kerber – Stephen Weatherhill (eds.; 2001): Party Autonomy and the Role of Information in the Internal Market. Berlin – New York.
Hart, Herbert L.A. – Tony Honoré (1985): Causation in the Law, 2nd ed. Oxford.
Head, John G. 1966. 'On Merit Goods' Finanzarchiv 25, pp. 1–29.
Hermalin, Benjamin E. – Avery W. Katz – Richard Craswell (2006): 'Chapter on the Law & Economics of Contacts' in The Handbook of Law & Economics, ed. A. Mitchell Polinsky – Steven Shavell, online: http://ssrn.com/abstract=907678.
Honoré, A.M. (1973): 'Legal Reasoning in Rome and Today' Cambrian Law Review 4, pp. 58–67.
Hynes, Richard – Eric A. Posner (2002): 'The Law and Economics of Consumer Finance' American Law and Economics Review 4, pp. 168–207.
Jolls, Christine – Cass R. Sunstein – Richard H. Thaler (2000): 'A Behavioral Approach to Law and Economics' in Sunstein (ed.), pp. 13–58.
Jolls, Christine – Sunstein, Cass R. (2006): 'Debiasing Through Law' Journal of Legal Studies 35, pp. 199–242.
Kaplow, Louis – Steven Shavell (2002): Fairness vs Welfare. Cambridge, Mass.
Kennedy, Duncan (1973): 'Legal Formality' Journal of Legal Studies 2, pp. 351–398.
Kennedy, Duncan (1976): 'Form and Substance in Private Law Adjudication' Harvard Law Review 89, pp. 1685–1778.
Klick, Jonathan – Gregory Mitchell (2006): 'Government Regulation of Irrationality: Moral and Cognitive Hazards' Minnesota Law Review 90, pp. 1620–1663.
Kornhauser, Lewis A. (1980): 'A Guide to the Perplexed Claims of Efficiency in the Law' Hofstra Law Review 8, pp. 591–639.
Korobkin, Russell (2002): 'Empirical Scholarship in Contract Law: Possibilities and Pitfalls' University of Illinois Law Review 2002, pp. 1033–1060.
Korobkin, Russell – Thomas Ulen (2000): 'Law and Behavioral Science: Removing the Rationality Assumption from Law and Economics' California Law Review 88, pp. 1051–1144.
Kötz, Hein – Hans-Bernd Schäfer (2003): Judex Oeconomicus 12 höchstrichterliche Entscheidungen kommentiert aus ökonomischer Sicht. Tübingen.
Kraus, Jody S. (2006): 'A Philosophical Approach to the Economic Analysis of Contract Law' [Scholarship Profile] Virginia Journal 9, pp. 7–23.
Meagher, Partick (2005): 'Microfinance Regulation and Supervision in South Africa' Essays on Regulation and Supervision, No. 6. (April 2005), online: http://www.microfinancegateway.com/files/25525_file_South_Africa.pdf
Menyhárd Attila (2004): A jóerkölcsbe ütközö szerzō dések [Contracts against Good Morals] Budapest.
Mitchell, Gregory (2002): 'Why Law and Economics' Perfect Rationality Should Not Be Traded for Behavioral Law and Economics' Georgetown Law Journal 91, pp. 67–167.
Musgrave, Richard A. (1987): 'Merit Goods' The New Palgrave A Dictionary of Economics, ed. John Eatwell – Murray Milgate – Peter Newman. New York – London, vol. 3, pp. 452–453.
Posner, Richard A. (1981): The Economics of Justice. Cambridge; Mass.
Posner, Richard A. (1995): Overcoming Law. Cambridge, Mass.
Posner, Richard A. (1998): Economic Analysis of Law, 5th ed. New York.
Rachlinski, Jeffrey J. (2003): 'The Uncertain Psychological Case for Paternalism' Northwestern University Law Review 97, pp. 1165–1225.
Rachlinski, Jeffrey J. (2006): 'The Psychological Foundation of Behavioral Law and Economics' Keynote address at the conference on Behavioral and Experimental Law and Economics: Applications and Methodology, University of Haifa Faculty of Laws, Haifa, Israel, June 26, 2006.
Rawls, John B. (1993): Political Liberalism. Cambridge, Mass.
Saint-Paul, Gilles (2004): 'Policy Consequences of Limited Cognitive Ability' Spanish Economic Review 6, pp. 97–105.

Sen, Amartya K. (1970): 'The Impossibility of a Paretian Liberal' Journal of Political Economy 78, pp. 152–157.
Sen, Amartya K. (2002): Rationality and Freedom. Cambridge, Mass.
Sugden, Robert (1998): 'The Metric of Opportunity' Economics and Philosophy 14, 307–337.
Sunstein, Cass R. (ed., 2000): Behavioral Law and Economics. Cambridge.
Sunstein, Cass R. – Richard H. Thaler (2003): 'Libertarian Paternalism Is Not an Oxymoron' University of Chicago Law Review 70, pp. 1159–1202.
Sunstein, Cass R. – Richard H. Thaler (2006): 'Preferences, Paternalism, and Liberty' Preferences and Well-Being (Royal Institute of Philosophy Supplement: 59), ed. Serena Olsaretti. Cambridge.
Symposium (1980): Efficiency as a Legal Concern. Hofstra Law Review 8, pp. 485–770.
Symposium (2004): Freedom from Contract. Wisconsin Law Review 2004, pp. 261–836.
Thaler, Richard H. – Sunstein, Cass R. (2003): 'Libertarian Paternalism' American Economic Review 93, pp. 175–179.
Trebilcock, Michael J. (1993): The Limits of Freedom of Contract. Cambridge, Mass.
Trout, J.D. (2005): 'Paternalism and Cognitive Bias' Law and Philosophy 24, pp. 393–434.
Ulen, Thomas S. (2000): 'Rational Choice Theory in Law and Economics' in Encyclopedia of Law and Economics Vol I. The History and Methodology of Law and Economics, ed. Boudewijn Bouckaert – Gerrit de Geest. Cheltenham, UK, pp. 790–818.
Van Hees, Martin (2004): Modeling Freedom: Formal Analysis and Normative Philosophy, online: http://www.philos.rug.nl/%7Emartin/vici/Vici_ModellingFreedomWV2.pdf
Wälde, Thomas W. (1979): Juristische Folgenorientierung: »Policy analysis« und Sozalkybernetik Methodologische und organisatorische Überlegungen zur Bewältigung der Folgenorientierung im Rechtssystem. Königstein.
Zamir, Eyal (1998): 'The Efficiency of Paternalism' Virginia Law Review 84, pp. 229–286.
Zerbe, Richard O. Jr. (2001): Economic Efficiency in Law and Economics. Cheltenham, UK.

Part II

Constitutionalism

Edited by
A. v. Aaken and *P. Policastro*

Anne van Aaken*

A Functional Approach to International Constitutionalism

The Value Added of a Social Science Contribution

Abstract:
Die Frage des "ob" und des "wie" der Interaktion zwischen Rechtswissenschaft und Sozialwissenschaften ist ein alte, immer wiederkehrende. Begreift man Recht als den wichtigsten Ordnungsfaktor der Gesellschaft wie auch der internationalen Gemeinschaft, so ist es sinnvoll, eine funktionale Betrachtungsweise einzunehmen. Dies gilt umso mehr in Zeiten der Globalisierung und Europäisierung, in denen sich gleichzeitig der Schwerpunkt der juristischen Tätigkeit insgesamt mehr und mehr von einer anwendungsbezogenen Interpretationswissenschaft hin zu einer steuerungsorientierten Handlungs- und Entscheidungswissenschaft verlagert. Aufbauend auf einer alten Kategorisierung von Hermann Kantorowicz, werden unterschiedliche methodische Aussagen der Rechtswissenschaft klassifiziert. Dies erlaubt es, Einfallstore (und Grenzen) für sozialwissenschaftliche Aussagen genauer zu umreißen und ein funktionales Verständnis der völkerrechtlichen Konstitutionalisierungsdebatte zu zeichnen. Die Auffindung und Verwendung gemeinsamer Verfassungsprinzipien im Völkerrecht sind nur ein erster Schritt; notwendig, aber nicht hinreichend, um dem Anliegen der Konstitutionalisierung des Völkerrechts Substanz zu verleihen. Es bedarf dafür weiterhin einer funktionale Betrachtungsweise, die sich sozialwissenschaftlicher Erkenntnisse bedient und die (rechtlichen) Mittel betrachtet, die notwendig sind, um den gemeinsam gefundenen Prinzipien Wirkung zu verleihen.

1 Introduction

"Eureka! Social Science discovers constitutionalism (and constitutional lawyers discover social science)" – so Joseph H.H. Weiler in 1997.[1] Is this wishful thinking or description of the status quo? He answers the question himself and not much has changed since then: "The principal, and uniquely rich, contribution to constitutionalism of the German literature has been, as in religion, to its dogmatics. With some notable exceptions, in the field of European Law, German (and most other Continental) constitutionalists have not sought to integrate social and political science into their work."[2] About the same diagnosis can be made for Public International Law (PIL) in the year 2008.

Though international constitutionalism is an ever more explored subject by international law scholars, many questions remain to be answered. What is the legal nature of international constitutionalism (descriptive dimension), how can it be explained and rationally construed (explanatory dimension), and what goals should it pursue (normative dimension)?[3] The first as well as the third question have been

* I would like to thank the participants of the IVR Special Workshops 2007 in Krakow as well as Stefan Voigt and Rekha Oleschak for very helpful comments.

1 Joseph H.H. Weiler, "The Reformation of European Constitutionalism", Journal of Common Market Studies 35 (1997), pp. 97–131, 102.

2 Ibid., p. 128.

3 For an analysis of the narratives of European Constitutionalism (whose basic tenets and problems do not differ that much from international constitutionalism, though it certainly is more progressed), see Matej Avbelj, "Questioning EU Constitutionalism", German Law Journal 9 (2008), pp. 1–26 (online journal).

explored already in more detail. I submit though, that the explanatory dimension is still largely missing in international legal scholarship, though not in neighboring disciplines, such as political science or economics. If the agenda of international constitutionalism is to be pursued (certainly not an uncontested goal, but taken as given here), the explanatory social science dimension cannot be missing. It is uniquely qualified for uncovering weaknesses in PIL as well as for showing possibilities to render PIL (constitutionalism) more effective. In other words: this dimension checks whether constitutional functions are effectively fulfilled de facto and do not only remain black letter law. Normative agendas or visions how the international order[4] is to be constructed without reality grounding and check are seldom successful. If a move beyond constitutional nominalism is desired, it needs to be backed up by solid social science research.

This paper tries to show that interdisciplinary work may be fruitful under certain conditions and if there is a precise understanding of the legal methodology as well as scientific theoretical background of the statements made within the work. To be clear: a so-understood functional approach to international constitutionalism necessarily needs to build on thorough doctrinal work and a legally systemic view. Furthermore, I am not proposing a normatively different view than that of international constitutionalism. My *petitum* here is to add one more useful element, the social science element, to the research on international constitutionalism, considering the reality grounding of constitutionalism as a more solid building brick. It is also necessary in a world where the (international) legal profession moves more and more from a perspective of pure legal application to a perspective of governance. This is all the more so in a time of globalization and Europeanization where the understanding of the governance mechanisms of trans-, supra- and international problems becomes a prerequisite even for the application of national laws.

The question of how legal and social science relate to each other and might or might not be fruitfully combined has been debated for a long time already. Different scholars find different answers and take very different views. Whether social science may have any place in (doctrinal) jurisprudence is at the heart of the matter. By understanding law as the most important ordering factor in a nation state as well as in the international community, a functional approach to law is taken, as this view enables to argue why and how the ordering works. I will thus concentrate on the question of how legal methodology may incorporate positive science (in the social science sense). The argument can be made *a fortiori* for questions of legal policy, institutional design as well as constitutional design, in the field of international constitutionalism. It is also a pressing and under-researched issue in the international constitutionalism debate which concentrates mainly on the descriptive and normative questions. The paper outlines the opening windows and connecting bridges to social science with legal methodology and hints at where those windows become more widely open in institutional design with a special view to international constitutionalism. The main submission of the paper is that it is time to move

4 Pierre-Marie Dupuy, "Taking International Law Seriously. On the German Approach to International Law", EUI-Working Papers Law No. 2007/34 (2007) primarily describes the German Scholarship as visionary, certainly explicable with a deep desire to re-integrate Germany in the international community after WW II.

on in the international constitutionalism debate: for those scholars who agree on the goal of constitutionalizing the international world order, it is not enough to state normative goals or values contained in the project, rather one needs to start with the back-breaking work of careful doctrinal description (done to a great part) enriched by social science which allows to construct effective institutions (not done yet). The article is – due to page restraints – necessarily nothing more than a methodological proposal, unable to do the exercise itself.

First, the article gives an overview on the debate on constitutionalism in international law scholarship (II.). It then moves on to explain the basic methodological tenets which are used, rather implicitly, in that debate. I propose to use a methodologically clear and explicit framework in order to first clarify the debate, and secondly clarify where the desiderata of further research lie (III.). In the next part, some examples are given of how to use social science, e.g. rational choice, in order to construct an effective international legal order (IV.). The last part concludes.

2 Constitutionalism in International Law

The term constitutionalism is to be found in national, European and – more recently – in international legal debates. Mostly, the debates on hierarchy, on fragmentation, on de-consensualization in PIL, on novel structures such as administrative networks are closely connected to the debate on international constitutionalism. This ever broader debate cannot be reflected here but will only be alluded to if necessary; I will concentrate on constitutionalism only. The understandings behind the term constitutionalism differ wildly, also due to different ideas hidden behind it, but some basic tenets can be filtered out. First, the terms constitutionalism (the perspective), constitution (the framework), and constitutionalization (the process) have to be clarified. Secondly, I will shortly sketch the legal phenomena which are mainly discussed in the international constitutionalism debate.

2.1 The Notion of Constitutionalism

Let me begin again with a quote from Joseph Weiler: "Constitutionalism is, too (some would say only), but a prism through which one can observe a landscape in a certain way, an academic artefact with which one can organize the milestones and landmarks within the landscape (indeed, determine what is a landmark or milestone), an intellectual construct by which one can assign meaning to, or even constitute that which is observed."[5] Of course, ideas create reality[6] and if ideas are taken as normative goals, they need to take the real world into account to become reality.

5 Weiler (Fn. 1), p. 99. Similar Anne Peters, "Compensatory Constitutionalism: The Function and Potential of Fundamental International Norms and Structures", Leiden Journal of International Law 19 (2006), pp. 579–610, 605, who correctly points out that the hermeneutic premise makes reconstruction of (legal) texts not only necessary but is unthinkable without interpretation.

6 As was wonderfully exposed by Umberto Eco, Il pendolo di Foucault 1988 for religious ideas.

Having said that, let us start with the definitions of constitutionalism in international legal scholarship.[7] There is no accepted definition of constitutionalism, neither in national law nor in PIL.[8] Rather, it has to be understood as a "frame of reference for a viable and legitimate regulatory framework for any political community".[9] It is the notional container used for "a legal argument which recommends and strengthens efforts (legal and political) to compensate for ongoing de-constitutionalization on the domestic level".[10] Here, it becomes clear already that the notion of constitutionalism has a strong normative agenda *de lege ferenda*, mixed with descriptive elements. What is missing is the explanatory social science basis.

In the current discussion, two foci can be distinguished.[11] Whereas some scholars have focused on the question whether there are international constitutional dimensions as a legally binding framework for international organizations,[12] states or the international community respectively,[13] the other parts have focused on defining the substratum, that is, the community for which the constitution is designed, e.g. on the question whether it is possible to filter a notional evolution for an international community without the necessary element of the state.[14] Both of these are "striving for a global legal community that frames and directs political power in light of common values and a common good,"[15] and are thus pursuing normative legal policy goals.

7 For a very good overview on the definitions, see Peters (Fn. 5), pp. 581 ff.

8 Cf. Lawrence Alexander, Constitutionalism, in: Contemporary Debates in Political Philosophy, ed. by Thomas Christiano/John Christman 2004, available at SSRN: http://ssrn.com/abstract=802885.

9 Erika de Wet, "The International Constitutional Order", International and Comparative Law Quarterly 55 (2006), pp. 51–76, 52 f.

10 Peters (Fn. 5), p. 579.

11 Christian Walter, "Constitutionalizing (inter)national Governance", German Yearbook of International Law 44 (2001), pp. 170–201, 171.

12 Often the foundational treaties of international organizations are viewed as partial constitutions, e.g. for the WTO, the WHO, the UN. Those functional constitutions thus embody the "legal framework within which an autonomous community of a functional (sectoral) nature realizes its respective functional goal, e.g. trade liberalization, human rights protection, or the maintenance of international peace and security, see de Wet (Fn. 9), 53 and Walter (Fn. 11), pp. 193 ff. For the WTO, see Ernst-Ulrich Petersmann, "Human Rights, Constitutionalism and the World Trade Organization", Leiden Journal of International Law 19 (2006), 633–667.

13 E.g. Pierre-Marie Dupuy, "The Constitutional Dimension of the Charter of the United Nations Revisited", Max Planck Yearbook of United Nations Law 1 (1997), pp. 1–33 and Bardo Fassbender, "The United Nations Charter as Constitution of the International Community", Columbia Journal of Transnational Law 36 (1998), pp. 529–619.

14 See instead of many Bruno Simma/Andreas L. Paulus, "The "International Community": Facing the Challenge of Globalization", European Journal of International Law 9 (1998), pp. 266–277; Andreas L. Paulus, Die internationale Gemeinschaft im Völkerrecht, München: Beck 2001 and Christian Tomuschat, "International Law: Ensuring the Survival of Mankind on the Eve of a New Century, General Course on Public International Law", Recueil des Cours / Académie de Droit International de La Haye 281 (1999), pp. 13–438, 161 f. See also Walter (Fn. 11), 172, citing Art. 42 lit. b and 48 Sec. 1 lit. b ILC Draft Articles on State Responsibility (UN Doc. A/CN.4/L.602/Rev.1.(2001)) which refers only to the "international community" but not the "international Community of States" as in Art. 53 VCLT.

15 Armin von Bogdandy, "Constitutionalism in International Law", Harvard International Law Journal 47 (2006), pp. 223–242, 223.

Constitutionalism has to be differentiated from constitution. Constitution is traditionally associated with nation states, even more so among German scholars, where this is even reflected in the notions used (Verfassungs*staat*, Rechts*staat*, *Staats*-volk) which makes it difficult for German scholars to think a constitution without a state and its demos.[16] This historical understanding of a constitution with its restrictive terminology (in German) is not used here as a functional approach is taken. Following others, I will understand constitution in a normative sense as the sum of the basic and materially most important legal norms which comprehensively regulate the social and political life of a polity and usually have special impediments for changeability.[17] The norms do not have to be written in one single document.[18] They include the most basic value of a polity as well as institutional and procedural organization of the same.

Constitutionalization denotes the process by which constitutional law comes into being; the emergence of constitutional law. There is broad consensus that PIL has developed immensely after WW II and is ever more restricting the sovereignty of states, their *domaine reservé* (how one judges that process is another normative question). Whereas most scholars draw a distinction between the old law of coexistence, the interim law of cooperation, and now the process of constitutionalization,[19] Tomuschat uses four steps to describe the evolution: first, PIL as a law of coexistence; second, PIL as a law of cooperation; third, PIL as a comprehensive blueprint for social life; and fourth, PIL of the international community.[20]

This process came about due to the de-territorialization of economic, environmental and social problems, creating an ever more problematic disability of the nation-state alone to continue to fulfill its traditional functions such as regulating social order and protecting its citizens. Increased global interdependence and transnational actions building up transnational networks call for more dense international norms: not only due to new real world developments, which require international regulation, but also in order to compensate for deficits of fulfilling the traditional functions of the state[21] and its subsequent disaggregation due to delegated

16 For a critique, see Brun-Otto Bryde, "Konstitutionalisierung des Völkerrechts und Internationalisierung des Verfassungsrechts", Der Staat 42 (2003), pp. 61–75, 61 f. Of course, there are substantive reasons behind this "thick" notion of constitution which is said to need a demos (Staatsvolk): see only Dieter Grimm, "The Constitution in the Process of Denationalization", Constellations 12 (2005), 447–463 and Josef Isensee, Staat und Verfassung, in: Isensee/Kirchhof, HdbStR I (1987), § 13.

17 See similarly Peters (Fn. 5), p. 581 who does not take into account the changeability.

18 As e.g. the British and the Israeli Constitutions show which are functioning without a formal, integrated, written constitution. In 1995, the Israeli Supreme Court held that the 11 periodically enacted Basic Laws would function as the nation's constitution, and that the Court would exercise an American-style power of judicial review.

19 See Peters (Fn. 5), p. 580 and Ronald MacDonald/Douglas M. Johnston (eds.), Towards World Constitutionalism: Issues in the Legal Ordering of the World Community, Leiden: Nijhoff 2005.

20 Tomuschat (Fn. 14), pp. 56–88. See also for an analysis of the General Course of Tomuschat, von Bogdandy (Fn. 15).

21 Peters (Fn. 5) who talks about compensatory constitutionalism. Anne-Marie Slaughter, A New World Order Princeton: Princeton University Press 2004, bases her assessment of the changing international order more on the less visible, but even more forceful regulatory and judicial networks.

norm generation of International Organizations, transnational cooperation of executive bodies in networks as, e.g., in the European comitology or in the Basel Committee for Banking Supervision,[22] as well as more prominent private standard setting.[23] Some scholars, however, view the possibility of compensation of the loss of constitutional functions as idealistic: "(…) it is inevitable that, for the time being, a bundling of constitutional functions as it has been achieved by the nation state will remain impossible. It has been lost in the level of the nation state and, at the moment, it cannot be achieved elsewhere."[24]

In order to illustrate the process of constitutionalization, authors mainly focus on substantive issue areas which show a tendency to restrict national sovereignty in a yet unknown way.[25] Those are foremost the basic values which constitute a common core of values of the international community (of states), fulfilling certain functions. A focus on the constitutional functions allows transposing the term constitutionalism to the European Communities as well as to the international sphere. Here therefore, international constitutional law is defined, following Peters, as "the bulk of the most important norms which regulate political activity and relationships in the global polity (consisting of states and other subjects of international law)."[26] Of course, there is no exact consensus of what constitutional functions are but again some common ground can be filtered out. More abstractly a constitution is supposed to limit, guide and legitimize politics.[27] There are different definitions of functions to be found – a more minimalist notion suffices with only organizing and institutionalizing a polity. A more specific notion relates to "rules and principles *fulfilling typical constitutional functions* … (that) constitute a political entity as a legal entity, to organize it, to limit political power, to offer political and moral guidelines, to justify governance, and, finally, to contribute to integration."[28] Peters defines a more normative value-laden function, namely to legitimize a constitution. Here, substantive functions are added, such as human rights, the separation of powers as necessary elements as well as other functions, such as democracy and a minimum of social security guarantees.[29] More specifically for the international sphere, Tomuschat views this thick constitutional function with respect to PIL in "safeguarding

22 See ibid. For financial markets, see Anne van Aaken, Democracy in Times of Transnational Administrative Law: The Case of Financial Markets, in: Perspectives and Limits of Democracy, ed. by Harald Eberhard/Konrad Lachmayer/Gregor Ribarov/Gerhard Thallinger, Vienna: WUV/Nomos 2008, pp. 41–61.

23 See Walter (Fn. 11), pp. 173, 188.

24 Walter (Fn. 11), p. 188.

25 E.g. Jochen Abr. Frowein, Konstitutionalisierung des Völkerrechts, in: Völkerrecht und Internationales Privatrecht in einem sich globalisierenden internationalen System, ed. by Klaus Dicke, Heidelberg: Müller 2000, pp. 427–447.

26 Peters (Fn. 5), p. 582 as well as de Wet (Fn. 9), p. 53: "This article extends the use of the term constitution … to describe a system in which the different national regional and functional (sectoral) constitutional regimes form the building blocks of the international community ("international polity") that is underpinned by a core value system common to all communities and embedded in a variety of legal structures for its enforcement."

27 Von Bogdandy (Fn. 15), and Peters (Fn. 5), p. 585.

28 Peters (Fn. 5), 585 and more extensively Anne Peters, Elemente einer Theorie der Verfassung Europas Berlin: Duncker & Humblot 2001.

29 Peters (Fn. 5), p. 585.

international peace, security and justice in relations between States, and human rights as well as the rule of law domestically inside States for the benefit of human beings, who, in substance, are the ultimate addressees of International Law."[30] Thus, classical functions of the nation state such as safeguarding individual liberty, freedom and safety are (partly) transferred to the international sphere. Nevertheless, there is no consensus, whether constitutionalism is to be viewed as a phenomenon for the whole of the international community or whether it takes place only in sectorial regimes, such as, e.g., WTO law.[31]

2.2 Legal Phenomena of International Constitutionalism

As mentioned, the "descriptive" or doctrinal case *de lege lata* to be found for international constitutionalism has to be unearthed in different sectoral developments, filtered out by inductive doctrinal work; the legal phenomena being the "empirical" material. A holistic view on these may hint to constitutionalization. The issue areas to be found are mainly international human rights which have a tendency to supersede national constitutional law, international humanitarian law, self-determination, international criminal law which holds individuals responsible under PIL, the ever more extensive legislating practice of the United Nations Security Council when acting under Chapter VII of the UN Charter, some aspects of international environmental law as well as international investment law, giving individuals and firms actionable rights for suing states without exhaustion of local remedies. More principle-based phenomena are also to be found in the ever more non-consensual norm generation on the international level, a continuous surge of obligations for states arising against their will,[32] hierarchization of PIL through *ius cogens* and Art. 103 UN-Charter, the emergence of *inter omnes* obligations as well as the emergence of individuals as subjects of PIL. Space does not permit an in-depth analysis of the different phenomena (this has also been done in the literature on international constitutionalism), rather my point here is to show the methodological way of proceeding when doing research on constitutionalism. In my view, a clear separation of assertions in the debate would be helpful.

30 Tomuschat (Fn. 14), p. 23.

31 Walter (Fn. 11), p. 195: "Constiutionalisation only occurs within the various sectoral regimes, but fails to reach the international community as a whole. Given the limited areas in which the Security Council may take legally binding decisions, this statement is also true for the United Nations." Differently: Ernst-Ulrich Petersmann, Constitutionalism, International Law and "We the peoples of the United Nations", in: Tradition und Weltoffenheit des Rechts. Festschrift für Helmut Steinberger, ed. by Hans-Joachim Cremer, Berlin, Heidelberg: Springer 2002, pp. 291–313. For the constitutionalization of WTO, see Petersmann (Fn. 12).

32 Christian Tomuschat, "Obligations Arising for States without or against their Will", Recueil des Cours / Académie de Droit International de La Haye 241 (1993-IV), pp. 199–374.

3 Clear Separation of Assertions: A Desideratum

Traditionally, three categorical statements are possible in legal science which in turn means that lawyers may take three different perspectives or roles.[33] The first scholar to introduce that kind of distinction was, to my knowledge, Hermann Kantorowicz,[34] followed by Max Weber[35] and Hans Albert[36] as well as some of the legal sociologists in the German speaking countries.[37] Of course, classifications are never right or wrong but only more or less useful. Kantorowicz composes an epistemological trilogy[38] consisting of the normative perspective (Wertwissenschaft)[39] (in the social science sense), the sociological perspective (Realwissenschaft), and the dogmatic perspective (Normwissenschaft). He also distinguished between the general level and the specific level within those three columns.[40]

The normative perspective includes questions of how (international) law ought to be. On a general knowledge level this is meant to be legal philosophy: what kind of goals ought PIL pursue. The discussion on which goals are to be pursued and how they are to be justified (e.g. efficiency, peace, certain human rights, preservation of global public goods) thus belong to the normative perspective. International Constitutionalists usually have a well-defined ideal that is to be pursued (though it differs in detail), but most take a neo-Kantian approach to humanistic values as democracy, accountability, equality, the separation of powers, the rule of law, and fundamental rights. Whereas that question is at the forefront of the constitutionalism debate in PIL, it is much more settled in the national sphere through national constitutions containing basic values to be pursued by a polity. The specific level includes legal policy questions, e.g. how to design international institutions (*de lege ferenda*) with a view on achieving the stated goals, including the effectiveness of the law. Thus, the question of how best to pursue certain normative goals necessarily includes social science knowledge; norm idealism without reality check is at best naïve, at worst untruthful. A purely deontological debate without consequentialist back-up is seldom pursued in adjudication, but is still to be found in academia.

33 See for an extensive discussion Anne van Aaken, Rational Choice in der Rechtswissenschaft (2003).

34 Hermann Kantorowicz, Rechtswissenschaft und Soziologie, Karlsruhe: C.F. Müller 1962 (first 1911).

35 Daniel Bodansky, International Law in Black and White, 34 Georgia Journal of International and Comparative Law 34 (2006), pp. 285–304 attributes this classification to Max Weber. Weber neither used this categorization in "Sociology of Law" (1921) nor in "Objectivity in Social Science and Policy" (1904) though he of course always made a sharp distinction (as Kantorowicz) between normative and empirical knowledge. Weber also knew the paper of Kantorowicz as he commented on the paper "Rechtswissenschaft und Soziologie in 1911, see Bibliography of Max-Weber Gesamtausgabe, http://www.mohr.de/mw/mwg_bibliographie_e.htm#begin.

36 Hans Albert, Erkenntnis und Recht. Die Jurisprudenz im Lichte des Kritizismus, in: Rechtstheorie als Grundlagenwissenschaft der Rechtswissenschaft, ed. by Hans Albert/Niklas Luhmann/ Werner Maihofer/Ota Weinberger, Düsseldorf: Bertelsmann Universitätsverlag 1972, pp. 80–96.

37 E.g. Manfred Rehbinder, Rechtssoziologie, Berlin: de Gruyter 2000; Hubert Rottleuthner, Rechtstheorie und Rechtsoziologie, Freiburg: Alber 1981.

38 Kantorowicz (Fn. 34), p. 69: "erkenntnistheoretischer Trialismus".

39 Bodansky (Fn. 35), p. 285 calls this the ethical perspective.

40 Kantorowicz (Fn. 34), p. 92: "generalisierende und individualisierende Erkenntnis".

The second column entails the sociological perspective or positive explanation in the social science sense. Here, descriptive (in the social science sense, not in the sense of describing what the law is), explanatory and prognostic questions are asked. Usually one proceeds by developing a hypothesis which may be (should be) empirically tested. Thereby, the causes and effects of PIL come to the fore, depending on whether PIL is used as *explanans* (independent variable) or *explanandum* (dependent variable). Only that kind of knowledge on PIL as *explanans* enables PIL scholars to look at the problem structure underlying PIL, and explain or prescribe certain law-making procedures or monitoring mechanisms for certain issue areas of PIL. Furthermore, explaining the effectiveness of, e.g., international human rights treaties or international trade treaties requires a view on the underlying problem structure (mostly modeled in game theoretic terms[41] using e.g. economic contract theory[42]) in order to know why some monitoring mechanism work in one issue area but not in the other.[43] Furthermore, a first attempt has been made to explain (and not only describe) the fragmentation of PIL (PIL as *explanandum*) by using a political economy approach.[44] Positive social science knowledge also enables normative critique. Here again, one may distinguish the general from the specific level. Whereas on the general level discussions on the merits of different social science theories and their respective hypotheses take place (e.g. rationalist vs. constructivist views on how PIL functions), on the specific level a scholar may work empirically on a specific issue and try to validate (by refuting) a hypothesis. Clearly more empirical work on, e.g. the effectiveness of international regimes, is desirable; much more work needs to be done. Rational choice analysis should be taken as a basis and a starting point but needs to be enriched.[45] Cooperation between social scientists and PIL lawyers would be very helpful, although European scholars tend make little use of this research potential.

41 Andrew Guzman, How International Law Works: A Rational Choice Theory, Oxford: Oxford University Press 2008 and Joel Trachtman, The Economic Structure of International Law 2008, Cambridge: Harvard University Press. A rational choice approach in the realist tradition is to be found in Jack L. Goldsmith/Eric A. Posner The Limits of International Law Oxford, Oxford University Press 2005. For a critique, see Anne van Aaken, "To Do Away with International Law? Some Limits to 'The Limits of International Law'", European Journal of International Law 17 (2006), pp. 289–308.

42 George W. Downs/David M. Rocke, Optimal Imperfection? Domestic Uncertainty and Institutions in International Relations Princeton: Princeton University Press 1995; Robert E. Scott/ Paul B. Stephan, The Limits of Leviathan. Contract Theory and the Enforcement of International Law Cambridge: Cambridge University Press 2006.

43 This is nothing else than the argument Andreas Zimmermann, "Is it Really all about Commitment and Diffusion? Why do States Incorporate International Law in their Domestic Constitutions?", Illinois Law Review 2008 (2008), pp. 253–264, makes with respect to the question of why there was never a state complaint under Art. 41 ICCPR (and only very few under Art. 24 ECHR). The relevant question is what kind of incentives are set by erga omnes obligations: do they carry their weak enforcement within themselves due to the incentive structure?

44 Eyal Benvenisti/George W. Downs, "The Empire's New Clothes: Political Economy and the Fragmentation of International Law", Stanford Law Review 60 (2007), pp. 595–631.

45 Anne van Aaken, "Towards Behavioral International Law and Economics? Comment on Kenneth W. Abbott", Illinois Law Review 2008 (2008), 47–59, see also Kenneth Abbott, "Enriching Rational Choice Institutionalism for the Study of International Law", Illinois Law Review 2008 (2008), p. 5–46.

Last, but not least, there is the third column which is the genuine domain of international lawyers, namely the doctrinal perspective, which Kantorowicz called "Normwissenschaft", that is, "Rechtsanwendungswissenschaft" (science of law application). European international lawyers tend to concentrate on that column.[46] The back-breaking work of stocktaking of different legal phenomena inductively and developing a prism or notion or principle which then orders the legal material is certainly one of the foremost works of a lawyer and it is also what is to be found in European scholarship about international constitutionalism. Especially German (PIL) Scholarship took a systemic approach to law by construing it with systemic coherence, logical consistency, using taxonomies, abstractness as well as precision and clarity of concepts.[47] Being myself a German trained lawyer, I cannot but think in those ways. Still, I believe that an essential element is missing and this highly appreciated scholarship could be enriched.

Here again, two levels may be distinguished: the level of methods of interpretation on the general level as well as the doctrinal analysis on the specific level. An example for the first would be the discussion whether an interpretation of the object and purpose of a treaty allows for the inclusion of the aspect of effectiveness (Art. 31 (1) VCLT), how other international obligations of a state may be taken into account when interpreting a treaty (Art. 31 (3) (c) VCLT), how far consequentialist arguments (Folgenargumente) are permissible as an interpretative method. Examples for questions on the second level are whether the invasion of Iraq violated the UN charter,[48] how to understand the potential victim requirement under the standing norms of regional human rights treaties or whether a country in severe economic crisis could justify its necessity measures under Art. 25 ILC Draft on State Responsibility or essential security escape clauses in Bilateral Investment Treaties respectively. Here, a PIL scholar takes the perspective of a judge, a legal advisor to government or a lawyer for her client and asks first of all what the law is. No matter what kind of norms (soft or hard) are relevant for changing states' behavior, only the sources of PIL as stated in Art. 38 (1) ICJ Statute are relevant for this task.[49] On

46 Benedict Kingsbury, "The International Legal Order", IILJ Working Paper 2003/1 (History and Theory of International Law Series), available at: http://ssrn.com/abstract=692626 (2003), 2; Dupuy (Fn. 4).

47 See in more details, equally praising but still going further in many of his articles, Eyal Benvenisti, "The Conception of International Law as a Legal System", German Yearbook of International Law 50 (2008), pp. 393–405, 394.

48 This example is taken from Bodansky (Fn. 35), p. 285.

49 The debate on the importance of soft law is exploding. Nevertheless, even if one assumes the importance of soft law for changing states behaviour, as e.g. Eibe Riedel, "Standards and Sources. Farewell to the Exclusivity of the Sources Triad in International Law?", European Journal of International Law 2 (1991), pp. 58–84, there seems to be a wide consensus that the sources of international law should not be extended (though of course there is a wide discussion on the importance of soft law as a means of interpretation of hard law or its role in forming customary international law). See instead of many Daniel Thürer, Soft Law, in: Encyclopedia of Public International Law, Vol. 4, ed. by Rudolf Bernhardt, Amsterdam: Elsevier 2000, pp. 452–460 and Prosper Weil, "Towards Relative Normativity in International Law?", American Journal of International Law 77 (1983), pp. 413–442. For a different view including soft law as a source of law, see Andrew T. Guzman, "A Compliance-Based Theory of International Law", California Law Review 90 (2002), pp. 1823–1887.

questions of legal validity, legal positivism is still the way to go.[50] Here, also, descriptive constitutionalism has its basis. If international constitutionalists make their point, they often analyze and describe legal constellations and developments which fulfill constitutional functions, such as the human rights protection, rule of law, eroding national sovereignty, implied powers by international organizations, commonly pursued goals as codified e.g. in environmental treaties, etc. This task is foremost a task *de lege lata*, and a necessary first step in the research agenda of international constitutionalism. Often, parallels are drawn to national constitutional functions.[51]

These columns or perspectives do not stand unconnected to each other, though a clear conceptual distinction is, in my view, desirable. Positive explanation can be used to derive normative critique and is indispensable for the pursuit of certain goals.[52] On questions of legal policy and institutional design, there is broad consensus that social science should be taken into account. The differences in view arise more forcefully on the question of law's application, that is the extent and the way by which the normative and the sociological perspective may enter the doctrinal perspective.[53] It is foremost a question of permissible interpretative methods. Here, the difference between European and American PIL Scholars may be the greatest; the latter being generally more open to the normative as well as the sociological perspectives than the former, although the wording of the text[54] is well accepted as a limit (with all its own known problems). There is more room for the integration of social science insights with regard to institutional design than with regard to law application. The difference of reception of social science insights between law-making and law application, though, is a matter of degree, not principle. Having said that, legal science as practiced in Europe and Germany lacks social science competence; the doctrinal perspective is strong as a hermeneutical science only. Once it is accepted that reality (and theories on it) enters (even) law application, lawyers are forced to look at their neighboring disciplines. All this sounds terribly familiar to US scholars but is still debated within German and European Scholarship. Some interpretative methods not only leave open a window for social science knowledge but even demand it, e.g. in teleological interpretation (object and purpose as mentioned in Art. 31 (1) VCLT), in comparative interpretation, in openly consequential-

50 This is a small problem for treaties: they are valid through consent even if not effective. Consent would also still be needed on a "constitutional level", even if there is a delegation of law making to International Organizations. See for a game theoretical analysis of the trend of eroding the traditional consent model in PIL, Laurence R. Helfer, "Participation, Compliance, and Non-consensual International Lawmaking", Illinois Law Review 2008 (2008), 71–126. The problem is greater with customary international law: here, sociological factors might be necessary in order to determine validity of Customary International Law and a fusion of a doctrinal and a sociological perspective might be necessary.

51 Laurence R. Helfer, "Constitutional Analogies in the International Legal System", Loyola of Los Angeles Law Review 37 (2004), pp. 193–236.

52 Daniel A. Farber, Positive Theory as a Normative Critique, Southern California Law Review 68 (1995), pp. 1565–1593.

53 See the old-new theoretical reflections on what constitutes "legal science" in Germany in Christoph Engel & Wolfgang Schön (eds.), Das Proprium des Rechts (2007) as well as Matthias Jestaedt & Oliver Lepsius (eds.), Was ist und wozu eine Rechtswissenschaftstheorie? (2007).

54 Art. 31 (1) VCLT "ordinary meaning to be given to the terms of the treaty".

ist argumentation, or within the principle of proportionality (e.g. necessity under Art. XX (b) GATT or Art. 1 of Protocol No. 1 to the ECHR). Thus, rational choice, if accepted as social science paradigm, may enter the interpretation of (International) Law through various interpretative methods – and already does so. The famous statement by Anne-Marie Slaughter that International Relations as a social science approach can make International Lawyers better *lawyers*,[55] reflects this understanding. One of the eminent PIL Scholars, Sir *Hersch Lauterpacht* has called for "the principle of effectiveness" when interpreting international law. This was meant to ensure that treaties effectively achieve their goals (even if that requires progressive interpretation).[56] I can only subscribe to that and plead for the integration of social science knowledge when assessing effectiveness. Although in Europe, elements of social science often enter the interpretation by everyday intuition of the respective law applier,[57] sometimes smuggled in either by her own social science intuition (sociological perspective) or hidden value judgments (thus a category from the normative/ethical perspective) without making the epistemological status of the argument clear and without thus enabling open critique and discussion.[58] Furthermore, in the US sometimes normative statements are hidden under the cover of positive science in economic analysis of law – not contributing to the acceptance of Law and Economics in Europe. Epistemological obscurities thus contribute to misunderstandings, especially concerning the application of Law and Economics; an epistemologically clear discussion could mitigate those misunderstandings, enable more rigorous analysis of PIL constitutionalism and foster more common research projects (interdisciplinary as well as transatlantic).[59]

55 Anne-Marie Slaughter, "International Law and International Relations: Millenial Lectures", Receuil de Cours/ Hague Academy of International Law (2001), 9–250, at 26. See also Anne-Marie Slaughter/Andrew S. Tulumello/Stepan Wood, "International Law and International Relations Theory: A New Generation of Interdisciplinary Scholarship", American Journal of International Law 92 (1998), 367–397 and for an early argument Kenneth Abbott, "Modern International Relations Theory: A Prospectus for International Lawyers", Yale Journal of International Law 14 (1989), 335–411 and Kenneth Abbott, "Enriching Rational Choice Institutionalism for the Study of International Law", Illinois Law Review 2008 (2008), p. 5–46.

56 Hersch Lauterpacht, The Development of International Law by the International Court London: Stevens 1958, pp. 227 et seq., 282.

57 Robert D. Cooter, "The Minimax Constitution as Democracy", International Review of Law and Economics 12 (1992), pp. 292–294, 292: "For two millennia lawyers and legal theorists in the West used the same reasoning as the man in the street to predict how people will respond to laws. Legal scholarship knew no behavioral theory beyond common sense." The same criticism can be found in Europe, e.g. Peter Noll, Gesetzgebungslehre Reinbek bei Hamburg: Rowohlt 1973, 27: "Wo empirische Überlegungen bei gesetzgeberischen und richterlichen Entscheidungen selbst beim Rückzug auf normenidealistische Positionen unvermeidlich sind, werden selten mehr als *vulgärsoziologische* oder *vulgärpsychologische* Erkenntnisse bemüht." (emphasis in the original). Though this still holds largely true, the German Constitutional Court recently reasoned for the first time openly with a law and economic approach, see BVerfGE, 1 BvR 2576/04 of 12th December 2006 (at para. 67 et seqq.).

58 The latter was one of Hans Kelsens main critique of his colleagues, see Hans Kelsen, Reine Rechtslehre (Pure Theory of Law) Darmstadt: Scientia Verlag Aalen 1994.

59 See for this attempt Anne van Aaken/Christoph Engel/Tom Ginsburg, "Public International Law and Economics: Symposium Introduction", Illinois Law Review 2008 (2008), 1–4.

4 The Social Science Contribution to the International Constitutionalism Debate

Let me take up two examples of legal phenomena of how to combine international constitutionalism with social science in order to illuminate what I have in mind. I will focus on two aspects often cited as phenomena of international constitutionalism. One is human rights and the other is non-consensual law-making.

International human rights treaties are viewed upon as one of the constitutional functions partially usurped by the international community. By ratifying human rights treaties, the state function of protecting human rights is partially outsourced to the international level. Almost all states are party to one or more international human rights treaties or regional human rights treaties. The so-called treaty-based procedures, established under the major U.N. human rights treaties, all include reporting procedures, individual complaint procedures, inter-state complaints procedures, and inquiry procedures. The committees also issue "general comments",[60] which are interpretations of the provisions of the human rights treaties clarifying the obligations of State Parties. Furthermore, in the early 1990s the treaty bodies started adopting conclusions and recommendations after examining the specific country reports.

A growing number of international bodies with jurisdiction to protect individuals against human rights violations committed by states within their own jurisdiction have been created.[61] It is sometimes claimed that we are living through a "human rights revolution in progress",[62] in which (i) the recognition of the objective character of obligations to protect human rights,[63] (ii) the acceptance of a collective

60 See the compilation of General Comments at <www.unhchr.ch/tbs/doc.nsf/0/ca12c3a4ea8d6c53c1256d500056e56f?Opendocument>.

61 Courts, commissions and committees are all dealt with together as they all allow for individual complaint mechanisms. Commissions and committees are not judicial bodies in the proper sense as they issue only non-binding decisions. In the text, the term "judicial body" is used to include all of them. Furthermore, compliance with decisions does not necessarily depend on their binding nature.

62 Thomas Buergenthal/Dinah Shelton/David P. Stewart, International Human Rights in a Nutshell St. Paul, MN: West Group 2002, at 24.

63 Human rights treaties are distinct from other treaties, which are characterized by mutual and reciprocal concessions and obligations, in that human rights treaties find inspiration in considerations of a superior order, the ordre public. In creating obligations for states vis-à-vis human beings under their jurisdiction, the norms of these treaties not only require States Parties to take joint action for human rights protection (i.e., through the exercise of a collective guarantee), but also, and above all, oblige each State Party to provide an internal legal order to enforce these rights, in relations between the public power and the individual. See instead of many Hermann Mosler, "The Protection of Human Rights by International Legal Procedure", Georgetown Law Journal 52 (1964), 800–823, at 818 et seq. considering the function of the European Commission. The European Court of Human Rights (ECtHR) and the Inter-American Commission (IACHR) understand the respective human rights treaties not only as a reciprocal treaty between states but as an objective order. The ECtHR stated in Ireland v. The United Kingdom (Appl. No. 5310/71), 25 Eur.Ct. H.R (ser. A) (1978), Judgment of 18 January 1978, at para. 239 that: "… unlike international treaties of the classic kind, the Convention comprises more than merely reciprocal engagements between Contracting States. It creates, over and above a network of mutual, bilateral relationships, objective obligations, which, in the words of the Preamble, benefit from a "collective enforcement" ". Likewise the I/A Court H.R., The Effect of

guarantee of compliance with these obligations and, last but not least, (iii) the right of individual complaints are all crucial parts. Nevertheless, it is also true that the institutions for the enforcement of human rights are still rather weak. Empirical research[64] shows that IHRL is largely ineffective.[65] Why is that so? International bodies carry out their task of human rights enforcement and compliance monitoring mainly based on self-reporting by states or on inter-state complaints. The reporting system is considered the backbone of monitoring compliance. Still, those procedures may be deemed insufficient for ensuring compliance. Inter-state complaints have been thoroughly and predictably underused.[66] In contrast, individual com-

Reservations on the Entry into Force of the American Convention on Human Rights. Advisory Opinion OC-2/82 of September 24 1982, at para. 29. More generally for different types of treaties, see Gerald Fitzmaurice, "Second Report on the Law of Treaties", UN doc. A/CN.4/107, Yearbook of the International Law Commission, Vol. II, 16–70 (1957), 54 f. called those obligations "integral". See for this distinction also Joost Pauwelyn, "A Typology of Multilateral Treaty Obligations", European Journal of International Law 14 (2003), 907–951, 933 especially for IHR Treaties.

64 Oana A. Hathaway, "Do Human Rights Treaties Make a Difference?", Yale Law Journal 111 (2002) 1935–2042.

65 Effectiveness and compliance are different but related notions. To determine whether a state complies with a treaty requires comparing the relevant state activity with the treaty's requirements. Effectiveness is directly related to, but distinct from, compliance and regards causality. A state may comply with a treaty, that is, its actions comport with the requirements of the treaty, but the treaty may nonetheless be ineffective in changing that state's practices. For these notions see: Andrew T. Guzman, "A Compliance-Based Theory of International Law", California Law Review 90 (2002), 1823–1887, for compliance theories Harold Hongju Koh, "Why do Nations Obey International Law?", Yale Law Journal 106 (1997), 2599–2659 and Laurence R. Helfer/Anne-Marie Slaughter, "Toward a Theory of Effective Supranational Adjudication", Yale Law Journal 107 (1997), 273–391.

66 Dinah Shelton, "The Participation of Nongovernmental Organizations in International Judicial Proceedings", American Journal of International Law 88 (1994), 611–642, at 613 and 615; Anne F. Bayefsky, The UN Human Rights Treaty System The Hague: Kluwer Law International 2001, at xv and Laurence Helfer/Anne-Marie Slaughter (Fn. 65), 298 f. Inter-state complaints are possible under the following agreements: Art. 24 of the European Convention on Human Rights and Fundamental Freedoms (ECHR); Art. 45 of the American Convention on Human Rights (ACHR); Art. 49 of the African Charter on Human and Peoples' Rights (African Charter); Art. 41 of the International Convenant on Civil and Political Rights (CCPR); Art. 11 of the Convention on the Elimination of Racial Discrimination (CERD); and Art. 22 of the Convention Against Torture and Other Cruel, Inhuman or Degrading Treatment or Punishment (CAT). Consequently, a State can lodge an application with a treaty-body when it has reason to believe that another State has violated a right guaranteed in one of these conventions. Up to 2001, the inter-state complaint procedures of the CCPR, the CERD and the ACHR have never been used, and the CAT has been used twice, however. Under the ECHR there have been 21 applications by states in 13 cases relating to no more than seven situations, see Søren C. Prebensen, Inter-State Complaints Under Treaty Provisions – The Experience Under the European Convention on Human Rights, in: International Human Rights Monitoring Mechanisms. Essays in Honour of Jakob Th. Möller, ed. by Gudmundur Alfredsson/Jonas Grimheden/Bertrand Ramcharan/Alfred de Zayas, The Hague: Nijhoff 2001, 533–559, 543. As Pieter van Dijk/Godefridus J. van Hoof, Theory and Practice of the European Convention on Human Rights, The Hague: Kluwer 1998, at 43 point out: [I]t is evident that the right of complaint of States has proved not to be very effective … [T]he contracting States have not been willing to lodge complaints about situations in other States where no special interest of their own was involved. Such a step generally even runs counter to their interest in that a charge of violation of the Convention is

plaint mechanisms are the only enforcement mechanism having at least a weak empirical significance of effectiveness.[67] Ratification of e.g. the First Optional Protocol to the International Covenant on Civil and Political Rights is associated with less rights violations.[68]

It is submitted that we should not simply accept the empirical finding that IHRL is largely ineffective on the whole, yet more effective if there is the possibility of individual complaint mechanisms. It seems insufficient for international human rights lawyers to stop short with the analysis at that point. Rather, we need to ask how those mechanisms can be rendered more effective. In order to achieve this kind of knowledge, one needs to undertake a social science analysis.[69]

Although states are the primary addressees of human rights obligations, since the nineties, the role of multinational enterprises in human rights protection has been analyzed, i.e., in order to mitigate the enforcement gap in developing countries.[70] The Special Representative of the UN Secretary-General has recently issued the final report on how the responsibilities between states and enterprises should be aligned,[71] after the "Draft Norms on the Responsibilities of Transnational Corporations and Other Business Enterprises with Regard to Human Rights"[72] have not been adopted. He rightly points out that responsibilities between enterprises and states drawn in an unclear way would lead to "strategic gaming".[73] Clearly, in order to draft a workable framework for including enterprises in human rights responsibilities, one need to analyze underlying incentives for corporate actors as well as governments, including all kind of restraints enterprises will be subject to, including

bound to be considered an unfriendly act by the other party, with all the political consequences that may be involved." Suggestion for strengthening the inter-state complaint mechanisms are given by Scott Leckie, "The Inter-State Complaint Procedure in International Human Rights Law: Hopeful Prospects or Wishful Thinking?", Human Rights Quarterly 10 (1988), 249–303.

67 Antônio Augusto Cançado Trindade, "The Consolidation of the Procedural Capacity of Individuals in the Evolution of the International Protection of Human Rights: Present State and Perspectives at the Turn of the Century", Columbia Human Rights Law Review 30 (1998), 1–27 also stresses the importance of the individual complaint mechanisms for recognizing that human rights are no longer simply "granted" by the state.

68 Hathaway (Fn. 64) 1999, Eric Neumayer, "Do International Human Rights Treaties Improve Respect for Human Rights?", Journal of Conflict Resolution 49 (2005), 925–953 finds the same result. Succumbing to individual complaint mechanisms might also have a positive signaling effect to other states, see David H. Moore, "A Signalling Theory of Human Rights Compliance", Northwestern University Law Review 97 (2003), 879–910, 905.

69 For one proposal to use ius standi as one mechanism to render International Human Rights more effective, see Anne van Aaken, Making International Human Rights Protection More Effective: A Rational-Choice Approach to the Effectiveness of Ius Standi Provisions, in: International Conflict Resolution, Conferences on New Political Economy 23, ed. by Stefan Voigt/Max Albert/Dieter Schmidtchen, Tübingen: Siebeck/Mohr 2006, 29–58.

70 For an overview, see John Ruggie, "Business and Human Rights: The Evolving International Agenda", American Journal of International Law 101 (2007), 819–840.

71 John Ruggie, "Report of the Special Representative of the Secretary-General on the Issue of Human Rights and Transnational Corporations and other Business Enterprises", UN Doc. A/HRC/7/3, 21 March 2011.

72 UN Doc. E/CN.4/Sub.2/2003/12/Rev.2 (Aug. 26 2003).

73 John Ruggie, "Report of the Special Representative of the Secretary-General on the Issue of Human Rights and Transnational Corporations and other Business Enterprises", UN Doc. A/HRC/8/5, 7 April 2008 (2008), para. 55.

the work of NGOs, the media and the world court of public opinion. Setting only desirable goals is insufficient and may lead to unintended consequences.

A further example I would like to mention is a second phenomenon often brought up in the constitutionalism debate: non-consensual law making in the international sphere. The Westphalian system was firmly based in the concept of state consent. Clearly, this is still the most important factor but non-consensual law making is getting ground. Non-consensual PIL making is to be found in many different sectors, the most prominent one being the "legislation" of the UN Security Council Resolutions after the terrorist attacks after 9/11.[74] In Resolution 1373,[75] the Security Council created not only a duty to prosecute and punish terrorists by setting up a detailed measure of how to deal with them and especially with terrorism financing, it also set up a committee monitoring the implementation of the measures, thereby creating an enforcement mechanism. It also ordered states to ratify different conventions against terrorism which hitherto did not have many state parties.

How is this development to be analyzed? Clearly, as economic contract theory tells us, states only enter international commitments if the expected benefit of it exceeds the expected costs, often framed in "sovereignty costs". If states deem those to be too high, they might either not enter a treaty, exit it, or not comply with the treaty.[76] Helfer[77] analyzes this trade-off between increasing participation and decreasing compliance, analyzing first recent examples from multilateral efforts to prevent transnational terrorism, to preserve the global environment, and to protect human rights, and second the underlying problem structure by making use of the game-theoretic framework of certain cooperation problems. He is able to show that law can create self-enforcing equilibria in which compliance is a dominant strategy. Thus, in certain situations, non-consensual lawmaking can reduce both the participation and the compliance deficits, but not in all. Conducting this kind of analysis helps not only for questions of institutional design but also for interpreting international treaties. Too strict interpretation might create a backlash. Most International Courts are well aware of that.

5 Conclusion and Outlook

The debate on international constitutionalism (in Europe) is foremost a normative one in the sense of Wertwissenschaft, that is, its main aim is to construct *de lege ferenda* with a view on certain goals or international values. The arguments used are

74 Instead of many: Paul C. Szasz, "The Security Council Starts Legislating", American Journal of International Law 96 (2002), 901–905.

75 Security Council Resolution S/RES/1373(2001).

76 Simon Schropp, Trade Policy Flexibility and Enforcement in the WTO. A Law and Economics Analysis, Cambridge: Cambridge University Press 2009; Anne van Aaken, International Investment Law between Commitment and Flexibility: A Contract Theory Analysis, Journal of International Economic Law, 12 (2009), 507–538.

77 See Helfer (Fn. 50). See for the use of market mechanisms for the effectuation of PIL: Anne van Aaken, Trust, Verify or Incentivize? Effectuating Public International Law Regulating Public Goods through Market Mechanisms, forthcoming in 104th Proceedings of the American Society of International Law 2011.

usually a mixture of doctrinal description of what is already there *de lege lata* and at the same time a formulation of a desideratum.

A descriptive stocktaking and the filtering of common principles (as landmarks viewed through the constitutionalism prism) is necessary but insufficient. Just as in comparative law, normative description is a first step, but only a first step. One needs to look at the functions of the legal institution, that is, the social problem that is to be solved. In order to answer that question, a view on the underlying problem structure is necessary, especially if one wants to take not only the constitutional text (Verfassungstext) or constitutionalizing treaties such as the UN-Charter or Human Rights treaties into account but also the constitutional reality ("Verfassungswirklichkeit"). Questions of compliance and effectiveness abound here: Normative agendas are valuable but in order to be able to fulfill them, one need to take a consequentialist turn and take a realistic look at how to achieve those desired values. That last step is unfortunately often not taken by international constitutionalists. If constitutional functions are to be taken seriously, a social science contribution, the explanatory dimension is necessary. Another "eureka" is needed: international constitutionalism should discover social science.

Pasquale Policastro

Constitutionalism vs. Economic Analysis

On the Use of Founding Theories and Complementary Theories in Constitutional Interpretation

Abstract:
Le droit, en tant que science sociale, traite des phénomènes pouvant également être étudiés par l'économie. Les différents paradigmes de recherche ont toutefois des horizons de connaissances différents. Pour cette raison, les phénomènes qui se produisent dans la société – comme par exemple les constitutions – ne peuvent être étudiés en une seule fois à partir des paradigmes des sciences juridique et économique. Le mieux que l'on puisse faire est de chercher des éléments complémentaires, qui devant être utilisés aux côtés des paradigmes d'analyse relationnelle et d'interprétation fonctionnelle, choisis comme théories-objet et métathéories et permettant leur définition successive. L'intégration des métathéories avec les théories complémentaires se perfectionne ainsi seulement à un niveau suffisamment élevé de définition. Aux autres niveaux, séparer le traitement dans l'argumentation des différents paradigmes scientifiques est toujours nécessaire. Toutefois, cette séparation sera toujours relative. C'est pourquoi la vérification à chaque pas de notre discours dans (la production et) l'interprétation du droit, devra toujours être considérée avant tout au regard de sa cohérence avec les hypothèses juridiques prises comme fondement constitutionnel. C'est uniquement en prenant ce point de départ qu'il est possible de tenir compte des implications de notre discours sur les sciences complémentaires, à travers un processus de motivation critique et consciente.

1 Normativeness and Complexity in economic theory and in legal theory

Any activity of the human mind appears directed to control a set of 'given' entities, which 'reality' manifests at different levels. For this reason the activity of theorizing appears to have, directly or indirectly 'normative' purposes. Such normative approach takes into account the perspective of the observer, and his/her aims. Therefore, the concept of normativeness, in its most general meaning, is a manifestation of any scientific-technologic approach. The specific aspects in which normativeness manifests constitute the realm of application of different sciences. For this reason, when we choose the variables whose understanding we aim to develop, we actually delimit the use of a certain science.

From such introductory remarks, we find first of all the need to highlight the potential relation between the different sciences that is due to their common finality, widely considered. A second conclusion is that in order to develop a scientific theory, and a scientific paradigm[1] we need a great deal of interpretation. We interpret the phenomena around us, according with abstract features, developed by us. We then perform a new interpretation when we have to adapt the abstract features to reality, in order to "execute" an abstract model that we wish to put into practice. A third is that the solution of a given problem through a theory may make use of other theories that were developed for the solution of different problems, however

1 Kuhn, The Structure of Scientific Revolutions, Chicago and London 1962, 3rd ed. 1996, pp. 17–18 passim.

linked to the basic problem – our object problem. Also in this case, the choice of the auxiliary theory with respect to the given problem, that may be either a complementary theory or a meta-theory, is highly arbitrary and depends from the 'theorizing' subject and the purpose he/she has.

From the former, introductory considerations, we see that the more the number of variables we aim to isolate and to control in our theory, the more we wish to take into account auxiliary theories with respect to our object, the more the theory attains a higher level to complexity. This is due to manifold relations existing between the object or the target of the enquiry and the purposes of the observer, who is at the same time inquiring, theorizing, creating and developing relations among the variable elements, and then executing the interpretation "models" into practice in order to attain his/her purposes.

The studies on scientific development highlighted the importance of models and of scientific paradigms for many sciences.[2] Economic analysis scholars stressed the importance of modeling for economic theory.[3] In addition, for legal science, we may consider each norm, legislative act, constitution, and legal principle etc. as a "model" or as a part of a model. The importance of the understanding of legal elements as "models" relates to the use of law as a tool to understand, describe and in the same time to influence reality. In this way, we highlight the "reasonableness" required to legal rules as a relevant predicate of its characteristics as a model. In this sense, we may say: if we rule the situation X, characterized by given features $X=(X_1 \ldots Xk)$ through a norm N_1, we may say that the class of events $E=(E_1 \ldots En)$ is likely or not likely to take place. This prediction aspect characterizes legal models, as well as models in other sciences. However, legal science has a special feature related to a specific attention to the questions of its reasonable character.[4] In order to analyze the object situation of legal activity, the target situation, that we aim to influence by legal rules when they will be determined and implemented, we need to perform different interpretations. In this process, we have to make use of different auxiliary theories, both complementary theories and meta-theories, in order both to determine the norm, to execute it, and to evaluate its effect basing on its feedback.

The specific complexity that characterizes the process of legal interpretation, is related to a number of factors. Among them, we may firstly include the wide range of heterogeneous phenomena that we aim to rule with law. Secondly, the wide range of theories considering such phenomena from different viewpoints and both with theoretical and practical aims. Thirdly, we may include the quantity of norms that

2 See at least R. Frigg, S. Hartmann, "Models in Science", in Stanford Encyclopedia of Philosophy, http://plato.stanford.edu/entries/models-science/, first published in 2006, and the literature quoted thereof. The authors point out that models are a tool to learn about the world, and that, however different aspects related to models – for example questions related to their nature as representation, have been giving rise to significant intuition, however much is to be done in the field of models. For this reason, it appears particularly interesting, in our view, to deal with models in law.

3 J.A. Schumpeter, History of Economic Analysis, London 1954; Italian abridged edition, Storia dell'analisi economica red. C. Napoleoni, translation P. Sylos-Labini, L. Occhionero, Torino 1972, p. 18.

4 An interesting and well documented approach to the reasonableness as an intrinsic and necessary attribute of law can be found in A. Cerri, "Ragionevolezza delle leggi" in Enciclopedia giuridica, Aggiornamenti, III vol., Roma 1994.

we find in each legal order and of subjects, which may interpret and apply them, evaluating their feedback on their situation. We may also take into account the interdependences between the different factors. In order to deal with the problems related with these issues, we need specific tools of analysis.

The complexity of such issues does not change, even if we concentrate our analysis in the constitutional norms, which contain the basic principles and rules, from which descend all the valid rules in a polity, or in a system or network of polities. Independently from such factors, however, all the processes relating to the development and the application of knowledge are based on sequential processes of interpretation. This holds true also with respect to the object of law. Such interpretations are operations through which we 'correlate' phenomena of the real world with the 'specific' features of legal norms, and vice versa. In legal theory, we often distinguish between "subsumption" and "balancing": the nature of these two operations may be considered analogous, within the "genus" of the process of interpretation. Indeed, also when we acknowledge relevance to some elements in order to give or to deny a predicate to an entity[5] we subsume, we give a weight to some events, and then we choose. It is worth considering that the monumental work of Emilio Betti, which is relating to the theory of interpretation, takes into account in a similar way the interpretation processes developed in the different fields. However, it seems to us, that this famous author tends to distinguish between the "historic consciousness" through which a given entity acquires a meaning, and the activity of the interpreter as such, for example with respect to the judgment of qualification of an entity.[6] This approach may not be considered incorrect as such, but it ought to be better explained, for example through the uses of the concept of semiosphere,[7] eventually understood by means of the Kolmogorov complexity, in its version adapted to legal modeling of reality.[8]

The problem on which we aim specifically to concentrate here is how to deal, for the sake of the legal interpretation, with the understanding of the reality by means of the economic science. We understand the economic process through forms of interpretation that, in economic science, concentrate on the phenomenon of production or on the phenomenon of exchange.[9] The classes of the models of production and of the models of exchange however centered on the phenomena and variables, that characterize altogether "the scope and method of political economy" when mutually confronted, present significant differences. Among them, we ought to underline that in principle, exchange models are normative, whilst produc-

5 E. Betti, Teoria generale dell'interpretazione, II volumes, ed. G. Crifó, Milano 1990 (1st ed. 1955) p. 328.

6 Ibidem, § 18a, p. 328–329 passim.

7 Y.M. Lotman, Universe of the Mind. A Semiotic Theory of Culture, translated by Ann Shukman, Introduction by Umberto Eco, Bloomington & Indianapolis 1990.

8 P. Nunziante, Sistemi cognitivi, Napoli 2000.

9 A. Quadrio Curzio, R. Scazzieri, Protagonisti del pensiero economico. I. Nascita e affermazione del marginalismo (1871–1990), Bologna 1977; Id. Protagonisti del pensiero economico. II. Tradizione e rivoluzione in economia politica (1890–1836), Bologna 1977; Id., Protagonisti del pensiero economico. III. Rivoluzione industriale e economia politica (1917–1948), Bologna 1982; Id. Protagonisti del pensiero economico. IV. Struttura produttiva, scambio e mercati (1848–1872), Bologna 1982; Id. Sui momenti costitutivi dell'economia politica, Bologna 1983; M. Baranzini, R. Scazzieri, Foundations of Economics, Oxford 1986.

tion models are descriptive. We make here use of the expression 'in principle', due to the fact that, many exchange models are based upon "comparative static" analysis,[10] which appears particularly suitable for short-term modeling, whilst many production based models are actually developing dynamic analyses which are suitable for long-term issues. The two classes of models have also different meta-theoretical foundation. For the exchange-based models, psychological assumptions or behavioral assumptions play a very important role. For production-based models, statistics plays instead a major foundation role. So basically, both the models may be used to advice in the process of government, although in different matters: the exchange models may appear better suitable for policy issues, while the production models appear somehow helpful to interpret constitutional and political issues. However, the models of the two classes are often mutually competing, due to the fact that they highlight different aspects of the reality, through methods that lead to partly different results in key issues, such as the ones related to labor and salary.

However, the importance of the "exchange-production duality" in economic analysis plays a very important role not only for the economist, but also for the lawyer. Indeed, the competition between production-based models and exchange based models manifests in periods in which the first paradigm had success over the second, followed by periods in which the second paradigm prevailed over the first. This kind of competition with alternate success has been taking place not only in general within the industrialized economies, but it has also been manifesting in different national systems. From such a competition there derived within the time a different kind of influence not only in the constitutions and in the policies of the states and of the international organizations. Such a competition contributed also to the transformation of the public opinion and to the development of the social expectation towards law and the purposes of the polities.

For this reason it has an outstanding meaning, to understand in which way we can make use of the contributions to economic analysis, in the process of legal interpretation. With the aim to contribute to this task, we will try to clarify, for the sake of our study, which are the characteristic of the legal, and first of all, the constitutional systems, with respect to the said features of economic models. For this reason, we will introduce the concept of static and dynamic concept of the constitution. Such concept however, shall not be mixed which the concept of static and dynamic economic models.

2 Static and Dynamic Concepts of the Legal Order vs. Static and Dynamic Concepts of the Constitution. Constitutionalism

One of the core concepts that permit us to qualify legal order is the concept of dynamic or "poietic" order. This concept is grounded on the idea that a legal system is characterized by rules that superintend the position of other rules.[11] In such a dynamic approach to law, the will of the individuals that have been 'authorized to

10 P.A. Samuelson, Foundations of Economic Analysis, Cambridge, Ma. 1953.

11 H. Kelsen, General Theory of Law and State, Cambridge, Ma. 1945; Italian version Teoria generale del diritto e dello stato 1994^6, p. 113, 114.

create a given norm' plays a deciding role. However, such an approach opens to the question that the norm does not exist in itself, if not by a quantity of given 'signs'. Every use of such a norm, starting from the act of 'recognition' of the existence of a binding obligation,[12] is based upon an extremely complex number of interpretative operations. If we take into account such questions, then we ought to revisit both the 'static' concept of a legal order, according with which all the specific norms in a legal order, may be obtained through an intellectual operation of inference from general to particular[13] and the approach according with which "legal reasoning has analogous features to moral reasoning". We ought in any case, to consider as a part of the legal theory, at least the results of the different scientific observations that we may use to develop our legal argument. Economic analysis is one of them. When we wish to take into account economic analysis for legal reasoning, we ought to take into account the overall scientific environment within which economic analysis develops: "in principle, let us remember that, Latin paleography is one of the techniques of economic analysis" – wrote Schumpeter in his "History of Economic Analysis".[14] Taking into account the whole range of scientific reflections related with the legal issues permits to see the complexity related to the good functioning of a legal order. Indeed, in the process of legal interpretation we deal not only with classes of complementary theory, as for example economic analysis. We deal also with theories that permit ourselves to "speak about", in other words to give a foundation to the concepts we use when we try to understand and to interpret law: the class of the 'meta-theories'.[15] We may conceive the ultimate meta-theory as the 'approach of the individual subject' to reality through his 'neural functions'. We may relate such functions to the perception of structures, (through the neural "hypotaxis"), the systemic arrangement of the perceived data (through the neural "hypertaxis") and the competitive comparison of arranged data, in the search of a feedback (through the "meta-taxis"). All these functions are altogether expressed by means of the sequential features of language.[16] We have many classes of meta-theories. We may consider philosophical enquiry[17] as one of such meta-theories: through it, we may study the logic of legal rules, for example according with the three-partition

12 H.L.A. Hart, "Law and Moral Obligation", in A.I. Melden, Essays in Moral Philosophy, Washington 1958; Italian version Contributi all'analisi del diritto, ed. By V. Frosini, Milano 1964, pp. 196–197 passim.

13 Kelsen, Teoria, p. 113.

14 Schumpeter, History, cit. p. 16.

15 We can see the reach of this concept, in the line that links the thought of Carnap to the one of Tarski. See R. Carnap, Meaning and Necessity, A Study in Semantics and Modal Logic, Chicago and London 1956 (first ed. 1947); A. Tarski, "The Semantic Conception of Truth and the Foundation of Semantics", Philosophy and Phenomenological Research, vol. 4, 1944, p. 13–47. The latter author tends to look at this concept in an opened approach to the object language, with which we sympathize due to the importance of the interaction between individual subject and legal reality in the process of interpretation. Kelsen appeared very aware of the need to give a final foundation to the legal theory. See, H. Kelsen, Allgemeine Theorie de Normen, Manzsche Verlags- und Universitätsbuchhandlung, Wien 1979; It. version Teoria generale delle Norme, ed by M. Losano, Torino 1985.

16 Nunziante, Sistemi, cit.

17 G. (Jerzy) Kalinowski, Introduction à la logique juridique, Paris 1965; Italian version, Introduzione alla logica giuridica ed. By M. Corsale, Milano 1971.

into: legal semiotic, theory of norms, theory of the legal reasoning. The classes of the theories and of the meta-theories, give rise to a "semiotic cluster" and a to "semantic cluster" through which we develop our interpretation processes, for the purposes of legal production and the implementation of legal norms. Although the distinction between complementary theories and meta-theories is highly arbitrary, we may see that complementary theories and meta-theories do not have the same function: the complementary theories have we may say a horizontal function: they link legal reasoning with the different branches of knowledge. Meta-theories, they relate legal reasoning to the different knots, through which legal concepts have been evolving and developing within the framework – obviously – of the human knowledge possibilities. A question that we may pose ourselves it is to consider the relationship between complementary theories to law, and meta-theories of law. For the purposes of this work we concentrate on economic analysis as a complementary theory. Instead, for what concerns the choice of our meta-theory, it is some time that we have been concentrating our attention to constitutionalism and to its paradigms.[18] Our choice is justified by the fact that, so far the different legal theories have been founded on a fact: so it is with Kelsen's normativism as we can see from the concept of Grundnorm, with institutionalism, both in its original versions that in the more recent approaches, and with realism.[19] The purpose of our approach to constitutionalism is indeed to overcome the said problems related to the foundation of the legal theory on abrupt facts. However, our approach to meta-theory tends to be relative to a bigger extent then the approach considered in general by logicians. Indeed, we consider constitutionalism as the "first" of a class of meta-theories that we need to use, in order to give a foundation to the legal process. The reason of our choice is that constitutionalism, according with our understanding, permits to consider the answer to the following questions and namely: 1) to which purposes political power is addresses; 2) through which tools it is exercised and 3) how it is exercised. In this way constitutionalism is not intended as a way through which one describes the features of one chosen system, but a way through which the 'languages', so to say, spoken by the different legal system, may be confronted on

18 P. Policastro, "La Costituzione di Weimar e la razionalizzazione democratica del potere politico tra metodo storico, paradigmi evolutivi del costituzionalismo e metodo" giuridico in: E. Amato A. Capo D. Viscido (eds.), Weimar, le letterature classiche e l'Europa del 2000; Id. "Political Parties, Participation and Representation Face to Globalisation, European Integration and Democratic Transition" in M. Granat, P. Policastro, J. Sobczak, (eds.), Partie polityczne we współczesnym konstytucjonalizmie, Lublin 2001; Prawa podstawowe w demokratycznych transformacjach ustrojowych. Polski przykład, Lublin 2002; Id. "On the Reconstruction of the Legal Strength of the Constitution in a World in Transition. Multi Level Constitutionalism Towards Multi Level Democracy" in: J. Nergelius, P. Policastro, K. Urata (eds.), Challenges of Multi-Level Constitutionalism, Polpress, Kraków 2004; XXI IVR World Conference: Lund 12–18 August 2003 – Proceedings of the Special Workshop "The Material Control of Constitutionality of Statutes: Constitutionalism, Multi-Level Democracy and Fundamental Values"; Id. "On the Descriptive and the Prescriptive Nature of the Constitution. Constitutionalism and the Legitimisation of the Constitution in the Practice of its Implementation" in L.J. Wintgens (ed.), The Theory and Practice of Legislation. Essays in Legisprudence, Ashgate, Aldershot 2005.

19 P. Policastro, Paradigmi del costituzionalismo, seminar held at the Università della Magna Graecia, Catanzaro on April 4th 2008, in the framework of the PhD. Program in jurisprudence, coordinated by Massimo La Torre, and in particular the final intervention of the latter scholar.

the base of a 'common reference framework' that is our first level meta language. It goes by itself that the same first class meta-language, has to be founded. We need a theory to refer to it. Indeed, when we speak about 'constitutionalism', also in our paradigm-based approach, we need to refer to other assumptions. For example, we may refer to some philosophical conception related to human rights. They, however, may give rise to some objections, of philosophical or of cultural nature. For this reason, to consider as the meta-theory, the philosophy at large (see Kalinowski infra) may not be sufficient. The point will be: Which philosophy? Which culture lies beyond that specific philosophy? The objection of 'cultural relativism' may be solved whenever we may find a 'comparing framework' to deal with the problem. May be such a meta-language logic, or the framework of logic?[20] We are keen to support the approaches that believe that at the bottom of these classes of meta-language[21] we ought not to locate a language, but the way in which the individual subject, the one who speaks, develops his thoughts formulating them into language.[22]

Constitutionalism is a theory that deals with the legal framework permitting the limitation of the political power through law. This limitation concerns, when the case, also the constitution of a polity and the exercise of its powers. In order to avoid dangerous ambiguities, we have to add that, as we had already the occasion to say,[23] while we can consider legal mediation as a universal[24] characteristic of societies, not all the forms of legal mediation may cope with constitutionalism. Constitutionalism emerges throughout the history, as a specific form of legal mediation, according with the exercise of political power is limited within the framework of three specific relations. Such paradigms, which theory we developed in former analyses,[25] may be

20 For what concerns an approach related to a cultural framework different from the European one, see SUN Zhongyuan, "Meta-research in Chinese logic", Front. Philos. China 2007, Vol 2 Section 1, pp. 50–69

21 See B. Russel, "Introduction" in the English version of L. Wittgenstein, Tractatus Logico Philosophicus 1922, revised edition printed in London and New York 1974; The "Tractatus" was first printed in 1921 in Annalen der Naturphilosophie.

22 P. Nunziante, Sistemi.

23 P. Policastro, "Constitutionalism, Comparison, Complexity. Prolegomena on Liberty and the Use of Language for a Predictive Theory of Law", in E. Castorina, P. Policastro (eds.), Liberty and Language. The Global Dimension of European Constitutional Integration, Torino 2010, pp. 15–109. A first version of the paper was presented as: "Constitutionalism, Comparison, Complexity. Prolegomena for a Predictive Theory of Law", Communication presented at the Örebro Conference on Comparative Law, Spring 2006. The said reflection had been already partly developed in the course of lessons, with the same title, given in the same year at the Master 2 "Recherche" in European and Comparative Constitutional Law at the University of Paris I, Panthéon-Sorbonne, as well as at the "Return of the Brains" PhD lessons given on "The Transformation of the Sources of Law in the Process of Globalization and European Integration" (at the University of Salerno, Department of Civil and Economic Relationships in the Comparative Legal Systems 2005–2008), and lately at the II yearly conference of the European Network of Constitutional and Comparative Law (ECONET) hold in Ragusa on April 19th 2008, on "Language and Constitution: A Key issue for European Integration".

24 D.M. Armstrong, Universals. An Opinionated Introduction, Boulder, Co., Westview Press,1989, especially page 135.

25 P. Policastro, "La Costituzione di Weimar"; Id. "Political Parties, Participation and Representation"; Id. "On the Reconstruction"; Id. "On the Descriptive and the Prescriptive".

considered as three classes of relations: a) the first is the relationship between the status of the individual and the achievement of collective goals; b) the second is the relationship between participation and representation; c) the third is the relationship between norms and their adaptation of reality.[26] We can find within the historical experiences of constitution, many significant insights on these paradigms. However, the content of these relations evolves, and through different forms of legal evolutions, legal transformations[27] or "legal revolutions", they took the contemporary features. Nevertheless, however we may confine our analysis from the process that starting in the Middle Ages,[28] develops throughout the Renaissance leading to the modern and contemporary ages, we still find ambiguities, that for example, lead some authors to deny the general values of constitutionalism, as marked by a specific cultural experience. This is indeed also the limit of the hermeneutic theory of interpretation,[29] the discourse theory of democracy, and of the theory of legal validity.[30] Instead, our problem is to try developing a theory that may compete with different approaches to legal mediation, without aiming either to develop a hegemonic culture or to support a hegemonic political approach. In this framework of analysis, we may then consider the economic analysis as a complementary theory with respect to constitutionalism: that is of a theory that may help us in evaluating what may be the role of economic processes for the achievement of constitutional goals.

For this reason, we need to develop our system of comparative tools. To this purpose, I think worth here to introduce another concept related to the constitution: the constitution in a static sense and the constitution in a dynamic sense. This distinction is related to a significant extent with the horizontal relations between constitutional theory and complementary theories. However, it permits to take into account comparative issues in our theory of constitutionalism.

3 Static Constitution and its Interpretation

We will start now characterizing the concept of static constitution, and its features. We will give then a specific attention with respect to the use of the economic analysis, and the conclusions in terms of constitutionalism, that we may derive using the concept of static constitution. Later, we will do so, with reference to the dynamic concept of constitution.

We can characterize any political community by some basic principles that enable the distribution of income and wealth, of political influences and of social influences to take place. We can understand such rules, as the constitution of a community in a 'static sense'. Such concept, which applies both to the ancient and

26 Policastro, "Constitutionalism, Comparison, Complexity".

27 Policastro, Prawa podstawowe, especially chapters I, II, III.

28 B. Tawney, The idea of Natural Rights. Studies on Natural Rights, Natural Law and Church Law 1150–1625, Atlanta 1997; J.G.A. Pocock, The Machiavellian Moment. Florentine Political Thought and The Atlantic Republican Tradition, Princeton and Oxford 2003 (first ed. 1975).

29 E. Betti, Teoria generale, cit.

30 J. Habermas, Faktizität und Geltung, Frankfurt a. M. 1992, Italian edition, Fatti e norme, ed. by L. Ceppa, Milano 1995.

modern constitutions, presents a clear relation with some economic theories. Indeed, in the communities regulated by a static constitution, the subjects that are acknowledged a certain social influence participate also to the exercise of the political power. Therefore, they are also able to influence the making and the application of the rules through which income and wealth are distributed.

In such an approach the function of the constitution, as an expression of political power, is limited to take into account of factual situations determined by the existence and the functioning of different rules on the distribution of influence on the social, political and economic sphere. In such an approach, a legal theory of the constitution may have only a limited role. Instead, the main subject of studies is the system of relations that are developing under a given 'constitutional system'. To this respect, when confronted with the static approach to the constitution, the legal science studies the consistency of given rules within the framework of a given society. In this perspective, legal science may to be even predictive, since legal interpretation is linked with economic calculation.[31] Namely, through its formal and substantive characteristics, it could arrive to make sure that the respect of given rules may be consistent with the basic framework of distribution of social, political and economic influences. Therefore, jurisprudence may permit to develop a system of relations consistent with a given framework of constitutional principles. Jurisprudence as a science, in this perspective, deals with the making of those rules, both general and individual, that permit a given system to exist within a given constitutional framework. This framework, we have to stress, determines the distribution of political, social and economic influences of a community living in a given territory.

The production of general rules and the interpretation of rules by judicial means may however, in a static constitutional context, arrive to embody and support different values then those that we may immediately refer to the permanence, within the time, of a given framework of constitutional rules in the static sense. Notwithstanding the efforts to separate the constitutional framework from the sociological ground from which they derive, the legal rules may in the long run exclude large parts of the society from the possibility of participating in law making and in having their needs represented in the exercise of the political power. This happens especially with respect to the rules that guarantee a given model of distribution of influences on politics, on society and on nation's economy. Indeed, the forces at power may show "autopoietic" tendencies.[32]

Therefore, within a constitution understood in a static sense, we may define jurisprudence as the science that permits the achievement of the given purposes of the different subjects operating within a constitutional framework. These subjects may be also individuals. Their goals may be obviously subjective, but their achievement is subject to the 'constitutional constraint'. Namely, their achievement may take place if the scheme of distribution of income and wealth, of social influences and of political influences on the community remains without change. Here, we have a formulation of the 'Pareto optimality' in constitutional terms, where the level

31 M. Weber, Wirtschaft und Gesellschaft, ed. J. Winckelmann, Tübingen 1972 (first ed. 1921–1922), p. 503–511, esp. 508–509; E. Forsthoff, Rechtstaat im Wandel, Stuttgart 1964; Italian version Stato di diritto in trasformazione, ed. by C. Amirante, Milano 1973, p. 43.

32 Among the different works of Niklas Luhman, we may refer here to, Politische Planung, Opladen 1978; Italian edition Stato di diritto e sistema sociale, Napoli 1990.

of benefit of the other members of the society is substituted by the constitutional expression of the existing framework of distribution of income and wealth, of political influences, and of social influences. If we do so, we can understand how a static approach to constitution may coexist with the acknowledgement of other values then those ones related to the existence and the reproduction of the constitutional framework. From this, we can understand how it took place the approach to the constitution by means of doctrinal schemes having the purpose to outweigh rights and interests by means or other rights or interests. We find in this approach, the tendency to give a general significance to operations of 'balancing',[33] by transforming the legal interpretation in a constrained moral discourse.

We may very well look at this jurisprudential approach to the optimization of the individual situation within a given constraint as one perspective to approach the concept of constitutionalism. Indeed many authors have been looking at constitutionalism, as a way to limit the exercise of the political power to those activities needed to maintain a given constitutional framework, and thus living a space for freedom and for the achievement of the individual goals. This kind of formulation of the Pareto optimality within a constitutional framework, presents the same weaknesses of the principle, as observed by economic theory: namely that in the period in which economic expands, many people may be better off,[34] without changing the distribution of the social, political and economic power. However, this may not be true in general, and therefore economic negative cycles, may easily turn in negative constitutional cycles, characterized by significant limitation of freedom.[35]

In this sense, we understand that an approach to the limitation of the power within the internal sphere of a constitutional legal system, or within the external sphere by means of international law, may coexist with different political, economic, and social frameworks. From the external point of view, it can coexist with the development of an empire (as in the former European history), with the development of a two-block international hegemonic system or even with the hegemony of a single and coordinated power. From the internal point of view, it may coexist with the principles of separation of powers, with parliamentary sovereignty, with an authoritarian state and with a socialist rule. It may not instead coexist with the totalitarian state, since we are supposing the existence of a well-defined rule of repartition of income and wealth, of social influences, and of political influences, and not merely the rule of a 'leading will', although the latter may be coordinated with the principles of a given framework of influences.

The approach to constitutional law embodied in the static approach has been giving rise to a wide, interdisciplinary approach to law making and legal interpretation. It appears to be consistent with different sociology-based theories of the exercise of the political power, such as various kinds of 'institutional' approaches or Habermas[36] discursive theory. It appears also consistent with economic based theories of politics and law, such as the theory of collective choices started by Arrow[37] or

33 A. Peczenik, On Law and Reason, Dordrecht, Boston, London 1989.

34 L. Campiglio, Appunti di Politica Economica, book I and II, without date, Milano (CUSL), especially book I, p. 81–85.

35 Policastro, "On the Reconstruction", cit.

36 Habermas, Faktizität, cit.

37 K.J. Arrow, Social Choice and Individual Values, New York and New Haven 1963, (first ed.

the economic analysis of law developed, among others, by Richard Posner.[38] We ought to consider with attention the 'consistency' between the static approach to constitution and specific aspects of economic theory. The assumptions of the economic models influence indeed in a significant way their use in the legal and constitutional understanding and in the legal reasoning. With this attention, we can develop a deeper insight to different approaches to the relationship between economic analysis and legal interpretation. In relations to this we will refer to some remarks developed by Richard Posner.[39] According with this author, "the new law and economics" began with Guido Calabresi and Ronald Coase.[40] However, continues Posner, we find in the thought of modern thinkers, including Cesare Beccaria[41] and Jeremy Bentham,[42] earlier attempts to apply economic analysis in areas that are not strictly related with economic relations. Nevertheless, Posner adds, we can find some basic reflections leading to the most recent approaches in the thought of Pigou.[43] Driving the attention to Arthur Cecil Pigou appears to be very interesting for our purpose, as we can highlight considering for example the reference of the analysis of Pigou to the one of Vilfredo Pareto.[44] One of the question relates to the question of the so-called "personal distribution of income curve", of which some 'glimmering' may be found in the work of Pigou, with special reference to his commentary of Pareto's argument according with which the increase of the minimum income or the diminishment of the inequality "is substantially equivalent to an in-

1951); Id. "Extended Sympathy and the Possibility of Social Choice", The American Economic Review, Vol. 67, No. 1, Papers and Proceedings of the Eighty-ninth Annual Meeting of the American Economic Association (Feb. 1977), pp. 219–225. Especially in the last paper, we see that the author underlines the problems arising when we try to generalise an individual approach to the utility function, with individual preferences given before, and an interpersonal comparison and ordering, which may found a theory of justice. Such problems are finally deriving form the specific character of each individual.

38 R. Posner, Economic Analysis of Law, Austin, Boston, Chicago, the Netherlands 2007. Indeed, we may see that the said author considers the question of the economic analysis of law, within the long line of thought that starts for utilitarianism.

39 Ibidem, p. 23–24.

40 R. Coase, "The Problem of Social Cost", Journal of Law and Economics 1960.

41 A significant reference to the utilitarianism of Cesare Beccaria, may be found in the study of G. Zarone, Etica e politica nell'utilitarismo di C. Beccaria, Napoli 1971.

42 We may look at all the philosophical, political activity of this author. However, we will limit on to quoting the Leading Principles of a Constitutional Code for any State. The work starts that such a constitution, "has for its general end in view, the greatest happiness of the greatest number; namely, of the members of this political state: in other words the promotion or the advancement of their interests. By the universal interest, understand the aggregate of those interests". See The Works of Jeremy Bentham, ed. by J. Bowring, Edinburgh 1839, Part VII.

43 A.C. Pigou, The Economics of Welfare, London 1932, first published 1920.

44 See especially V. Pareto, Cours d'economie politique professé à l'Université de Lausanne, vol I and vol. II, Lausanne 1896. We have to take into account that it is due to Pareto one of the most important remarks founding the welfare economics, namely that the difficulties of the interpersonal comparison of the utilities do not invalidate those propositions of the welfare economics that create advantages or disadvantages for some elements of the society without creating advantages or disadvantages for the others. This case, as Schumpeter (History, p. 612) points out, includes also the cases where all the individuals receive an advantage or a disadvantage. This paves the way, also within the Pigou's approach, to the activity of a legislator or another agent who 'weights' or 'sets the weights' to the wishes of the members of the society (Ibidem, p. 613).

crease of the absolute share of dividend accruing to the poor". This approach is related to a constitutional approach where the influences on the model of distribution of wealth between the people remain the same. The commentary of Arthur C. Pigou[45] to this thesis, is that it "on the one hand, anything that increases the national dividend must, in general, increase also the absolute share of the poor, and, on the other hand – and this is the side of it that is relevant here – that it is impossible for the absolute share of the poor to be increased by any cause which does not at the same time increase the national dividend as a whole". For this reason, in his Economics of Welfare, Pigou confirms and takes further consequences for Pareto analysis. The increase of the national dividend, and not the transformation of the share between rich and poor social groups becomes the substantive purpose to be followed by the polities. So the question of the inequalities becomes substantively approached by the strife within each political community to increase its 'own' dividend. This approach has been leading to search the welfare through the growth of the economic dividend of the nations, irrespective not only of the effects it would have on other political communities, but irrespective of the effect that the strife for the increase of the national dividend may have on functioning of the internal institutions. The general criticism developed by Franz Neumann with reference to the changes in the function of the statutes in the bourgeois societies, appears revealing, to this extent, a deep insight.[46] Other more articulated forms of criticism, such as the ones of Altiero Spinelli and Ernesto Rossi, in the "Manifesto of Ventotene"[47] highlight with bigger detail the consequences of the "race" for the increase of the "national dividend" for individual rights, for the national politics and for the international relations. We may say that also John Maynard Keynes'[48] theory, remains linked to the 'national economy' as such, however within an approach that appears more linked to interdependences between the different elements of the societies and international interdependences. This may be seen not only – however partly – in the "General Theory" but also in the former "Economic Consequences of Peace"[49] and mostly in the contribution of Keynes to the debate on the foundation of the International Monetary Fund, markedly on the question of the international currency unit – the "Bancor".

45 Pigou, The Economics, IV.II.1.

46 F. Neumann, "The Change in the Function of Law in Modern Society", in The Democratic and the Authoritarian State, ed. by H. Marcuse, New York 1957, Italian version "Mutamenti della funzione della legge nella società borghese", Lo Stato democratico e stato autoritario, ed. by N. Matteucci. The criticisms set by the German author to the 'paradoxes' of the 'general character' of statutes, shows by means of constitutional and political remarks another side of the criticism moved by Schumpeter to the "normative" welfare economics, which in the search for a 'certain' and 'limited' equality in a given moment of time, does not take into account the effects of such conforming deliberations aiming to 'equality' and 'justice' to the cultural and economic evaluation (Schumpeter, History, p. 614).

47 A. Spinelli, E. Rossi, "Per un'Europa libera e unita. Progetto d'un manifesto", in Problemi della Federazione European, Roma 1944 now in Il Manifesto di Ventotene, with a preface by E. Colorni and a presentation by Tommaso Padoa-Schioppa, Milano 2006.

48 John M. Keynes, The General Theory of Employment, Interest and Money, Amherst, N.Y. 1997, fist published 1936.

49 Id., The Economic Consequences of Peace, New York 1920.

The model of the theory of welfare economics proposed by Pigou, has, notwithstanding its success, been set apart from the further developments, however framed within the long way developing from economic utilitarianism, liberalism and the theory of choice. The economic theory of law has been making a step forward postulating the need to take into account the overall consequences of the different actions, as in the case of Coase to damage.[50] The result is a new approach to responsibility. In this sense, the relative power of the wealthy part of society with respect to the one of the poors, leads the rich part to develop forms of production of goods and services, that for the same fact that they are developed, are deemed to be useful. For this reason, such endeavors, ought to be subject to a 'balancing' in the case of damage. But here we see that the postulate of the welfare through production of "social product" ends finally to affect the relative distribution of wealth itself. And finally, it leads to a 'global need' of accepting the 'beneficial effects' of the activity developed by the 'richer parts of society(-ies), without any accountability hic et nunc.[51] In this developments we see the danger of a unaccountable hegemony of such richer classes, whose effects on the world situation we see in the present crisis. Such a danger seems to have been seen, however within the range of the economic perspective by Schumpeter, in his criticism to normative economics of welfare,[52] and, more recently, by Sen.[53] The latter author has furthermore developed important glimpses in the relationship between principles of distribution of the influences on politics, on the society and on nation's economy, showing for example some paradoxes that may occur when we rely only on such criteria – for example the paradox of cyclical deliberation. However, we need an approach to constitutional principles, which may permit law to operate in a "counterfactual"[54] direction, therefore overcoming the unresolved difficulties and the ambiguities of a 'contract' based approach to balancing[55] and of an approach to law based upon 'facts'.

50 R. Coase, "The Problem of Social Cost", Journal of Law and Economics, October 1960.

51 The most sensitive authors in the field of constitutional law have perceived such problem; see C. Amirante, Dalla forma Stato alla forma mercato, Torino 2008.

52 See supra footnote 35.

53 A. Sen, "Maximization and the Act of the Choice", Econometrica, Vol. 65, No. 4, July 1997, 745–779. In particular the attention to the tension between maximization ant optimization behaviours, appears particularly interesting (especially p. 767–769). However, the limitation of the volition act envisaged by the author, with reference to the works of Smith (p. 769 passim) and Kant (p. 771 passim), and related to the importance of habits, does not take into account the process through which the human person develops the volition act. In relation to this it does not take into account the relationship between "rational behaviour" and reasonableness conceived in probabilistic terms, rather then confining itself to a systemic ground represented by the normative character of habits.

54 D. Lewis, Counterfactuals, Malden Ma., Oxford, Carlton Vi. (Aus.) 1973.

55 J. Rawls, A Theory of Justice 1971, Polish version Teoria Sprawiedliwości, Warszawa 1994.

4 Constitutionalism, Market and the Theory of Static Constitutions

From the analysis done so far on the relationship between the static theory of constitution and economic theories, we may see that the static approach to the constitution permits a good use of tools such as utility functions, the choice approaches, and the convexity hypothesis. In this context, free competition markets, with no costs of transaction – and the gradual correction of these hypotheses – have been playing a very important function as theoretical instruments. It is worth mentioning, that in the context of a static approach to constitution, market seems to play only the role of a mechanism, an institution through which the individual subjects can achieve their particular goals permitted within a given constitutional framework.

However, in order to give a deeper insight in a static-based approach to constitution, we have to underline that the market has different functions. Among them, we have firstly the regulative function, permitting to set the best possible achievements of individual goals that are compatible with the framework of a given static constitution. Secondly, we have the instrumental function of the markets, permitting the operative achievement of some individual goals that are compatible with the existent static constitution. Thirdly the market, understood as a free competition market, plays the function of 'an ideal' reference system for studying the possibilities for the optimal achievement of the individual goals in a given constitutional framework. Indeed, the 'normative' character of the market frame rests upon the 'univocal' relationship between the fulfillment of the free market hypotheses and the achievement of the constrained optimum. Whenever such optimum may not be satisfactory, then the legal norms will have the task of 'approaching' the fulfillment of the hypotheses that make the market institution a 'system' of 'interdependent' actors.[56] Such actors independently, but 'simultaneously' reach the optimization of their utilities or goals. In this context the terms "causation" may be used only with respect to a change in external data.[57] However, also within an interpretation that is different from the one of comparative static, characterizing the thought of Samuelson, namely within the dynamic, vertically-integrated Pasinetti approach,[58] the approach to the rate of profit as an historical constant in the industrial economies,[59] allows also the dynamic constitutional models to be compatible – or actually linked with – a static constitutional approach.

But if we see that the marginal approaches, starting from the seminal contributions of Jevons,[60] Menger[61] and Walras[62] appear heavily related to market economy, the ambiguities between the fulfillment of the market hypotheses and the failure of

56 P.A. Samuelson, Foundations of Economic Analysis, Cambridge Ma. 1953 p. 9; for another approach to interdependence see L.L. Pasinetti, Structural Dynamics and Economic Growth. A Theoretical Inquiry in the Structural Dynamics of the Wealth of Nations, Cambridge 1981.

57 P.A. Samuelson, Foundations, cit.

58 L.L. Pasinetti, "The Notion of Vertical Integration in Economic Analysis", Metroeconomica, vol. 25 1973, Italian version "La nozione di settore verticalmente integrato nell'analisi economica", in Id. Contributi alla teoria della produzione congiunta, Bologna 1977.

59 Pasinetti, Structural Dynamics, p. 77–79 esp. fn. 14 p. 79.

60 W.S. Jevons, The Theory of Political Economy, London, 1871.

61 C. Menger, Grundsätze der Volkswirschaftslehre, Vienna, 1871.

62 Walras, Elements d'économie politique pure, Lausanne, 1874.

the market, especially within the process of globalization, may call for further inquiries and other solutions. As we will see, it is not so easy taking into account the sole economic models. A different approach to constitution instead, based upon a role of the law permitting to constitutions to drive to transformation of the principles of distribution of the influences on the political sphere, on the social sphere and on the economic sphere, may lead to interesting consequences. For example, it may reasonably indicate, on the base of legal elements, that when the development of the production of goods and services on the global sphere goes beyond certain limits, the absolute amount of wealth produced by companies and the level of profit accruing to richer classes, may permit the development of forms of domination that – on the global sphere – may lead to unwanted transformation of the constitutional distributions of influences, at the disadvantages of the subjects with relatively smaller incomes and power. The use of the dynamic constitutional paradigm in order to evaluate the reasonableness of the use of the economic framework of the analysis needs however, a deeper analysis of the static constitutional principle.

In the static constitutions, we have to consider the existence of a political constitution that sets the principles of repartition of income and wealth, as well as of the exercise of the social and political influence. The goals of individuals (and groups) may be achieved within the constraints of such principles of distribution. Law acts here as a principle related to the maintaining of a given social (political and economic) order, permitting at the same time the development of the attainment of the individual goals compatible with that given order. Law in this sense works as a rule to achieve an "optimum", permitting the permanence of the constitutional rule of repartition and the achievement of individual and particular goals. It maximizes the subjective possibilities to achieve individual and particular goals, while minimizing the interventions needed to maintain, with the maximum probability possible, the existing rules of repartition. This approach to law appears however consistent also with a subjective approach to law.[63] Furthermore, it relates to the theory of the 'limited exercise of political power' that is the approach to constitutionalism characterizing the Anglo-Saxon legal tradition, as we can see for example by McIlwain.[64] Such an approach to constitutionalism has been developing, although in a later time also in continental Europe, with very significant results, that for example we can find in German thought[65] although in different perspectives, and however not without critical insights on the different problems arising within what we may call the 'constitutionalism of the static constitution'.[66] The ontological features of law showing its function to achieve the optimum of the achievement of the maximum of individual particular goals under the permanence of given repartition principles, may be shown by the general principles of legal protections that emerged in the Western tradition. We may mention among them the due process of law, the habeas corpus, nullum crimen, nulla poena sine lege, freedom of beliefs and of thought,

63 A. Sen, "Maximization", p. 759, 769 passim.

64 C.H. McIlwain, Constitutionalism: Ancient and Modern, New York 1947; Italian edition, Costituzionalismo antico e moderno, ed. by N. Matteucci (które wyposażył wstępem) 1990².

65 as in E. Forsthoff, Rechtstaat, cit.

66 G. Radbruch, Rechtsphilosophie, Heidelberg 2003² first published in Leipzig 1937, p. 38, pp. 128–135 passim; even clearer Id., Der Geist des englischen Rechts, Göttingen 1958; Italian version ed. by A. Baratta, Lo spirito del diritto inglese, Milano 1962, pp. 25–32 passim.

the general legal protection to freedom, property, equality before law. To them we may add the possible limitation of freedoms and rights only by means of statutes, the representative principle, the right of a fair trial, as well as the principles of proportionality and reasonableness in the application of law. So, a dynamic theory of the constitution may not think of a derogation of such principles, but their formal and substantive reinforcement.

The economic theory of the static constitution appears at the very first glance related with an approach where the 'status quo' represented by the existing model of influences on politics, on the economic system and the societies, may be consistent with a limited social improvement by means of a 'Pareto optimality approach'. Since the we deal with a society where not only individuals are confronting, but where we may distinguish between the different degree of influence on the political, social and economic power hold by different groups, we may see that any sort of 'constrained optimization' under a given constitutional 'status quo' has in itself the worm of dubious processes in which the factual situation through which the current system develops tends to endure within time. Furthermore, it may be factually consistent with processes of 'concentration of political, economic and social influences' – as we observed them in the rise of the authoritarian state in Europe. It may be also consistent with the development of a 'super'-national economic power, as in the process of present globalization, where the big corporation appear keen to 'dictate' their condition to the statehood, in terms of legal conditions through which their activity takes place. We have been observing such developments, with growing clarity since the last decade of XX century. We have also been observing and also in terms of extraordinary public intervention in order to support them in times of crisis, such as we observed in the economic crisis of the 2008.

To this extent, if we consider the literature developed following Marshall[67] approach, Pareto approach as well as a great deal of the European approach to marginalism we see that the equilibrium solution is somehow dependent on the assumptions concerning patterns of behavior of individual, groups and collectivity. Such assumptions refer also to questions arising from the interaction between subjects having a different power. Nevertheless, the question of how to attain such patterns of behavior in the reality, not only the one related with the European continent but also on the global sphere, when we deal with societies characterized by significant differences in the degree of influence to the exercise of political, economic and social power stays opened. As a matter of example, even in the attempt to overcome the crisis of the national state after World War II, Altiero Spinelli and Ernesto Rossi[68] and Friedrich August von Hayek,[69] gave a political proposal that seemed to converge: the international state, and the development of federative processes on an international scale. These proposals were basing on very different economical and political perspectives: notwithstanding such apparent consensus, however, such approaches appeared full of unknowns from the perspective of their legal implementation.

67 A. Marshall, Principles of Economics, London 1920, first edition 1890.
68 Spinelli, Rossi, "Per un'Europa", cit.
69 F.A. von Hayek, The Road to Serfdom, Chicago 1994, first published 1944.

5 The Dynamic Approach to Constitution and the Legal Rationalization of Power as a Problem of Reasonableness of Legal Reasoning: A Further Inquiry Economic Models and Their Relation with Economic Theory

At this point of our analysis we would like to point out that, the question of the adoption of a dynamic approach to the constitution, that is a legal approach to constitutional rules, permitting the latter to develop a gradual transformation from the model of repartition of the influences on political processes, on society and on wealth distribution may gradually change, presents specific legal features. Namely, it requires an approach to reasoning that is specific for legal analysis. An approach consisting in the description of the complexity of the reality within the complexity of the values that we wish to protect by law, and afterwards, in assigning different weights to the different values protected, according with the importance that given values have in their basic reconstruction. These operations of "subsumption" and "balancing"[70] are themselves including induction processes as well as choices between theories. The results we obtain are families of descriptions, different the one from the other. All these descriptions are then to be related to reality, through a process of induction that includes taking into account the results of other sciences, and so choices between theories. Such choices relate also to choices between economic theories. The result of these reasoning gives rise to practical choice, which is then fed-back, comparing them with the reality. In this context we may see a specific reasonableness of law, directed to improve the legal systems. The reasonableness of legal science relates to its ability to include different processes on subsuming and balancing, in sequence. The passage to the single subsumption and the single balancing to a sequential process, based on several feed-backs, may permit to overcome the problems arising from the excessively rigid assumptions in economic theories, making a full use of the contribution of each of them in the process of legislating, implementing and applying law. Furthermore, it may allow using economic models and legal theories, within the specific realm of questions they are designed for. In this way, the mutual relations about the findings of economic models and the requirements of the economic models are to be found in the relations between two open systems within a probabilistic approach.

In this respect the rationalization of the political power by means of law may be developed taking into specific account the characteristics of legal reasoning, based on the typically legal approach to reasonableness and the specific model of inference of other sciences. In fact, the rationalization of the political power by means of law necessitates taking into account the manifold dimensions through which power takes place. Power itself is not a resource. It rather is a factual state. Power founds the existence of institutions, that we may here understand as a means to distribute resources.

We may treat power as a pre-juridical concept. In this case, we may link it, for example, with the possession of resources. Our approach to the constitutions as the legal framework for a system of distribution of influences permits nevertheless an

70 R. Alexy, "Die Gewichtsformel", in J. Jickeli, P. Kreutz, D. Reuter, Gedächtnisschrift für Jürgen Sonnenschein, Berlin 2003, p. 771 f.

approach to power in juridical terms. To this extent, to explore the constitutional relations making use of the results of the economic theory may be important not only for reason of developing knowledge. It may also important in order to understand the relation between 'individual' and 'groups' in the 'counterfactual' processes of transformation of the principles of repartition of the influences on: the political processes, the social processes, and on the distribution of wealth. Such dynamic constitutional processes may lead, through the implementation of the legal principles, to produce a 'better' constitutional framework of distribution. We may understand this concept as an adaptive and a perspective concept, relating with our theorizing of the means and the results permitting the variety of the values and of the rights protected under the constitution to be applied in a fuller way. In the different processes of reasonable connection of the states related to our perception of the reality, and of our perception of the legal principles and legal values that we aim to protect and our consequent definition of rules of action to intervene in the reality we may make – at different stages – use of different theories. We may include different economic theories, sociological theories, and moral theories. The choice of such theories ought to take place as a conscious step for the development of a reasonable legal reasoning. To this extent, the distinction between complementary theories and meta-theories, permits to overcome some of the ambiguities that Jerzy Kalinowski showed in his legal logic, articulated in semiotic analysis, theory of the norms and legal argument, where he took into account merely a meta-theory, and choosing philosophy to this purpose.[71] Indeed, also, philosophy ought to be founded, and for this reason we prefer to take into account our cognition through our brain operations, that permits to consider philosophy within the realm of complementary theories.[72] In this way the use of complementary theories will be an element of our legal justification. It will be compounded, through our use of the meta-theories as an hypertext, which is itself not a theory but that permits to bridge up between our complementary theories, and our object theory of law. In this process, it intervenes the use of sequential meta-theories, as theories centered to the understanding of our object-theory – law – compounded with complementary theories. However, we ought to integrate constitutionalism, as a first order legal theory, with different orders of meta-theories, related to a gradual clarification of our understanding of the concepts we develop, firstly in terms of their use through the languages that interact, including natural languages. Secondly, in a hypertext that permits to overarch the different natural languages through which we express constitutionalism and its components, and though which we express our legal reasoning and justify it in terms of reasonableness. Such hypertext development acknowledges the complementary theories that we use in order to justify the different elements of our legal reasoning.

We have to take into account also that these sequential processes, that include induction and choice of different ways of interpreting and acting, take place within time. We describe the result of our operations of structure, systemic and competitive evaluations, we perform in our brain, in a way that can be communicated, by means of time sequences of expressions.

71 Georges (Jerzy) Kalinowski, Introduction à la logique juridique, Paris 1965, Italian version by M. Corrale, Introduzione alla logica giuridica, with a Presentation of Ch. Perelman, Milano 1971.

72 Policastro 2008.

Ultimately, in the process in which we perceive and evaluate, in which we communicate and we receive a feed-back in time, when we re-consider our understanding performing operation of confrontation of models with reality, we may undergo changes: i) on the perception of the reality and of the significant elements, ii) on the perception of the principles to be protected by law, iii) on the change of our rules of action to intervene. Such changes occur to all the participants in this communication process, directly or indirectly. In this way reasonableness is a reasonableness that occurs within time. Reasonableness is a reason that takes into account the time. For this reason, a dynamic theory of the constitution that takes into account the change of its paradigms of distribution, may well develop predictivity features concerning a reasonable paradigm of distribution. A dynamic constitution therefore, may significantly include a reasonable change in the paradigms of distribution.

In this sense we have to see the operations that we perform as subjective, and therefore different for any subject that performs them. Such differences are related to the specific situation of each individual, to his/her cultural background, to the specific problems on which he/she is concentrating.

For this reason, the inclusion of these elements into a probabilistic approach shows another specific aspect of the reasonableness of legal reasoning and legal practical activity, may need to refer to logic of the possible worlds,[73] logic of classes and universals,[74] counterfactual logic,[75] neuristic and hipercomplexity logic.[76] The recourse to meta-sciences, including moral philosophy, history and economic ought to be considered as important parts of the process of legal interpretation – for the use of legislation, and application of legal norms – but not mutually identified. Reductions of legal science into another science, does not appear to be possible.

The approach of normativeness that we obtain displays the overarching connection of many operations of reasonable connection, between the reality as we perceive it, the framework of principles that we wish to protect and the goals we wish to attain, and the principles of action we envisage.[77] The importance of taking into account the specific aspects of legal science, the subjectivity of the approach to legal understanding and to legal interpretation, the interaction between legal sciences and other sciences, but not its final reducibility, tends to highlight that, reasonable-

73 S. Kripke, Naming and Necessity, Cambride Ma. 1972 1980; Id., Wittgenstein on rules and Private languages, Cambridge Ma. 1982

74 D.M. Armstrong, Universals. An Opinionated Introduction, Boulder and London 1989.

75 D. Lewis, On the Plurality of Worlds, Malden, Oxford, Victoria 1986.

76 For what concerns Kolmogorov complexity, see at least Ming Li and Paul Vitányi, An Introduction to Kolmogorov Complexity and Its Applications,1997 2008, New York. In the introduction to the first edition, the authors widely relate Kolmogorov complexity to Ockham razor's criterium of choice of the simplest description. Furthermore, they consider the relation between Ockham razor and the solution proposed by Kolmogorv complexity approach in term of feasibility of inductive logic. Paolo Nunziante, in his Introduzione, cit., appears to strive to take into account all the possibility developed by Kolmogorov approach, in terms of iper-inductive logic or para-inductive logic from which it follows a theory of the hipertext, that permits to consider the prospective of a 'semiotic machine' joining the different semiosperes in a open sphere. With reference to the attention to the dimension of induction process and its possibilities of description by the human subject, such logic may be said to be 'neuristic'.

77 An initial approach to the problem may be found in Policastro, "On the Descriptive and the Prescriptive", cit.

ness in legal science is a reason participated by many reasons. And this aspect permits us to consider what is the relationship between legal reasonableness and constitutionalism. Namely, such an articulated sequence of operations, including structural consideration on existing phenomena, induction, choice, between different explanations, their linguistic expression, the different perception and the different explanation performed by the different subjects, may permit us to understand constitutionalism as an approach permitting us to develop a legal approach on how constitution itself – as a complex of principles of distribution – may evolve.

The possibility to make use of the dynamic approach to constitution in a way that constitution itself may be employed in a predictive way is the purpose of a conscious use also of different meta-theories, including economics. Such an approach is important due to the fact that when events not foreseen by constitution take place, one of the reactions that may follow, may consider the constitutional principles and constitutional practices of the constitution not applicable at all or partly. We have been seeing this, in the case of the Gulf Wars, the fight against terrorism, and last but not least the recent economic crisis of 2008. Another reaction may be to neglect, totally or partly, the new events: this is for example what has been happening for many years, with the questions relating to global warning. A third reaction, may be to change the constitution with a strong counterfactual accent, and associating the new constitution with a given family of meta-theories, for example political liberalism and economic liberalism, as it has been taking place in Russia in Eltsin times,[78] or in Poland after 1989.[79] In this way, the counterfactual approach may be unsuccessful, due to the fact that the theories posed as the ground to this counterfactual transformation do not take into a due account the complexity of the events that legally reasonable solutions ought to take into consideration. The risk may be constitutional cycles,[80] or even the failure of different projects of reform.

For this reason we will continue our analysis, by considering how other economic models, may be referred to, with respect to the need of the dynamic approach to constitutions and constitutionalism. In particular we would like to examine the question of the relationship between production-based theories and their eventual constitutional assumptions. We would also like to present a limited attempt to consider the cybernetic paradigm in economic analysis[81] with some detachment, however, from the political environment in which it was developed.

78 Uliukajev A., Reforming the Russian Economy 1991–1995, London 1996.

79 Policastro P., Constitutional Reflections on the Potentialities of a Pasinetti's Agency for Full Employment during the Economic Transformation in Poland, paper presented at the IX International conference on "Structural Dynamics in Economic Theory". Monte Verità, Canton Ticino, Settembre 1998.

80 P. Policastro, "On the Reconstruction", cit.

81 O. Lang, "Cybernetyka a Ekonomia" 1965 in O. Lang, Dzieła, vol 7, Cybernetyka, Warszawa 1977.

6 The Dynamic Constitutional Approach and the Dynamic Economic Approach

6.1. The dynamic approach to the economic analysis may present in its own approach, different consequences related to legal institutions. However, we also see in the exchange-based models that the institutions of the free market appear as a normative consequence of the model itself. A first attempt to consider the use of such theories in a theory of constitutions and of constitutionalism ought then to try to consider the context in which such theories developed. This context is important in order to see which kind of reasoning we may relate with the use of such theories as complementary theories or as founding theories with respect to the theory of constitution and constitutionalism.

If we look at the thought of the 'classical' economic thinkers, we may relate their reasoning with one of their most fundamental concerns: that is to overcome the institutions related with the remnants of the feudal system. There is to this respect continuity between the thought of the classics and the pre-classical economic thought. The fact that the pre-classical economic thought was not yet formalized according with the canons of modern economic sciences, enables to show a significant relationship between economic thought and the development of 'science of the state' (Staatswissenschaft). So classical economy may be read both in the perspective of a dynamic constitutional development with respect to the institutions of the "Ancient regime" and in the perspective of the consolidation of the institutions of the process of accumulation and distribution, which characterized the first stage of European capitalism. From this we see the criticism moved to the model of capitalistic accumulation by Karl Marx, starting from the approach of the human rights of the French Declaration of 1789, considered as the legal background for the dominating role of bourgeoisie. Furthermore, the criticism of Karl Marx went as far as to put in evidence the relationship between the cyclical crises of the capitalist economies and the institutions of the 'capitalistic' mode of production. Such criticism was calling for a 'transformation' both to the economic theory and to constitutional theory and therefore highlighted the question of the constitutional transformation related to the capitalistic accumulation.[82] We see the influence of the competition between the different "classical" approaches to the theory of distribution and accumulation of capital, also in the theory of the constitution and of the legislation also in the constitutions approved in the aftermath of World War I. We may look, however, at such a competition as if it would take place between different institutional grounds supporting the classical approach to economics. This opposition of the institutional grounds supporting a similar analytical approach to the economic theory, and based on the search of the "causes" of the process of distribution and accumulation, had however some ambiguities. Indeed, it did not permit to abandon completely some of the 'mechanisms' related with the institutional background of the one approach to classical theory, within the other competing "classical"-based

82 Indeed, and among other things, Marx points out that capital is not a thing but a social relation among people, mediated by things, see K. Marx, Das Kapital. Kritik der politischen Ökonomie, London 1872, first ed. 1867, and of the II and III books 1885, Italian version Il capitale. Critica dell'economia politica, ed. by E. Sbardella, Roma 1996, p. 550.

approach. Indeed, also within Marx criticism of classical economic theory, and the "bourgeois" political order,[83] and in the context of a newly radical approach to the legal and political mediation of the Bolshevik U.S.S.R., the "New Economic Policy" of Lenin's time was making[84] – we find a limited use of the mechanisms of production and of exchange. The latter elements appear, then, as inherent to the reasoning of the classical economic approach.

We may look at this ambiguity as if it would suggest us that the opposition between the production models and of the exchange models of economic analysis, in terms of their institutional background, may take place only 'prima facie'. Furthermore, that such an opposition fades somehow away when we need to explain such institutional approaches in depth, that is through a justification for the uses of legal theory. Indeed, as we had already the occasion to stress, the complexity of the operations of interpretation that we use in legal theory requires in general – as we stressed above – families of founding theories. It requires also families of complementary theories, which results and methods permit to integrate the argument we develop. In all these cases, the awareness of the range of definition and of application of each (founding and each) complementary theory has a key meaning. This is also because in the process of coordination of different theories within an articulated legal argument, which includes reference to its foundation, the choice of the complementary theories and a significant part of the choice of the founding theories take place already when we display the matters of the argument. That is, it takes from the 'prima facie' but affect all the following parts of the justification and of its communication to third parties.

6.2. On the ground of these remarks, we may then reflect on the exchange-production duality that characterizes economic history and economic analysis. Namely, as some scholars observed, in different periods there has been a prevalence of interest to production-based phenomena, whilst in other historical periods exchange-based phenomena prevailed. Such prevalence has been affecting not only the development of economic theory, but it led in different periods economic models centered on different paradigms to exercise a dominant influence on legal institutions and on constitutions. When we deal with the distinction between production-based models and exchange-based models,[85] one of the most interesting difference that scholars have been highlighting is that the first ones are supposed to be 'descriptive' and the second ones 'normative'. From this distinction, the scholars have been arguing that the 'production' based models are studying historical series of data, whilst normative models are based upon 'psychological assumptions', and on this ground, they can be considered as 'predictive'. Anyhow, both these approaches appear to be 'explicative' with respect to a 'pre-existent' constitution, related, directly or indirectly, with the assumption of the models. Directly, when we deal with the framework of the production based model and their 'institutional' assumption, however

83 M. Dobb, Political Economy and Capitalism, London 1940, first edition 1937, Italian version Economia politica e capitalismo, Torino 1972.

84 A. Nove, The Soviet Economic System, London 1980, first edition 1977.

85 Baranzini M., Scazzieri R. (eds.), Foundations of Economics, see especially the introductory essay of M. Baranzini and Roberto Scazzieri and the final essay of Alberto Quadrio Curzio and Roberto Scazzieri, which deal in particular with the dichotomy "production-exchange" as two paradigms of economic analysis.

limited. Indirectly, when we deal with models based upon psychological or behavioral assumptions that aim to optimize the variables objective within an institutional framework.

So, however predictive, or simply analytical, the models developed by the two approaches are based upon a 'constitution' derived from the past or inherent to the assumptions of the model. In both cases we have then that such classes of models alone, are not in principle able to give indication on the future developments of a constitution. This is because either they refer to a constitution taken from the reality they observe, with its principle of distributions, or they require the existence of an institutional order – the free market order in particular.

So, the two classes of models, the economic models of production and of exchange appear to support either a static approach to constitution or being indifferent to the constitutional problem. We may understand such indifference as incapability to deal in a systemic way with the consequences on the change of the model of repartition of political influences, of the model of repartition of the influences on the society, and the model of repartition of the influences on the production and the distribution of wealth. We may look at such incapability as evidence, that the object of economic analysis and the object of constitutional theory are different.

Continuing our consideration on these issues, we may not deny to the classics a significant interest to a constitutional order that may have been in the condition to overcome unjustified constraints to the display of economic activeness. The so-called pre-theoretical approaches, such as the one of Galiani and the one of Genovesi,[86] shared such interest. We will simply mention the far-reaching criticism of Marx to the constitutional and institutional framework of the capitalistic system. We may also acknowledge a significant interest to the relationship between constitution and policy in the marginalistic school. The attempt of such schools was indeed to combine the institutional framework and the policy in order to permit the good functioning of the market forces. Anyhow, the marginalistic frame of mind with respect to the constitutional framework shows ambiguities that we may not neglect in our analysis. Indeed, it appears applicable even in the systems where the state owns the means of production and centrally plans the economic processes, an approach influenced by cybernetics line of research.[87]

The results developed in the marginalistic theory appear anyhow addressed to show the results of some 'relations' within an economic system that show how 'market' structures may function. The 'competing' economic theories centered upon the production paradigm and starting from 'structural' data also make possible some interesting consideration concerning constitutional issues. However, such considerations were not always free of ambiguities. For example, the structural approach

86 Schumpeter, Storia, cit.; Pasinetti "Theory of Value – a Source of Alternative Paradigms in Economic Analysis" in Baranzini, Scazzieri, Foundations, cit., esp. p. 411–414.

87 See the importance acknowledged by Oskar Lange to the essay of E Barone "Il Ministro della Produzione nello Stato collettivista", Giornale degli Economisti, Sept./Oct., 2, pp. 267–293, English version "The Ministry of Production in the Collectivist State", in F.A. Hayek, ed. (1935), Collectivist Economic Planning, pp. 245–90; see O. Lange, "On the Economic Theory of Socialism", Review of Economic Studies 1936 n. 1; Id. "The Economists's Case for Socialism", Review of economic Studies 1937; for the Polish version "O ekonomicznej teorii socjalizmu" in Id. Wybór Pism. 1. Drogi do socajlizmu, Warszawa 1990, p. 139–194.

developed also by means of refined mathematical considerations, such as the ones of von Neumann, who attempted to consider the economic system defining its 'physical state' in a given moment by means of input-output data, and analyzing its development by means of sequences of state-descriptions of the economic system.[88] The 'viability conditions' used by von Neumann may be given different economic interpretation, supported by different grounds of assumptions backgrounds. For example, we may mention the approach of Arrow-Debreu[89] in which perspective based upon the exchange paradigms each individual may consume out of his initial stock in a feasible way, and still have a positive amount of each commodity available for trading in the market. We may underline only that, in the production-based perspective, it implies a very clearly defined destination of the net product, in form of profits, and their destination to accumulation (Pasinetti, 1975, p. 236 s.). In this perspective, the problem of von Neumann is to search those relative quantities related to the rate of growth, and simultaneously those relative prices and rates of profit that may be constant within time (Pasinetti, ibidem). The structural nature of the problem is important, due also to the theoretical features of the von Neumann approach. In fact, such an approach lies between the models founded on the exchange paradigm of economic research, and the models based upon the production paradigm of research. The first ones envisage their equilibrium on the base of institutional conditions, which may be seen as 'prima facie' static constitutional conditions, while the second kind of models, the production-based models are more indifferent to institutional issues. Notwithstanding such apparent indifference, the clear position of the 'viability conditions' has been permitting the practical use of the von Neumann approach also for what concerns the study of the general equilibrium within production-based models. Of noteworthy importance we find in this field the studies developed by Leontjef.[90] The Neumann approach to the 'viability' condition for the general equilibrium,[91] has been leading also to important develop-

88 The importance of the studies of J. von Neumann is extremely relevant also due to its contribution to the cybernetic 'line of research' in economic theory. Here we can refer to his seminal contribution "Über ein ökonomisches Gleichungssystem und eine Verallgemeinerung des Brouwereschen Fixpunktsatzes", in K. Menger (ed.), Ergebnisse eines Matematischen Kolloquiums, vol. VIII, Vienna 1937; English version "A Model of Genertal Equilibrium", The Review of Economic Studies 1945–46. For what concern the developments of the author into the cybernetic line of research, see at least Probabilistic Logic and the Synthesis of Reliable Organisms from Unreliable Components 1952, in C.E. Shannon, J. McCarthy (eds.), Automata Studies, Princeton 1956.

89 K. Arrow G. Debreu, "Existence of an Equilibrium for a Competitive Economy", Econometrica, Vol. 22, Issue 3 (July 1954), p. 265–290 esp. p. 270.

90 W.W. Leontjef et al., Studies in the Structure of the American Economy, New York 1953; Id. (ed.), Structure, System and Economic Policy, London, New York, Melbourne 1977.

91 On the base of the fixed point theorem, according with which each contraction defined in a complete metric space has one and only one fixed point. See A. Kolmogorov, S. Fomin, Elementy teorii fukntsij i funktsional'nogo analiza, Moskva 1980; Italian version, Elementi di analisi funzionale e teoria delle funzioni, Moskva, p. 76f., where the authors develop the questions related to the use of the principle for the proof of the existence and unicitiy, as well as for the development of methods to find the solution of different kind of families of systems of equations. The importance of such findings is related to all the sequent theory of topological spaces. Such theory, within the understanding of mathematical modelling, may be indeed related to different mathematical 'rules of reason' and mathematical 'possible worlds'.

ments that permitted to get with more precision some specific structural features of economic systems. We can see this in the Sraffa,[92] approach that made possible to concentrate the study of the viability conditions with reference only to the sub-system of the basic commodities (Pasinetti 1975, Sraffa 1960). The developments of the studies on the viability conditions in the input-output approaches, permitted them to develop a number of reflections concerning not only policy issues, but also the constitutional framework. For example, we may mention property law and competition legislation issues, related to the marginalistic perspective, whilst from the production theory approach, we may refer to the study of those interventions in economic structure that permit the equilibrium of the sub-system of the basic commodities, including nationalization, public aids to the research and so on. Indeed, we may say that von Neumann approach develops a far-reaching coordination between mathematical methodology – and its different application for example in quantum theory physics – and economic theory. Such coordination supports the foundation of the different economic models, as well as the reasonableness of its results, but within the specific range of their assumption and their specific modeling perspective.

However, we may grant to such modeling and to such reasoning, a specific meaning within the reasonableness characterizing the legal interpretation.

7 On the 'Prima Facie' Institutional Implications of the Production Based Models

We can find a remarkable example of the said theoretical developments in the Pasinetti approach that, in the attempt to overcome the problem of the fixed-coefficients in the input-output models, developed a vertically integrated dynamical analysis. Concerning the viability conditions, the Pasinetti model shows a two-step approach, in which the first part is the explicit expression of the economic structure by means of vertically integrated labor coefficients. The "vertical integration" appears as a way to explicit the viability conditions in the Leontjef model, highlighting in the same time the "rounds" of production that contributed to the development of the initial structure.[93] The "rounds" of production are ordered in a time sequence. For this reason the Pasinetti approach shows the definite overcoming through the models developed after von Neumann of an analytical approach based on the structure of given economic relations, centering instead the attention on the economic system.[94] This aspect appears in the final formulation of the viability conditions in

92 P. Sraffa, Production of Commodities by Means of Commodities – Prelude to a Critique of Economic Theory, Cambridge 1960; Italian version, Produzione di merci a mezzo merci. Preludio di una critica dell'economia politica, Torino 1960.

93 L.L. Pasinetti, Lezioni di teoria della produzione 1975, p. 87–88, in relation to p. 96–97 and to Pasinetti, Structural Dynamics, cit. 1981, p. 112–113.

94 See L.L., Pasinetti 'Vertical Integration in Economic Analysis', published in Metroeconomica 1973; Italian version of the essay: "La nozione di settore verticalmente integrato nell'analisi economica", in L.L. Pasinetti, Contributi alla teoria della produzione congiunta, Bologna,1977, p. 37 n. 1.

his multi-sector model of economic growth[95] as one sum, extended to all the commodities demanded, where each addendum is the quantity of vertically integrated labor needed for the production of one unit of a given commodity (the technical coefficient) times the average demand pro-capite of a of a given commodity. Each addendum is considered in its time dimension, as a changing quantity, and the overall sum represents "the effective demand condition for keeping full employment through time".[96] In order to preserve the dynamic equilibrium such a sum shall be identically equal to one. Such an identity shows in the approach to the model, the attention to the systemic aspect of the economic process.[97] It is not a 'numéraire' but we can consider it as a 'metric' element. This appears consistent, however, with the understanding of the production paradigm of analysis, followed by the same Pasinetti, who seems to continue the research, started by the classical economists, directed to "identify the values which are needed for the weighing of the social product". Such process of weighing, as John Hicks has been underlining,[98] appears addressed to consider the different commodities within a "common measure". Notwithstanding the evolution in the attention of the economic thinkers, put in evidence by the same Hicks, the search of a common measure, that is a series of general structural relations for all the system, may be seen as a feature that characterizes also general equilibrium models, developed within the approach to marginal analysis. So the fact, that marginal analysis approach is based on exchange, does not change the terms of the problem. The search of a common measure, takes place, however, in all the different economic theories, although with a different approach to the hypotheses of the models, and to the paradigms of research. We may reach such a conclusion from an intuition-based approach to the problems of general equilibrium that relates to the finding of values that 'clear-out' a system of linear relations, which seems the approach followed by Samuelson.[99] We may reach similar conclusions considering the geometrical interpretation of the determinant of a matrix,[100] which instead may be referred to the approaches used within the production theories. Both the approaches appear however consistently related with the von Neumann perspective of the minimax principle,[101] which, however extending the maximization approaches outside the range of the mere marginal analysis, did confirm the significance of this tool. Such common measures, although different between the different paradigms, create not only competition among them but also an inner dimension of reasonableness for each paradigm of economic theory.

In the case of the Pasinetti dynamic equilibrium, for example, the above said 'common measure' is the relationship between demand coefficient and technical

95 Pasinetti Structural Dynamics, cit., p. 86.

96 Ibidem, especially equation V.4.4.

97 Ibidem, p. 109–117.

98 J. Hicks (1976), "Revolutions" in Economics, in Latsis S.J. (ed.), Methods and Appraisal in Economics, Cambridge, p. 207–218; it. ed. "Rivoluzioni" in economia in John Hicks (1985), Moneta, capitale, benessere. Saggi di teoria economica, ed. by C. Casarossa, S. Zamagni, p. 291.

99 Samuelson, The Foundations, cit. 1953, p. 5.

100 V.I. Arnold, Obiennovenneye differenzialnye uravnenia, Moskva 1979, Italian version, Equazioni differenziali ordinarie, p. 126–127.

101 Which is a core principle in game theory. See, V. Neumann, "Zur Theorie der Gesellschaftsspiele", Mathematische Annalen', vol. 100 (1928), pp. 295–320.

coefficient within time, in condition of full employment. Outside such 'systemic' condition, the economy will be in disequilibrium. The quoted author claims that this equilibrium may not be reached automatically, and therefore gives rise to a number of necessary activities, to be performed by public and by private actors. The necessity of such activities may tempt many people to consider such activities as true "constitutional implications" of such a model. For example this is the case of the "Central Agency entrusted with the task of keeping full employment.[102] This may be also the case of the free market condition permitting the general equilibrium in the marginal economic analysis of Samuelson. However, in both the approaches, the one of Samuelson, championing the exchange based theory, and Pasinetti approach, championing the production based theory, the purpose to develop generally valid theorems appears very strong. Samuelson speaks about the development of "meaningful theorems", that is "an hypothesis about empirical data which could conceivably be refuted".[103] Also, Pasinetti tries to develop the features of 'the natural economic system',[104] an economic system characterized by properties independent from any specific institutional constraint. However, we may see that when the two approaches, the one of Samuelson, and the one of Pasinetti, when applied to reality, lead to different theoretical results, as for example the famous ones related to relevance of the worker's saving rate in the model of distribution.[105] The difference of hypotheses does not appear sufficient to justify the differences. As we see in the analysis of Nicholas Kaldor,[106] we deal with a different approach to economic reasoning and the conception of the economic process.[107]

We may be tempted to look also at the models that consider the 'natural system' as free from institutional constraints, as models characterized by an 'hidden or an implicit constitution'. For what concerns the content of such 'natural constitution' in the Pasinetti model we see that a process of technical progress developing continuously with the time according with the improvement of the dexterity following the application of human labor to given productive operations, embodies at least the assumption that we do not deal with a system where technical development is centrally steered. Some other authors have been seeing in the Pasinetti approach some reference to a 'democratic enterprise'. We will refrain here from a deeper analysis of the issue, but we have to point out that the approach to the 'natural economic system' that has been developed so far may take into account the existence of an 'implicit' constitution, where freedom of opinion and rights of the individual to actively 'participate' to the economic processes are acknowledged and are legally enforceable. Secondly, Pasinetti reflections show the necessity of public authorities that are able to perform 'public duties', by means of policies. In particular, they ought to be able, in order to maintain the 'dynamic equilibrium' to monitor the

102 Pasinetti, Structural Dynamics, cit., p. 91.

103 Samuelson, Foundations, cit., p. 4–5.

104 Pasinetti, Structural Dynamics, cit.

105 N. Kaldor, "Marginal Productivity and the Macro-Economic Theories of Distribution: Comment on Samuelson and Modigliani", The Review of Economic Studies, vol. 33 1966, n. 4; Italian version: "La produttività marginale e le teorie macroeconomiche della distribuzione", in Id. Equilibrio, distribuzione e crescita, ed. by F. Targhetti, Torino 1984, p. 203–204.

106 Ibidem.

107 Ibidem.

transformation of the internal and the external demand. They ought also to be able to intervene supporting the sectors that produce goods which rate of growth of the demand is 'speeding up', as well as 'helping' the structural change of the investments and the labor inputs for those sectors which tempo if growth of the demand is diminishing. Such forms of intervention may include labor and social policies as well as policies supporting research and schooling. A third feature of the 'implicit' construction of the constitution in the "natural economic systems" à la Pasinetti is the constitutional support for a system of free international exchanges and co-operation in a politically peaceful environment. These requirements, however, may be shared also by the exchange-based theories.

A forth feature of the Pasinetti model is the specific approach to the relationship between variables and constants that concentrated on the constant character of the rate of profit on a secular scale. Such a constant, however was measured within a period were the capitalistic processes of production flourished. Although such a relationship has a fundamental meaning in the construction of the economic features of the model, it has been giving rise to specific debates related to the level of the salaries and capital-labor relations.

However, analogously as what happens for the exchange-based model, the consistency between the approaches of the production-based models and some constitutional grounds may hold only 'prima facie'. Indeed, each of the economic paradigms of research that we have been studying so far presents its own reasonableness. Such difference stems from the choice of the ground of the modeling and affects the understanding of the economic process. This choice is specific for the problems being the object of the economic analysis, and it can be used only as complementary theory respect to the understanding of law.

8 Constitutionalism and Legal Reasoning: The Search of a Hypertext as a Way to Conjugate the Use of Complementary Theories to Law with Constitutionalism as a Founding Theory of Law

Our brief inquiry on the constitutional 'features' embodied in the different production-based models, including what has been called the "natural economic system" shows that, similarly as in the case of the marginalistic approaches, a complementary approach to constitution, that can be obtained by economic modeling, may not in principle deal with the articulated and complex aspects of the constitutional order. It may be not in particular deal in a satisfactory way both with the paradigms of constitutionalism, nor with the questions of constitutional change.

The range of variables that are related with the functioning of the economic models is very different from the object of constitutions, considered in their overall complexity and articulations. For example the assumptions done concerning constitutions, as for example in institutional approaches to economics, are addressed to phenomena or in a way that is relevant for economic science, or in an approach that makes use of the specific reasonableness used in economic reasoning. That is, without taking into account the need of a specific legally grounded justification when dealing with phenomena that, such as constitution, are the specific object of legal knowledge and interpretation.[108] For this reasons, the results of the economic models may be used within the legal reasoning, but after the transposition of the yielding of the economic models, within the terms of legal reasoning, its relation with an overall and complex constitutional construction, and constitutionalism. Therefore, generally speaking, we may not make use of the economic approach as a general way to argue in laws. In laws, the quality of relations between individuals, between individuals and communities, between communities play a fundamental role, that affect the purposes and reasoning used in legal interpretation. Although, obviously, political economics general statements interface with the constitutional principles, within the development of the legal reasoning we have to take into account the achievement of constitutional goals, and the results expressed by economic models ought to be resolved within the approach to the achievement of such goals. Furthermore, we ought to consider the issues related with the achievement of constitutional goals, within reasoning that takes into account the paradigms of constitutionalism. In this way, constitutional interpretation may be consistent with the different needs that appear in the process of European integration and in the process of strengthening legal and economic interdependence between individual and communities in the global arena.

If we then see a certain analogy between given constitutions and some economic modeling, we ought to take into account that such analogy is "prima facie" and is not in general related to a deep constitutional justifications, grounded upon constitutionalism. The use of the results of the economic models in constitutional interpretation ought to take into account their role of complementary theories, and of the need to explain the economic reasoning within the framework of a legal reasoning. This has to be done using founding theories, and first of all constitutionalism. Especially when we deal with constitutions having dynamic purposes, aiming to lead to a change in the model of distribution of wealth, of the influences on politics and of the influences on society, we shall highlight the importance of the correct use of complementary theories and meta-theories.

A summing up reflection is that, as we have been seeing throughout this paper, the economic models related to the different paradigms of production and of exchange, present different rationales, which embody the assumptions of each author and the phenomena studies as the core object of economic theory. However, both for what concerns the paradigm of production and the paradigm of exchange and the different lines of research that stem out from them, including the cybernetic one and the institutional line of research, we do not find, except some *prima facie* elements, evidence that reasonableness considered within the different economic mod-

108 We shall limit ourselves to quote J. Buchanan, "The Constitution of Economic Policy", The American Economic Review, Vol. 77, No. 3, June 1987, pp. 243–250. The article is the text of the Nobel price lecture, delivered by James Buchnan in Stockholm on December 8th 1986, containing many references to the Swedish economist Knut Wicksell. The text shows the tendency of Buchanan to look, within a perspective that he relates – among others – to the thought of Wicksell, to constitution within an approach that is peculiar for economic reasoning, within an exchange-based approach, and basing on a priori defined constitutional assumption. This approach very difficult to apply, and when applied, may give rise to serious problems, in a context where different approaches to law and constitution interact. Furthermore, it makes it almost impossible to use constitutionalism in counterfactual terms.

els resembles the one embodied within legal theory. This is a consequence of the difference between the assumptions and the objects of economic and of legal theory. For this reason, the results of the different economic models, may become included in the legal reasoning only if this appears reasonable within legal theory, once considered in depth the assumptions of the legal models and compared with constitutional principles, values and rights. It derives from this conclusion that no "economic analysis of law" may be possible, whenever we may understand by such concept the straightforward use of tools manifesting the reasonableness embodied in economic models. These conclusions appear to hold, independently of the paradigm of economic analysis that we may take for reference.

However interesting and inspiring the results produced by the tools developed for reasoning within economic models may be for lawyers, the acknowledgment of the results within the legal theory ought to be submitted to specific tests, in order to consider their consistency and its possible use within legal reasoning. Such tests relate, among others to verify if, and in which measure, the criteria used make sense within the reasoning approach related to the paradigms of constitutionalism.

For this reason we may say, trying to answer to the general questions we set at the beginning of our paper concerning the use of one theory as a complementary theory to another one – an object theory. Such use is submitted to the requirement that both the object theory and the complementary theory ought to be understood with reference to the same grounding 'language'. In particular the use of economic analysis for the sake of legal understanding and legal interpretation, is submitted to the requirement that the assumptions, the tools and the reasons used in complementary theories, have to be considered within the language used in order to clear up the purposes of the object theory. For this reason for example, the rules considered in engineering science are important and extremely significant for law, due to the fact that the security and the permanence of buildings different constructions is essential for legal security. For the same reason, the lawyer may always question the use of the specific assumptions used by the engineers in consider a building problem, for the sake of obtaining a more precise and punctual statement. Such a statement, in its turn, may guarantee legal security at a higher extent, and therefore guarantee the predictability of legal science. *A contrariis*, the use of a concept of constitution of an economic model, when oversimplified – for what concerns the requirements of constitutional theory, as we find in many approaches to collective choice in economic analysis – may even lead to conflicting solutions with respect to the ones developed by legal theories, but may not be significant for law as such. Similarly the use of methods developed within economic analysis, for example in trading off between goods in order to attain constrained equilibrium may not be in condition to replace the operations that we use to balance in legal science. Also the use of more sophisticated tools such as game theory, may be fallacious without an adequate description of the variables – functionals – involved.

Therefore, the search of an adequate meta-theory, useful for the practical needs law has to accomplish, relates to the ability to find a true hypertext, which is able to match complementary theories without leading to paradoxes, justifies the search of methods permitting to compare theories. Such a complex analysis, may serve to consider in more detail constitutionalism, as a meta-theory permitting to confront solutions adopted in different systems of government related to substantively different forms of political organization. Such an approach to complexity, based upon the comparison between theories as well as to the comparison between political systems, may better fit to today's needs where the "dream" of a diffusion in Europe and worldwide of the institutions of the constitutional state is fading away, due also to the hardships of the present economical and political situation in the global arena. We may remember here that at the beginning of the science of comparative law the substantive difference among the constitutions was based on factual evidence.[109] For this reason, the achievements of constitutionalism may help – when adequately supported by the reconstruction of the legal semiosphere – finding a common language permitting a counterfactual and predictive function of law. Together with this a dynamic approach to law and constitution may help coping better with human needs, although in the present situation of global diversity.

109 Aristotele, Politica, ed. by R. Laurenti, Roma-Bari 1993.

Jelena von Achenbach

Vorschläge zu einer Demokratietheorie der dualen demokratischen Legitimation europäischer Hoheitsgewalt

Abstract:
As Art. 10 of the Treaty of the European Union states, the democratic legitimacy of the European Union's public power is based on two political subjects and two forms of political representation:

> "The functioning of the Union shall be founded on representative democracy. Citizens are directly represented at Union level in the European Parliament. Member States are represented in the European Council by their Heads of State or Government and in the Council by their governments, themselves democratically accountable either to their national Parliaments, or to their citizens."

This dual model of democracy poses several questions which need to be investigated from a democratic theory point of view: How is the co-existence of two political subjects of the European Union – the Union citizenry on the one hand and the peoples of the Member States on the other hand – to be conceptualized? Of which kind are the structural differences between them? And how do the two representative organs of the Union, European Parliament and Council, relate to each other? Can they substitute each other as democratic organs of the Union? Or does one of them mediate more, or superior democratic legitimacy?

In engaging with these questions, the article proposes a normative theory of the dual democratic structure of the European Union.

1 Offene Fragen zum Konzept dualer demokratischer Legitimation europäischer Hoheitsgewalt

Die demokratische Legitimation der hoheitlichen Gewalt der Europäischen Union beruht auf zwei Legitimationssträngen. Sie verlaufen über das direkt von den Unionsbürgerinnen und -bürgern gewählte Europäische Parlament und den Rat, der sich aus den Regierungsvertretern der Mitgliedstaaten zusammensetzt. Nach den Lissabonner Reformen ist dieses duale Legitimationsmodell durch Art. 10 Abs. 1 und 2 EU nunmehr rechtsprinzipiell in den vertraglichen Grundlagen der EU verankert:

> „Die Arbeitsweise der Union beruht auf der repräsentativen Demokratie. Die Bürgerinnen und Bürger sind auf Unionsebene unmittelbar im Europäischen Parlament vertreten. Die Mitgliedstaaten werden im Europäischen Rat von ihrem jeweiligen Staats- oder Regierungschef und im Rat von ihrer jeweiligen Regierung vertreten, die ihrerseits in demokratischer Weise gegenüber ihrem nationalen Parlament oder gegenüber ihren Bürgerinnen und Bürgern Rechenschaft ablegen müssen."

Dieses Modell der demokratischen Legitimation eröffnet eine Reihe von demokratietheoretischen Fragen: Wie verhalten sich die beiden primärrechtlich eingesetzten Legitimationssubjekte der EU, die Gesamtheit der Unionsbürgerinnen und -bürger und die mitgliedstaatlichen Staatsvölker, zueinander? Gehen die beiden über Rat und Parlament verlaufenden Legitimationsstränge europäischer Hoheitsgewalt von zwei strukturell unterschiedlichen Legitimationssubjekten aus oder ist ihre legitimatorische Grundlage letztlich eine einzige?[1] Wie verhalten sich Europäisches Parlament und Rat als demokratische Vertretungsorgane zueinander? Stehen sie jenseits ihres gesetzgeberischen Zusammenwirkens in ihrer demokratischen Funktion miteinander in Beziehung? Vermittelt eines der Organe europäischer Gesetzgebung ein höheres Maß oder qualitativ höherwertige demokratische Legitimation als das andere? Können Rat und Parlament einander in ihrer demokratischen Funktion ersetzen?

Diese Fragen sind nicht allein von demokratietheoretischer, sondern zugleich von praktischer Bedeutung: Europäisches Parlament und Rat wirken bei der Ausübung der legislativen Gewalt der Union in unterschiedlichen Formen zusammen.[2] Abhängig davon, welches Gesetzgebungsverfahren zur Anwendung kommt, sind die formale gesetzgeberische Verantwortung und die Möglichkeiten inhaltlicher Gestaltung der Gesetzgebung zwischen ihnen unterschiedlich verteilt. Die verschiedenen Verfahren gewichten so zugleich die durch die beiden Organe institutionalisierten Legitimationsstränge im Verhältnis zueinander: Die kompetenzielle Ausstattung des Europäischen Parlamentes und des Rates bei der Gesetzgebung bestimmt, in welchem Umfang die beiden Organe jeweils demokratische Legitimation vermitteln. Bedarf wie im Fall des Anhörungsverfahrens der Erlass eines Gesetzes nicht der Zustimmung des Parlaments und kann dieses den Inhalt eines Gesetzgebungsvorhabens nicht unabhängig vom Wohlwollen des Rates oder der Kommission mit seinen politischen Präferenzen beeinflussen, fehlt es an der Bindung der Gesetzgebung an die parlamentarische Willensbildung, über die das Parlament seine demokratische Legitimation zu vermitteln vermag.

Die Frage nach dem Verhältnis von Europäischem Parlament und Rat als Vermittler demokratischer Legitimation lässt sich vor diesem verfassungsrechtlichen Hintergrund konkreter reformulieren: Vermitteln sämtliche der verschiedenen Gesetzgebungsverfahren der Europäischen Union der europäischen Gesetzgebung das gleiche Maß an demokratischer Legitimation oder bestehen in dieser Hinsicht Unterschiede? Ist Gesetzgebung, die nach bloßer Anhörung des Parlamentes ergangen ist, ebenso demokratisch legitim wie solche, die im Verfahren der Mitentscheidung zustande gekommen ist? Oder sind, respektive wären, bestimmte Formen des gesetzgeberischen Zusammenwirkens von Europäischem Parlament und Rat demokratisch defizitär?

Mit dem vorliegenden Beitrag werden Überlegungen zu den aufgeworfenen Fragen skizziert und damit zugleich Thesen zu einer Demokratietheorie der dualen

1 Armin von Bogdandy, Grundprinzipien, in: Bogdandy/Bast (Hrsg.), Europäisches Verfassungsrecht 2009, 13, 64.

2 Zwar ist nunmehr das Mitentscheidungsverfahren das ordentliche Gesetzgebungsverfahren (Art. 289 Abs. 1, Art. 294 AEU), weiterhin aber kommen daneben als besondere Gesetzgebungsverfahren das Verfahren der Anhörung und das Verfahren der Zustimmung zur Anwendung. In ersterem gibt das Parlament zu einem Gesetzesvorhaben lediglich eine Stellungnahme ab, an die der Rat nicht gebunden ist. In letzterem kann das Parlament der Annahme eines Gesetzes des Rates zustimmen oder seine Zustimmung verweigern, aber keine Änderungen einbringen. Der Rat kann in diesem Verfahren ein Gesetz jedoch nicht erlassen, solange das Parlament nicht mit der absoluten Mehrheit seiner Mitglieder zustimmt. Im Verfahren der Mitentscheidung bedarf die Annahme eines Gesetzes der beiderseitigen Zustimmung von Parlament und Rat, beide Organe können Änderungen am Gesetzgebungsvorhaben einbringen.

demokratischen Legitimation europäischer Hoheitsgewalt zur Diskussion gestellt.[3] Den Ausgangspunkt bildet im folgenden Abschnitt die Darlegung der zugrunde gelegten demokratietheoretischen Annahmen (2.). Es folgt eine demokratietheoretische Auseinandersetzung mit dem dualen Demokratiemodell des Primärrechts (3.).

2 Demokratietheoretische Grundlagen

Die Untersuchung des Modells einer dualen demokratischen Legitimation europäischer Hoheitsgewalt hinsichtlich der einleitend aufgeworfenen Fragen bedarf der demokratietheoretischen Grundlegung. Notwendig ist zum einen die Referenz auf eine normative Theorie des Subjekts der demokratischen Legitimation hoheitlicher Gewalt, des *demos* der Demokratie.[4] Erst auf dieser Basis kann das primärrechtliche Modell zweier demokratischer Subjekte der Europäischen Union, das wesentlicher Bestandteil des Modells des Art. 10 EU ist, demokratietheoretisch reflektiert werden. Des Weiteren ist die Grundlage eines normativen Konzepts demokratischer Repräsentation und der legitimatorischen Funktionsweise der Rückkopplung legislativer Organe an Wahlen erforderlich.

2.1 Das Subjekt demokratischer Legitimation und demokratische Gleichheit

Zentrale Annahme zum Subjekt demokratischer Legitimation ist vorliegend, dass hoheitliche Gewalt jedem Individuum gegenüber rechtfertigungsbedürftig ist, das durch sie rechtlich gebunden ist. Dies trifft für alle Individuen zu, die von der Geltung von Gesetzgebung erfasst sind, auch ohne dass sie durch die Erfüllung der Anwendungsvoraussetzungen eines legislativen Rechtsakts aktual betroffen sind. Legitimationssubjekt hoheitlicher Gewalt ist damit das Rechtssubjekt.

Im Rahmen rechtlicher Ordnung besteht die Freiheit des Individuums in den Grenzen des Rechts.[5] Hoheitliche Gewalt kennzeichnet als Rechtserzeugung die Betätigung individueller Freiheit entlang der Unterscheidung Recht/Unrecht, rechtmäßig/rechtswidrig und knüpft hieran Folgen. Dadurch wird die Reichweite individueller Freiheit definiert. Die objektive, von der individuellen Zustimmung unabhän-

3 Für eine eingehende Ausarbeitung der in dem Beitrag behandelten Fragen s. Jelena von Achenbach, Das Mitentscheidungsverfahren des Art. 294 AEUV als demokratisches Gesetzgebungsverfahren der Europäischen Union, insbesondere im Bereich der Biomedizin und Humanbiotechnologie, Ms. 2010.

4 Formulierung in Anlehnung an die Wendung das Volk der Volkssouveränität von Ingeborg Maus, Zur Aufklärung der Demokratietheorie 1992 191 ff.; Der Monismus der Volkssouveränität und der Pluralismus der Gesellschaft: das „Volk“ der Volkssouveränität.

5 Dies gilt unabhängig davon, ob man die Freiheit des Individuums als jeder positiven Rechtsordnung bereits vorausgehendes Recht mit nicht-positivem Geltungsgrund denkt, oder als allein positiv begründetes Recht. Zur Ablösung der Lehre des subjektiven Rechts von der metaphysischen Begründung durch das natürliche oder vor allem das moralische Recht Jürgen Habermas, Faktizität und Geltung, 112 ff.

gige Geltung der Definition[6] ist unter dem Gesichtspunkt der Geltung gleicher Freiheit das legitimationsbedürftige Moment hoheitlicher Gewalt.[7]

Um dem demokratischen Gleichheitsanspruch gerecht zu werden, ist die Gleichberechtigung der Rechtssubjekte zur Teilhabe an der hoheitlichen Gewalt erforderlich. Die demokratische Legitimation hoheitlicher Gewalt erfordert daher die Konstitution der Rechtssubjekte zu einem demokratischen Subjekt, indem zwischen ihnen politische Gleichheit etabliert wird. Demokratischer Teilhabemodus sind Wahlen, insoweit sie entlang des Formprinzips gleicher Freiheit verfasst sind: Die demokratische Funktion von Wahlen setzt voraus, dass das Wahlrecht den demokratischen Grundsatz der politischen Gleichheit verwirklicht. Das Wahlrecht muss seinen Trägern in formal gleicher Weise eingeräumt sein und den einzelnen Wahlakten muss das gleiche Gewicht zukommen. Es wird als grundlegendes Prinzip demokratischer Wahlen betrachtet, dass jeder Wähler über die gleiche Anzahl von Stimmen verfügt und dass alle Stimmen bei der Organbesetzung den gleichen Wert haben.

Dieser Ansatz zum Subjekt demokratischer Legitimation kann in der Auseinandersetzung mit der dualen Legitimationsstruktur der Europäischen Union mit zweifacher Bedeutung zum Tragen kommen. Zentral ist seine Funktion als analytische Perspektive der demokratietheoretischen Rekonstruktion der beiden Legitimationsstränge der Union, ihrer demokratischen Leistungsfähigkeit und ihres Verhältnisses zueinander. Hierbei entfaltet er zugleich seine zweite Bedeutung, nämlich seine Funktion als kritischer Maßstab, als normative Position sowohl gegenüber Argumentationen, die im Diskurs über Demokratie auf europäischer Ebene präsent sind, wie auch gegenüber dem primärrechtlichen Konzept des Legitimationssubjekts europäischer Hoheitsgewalt selbst.

2.2 Die elektorale Konstitution der Legislative und ihre pluralistische Kapazität

Das Primärrecht sieht die politische Repräsentation als Demokratiekonzept der Europäischen Union vor: Nach Art. 10 Abs. 1 beruht die Arbeitsweise der EU auf der repräsentativen Demokratie. Mit der Co-Gesetzgeberschaft des Europäischen Parlamentes und des Rates im ordentlichen Gesetzgebungsverfahren sieht das Primärrecht eine zweifache Rückkoppelung der Gesetzgebung an Wahlen als Standardmodus der demokratischen Legitimation vor. Voraussetzung der Entwicklung einer Demokratietheorie des Modells der dualen Legitimation ist deshalb eine normative

6 In Anschluss an Hans Kelsens realistischen, soziologisch aufgeklärten Begriff sozialer, auch rechtlicher Ordnung, s. Hans Kelsen, Vom Wesen und Wert der Demokratie (2. Auflage 1929), in: Jestaedt/Lepsius (Hrsg.), Verteidigung der Demokratie 2006. Die Reichweite individueller Freiheit kann in rechtlicher Ordnung in verschiedenen Formen bestimmt werden; die subjektive Berechtigung wie die subjektive Verpflichtung, die Erlaubnis, wie das Gebot bzw. das Verbot sind ohne weiteres als Fälle der rechtlichen Definition des Raums individueller Freiheit zu erfassen.

7 Eine klassische Position, die dem Recht eine instrinsische Legitimation zuschreibt, ist die Kantische Lehre, dass das Recht „der Inbegriff der Bedingungen [ist], unter denen die Willkür des einen mit der Willkür des anderen nach einem allgemeinen Gesetze der Freiheit zusammen vereinigt werden kann“.

Theorie zu der Frage, auf welche Weise die elektorale Rückkopplung der Legislative der Gesetzgebung demokratische Legitimation vermittelt.

Die Berechtigung des Individuums zur politischen Teilhabe ist legitimatorische Voraussetzung seiner Bindung durch hoheitliche Gewalt – demokratische Legitimation wird durch die Berechtigung des Rechtssubjekts zur politischen Teilhabe an der hoheitlichen Gewalt hervorgebracht. Dies impliziert die demokratische Funktion und Funktionsweise der elektoralen Konstitution der Legislative. Die Herstellung von Repräsentation durch Wahlen hat nicht nur den Zweck, das gewählte Organ formell als Stellvertretung des Legitimationssubjekts zu legitimieren. Ihr Zweck ist darüber hinaus die Ausrichtung der hoheitlichen Gewalt an den Präferenzen der Rechtssubjekte. Heidrun Abromeit hat formuliert, dass Demokratie ihren Sinn verfehle, „wenn zwar das Individuum als solches, nicht aber seine Präferenzen in den Mittelpunkt gerückt werden; denn warum sollte ihm an Beteiligung gelegen sein, wenn nicht um der größtmöglichen Umsetzung seiner Vorstellungen willen?".[8] Repräsentation als Form der – zunächst einfach – vermittelten politischen Beteiligung durch Wahlen eröffnet die Möglichkeit der materiellen Einflussnahme und Gestaltung: Wahlen befähigen die Rechtssubjekte dazu, ihren Willen in Bezug auf die inhaltliche Ausrichtung der gesetzgebenden Gewalt demokratisch zu artikulieren. Das durch regelmäßige Wahlen etablierte Verhältnis der politischen Verantwortlichkeit zwischen der Legislative und den Wählern bindet die legislative Willensbildung an die Präferenzen der wahlberechtigten Rechtssubjekte zurück.

Die Gesetzgebung durch ein gewähltes Organ ist die zentrale Funktionsweise repräsentativ-demokratischer Verfasstheit. In der verfassungstheoretischen Perspektive ist dabei im Rahmen der Gesetzgebung Repräsentation nicht die Aufgabe eines einzigen Individuums, sondern die einer Menge von Individuen – einer Versammlung, eines Parlaments.[9] Die Verfassung der Legislative als gewählte Versammlung ermöglicht den Ausdruck von Uneinigkeit, die Artikulation einer Pluralität von Präferenzen mit Blick auf den Inhalt von Gesetzgebung in der legislativen Willensbildung.[10] Der Versammlungscharakter der Legislative erlaubt die Artikulation differierender, konfligierender politischer Positionen im Rahmen der legislativen Willensbildung.

8 Heidrun Abromeit, Wozu braucht man Demokratie? Die postnationale Herausforderung der Demokratietheorie, S. 165.

9 Die Konstitution der Legislative als gewählte Versammlung ist verfassungstheoretisch die typische Form, die gesetzgebende Gewalt demokratisch zu verfassen. S. auch Jeremy Waldron, Law and disagreement 1999, 49: „Almost everywhere sovereign legislatures are assemblies rather than individuals; in almost every legal system, legislation bases its final authority as law on the fact that it is the product of (or its production has been authorized by) a large popular assembly." Bernard Manin, The principles of representative government 2002 (1997), 184 f.: „Representative government has always been conceived and justified as a political system in which an assembly plays a decisive role. One might imagine [...] that representation could be the privilege of a single individual, appointed and authorized by the people. It is nonetheless undeniably true that representative government was neither proposed nor established as a regime in which power was entrusted to a single indivdual chosen by the people, but as one in which a collective authority occupied a central position."

10 Dahingehend Waldron (Fn. 9), 21 ff., 49 ff. Zur pluralistischen Deutung demokratischer Repräsentation oben 1.

Dass die Legislative die Kapazität zur politischen Artikulation gesellschaftlicher Heterogenität bereitstellt, ist wesentliches Moment der demokratischen Funktion von Gesetzgebung.[11] Demokratische Gesetzgebung ist angesichts gesellschaftlicher Heterogenität nicht zufällig, sondern *wesentlich* durch ihre Erzeugung durch eine Versammlung gekennzeichnet.[12] Teilweise wird die Versammlungsform der Legislative bereits als Grund und Bedingung der Geltung von Gesetzgebung (*authority of legislation*) und der Anerkennung von Entscheidungen mit dem Anspruch allgemeiner Geltung als Recht gesehen (*recognition of a general measure of principle or policy, put forward by the powerful, as law*[13]).[14] Jedenfalls aber ist der Versammlungscharakter der Legislative eng mit ihrer demokratischen Funktion verknüpft. Die demokratische Legitimation von Gesetzgebung ist wesentlich eine Leistung der pluralistischen Kapazität der Willensbildung der gewählten Legislative. Demokratische Legitimation leisten Verfahren der Gesetzgebung, indem sie kollektives Handeln auf der Grundlage einer pluralistischen Willensbildung ermöglichen: *action-in-concert in the face of disagreement.*[15]

2.3 Legitimationsketten

Wegen der Mittelbarkeit der Rückbindung des Rates an Wahlen erfordert die demokratietheoretische Rekonstruktion der dualen Legitimationsstruktur der Union eine normative Theorie mehrfach vermittelter, indirekter Repräsentationszusammenhänge und die Bewertung ihrer Legitimationsleistung. Verfassungstheoretisch wird diese Konstellation einer indirekten elektoralen Rückbindung – in Anlehnung an die Lehre des Bundesverfassungsgerichts – über die Figur der *Legitimationskette* konzipiert. Danach kann ein Ableitungszusammenhang, der von der demokratischen Legitimation des Parlaments ausgeht, politischen Akteuren demokratische Legitimation vermitteln: Politische Akteure sind personell-organisatorisch legitimiert, wenn sie parlamentarisch gewählt oder durch Amtsträger gewählt, bestellt oder ernannt sind, die ihrerseits personell parlamentarisch legitimiert sind.[16] Formal ist ein Ent-

11 Waldron (Fn. 9),S. 49ff.

12 Waldron (Fn. 9), 10.

13 Waldron (Fn. 9), 51.

14 Waldron (Fn. 9), 49ff.

15 Waldron (Fn. 9), p. 108: „A piece of legislation deserves respect because of the achievement it represents in the circumstances of politics: action-in-concert in the face of disagreement."

16 Die Legitimationskettentheorie des Bundesverfassungsgerichts in BVerfGE 47, 253 (275); BVerfGE 77, 1 (40); BVerfGE 83, 60 (72); BVerfGE 93, 37 (66f.); diese Lehre geht auf Ernst-Wolfgang Böckenförde zurück, s. Ernst-Wolfgang Böckenförde, § 24, Demokratie als Verfassungsprinzip, in: Isensee/Kirchhof (Hrsg.), Handbuch des Staatsrechts der Bundesrepublik Deutschland, 429, Rn. 16, wonach die organisatorisch-personelle demokratische Legitimation in einer ununterbrochenen, auf das Volk zurückführenden Legitimationskette für die mit der Wahrnehmung staatlicher Angelegenheiten betrauten Amtsträger besteht. Diese Legitimation muss nach Böckenförde nicht unmittelbar auf das Volk zurückführen, mittelbare wie unmittelbare Berufung durch das Volk sind nach dem Legitimationskettengedanken gleichermaßen zulässig, wenngleich die unmittelbare Berufung eine höhere demokratische Dignität begründe. Die Kette individueller Berufungsakte vom einzelnen Amtswalter bis hin zum Volk als Inhaber der Staatsgewalt müsse lückenlos sein. Zur personell-organisationellen demokratischen Legitimation derselbe a.a.O., 429, Rn. 16ff.

scheidungsträger legitimiert, wenn seine Einsetzung auf eine Entscheidung des demokratischen Subjekts zurückführbar ist. Mit Blick auf den Rat besteht eine solche Legitimationskette ausgehend von den Wahlen der mitgliedstaatlichen Parlamente, die ihrerseits jeweils die Regierung wählen, welche einen handlungsbefugten Vertreter auf Ministerebene in den Rat entsendet.

Die demokratische Legitimation des Handelns von Akteuren, deren Einsetzung formal über eine Legitimationskette auf das demokratische Subjekt rückführbar ist, setzt aber nach dem bereits Gesagten auch die inhaltliche Rückbindung an die Willensbildung des demokratischen Subjekts voraus.[17] Beide Aspekte müssen zusammentreffen, damit hoheitliches Handeln demokratisch legitim ist.[18] Für die Ausübung von legislativer Gewalt vermitteln Wahlen und die damit begründete politische Verantwortlichkeit gegenüber dem demokratischen Subjekt beide Aspekte.

Die in der Politikwissenschaft für Wahlen entwickelte Delegationstheorie betont, dass entlang einer Reihe von Delegationsakten das Verantwortlichkeitsverhältnis zwischen dem originären politischen Prinzipal (d.h. der Wählerschaft) und einem politischen Akteur nur so effektiv ist wie die Verantwortlichkeitsverhältnisse in den einzelnen Delegationsbeziehungen, die den indirekten Verantwortlichkeitszusammenhang vermitteln.[19] Ausgehend von einem ersten Delegationsakt steigert jede weitere Delegation die Gefahr des *agency loss* des originären Prinzipals gegenüber dem ihm zurechenbar handelnden Akteur, d.h. die Gefahr einer Unterbrechung der vermittelten Verantwortlichkeit zwischen dem ersten Prinzipal und dem handelnden Akteur.[20] Eine mehrgliedrige Kette von Vermittlungs- und Ableitungsakten reicht Legitimation formal weiter, verringert aber die Chancen der Mitglieder des Legitimationssubjekts, materiellen Einfluss auszuüben und konkrete politische Entscheidungen zu gestalten.

Führt man diese Einsicht mit der Erkenntnis zur Bedeutung des Versammlungscharakters der Legislative zusammen, folgt daraus, dass entlang einer „Legitimationskette" der Verlust an inhaltlicher Rückbindung an die Willensbildung des demokratischen Subjekts noch zunimmt, wenn die Delegation hoheitlicher Gewalt mit einem Verlust pluralistischer Kapazität einhergeht, vor allem also, wenn am Ende der Legitimationskette monokratisch gehandelt wird.

17 S. auch verfassungstheoretisch Böckenförde (Fn. 16), 429, Rn. 23.

18 Böckenförde (Fn. 16), 429, Rn. 23.

19 Kaare Strøm, European Journal of Political Research 37 (2000), 261, pp. 277; so auch Arthur Lupia, Delegation and its Perils, in: Strøm/Müller/Bergman (Hrsg.), Delegation and accountability in parliamentary democracies 2006, 33, 52: „Suppose, […] that a country's chain of delegation is a straight line – one link connects voters to MPs, one link connects MPs to governments, and so on. In such a chain, a broken link implies a broken chain. So, for citizens at one end of the chain to hold accountable civil servants at the other end, every link of the chain must be strong. Reducing agency loss in such cases requires that the necessary conditions for successful delegation are satisfied at every link in the chain. If this condition is not satisfied, the chain is broken. As a result, principals on one side of the break have no direct control over agent actions on the other side of the break."

20 Zum Anwachsen des Potentials eines agency loss mit der Zahl der Delegationsakte Strøm (Fn. 19), pp. 261, 277; Lupia, Delegation and its Perils, in: Strøm/Müller/Bergman (Hrsg.), Delegation and accountability in parliamentary democracies 2006, pp. 33, 52. Zum Problem des agency loss, d.h. des Ausfalls politischer Verantwortlichkeit bzw. der Dysfunktionalität formeller Mechanismen politischer accountability überblicksweise Strøm (Fn. 19), pp. 270f.

3 Das Verhältnis von Europäischem Parlament und Rat als Mittler demokratischer Legitimation

Nach Art. 10 EU bezieht die duale Legitimationsstruktur der EU diese legitimatorisch auf zwei politische Subjekte: Das Europäische Parlament vertritt nach Art. 10 Abs. 2, Art. 14 Abs. 2 EU die Bürgerinnen und Bürger der Europäischen Union. Im Rat werden die Mitgliedstaaten von dem jeweiligen Staats- oder Regierungschef und von ihrer jeweiligen Regierung vertreten, die ihrerseits gegenüber dem jeweiligen nationalen Parlament oder unmittelbar gegenüber den jeweiligen Bürgerinnen und Bürgern demokratisch verantwortlich sind, Art. 10 Abs. 2, Art. 16 EU. Der Rat ist damit über eine Delegationskette an die Willensbildung der mitgliedstaatlichen Staatsvölker zurückgebunden.

Teile der Literatur schlagen demgegenüber vor, Europäisches Parlament und Rat als Repräsentanten eines einheitlichen, aber in zwei rechtlichen Verfasstheiten auftretenden Legitimationssubjekts zu betrachten. Die mitgliedstaatlichen Staatsvölker und die Unionsbürgerschaft verfassen auf Grund der Akzessorietät des europäischen Bürgerstatus zur mitgliedstaatlichen Staatsbürgerschaft (Art. 9 EU, Art. 20 AEU) grundsätzlich dieselbe Menge von Individuen.[21] Im Mehrebenenzusammenhang von supranationaler Union und Mitgliedstaaten seien daher dieselben Menschen Träger und Zurechnungssubjekt beider Handlungsebenen, die auf sie einwirken, für sie handeln und Recht setzen: *„Als Staatsbürger sind sie* […] *über ihre Parlamente und Regierungen repräsentiert im Rat, als Unionsbürger durch die Abgeordneten im Europäischen Parlament.“*[22]

Die beiden verfassungsrechtlich eingesetzten demokratischen Subjekte der Union lassen sich aber nicht nur aus der verfassungstheoretischen, sondern auch aus der demokratietheoretischen Perspektive auf die gleiche legitimatorische Grundlage zurückführen. Aus der Perspektive des Demokratiebegriffs, der hier zugrunde gelegt wird, ist sowohl die Gesamtheit der Unionsbürgerinnen und -bürger wie die Gesamtheit der mitgliedstaatlichen Staatsvölker eine Verfasstheit der Menge von Individuen, denen gegenüber europäische Hoheitsgewalt demokratisch rechtfertigungsbedürftig ist. Der demokratische Anspruch der Geltung politischer Gleichheit for-

21 Ausnahmen gelten nach der sog. Gibraltar-Rechsprechung des EuGH.

22 Ingolf Pernice, Zur Finalität Europas, in: Schuppert/Pernice/Haltern (Hrsg.), Europawissenschaft 2005, 743, 760; ders., Der Europäische Verfassungsverbund auf dem Wege der Konsolidierung, in: Häberle (Hrsg.), Jahrbuch des öffentlichen Rechts der Gegenwart 2000 205; *ders.*, European Law Review 27 (2002), p. 511. In diesem Sinne auch Anne Peters, Elemente einer Theorie der Verfassung Europas 2001, 566: „Die Individuen handeln […] in verschiedenen Rollen, in denen sie ihre Repräsentanten wählen. Als Staatsbürger wählen sie das nationale Parlament, als EU-Bürger wählen sie das Europäische Parlament. […] Die Staaten (im Rat oder in einer potentiellen Staatenkammer) vertreten die Bürger, in ihrer Rolle als Staatsbürger. Das Europäische Parlament vertritt ebenfalls die Bürger, in ihrer Rolle als EU-Bürger.“ Siehe auch die Stellungnahme von Franz C. Mayer für den Deutschen Bundestag im Organstreitverfahren und zu den Verfassungsbeschwerden gegen die Zustimmungs- und Begleitgesetzgebung, F. Mayer, Stellungnahme des Bundestages in dem Organstreitverfahren 2 BvE 5/08 und zu den Verfassungsbeschwerden 2 BvR 1259/08, pp. 70f., nach dem „auch die Hoheitsmacht der einzelnen Ratsmitglieder letztlich von den einzelnen Unionsbürgerinnen und -bürgern ausgeht und – genauso wie beim Europäischen Parlament auf diese als Legitimationssubjekte zurückgeführt werden kann.“

dert die Berechtigung des Rechtssubjekts zur politischen Teilhabe. Auf dieser Grundlage ist das Individuum, das von der hoheitlichen Gewalt der Union gebunden ist, das Subjekt ihrer demokratischen Legitimation. Europäische Gesetzgebung begründet individuelle Rechte und Pflichten durch unmittelbar anwendbare Gesetzgebung in der Form der Verordnung. Erfasst vom Anspruch demokratischer Legitimation ist aber auch Unionsgesetzgebung, die in der Form der Richtlinie an die Mitgliedstaaten adressiert ist. Richtlinien können den herzustellenden Zustand der mitgliedstaatlichen Rechtsordnung absolut bestimmt bezeichnen.[23] Im Fall der Nichtumsetzung können Richtlinien mit direkter Wirkung die Rechtsposition von Individuen betreffen.[24] Der europäische Gesetzgeber vermag daher den mitgliedstaatlichen Gesetzgeber durch eine Richtlinie in seiner Willensbildung zu determinieren. Daher ist die rechtliche Definition individueller Freiheit, die durch den mitgliedstaatlichen Umsetzungsakt gilt, unter dem Gesichtspunkt der demokratischen Funktion gesetzgebender Gewalt dem europäischen Gesetzgeber zurechenbar. Die Richtlinie steht daher unmittelbar anwendbarer europäischer Gesetzgebung unter dem Gesichtspunkt des Rechtfertigungsbedürfnisses im Verhältnis zum Individuum gleich.

Die Berechtigung des Rechtssubjekts zur politischen Teilhabe legitimiert seine Bindung durch hoheitliche Gewalt. In der Makroperspektive ist so die Menge der Rechtssubjekte das Subjekt der demokratischen Legitimation europäischer Hoheitsgewalt. Die Gesamtheit der Unionsbürgerinnen und -bürger und die mitgliedstaatlichen Staatsvölker verfassen vermittels der politischen Teilhaberechte, die mit dem jeweiligen Bürgerstatus verbunden sind, die Menge der Rechtssubjekte europäischer Hoheitsgewalt jeweils zu einem politischen Subjekt.[25] An die kollektive Willensbildung dieser beiden politischen Subjekte ist die europäische Hoheitsgewalt über das Europäische Parlament respektive den Rat rückgebunden. Die Frage nach der legitimatorischen Grundlage beider Organe ist damit beantwortet: Es ist dieselbe.

Folgt aber aus dieser Erkenntnis, dass sich Parlament und Rat als demokratische Organe gegenseitig ersetzen können? Nach einer hier als Kompensationstheorem bezeichneten Argumentation kann der durch den Rat repräsentierte intergouvernementale Legitimationsbeitrag desto niedriger ausfallen, je mehr das Europäische Parlament europäische Hoheitsgewalt demokratisch legitimiert. Umgekehrt müsse die Legitimationsleistung des Rates umso höher sein, je weniger das Europäische Parlament demokratische Legitimation vermittelt.[26] Von diesem Standpunkt aus be-

23 Dazu mit Nachweisen Martin Nettesheim, Art. 249 EG, in: Grabitz/Hilf (Hrsg.), Das Recht der Europäischen Union, Rn. 133 ff.; Matthias Ruffert, Art. 249 EGV, in: Calliess/Ruffert (Hrsg.), EUV, EGV, 2007b, Rn. 45 ff.; Gudrun Schmidt, Art. 249 EG, in: Groeben/Schwarze (Hrsg.), Kommentar zum Vertrag über die Europäische Union und zur Gründung der Europäischen Gemeinschaft, Rn. 38 ff.

24 Mit Nachweisen der Rechtsprechung des EuGH hierzu Nettesheim, (Fn. 23), Rn. 124 ff.; Ruffert, (Fn. 23), Rn. 36 ff.

25 Zu beachten ist, dass über beide Bürgerschaftstatus nicht alle Rechtssubjekte mit Blick auf die europäische Hoheitsgewalt politisch berechtigt werden; man denke etwa an Drittstaatsangehörige, die von der Geltung von Unionsrecht erfasst sind. Ausgehend von der grundlegenden Annahme der demokratischen Rechtfertigungsbedürftigkeit der Bindung individueller Freiheit können legislative Regelungen im Verhältnis zu dem politisch nicht Berechtigten nicht als demokratisch legitim betrachtet werden.

26 So Christian Calliess, Das Demokratieprinzip im Europäischen Staaten- und Verfassungsverbund, in: Bröhmer/Bieber (Hrsg.), Internationale Gemeinschaft und Menschenrechte, pp. 399,

trachtet, kann der Legitimationsbeitrag eines einstimmigen Ratsbeschlusses die fehlende Vermittlung demokratischer Legitimation durch ein bloß angehörtes Europäisches Parlament ausgleichen. Umgekehrt kompensiere die Mitentscheidung des Parlaments die angenommene geringere Legitimationsleistung des mit Mehrheit beschließenden Rates.[27]

Gültigkeitsbedingung des Kompensationstheorems ist, dass beide Organe dasselbe Maß und qualitativ gleichwertige demokratische Legitimation vermitteln. Anderenfalls könnte – mit der Folge eines Legitimationsdefizits – eine fehlende oder geringere Legitimationsvermittlung nicht durch den Legitimationsbeitrag des jeweils anderen Organs ausgeglichen werden. Ausgehend von der demokratietheoretischen Grundlegung lässt sich die Legitimationsleistung der beiden Organe komparativ untersuchen. Dabei zeigt sich, dass die Legitimationsleistung der beiden Organe nicht dasselbe Maß erreicht. Damit ist das Kompensationstheorem nicht haltbar.

Als gewählte Versammlung betätigt das Europäische Parlament seine legislativen Befugnisse auf der Grundlage eines Prozesses der legislativen Willensbildung, in dem die Möglichkeit der Artikulation und Behauptung einer Mehrzahl politischer Positionen und damit die Möglichkeit des politischen Ausdrucks der Heterogenität der Unionsbürgerinnen und -bürger als demokratisches Subjekt besteht. Die Verfasstheit des Europäischen Parlaments ist dabei – mittels der degressiv-proportionalen Verteilung der mitgliedstaatlicher Sitzkontingente[28] – einerseits daraufhin zuge-

403 und *ders.*, Art. 6 EU, in: Calliess/Ruffert (Hrsg.), EUV, EGV, 2007, Rn. 17, „[J]e höher die Legitimationsvermittlung durch das Europäische Parlament [...], desto niedriger kann der mitgliedstaatliche Legitimationsbeitrag ausfallen. Umgekehrt muss die Vermittlung demokratischer Legitimation [...] über den Rat umso höher sein, je niedriger die Mitwirkungsmöglichkeiten und damit die Legitimationsleistung durch das Europäische Parlament ist [...]" in Anschluss an Peter M. Huber, Recht der europäischen Integration 2002, 69, Rn. 39: „Je höher [...] das unional vermittelte Legitimationsniveau ist, desto eher kann auf eine Optimierung der mitgliedstaatlichen Legitimationsbeiträge [meint: Einstimmigkeitserfordernis im Rat] verzichtet werden. Je niedriger das unional vermittelte Legitimationsniveau ausfällt, und das gilt insbesondere dort, wo das Europäische Parlament auf das Verfahren des Art. 252 EG oder gar auf Anhörungsrechte beschränkt ist, desto höher muss die Legitimationsvermittlung über den Rat [...] sein. Das setzt Vetorechte der Mitgliedstaaten, Einstimmigkeitserfordernisse [...] voraus, weil nur so die Möglichkeit einer effektiven Kontrolle des Rates durch die Regierungen und Parlamente der Mitliedstaaten besteht. Nicht nur die unionsrechtlichen Partizipationsmöglichkeiten bedürfen freilich der Kompensation. [...]"; Frauke Brosius-Gersdorf, Europarecht 34 (1999), pp. 133, 167 f.: „Beide Legitimationsformen [die gemeinschaftsrechtliche, „die ihren Ursprung in der Aktivbürgerschaft der Europäischen Union" hat und die intergouvernementale] stehen in einem Verhältnis wechselseitiger Komplementarität. [...] Defizite in der gemeinschaftsrechtlichen Legitimationsstruktur [...] können durch entsprechende Verstärkung nationaler Legitimationselemente kompensiert werden und umgekehrt."; Hervorhebungen der Verf.

27 Zur Bedeutung des Mehrheitsprinzips für Ratsbeschlüsse für die Legitimationsleistung des Rates unten Kap. 8. Für die geringere Legitimationsleistung des mehrheitlich beschließenden Rates etwa Felix Hanschmann, Der Begriff der Homogenität in der Verfassungslehre und Europarechtswissenschaft 2008, 30 ff.; Stefan Kadelbach, Demokratische Legitimation zwischenstaatlichen Handelns, in: Vöneky/Hagedorn/Clados u. a. (Hrsg.), Legitimation ethischer Entscheidungen im Recht 2009a, 147, 155 f. Anderer Ansicht aber Matthias Ruffert, Europarecht 39 (2004), pp. 165, 184: „Allein in der Möglichkeit des Überstimmtwerdens kann nach der Logik von Mehrheitsentscheidungen noch kein Demokratiedefizit liegen."

28 Zur elektoralen Konstitution des Europäischen Parlaments s. Felix Arndt, Ausrechnen statt aushandeln: Rationalitätsgewinne durch ein formalisiertes Modell für die Bestimmung der Zusam-

schnitten, Kapazität zur Artikulation der föderalen Vielfalt der Europäischen Union bereitzustellen. Das Verfahren der legislativen Willensbildung des Parlaments ermöglicht es aber gleichfalls, eine Pluralität politischer Präferenzen zu artikulieren. Zwar wird das Europäische Parlament in nationalen Wahlen mitgliedstaatlicher Abgeordnetenkontingente gewählt. Die Strukturähnlichkeit der politischen Artikulation der mitgliedstaatlichen Völker in den Wahlen zum Europäischen Parlament aber integriert diese politisch zu einer europäischen Wählerschaft.[29] Indem das Parlament seine legislative Verantwortung richtungspolitisch und nicht entlang mitgliedstaatlicher Positionen betätigt, vertritt es seine Wählerinnen und Wähler primär mit ihren Präferenzen als Mitglied eines sich politisch in Richtungen, nicht als Menge nationaler Einheiten entlang dieser artikulierenden demokratischen Subjekts. Das Europäische Parlament vermittelt der Gesetzgebung der Union daher über seine Co-Gesetzgeberschaft demokratische Legitimation als parlamentarische Vertretung der Unionsbürgerinnen und -bürger.

Demgegenüber ist ein erster Faktor der demokratischen Minderleistung des Rates seine Struktur als Kompositum monokratischer, durch eine einzelne Person geleisteter Vertretungen demokratischer Subjekte. Die demokratische Vertretung des einzelnen Staatsvolks durch einen Regierungsvertreter im Rat stellt keine Kapazität für den politischen Ausdruck der Heterogenität der politischen Präferenzen seiner Angehörigen bereit. Pluralistische Kapazität entfaltet der Rat als Kollegium lediglich für die politische Artikulation der föderalen Vielfalt der EU. Der Rat ist keine gesetzgebende Versammlung – die legislative Verantwortung einer gewählten Versammlung aber ist zentrale Funktionsweise der demokratischen Legitimation von Gesetzgebung.

Ein zusätzlicher Faktor der Legitimationsleistung des Rates ist die begrenzte Effektivität der politischen Verantwortlichkeitsverhältnisse, die von den mitgliedstaatlichen Staatsvölkern jeweils zu ihrem im Rat handelnden Vertreter führen. Zwar verfügen die im Rat handelnden Regierungsvertreter über personelle demokratische Legitimation. Die sachlich-inhaltliche demokratische Legitimation ihres Handelns vermittels eines effektiven politischen Verantwortlichkeitsverhältnisses zum demokratischen Prinzipal, dem jeweiligen Staatsvolk, leidet aber unter einer Reihe von Schwächen. Zum einen können die nationalen Parlamente das Handeln der Regierungsvertreter kaum effektiv kontrollieren und steuern, so dass die inhaltlich-sachliche Rückbindung des Handelns der Regierungsvertreter an die demokratische Willensbildung des jeweiligen politischen Subjekts schwach ausgeprägt ist. Zum anderen unterbricht die Geltung des Mehrheitsprinzips die Bindung des legislativen Handelns des Rates an die demokratischen Positionen der Mitgliedstaaten.

Das Mehrheitsprinzip bedeute, so wird vielfach befunden, eine mindere demokratische Legitimation von Mehrheitsentscheiden des Rates gegenüber dem Einstimmigkeitsprinzip: Selbst wenn die nationalen Parlamente effektiv Einfluss nehmen könnten auf das Verhalten des jeweiligen im Rat handelnden Regierungsvertreters, unterlaufe dessen Überstimmbarkeit diese Einflussmöglichkeit auf die legisla-

mensetzung des Europäischen Parlaments, Zeitschrift für ausländisches öffentliches Recht und Völkerrecht 68 (2008), pp. 247–279.

29 S. hierzu grundlegend Daniele Caramani, Is there a European electorate and what does it look like?, Evidence from electoral volatility measures 1976–2004, West European Politics 29 (2006), pp. 1–27.

tive Politik des Rates.[30] Dagegen wird vereinzelt argumentiert, allein in der Möglichkeit des Überstimmtwerdens von Mitgliedstaaten im Rat könne nach der Logik von Mehrheitsentscheidungen noch kein Demokratiedefizit liegen. Das Mehrheitsprinzip sei Funktionsprinzip demokratischer Willensbildung.[31]

Das Mehrheitsprinzip ist grundsätzlich keine Begrenzung der demokratischen Legitimation von Entscheidungen, sondern originär demokratischer Entscheidungsmodus. Mit Blick auf den Rat ist es allerdings wegen seines Kontexts differenziert zu beurteilen. Ist das Mehrheitsprinzip für parlamentarische Beschlüsse Modus der Erzeugung einer Entscheidung, die dem demokratischen Subjekt zugerechnet werden kann, ist es dies im Rat gerade nicht. Der Rat ist nicht die demokratische Vertretung eines einzigen politischen Subjekts, sondern Kompositum demokratischer Vertretungen einer Menge politischer Subjekte. Diesen politischen Subjekten ist die Stimmabgabe des jeweiligen Regierungsvertreters im Rat formal als Willensartikulation zurechenbar.[32] Das Mehrheitsprinzip ist damit im Rat Mittel der Negation des demokratischen Willens politischer Subjekte, nicht demokratischer Modus der Willensbildung eines politischen Subjekts.[33] Bereits seine Geltung – nicht erst seine Betätigung – prägt die Willensbildung des Rates, weil in dieser unter der Bedingung des Mehrheitsprinzips demokratische Positionen in Verhandlung und Diskussion marginalisiert, negiert und formal ungleich behandelt werden können.[34] Das Mehrheitsprinzip unterläuft die pluralistische Kapazität des Rates in Bezug auf die föderale Vielfalt der Positionen der Mitgliedstaaten.

Ein weiterer Faktor der demokratischen Leistungsfähigkeit des Rates ist, dass wesentliche Teile der inhaltlichen Willensbildung des Rates auf dessen Arbeitsebenen nicht-öffentlich und außerhalb der Reichweite der politischen Kontrolle der nationalen Parlamente stattfinden. Auch dies begründet einen Mangel der sachlich-inhaltlichen demokratischen Legitimation des legislativen Handelns des Rates. Zwar findet auch im Europäischen Parlament die Befassung mit Gesetzgebungsvorhaben wesentlich auf einer Arbeitsebene, den Ausschüssen, statt; doch tagen diese zum einen grundsätzlich öffentlich, zum anderen existiert das parlamentarische Plenum – wie die in den Protokollen der parlamentarischen Beratungen dokumentierten Debatten zeigen – als Ort der substantiellen Auseinandersetzung mit den Inhalten von Gesetzgebung. Dies ist im Rat anders; politikwissenschaftliche Studien zeigen,

30 So Karl Doehring, Deutsches Verwaltungsblatt 112 (1997), 1133, 1134; für die geringere Legitimationsleistung des mehrheitlich beschließenden Rates etwa auch Hanschmann (Fn. 27), 30 ff.; Kadelbach, (Fn. 27), pp. 147, 155 f.

31 Matthias Ruffert, Europarecht 39 (2004), 165, 184: „Allein in der Möglichkeit des Überstimmtwerdens kann nach der Logik von Mehrheitsentscheidungen noch kein Demokratiedefizit liegen."

32 Dies ist die Bedeutung der eingangs rekonstruierten demokratischen Delegationskette, die die personelle demokratische Legitimation des handelnden Regierungsvertreters leistet.

33 Dahingehend wohl die Formulierung von Doehring (Fn. 30), pp. 1133, 1134: „Wenn eine Entscheidung kommt, ist sie jedenfalls nur von einem Teil der europäischen Staatsvölker demokratisch legitimiert. Man kann auch sagen, dann, wenn die Gesamtregierung – hier die Gesamtheit des Ministerrats – nicht von einem Volk legitimiert ist, gibt es auch keine Volksherrschaft."

34 Dahingehend auch Ingolf Pernice, Art. 23, in: Dreier/Bauer (Hrsg.), Grundgesetz 2006, Rn. 57, wonach der Weg der Legitimation über die nationalen Parlamente gangbar bleibe, solange der Rat als Angelpunkt eines Konkordanzsystems handeln könne, d.h. jede Regierung gleichermaßen für einen Rechtsakt Verantwortung trägt.

dass die Ministerebene kaum Akteur der inhaltlichen Willensbildung, sondern vielfach bloß formales Ratifikationsorgan für politische Einigungen auf der Arbeitsebene ist.[35]

Die demokratische Leistungsfähigkeit des Rates wird zudem durch dessen Sektoralisierung beschränkt. Die Gliederung des Rates in jeweils legislativ verantwortliche Ratsformationen verhindert die sachlich-inhaltliche, materielle Allgemeinheit der legislativen Willensbildung des Rates. Auf Grund der fachlichen Fragmentierung des Rates ist seine legislative Willensbildung strukturell nicht zur Artikulation und Einbeziehung aller relevanten Aspekte verfasst. Zwar ist die Willensbildung des Europäischen Parlamentes mit den fachlich spezialisierten Ausschüssen ebenfalls durch Strukturen sachlicher Ausdifferenzierung geprägt. Im Parlament aber besteht anders als im Rat das Komplement eines im Rahmen der legislativen Kompetenzen des Parlaments allgemein zuständigen Plenums. Im Vergleich hierzu kann – und solche Konstellationen sind für die Praxis dokumentiert[36] – eine gesetzgeberisch handelnde Ratsformation in ihrer Zuständigkeit durch die Zuordnung zusammenhängender Sachmaterien zu verschiedenen Ratsformationen begrenzt und daher nicht umfassend zur Betätigung ihrer legislativen Willensbildung befähigt sein.

Der Vergleich ergibt, dass die demokratische Leistungsfähigkeit des Rates hinter der des Europäischen Parlaments zurückbleibt – dies vor allem auf Grund der intergouvernementalen Struktur und Logik seiner Willensbildung, die einer demokratischen Verantwortlichkeit des einzelnen Regierungsvertreters gegenüber dem mitgliedstaatlichen Parlament ebenso zuwiderläuft wie seine interne Arbeitsweise, wegen seiner Sektoralisierung und wegen allgemeiner Probleme seiner Transparenz.

In Anlehnung an die Formulierung des Urteils des EGMR in der Sache Matthews[37] ist das Europäische Parlament in seiner demokratischen Leistungsfähigkeit als prinzipaler Mechanismus der demokratischen Verantwortlichkeit auf der Ebene der EU zu beschreiben. Das Parlament ist als demokratisches Organ nicht ohne Defizite, vor allem in Hinblick auf die Gleichheit der Wahl. Daneben bestehen nachhaltige Probleme seiner Wahrnehmung durch die Öffentlichkeit.[38] Das Europäische Parlament vermag gleichwohl europäischer Gesetzgebung im Vergleich zum Rat ein höheres Maß demokratischer Legitimation zu vermitteln. Die Legitimationsleistung des Rates bleibt qualitativ hinter der des Europäischen Parlamentes zurück. Ausgehend hiervon ist europäische Gesetzgebung im Anhörungsverfahren,

35 S. hierzu Michael Häge, Journal of Legislative Studies 13 (2007), pp. 497, 505.

36 Ratspräsidentschaft Österreich 2006, INFORMATION DES JI-RATES ÜBER JI-RELEVANTE THEMEN IN ANDEREN RATSFORMATIONEN 2006.

37 Europäischer Gerichtshof für Menschenrechte, 18. Februar 1999, Appl. 24833/94, p. 52.

38 Die Frage nach der Existenz einer europäischen Öffentlichkeit ist hier nicht adressiert worden; s. für eine kritische Aufarbeitung der Diskussion zu den Entstehungsbedingungen europäischer Öffentlichkeit, ihrer Gestalt und zur Frage der Bedingtheit europäischer Demokratie durch eine einheitliche europäische Öffentlichkeit Hanschmann, (Fn. 27) pp. 196 ff.; wichtig im Diskurs die Position von Dieter Grimm, European Law Journal 1 (1995), 282, 292 ff. Aus der Perspektive der Rekonstruktion der demokratischen Leistungsfähigkeit des Parlamentes nach seiner primärrechtlichen Verfasstheit und in seiner Praxis als Co-Gesetzgeber interessieren hier die rechtlichen Gewährleistungen der Transparenz und Öffentlichkeit der legislativen Willensbildung der Co-Gesetzgeber und ihre praktische Transparenz und Öffentlichkeit, insbesondere mit Blick auf die Informalisierung der Verhandlung zwischen den Verfahrensbeteiligten der Mitentscheidung in der Praxis.

die auf Grund einer Ratsentscheidungen nach bloßer unverbindlicher Anhörung des Parlamentes ergeht, demokratisch defizitär.

4 Schluss

Art. 10 EU verankert eine duale Legitimationsstruktur der Europäischen Union verfassungsprinzipiell. Die beiden demokratischen Unionsorgane, Europäisches Parlament und Rat, sind verfassungsrechtlich auf zwei unterschiedliche Legitimationssubjekte bezogen; einerseits die Menge der Unionsbürgerinnen und -bürger, andererseits die Staatsvölker der Mitgliedstaaten. Demokratietheoretisch lassen sich beide demokratischen Subjekte der Union aber auf eine einheitliche legitimatorische Grundlage zurückführen, nämlich die Menge der Rechtssubjekte europäischer Hoheitsgewalt. Diesen gegenüber bedarf europäische Gesetzgebung in der Form von Verordnungen und Richtlinien als einseitige, objektive Definition individueller Freiheit der demokratischen Rechtfertigung. Demokratische Rechtfertigung, demokratische Legitimation vermittelt die Gleichberechtigung der Rechtssubjekte zur politischen Teilhabe. Sowohl der Unionsbürgerstatus als auch die mitgliedstaatliche Staatsangehörigkeit vermitteln mit Blick auf europäische Gesetzgebung über Wahlen politische Teilhabe. Die zwei verfassungsrechtlich konstituierten politischen Subjekte und die sie repräsentierenden Gesetzgebungsorgane weisen dabei Gleichheitsstrukturen auf, die dem demokratischen Prinzip absoluter bürgerschaftlicher Gleichheit nicht vollständig entsprechen. Föderale Strukturen überformen die bürgerschaftliche Gleichheit in der EU, wie vor allem die degressiv-proportionale Verteilung nationaler Sitzkontingente im Europäischen Parlament zeigt.

Trotz der Gleichheitsdefizite in seiner elektoralen Konstitution stellt das Europäische Parlament die prinzipale, notwendige Form demokratischer Willensbildung auf europäischer Ebene bereit. Es bringt als legislative Versammlung pluralistische Kapazität für richtungspolitische Entscheidungen ein und ist in höherem Maß politisch verantwortlich als die den Rat konstituierenden Regierungsvertreter. Auch einstimmige Ratsentscheidungen können nicht die Legitimationsleistung eines gesetzgeberisch verantwortlichen Parlamentes ersetzen. Aufgrund der intergouvernementalen Struktur und Logik der Willensbildung des Rates bleibt dessen Legitimationskapazität qualitativ hinter der des Europäischen Parlamentes zurück.

Raffaele Lapenta

The Right of Defence in the Framework of Multilevel Constitutionalism

Abstract:
Avec le processus de stratification des pouvoirs internationaux, supranationaux et entre-étatique, nous observons des croissantes différentiations du système des droits, et l'affirmation de différents niveaux de protection, qui sont la manifestation du dépassement graduel du dogme, caractérisant le constitutionnalisme classique, du monopole de l'État en matière des droits. Cet phénomène c'est intensifié à travers le processus d'intégration communautaire. Pour cela, notre premier bût a été de comprendre si le processus d'intégration européenne c'est évolué au point de garantir une effective protection des droits fondamentaux de la personne, et avant tout le droit de défense, comme garanti par les Constitutions nationaux et par la CEDH.

Des perplexités signifiants naissent quant à l'analyse des dispositions que, au paravant la "Constitution européenne" et, après le Traité de Lisbonne que, à travers un explicite renvoi qui a attribué efficace contraignante à la Charte des droits de Nice, sont dédiés à la question de la justice. Ce sont des principes qui sont amplement consacré comme fondamentales dans les constitutions nationaux: inviolabilité du droit à la défense, contradictoire, parité des parties, publicité du débattement, indépendance et impartialité du juge. Ces principes ont toutefois une signification implicite et parfois dérisoires au niveau européen, où sont prévalants les quatre libertés à caractère économique, assurés aux citoyens européens par rapport aux droits sociaux.

C'est justement l'analyse des standards de protection des droits dans les constitutions nationaux, qui permette nous déterminer un idéaltype de protection de la personne, articulé sur les droits différents, qui pourra être considéré un référent de comparaison. Sur sa base nous pourrions évaluer l'aptitude du droit communautaire à garantir la protection à la quelle il aspire, aussi dans la perspective de compléter dans le future le processus d'intégration selon une logique plus correspondante aux exigences "sociaux" des communautés.

1 Introduction. The Protection of Rights in the European System at Several Levels

For a long time, and even more so over the last few years, the processes of "stratification" of powers at different levels – international, supranational and infra-state – have revealed growing differentiations in the system of rights. This comes with the assertion that there are different levels of protection which, despite some elements of crisis, show problems and moments of stabilization,[1] they increasingly indicate that in the matter of rights, the dogma of Classical Constitutionalism of state monopoly is being overcome.[2]

If we consider the protection of rights to be a prerogative particular to the Nation States, over the years we have witnessed the gradual birth of the protection of rights on an international and supranational level (with the European Community experience) and, more recently, at least in Italy, also on an interstate level.

1 P. Bilancia, E. De Marco, La tutela multilivello dei diritti. Punti di crisi, problemi aperti, momenti di stabilizzazione, Milano 2004.

2 S. Cassese, La crisi dello Stato, Laterza, Roma – Bari 2002.

This phenomenon presents advantages and disadvantages.[3] With regard to the former, it is fundamentally a question of offering a protection of rights from different perspectives to make it as complete and effective as possible. Regarding the latter, some problems arise, as some constitutionalists have pointed out, speaking of a "garden of rights", which indicates some antinomies and contradictions that can arise from this phenomenon.[4]

It is an irrefutable fact that international law with supranational or universal overtones influences both domestic and international policy, and not only economic policy, of any country. It imposes decisions regarding the proceedings and deadlines that result in upsetting the traditional competences of the constitutional State.

This new way of re-organizing the legal system focuses on, above all, the system of the sources of law in Europe, that is to say the Kelsenian criteria of the pyramidal hierarchy of sources with the constitutional State at the top.

Of a legal system tied to a hard, hierarchical principle – on the line of Constitution/laws/secondary sources – a system steps in which is based on the supremacy of the sources of supranational law and on the coordination and collaboration among the supranational and national institutions which produce laws and among the Courts, which are competent to deal with and solve arising problems.

In this process of constant change, the risk is that the fundamental functions of the Constitution of the Nation States are lost, or at least, drastically limited: *in primis*, the direct and indirect participation of citizens through the instruments of democratic pluralism (parliament, parties, trade unions, etc) must not be denied.

A decisive factor for the theory and the praxis of the sources of law, with particular regard to freedom, fundamental and social rights, is the impact that the rules have on these rights: rules that are born from the plurality of supranational sources of law where the "owners" of these rights are often defenseless. This situation results in a "sort of a negative integration: while the community institutions set down some rigid financial and budget rules in the name of the market and competition, it is then up to each national government to reach the complex objectives of developmental support, redistribution of wealth and work policy, obviously with very strict operational margins".[5]

The prevalence of the four freedoms guaranteed to European citizens by the community treaties – free movement of persons, goods, capital and services – on social rights, for someone, makes pathetic the affirmation of the right of personality and of equality in a real sense and, maybe even more so, the right to work.[6]

3 C. Amirante, Costituzionalismo e costituzione nel nuovo contesto europeo, Torino 2003; I. Pernice, Multilevel Constitutionalism in the European Union, in European Law Review 2002; P. Bilancia e F.G. Pizzetti, Aspetti e problemi del costituzionalismo multilivello, Milano 2004; E. De Marco, Percorsi del "nuovo costituzionalismo", Milano 2005.

4 M. Patrono, I diritti dell'uomo nel paese d'Europa: conquiste e nuove minacce nel passaggio da un millennio all'altro, Padova 2000.

5 C. Amirante, Costituzionalismo e costituzione nel nuovo contesto europeo.

6 Indeed, with normative practices being more flexible, a different way of understanding and interpreting the relationship between authority and freedom, public and private, in the name of the return to a civilised society. If more space is given to economic lobbies, space is progressively taken away from the forms of citizen participation. (C. Amirante, op. cit.).

Therefore, moving from a hierarchical system of the sources of law (with the Constitution at the top) to a legal system which is polycentric and multilevel (from where it's difficult to establish the complex vision and the systemic elements and, in which, the International and supranational Court have an fundamental role), there is further confirmation of the risks that the change from the *hard law* to the *soft law* involves. In other words from the classical forms of modern law to different, more flexible forms, both for fundamental rights and social rights, following the negative nature of integration promoted in the first thirty years of jurisprudence of the European Court of Justice). However, the critics of the current EU believe that above all social rights require an economic policy, which currently does not exist. In addition to this, they also believe the budget should allow for more spending than at present. The hard rules of the Maastricht treaty make it difficult for the States to achieve adequate promotion of social rights in line with the demands and requirements of citizens.

On one hand the multiplicity of supranational and international Courts seems to enrich and improve, but on the other it makes it more difficult for the citizen to understand who his "natural judge" is, in other words the Court where he can assert his rights.[7]

With reference to political legitimacy, it is above all the distance between the sources of production and the regulation of rights that makes it difficult for the person (either *uti singulus* or *uti socius*) to know and assert his own rights, above all with regard to collective rights (work, strikes, environment, public services, health, etc.). This is also because the supranational courts take the role of arbitrators, able to solve through mediation, the cases of violation of rights and – with the exception of the European Court of Justice which has limited competence in cases of Human Rights – they have the power to impose a compensation for damages charged to the State that violates a right, but not to reintroduce the violated right.[8]

2 The Fundamental Rights on the Road to a European Constitution

The Treaty establishing a Constitution for Europe signed by the representatives of twenty-five States of the European Union (today twenty-seven) on October 29th 2004 in Rome, in the same city where forty-seven years before had witnessed the beginnings of the economical, political and cultural dream of an united Europe. It represented the synthesis of all treaties signed over the last fifty years, with the exception of Euratom Treaty.

Its purpose, other than replacing the various existing treaties which constituted the legal basis of the EU, was largely to give the EU a clear, permanent political set-up with regard to its institutions, competences, decision-making procedures, and

7 In reality, interpreters have many difficulties, with the variety of laws from several sources, the rules to follow for a specific aim or to resolve a controversial case, even more so if the citizen experiences this new legal system as "an inextricable cobweb, where he moves around with increasing difficulty" (C. Amirante, op. cit e Id., I diritti fondamentali fra legislazione e giurisdizione? In L. D'Avack [ed.], Sviluppo dei diritti umani e protezione giuridica, Napoli 2003).

8 C. Amirante, op. cit.

foreign policy.[9] The so-called European Constitution would come into force with the notification by the Members States of the ratification of the Treaty in accordance with their respective internal requirements (i.e. by parliamentary procedure and/or by referendum). Nevertheless, with the vote opposed to the Treaty in both France and in the Netherlands in 2005, such an eventuality became shelved.

From this point of view it can be said that if the European Constitution would have come into force we would have all acquired the *status* as 'citizens' of a new, unified, constitutional Europe. Shall we hope so? Does it happen the same with the Treaty of Lisbon? The question pre-empts what we are all thinking, in view of the unanswered questions and of the persisting doubts in the legal arena put forward by the Constitution with regard to "Justice" and to the right of defense, above all in a court of law.[10] Doubts that growth as a result of the uncertainty of the ratification of the mini-treaty[11] and that persisted throughout the period before the ratification of the Treaty of Lisbon, and even more so with regard to the regulations laid down in the Charter of Nice, an area of much discussion.[12]

9 Despite the name, it is not a true constitution which sanctions the birth of a sovereignty (like the Federal Constitution of the United States of America), but rather a kind of unique text where, as anticipated, the existing judicial texts have been acknowledged and reordered, with very few changes and no move to sovereignty.

10 G. Liut, I diritti della difesa nella nuova Europa unificata e costituzionale, during the congress "L'integrazione europea e la cooperazione giudiziaria in materia penale", Roma 2005. G. Zagrebelsky (ed.), Diritti e Costituzione dell'Unione europea, Roma-Bari 2005; C. Curti Gialdino, La Costituzione europea. Genesi – natura – struttura – contenuto, Roma 2005.

11 After the "period of reflection" of European leaders, following the "no" on the part of the French and the Dutch, there were essentially three possibilities to be considered: 1) to proceed with the ratification of the remaining states, and if there should be only a minority opposing the treaty, to call a new referendum in those countries that rejected the treaty. The idea was turned down outright by France and the Netherlands. 2) To open the road to closer cooperation: the Constitution would come into force only in the countries in favour of the treaty. Although theoretically possible, the hypothesis was rejected in order not to leave two of the founder members out the European Community. 3) Draw up a new simplified Treaty, with no constitutional descriptions, to be approved only by parliament. In the end the last solution was chosen. With the declaration of Berlin on the 25th of March 2007, on the occasion of the 50th anniversary of a united Europe, the German Chancellor Angela Merkel and the Italian Prime Minister Romano Prodi expressed the desire to resolve the problem within a few months to allow for a new treaty to come into force by 2009, the same year of the elections for a new European Parliament. Led by the German presidency, the summit of Brussels was held between the 21st and the 23rd of June 2007, reaching an agreement on the new Reform Treaty. On September 13 2007 the representatives of the 27 Member States of EU undersigned the Treaty of Lisbon (which came into force on December 1 2009), which introduced a deep change in the Treaty establishing the European Economic Community of 1957 (TEC) and the Treaty of Maastricht on European Union (TEU). Its final ratification puts an end to the long period of reflection on the reform of the community legal order, opened with the European Council of 2005 following the failures occurred in the ratification of the project of European Constitution of 2004.

12 It is important to point out that the heavy criticisms of the constitutional text were based on opinions which are often diametrically opposed. A good number of the criticisms and the "no" with regard to the Constitution came from public opinion who have no real interest in politics, the so-called "euro-sceptics" who rejected the European Union for the way in which it has been structured, considered to be too bureaucratic and not very efficient in dealing with the real interests of citizens. Criticisms have also came from a religious point of view, regarding the fact that no space has been given to the Judaic-Christian roots which are an essential part of Euro-

In 2009 a very long procedural process came to an end. The treaties which followed over the years constituted fundamental stages on the road towards true, effective constitutional coverage of Europe:

- The Single European Act (SEA), signed in Luxembourg and Aia which came into e effect on the 1st of July 1987 – set out the required adjustments for a single market by 1992;
- The European Union Treaty – signed in Maastricht on the 7th of February 1992, becoming effective on the 1st of November 1993 – changed what had previously been known as the European Economic Community to the "European Community". Moreover, it introduced new forms of cooperation between the governments of the Member States, regarding security, justice and internal affairs. This addition of intergovernmental cooperation to the already existing "Community", created a new three – pillared structure,[13] which is political as well as economical: this is known as the European Union (EU);
- The Treaty of Amsterdam – signed on the 2nd of October 1997 and came into effect on the 1st of May 1999 – modified and introduced a numbering system of the treaties of the EU and EC. The Treaty modified the order of the articles of the Treaty on the European Union, previously indicated by capital letters from A to S, replacing it with a numbering system. In addition, it confirmed the principles of freedom, of democracy, and of the fundamental human rights, defining the essential elements of a common policy in terms of freedom, security and justice;
- The Treaty of Nice – which was signed on the 26th of February 2001 and came into effect on the 1st of February 2003 – was mainly concerned with the institutional reforms which are necessary to guarantee the smooth running of the institutions, the number of Member States to increase in number to 25 in 2004 and 27 in 2007. The Treaty of Nice, the previous treaty on the European Union,

pean life. These are critics who, with a lack of European spirit, claim that it is deception to call the document a "Constitution", when that is not what it is. In the light of such considerations we may observe that, in the Treaty of Lisbon the Member States left away the idea to replace to the EC and EU Treaties a single text of constitutional nature, preferring to follow the traditional method to review the existing treaties following an inter-governmental negotiation. Therefore, following the Treaty of Lisbon, we keep having two treaties, notwithstanding the fact that we have now a single legal subject. According with art. 1.3 TEU, indeed "... The Union shall replace and succeed the European Community". For an analysis of the deeper reasons behind the present situation of stalemate and uncertainty regarding the future of the process of European integration in an ever-expanding Europe see C. Amirante, Il futuro dell'Unione europea dopo i referendum tra economia, espertocrazia e democrazia, in S. Gambino (ed.), Trattato che adotta una Costituzione per l'Europa, Costituzioni nazionali, diritti fondamentali, Milano 2006. U. Allegretti, Europa, che fare?, in Democrazia e diritto, n. 2 2005; F. Bilancia, Referendum, populismo e moneta unica. A proposito della Costituzione europea, www.costituzionalismo.it

13 The first pillar is represented by the European Community which proposes a single European market, economic and monetary union as well as a series of other competencies that have been added; the second relates to Common foreign and security policy, that is the construction of a single foreign policy; with the third pillar, Police and judicial co-operation in criminal matters, the intention is to create a European space of freedom, security and justice in which there is collaboration in the fight against criminality on a supranational level.

and the treaty which founded the European Community, have been combined in one single version.[14]

However, it was the declaration on the future of Europe, in the final act of the intergovernmental conference (IGC) in 2000, to lead the way for the drafting of a new reform treaty, the first step towards the European Constitution. On the 15th of December 2001 the Council of the European Union accepted the so-called "Laeken declaration", of primary importance because, apart from reiterating the problems talked about since Nice, a convention led by Valery Giscard d'Estaing as President was officially announced, with the task of preparing a rough draft of the European Constitution. After three years of work,[15] the definitive draft was complete. The Treaty founding the Constitution for Europe was officially ratified in Italy on the 7th of April 2005 n. 57.

In testimony of the constitutional importance of the treaty project, we can identify, albeit briefly (closed at our interest in this place): firstly, the preamble, with the list of values on which the Union is based (art. I-2) and a list of the objectives of the Union (art. I-3); and secondly, the introduction of the entire text of the Charter of the fundamental rights to the European Union (Part II), signed in December 2000 by the representatives of the countries of the Union Heads of State and Government or Sovereigns) in Nice in order to guarantee the fundamental civil rights to all citizens of the Member States.

However, the reality was that the text approved in Nice only had a political, declaratory value. It was actually a document which expressed plans, ideals and suggestions, lacking any real binding legal value. This aspect would become even more evident with its inclusion in the Constitution, but the fact that the latter has not come into force leaves wide open the debate on the legal strength of the Charter.[16] However, with the coming into force of the Treaty of Lisbon such debate appears clearly quieting down, due to the explicit reference of the Charter of Nice to the general values contained therein.

Before the Charter of Nice, it was the European Convention for the Protection of Human Rights and of the fundamental freedoms (ECHR) in 1950 which was the

14 With the signing of the Treaty of Nice in 2001, Community Law was founded on eight treaties, to which about fifty protocols and attachments were added. Rather than modifying the original EC treaty, other texts were drafted which were integrated into the document. The combination of all these acts has made the structure of Europe even more complex and even more remote from European citizens. See also C. Pinelli, Il momento della scrittura. Contributo al dibattito sulla Costituzione europea, Bologna 2002; Id., La Carta europea dei Diritti ed il processo di "costituzionalizzazzione" del diritto europeo, in (various authors), Riflessi sulla Carta europea dei diritti sulla giustizia e la giurisprudenza costituzionale: Italia e Spagna a confronto, Milano 2003

15 From the 28th of February 2002, when in the European Parliament in Brussels a meeting of the Convention was held, to the 17–18th June 2004, when during the course of the European Summit held in the Belgian capital the Heads of State and Government of the 25 member states, at the end of the negotiations the IGC 2003/2004, a compromise was reached on the constitutional text.

16 G. Ruiz-Rico Ruiz, Il catalogo dei diritti sociali nel trattato costituzionale dell'Unione europea in S. Gambino (ed.), Trattato che adotta una Costituzione per l'Europa, Costituzioni nazionali, diritti fondamentali; S. Gambino, Diritti fondamentali, costituzioni nazionali e trattati comunitari, in ibid.; N. Perez Sola, Le debolezze della garanzia della tutela giudiziaria effettiva nel trattato che istituisce una Costituzione per l'Europa, in Ibid.

main legal instrument of guarantee of the respect of Human Rights and Freedoms on a European level. Even though the European Community did not take part in this Convention, all the Member States are contracting parties, and as such are obliged to apply them in their own national legal system and to the benefit of all citizens, without exception.

To guarantee the respect of the fundamental rights in the European Union, the Court of Justice of the European Community, in the elaboration of its own system of jurisprudence, was based precisely on the principles outlined by ECHR, rather than on the common constitutional traditions of the Member States. Indeed, although ECHR is not officially Community Law, the list of rights it contains constitutes the common minimum of guarantees. There has been a gradual move towards a kind of protagonist attitude in the jurisprudence in the Courts of Justice of the European Community, and the two systems undoubtedly operate in the same States since all the Member States of the Union, as previously mentioned, are part of ECHR. And since 1974 (the so-called Casagrande case) the Court has stated that the fundamental rights are a part of the general principles of the Union which the institutions have the duty to protect. Over the years, sentence after sentence, the Court has seen fit to implement the number of rights it deems worthy to protect, recognizing as early as the 1980s the right to reasonable judicial protection and to a fair trial (for example, the sentence in the case of Johnson, Chief Constable of the Royal Ulster Constabulary in 1986 and that of Pecastaing in Belgium in 1980).

As we previously referred (see footnotes 11 and 12), The Heads of State and Government of the Member States of EU undersigned on December 13, 2007 the Treaty of Lisbon, which came into force on December 1, 2009, which deeply modified the two treaties that ruled the institutional structure and European policies. At a first glance, it may look like another Treaty that, following The Single European Act of 1986, the Treaty of Maastricht of 1992, the Treaty of Amsterdam of 1997 and the Treaty of Nice of 2001, introduces adaptations to the founding treaties.

However, this new treaty was approved through very complex events that, starting from the ambitious project to give to the European Union its own constitutional text, develops a fine weighted reform apparently introduced to take into account all the viewpoints manifested in the negotiations, but that substantively guards many of the modifications that were introduced in the European Constitution.

With the Treaty of Lisbon there were deeply modified the Treaty establishing the European Economic Community of 1957 and the Maastricht Treaty of 1992. It disappeared, however the distinction between the two organizations, that assumed the sole denomination of European Union. Following the explicit indication of the European Council, the new treaties do not have a constitutional character. The terminology used in all the text of the treaties reflects such change: the word "Constitution" has not been used.

The new TEU preserves the old denomination and maintains substantially without change the new its previous structure, with the exception of the introduction of some elements, that were characterizing the aborted constitutional project as well as of a new chapter dedicated to the provisions on democratic principles (Title II).

The old TEC obtained the new denomination of Treaty on the Functioning of European Union (TFEU) and includes many of the innovative elements that characterized the constitutional text, among other: new aims for the EU (among others peace, full employment and sustainable development), the transformation of the co-decision procedure with vote with qualified majority in the Council as ordinary legislative p[rocedure for the adoption of the acts of the Union; the distinction between legislative and non legislative acts.

3 The Right of Defense in a Unified (and Constitutional?) Europe

Aside from the constitutional provisions of the national legal system, within the "constitutional" legal system of the EC it is obviously possible to find some important principles of justice taken from the Charter of rights of the European Union, referred to in the new reform treaty. It should be pointed out, however, as it has been claimed, that the process of European constitution making, while lacking in legal value, also appears to be incomplete in terms of the definition of a system of workable guarantees.[17] In terms of justice, it is worth noting that the Charter of rights, is largely inspired by the principles contained in the European Convention on Human Rights, the first true European document on the subject of justice and jurisdiction, even though the content of the Constitution summarizes only some of the principles expressed in more detail by ECHR.[18]

Indeed, analyzing the principles and the values on which the Union is founded it appears legitimate to prospect a normative construction where the issues concerning justice are coherent with the respect if the rule of law and the human rights. However reading the Title IV – Justice – of the Nice Charter we find only four articulated articles related to justice. Of these, art. 47 (previously art. II-107 of the project of European Constitution) sanctions the right to an effective remedy and to a fair trial (with an independent and impartial judge previously established by law)[19]; the art. 48 (before art. II-108 of the European Constitution) sanctions the presumption of innocence and the right to defence;[20] the art. 49 (art. II-109 European constitution) sanctions the principles of legality and proportionality of criminal offences and penalties;[21] the art. 50 (art. II-110 European Constitution) sanctions the

17 G. Moschella, Giustizia, organizzazione giudiziaria e tutela dei diritti nell'ordinamento costituzionale europeo, in S. Gambino (ed.), cit.

18 Taken from art. 6, 7, 10, 13 ECHR. These previsions are subsequently included in art. 47–50 of the Charter of Nice (and inserted in the original constitutional project, in title VI – Justice of the constitutional Treaty in art. II-107/II-110).

19 Art. 47. Right to an effective remedy and to a fair trial – 1. Everyone whose rights and freedoms guaranteed by the law of the Union are violated has the right to an effective remedy before a tribunal in compliance with the conditions laid down in this Article. 2. Everyone is entitled to a fair and public hearing within a reasonable time by an independent and impartial tribunal previously established by law. Everyone shall have the possibility of being advised, defended and represented. 3. Legal aid shall be made available to those who lack sufficient resources insofar as such aid is necessary to ensure effective access to justice.

20 Art. 48. Presumption of innocence and right of defence – 1. Everyone who has been charged shall be presumed innocent until proved guilty according to law. 2. Respect for the rights of the defence of anyone who has been charged shall be guaranteed.

21 Art. 49. Principles of legality and proportionality of criminal offences and penalties – 1. No one shall be held guilty of any criminal offence on account of any act or omission which did not

right not to be tried or punished twice in criminal proceedings for the same criminal offence.[22] Of these four, two – the article 49 and the article 50 – are of minor importance in our mentioning, which is essentially procedural, and so about trial and, in general, proceedings. So in our last analysis, we could affirm that the articles of the European Constitution about justice are just two, the articles 47 and 48.

However, if we read article 47 more closely – and compare it to article 48, which talks about "everyone who has been charged", the defendant, in the first paragraph, and it's about the "rights of the defense of everyone who has been charged", in the second paragraph – it would seem that the article 47 had been written regarding "civil" laws, or rather regarding procedural civil laws. It is not possible to give a different meaning to the expression "remedy" for the protection of "rights" and for the protection of the "freedoms guaranteed by the Law of the Union", when a person says that they have been "violated". But if this is the case, it is logical that the only article of the European Constitution about (penal) justice is the art. 48 which claims: "Respect for the rights of the defense of anyone who has been charged shall be guaranteed".[23]

A few words that, as was the intention of the redactors of the Charter of Nice, as well as of the members of the Convention responsible for writing the constitutional text, sum up – or should in any case – all the rights which in Italy guaranteed at the highest level in the system of the sources of rights. The reference is to the inviolable right to defense at every step and stage in the proceedings; the right for individuals to be able to defend themselves before every type of jurisdiction, even when they are not in the financial position to do so (see art. 24, Italian Constitution). With reference to this point, it is important to highlight some relevant aspects found in the new art. 111 of the Italian Constitution (it states that "jurisdiction takes place by means of a fair trial regulated by the law"):

Cross-examination. The right to appear before a judge to deny and rebut the claims put forward by the opposing parties in a court of law, in equal measure. This is where the right of defense is put into practice.[24]

Equality of both parties. By means of the principle of cross-examination, this refers to the possibility that both parties are given in a court of law to present their case in a way that does not give them a disadvantage compared to the opposing side, thus ensuring an a fair balance for both parties.

constitute a criminal offence under national law or international law at the time when it was committed. Nor shall a heavier penalty be imposed than that which was applicable at the time the criminal offence was committed. If, subsequent to the commission of a criminal offence, the law provides for a lighter penalty, that penalty shall be applicable. 2. This Article shall not prejudice the trial and punishment of any person for any act or omission which and at the time when it was committed, was criminal according to the general principles recognised by the community of nations. 3. The severity of penalties must not be disproportionate to the criminal offence.

22 Art. 50. Right not to be tried or punished twice in criminal proceedings for the same criminal offence – No one shall be liable to be tried or punished again in criminal proceedings for an offence for which he or she has already been finally acquitted or convicted within the Union in accordance with the law.

23 Theory efficiently illustrated by G. Liut, op. cit.

24 P. Mazzina, Il diritto di difesa nell'ordinamento comunitario, in M. Scudiero, Il diritto costituzionale comune europeo. Principi e diritti fondamentali, t. III.

The trial should be publicized. Every individual has the right to a public hearing. In addition, this is one of the means which contributes to maintaining the trust in the courts and the justice system. The guarantee of a fair trial is recognized as one of the fundamental principles of democratic societies.

The principle of the independence and the impartiality of the judge. Every jurisdictional decision must conform to the law. Constitutional bills do not allow for forms of control by members connected with the government. Hence the affirmation in art. 101, which states that the court must work independently from the state.

With particular reference to criminal trials, the art. 111 of the Constitution also recognizes: the right of the accused person to be informed, in as short a time as possible, about the nature of the crime for he is being charged with; the right to the time and the conditions necessary to prepare his defense, the right to question the people who give evidence for or against him in the presence of the judge; the right to summons witnesses to give evidence for his defense in the same way the prosecution does, and to be given the chance to find the evidence for his defense; the right to have the assistance of an interpreter. Moreover, the right to the formation of evidence, following the rules of cross-examination; the principle that the guilt of the accused person cannot be proven on the basis of declarations given by a witness who has not been questioned by either the defendant or the Attorney for the Defense, the right to understand the grounds of every jurisdictional measure, the right to appeal against sentences and the measures with regard to personal freedoms.

From this point of view, even the panorama of constitutionalism in Europe appears to be particularly rich. Art. 24 of the Spanish Constitution sanctions the right to a public trial without undue delays and with all guarantees ensured, while the Constitution of Sweden (art. 9) and the Netherlands (art. 15), with regard to cases where the defendant is in custody, respectively insist that the trial take place within a reasonable time and without delay. The Constitution of Sweden also states that in all other cases the trial of the defendant must take place without unjustified delay. According with the Constitution of Finland (art. 16) the trial must take place without unreasonable delays. The art. 32 of the Portuguese Constitution states that, in relation to a criminal trial, every defendant must be tried in as short a time as possible compatible with the guarantees of defense. The art. 103 of German Law, states that in every court of law every individual has the right to be heard.

What conclusion may we derive from the analysis of such rules? In the Charter of the fundamental rights of Nice – that before was the part II of the constitutional project that was later definitively set apart – a real prevision of the judicial rights and the principles of the due process of law seem to be lacking. Even the references to a fair trial (art. 47), appear generalized, undefined, and without legal importance. In reality, they are not stylistic imperfections or any peculiar legislative technique; the text of the treaty is the result of a compromise agreed upon by representatives of the different legal orders, including the judicial systems of the Member States of the Union: consider, for example, the structural incompatibility between the accusatorial model of proceedings (now in force in Italy) and the inquisitorial one typical of the majority of Continental Europe.[25]

25 In terms of the legal deficit, justifications can be found in cornerstones around which the Laws European Constitution was based. Consider the following factors: the unification of the treaties

But consider, above all, the common foreign and security policies of the European Union,[26] to which the community legislator dedicates some rules. Indeed, from a structural perspective, already in Part I of the constitutional text in its original formulation we find a number of articles on security and common defense, and so, we can find them in the first part of the text of the Constitution, made up of 60 articles (ref. art. 3 paragraph 4, 16, 40, 41, 42, 43). This data is not to be overlooked and we have to wonder why it is that the members of the Convention put justice, in its greatest sense, just in four articles, while they give more space to security and common defense, not monitoring the real numerical element.

In a similar way, we can look at the subject of "European juridical space" (Chapter IV of Part III of the original project of European constitution). Reading the articles briefly, there is an evident disparity between the issues regarding justice and those regarding security.

This subject represented the so called "third pillar" of the Union, referred to as the constitution of a single space of freedom, security and justice, first noted in the Treaty of Amsterdam in 1997. The aim was to prosecute and punish the crimes generally considered to be common to EC countries, through very close cooperation with the police and penal justice service.[27] This was one of the most important aims, the project of a constitution in its entirety, creating a kind of framework, almost more of an instrument of repression than the protection of freedoms and rights, which made the Constitution a Charter of the rights of the States rather than the Charter of the rights of citizens.[28]

All in all, if this is the context we are working in, then the judgment of the project cannot be anything but negative. Any other judgment could not be possible, even if we read the Council's Proposal regarding the procedural rights in criminal proceedings in the territory of the European Union, introduced by the Commission in April 2004.[29] Many objectives are set out in the proposal: the access to legal assistance (the right of "technical defense") – either in the phase of the investigation or of the trial – the access to an interpreter or translator, the right to information for sake of guarantee, the protection of defendants (or those under police investigation)

currently in force in one single legal source, the inclusion sic et simpliciter of the Charter of the fundamental rights of Nice, the fusion of the so-called three pillars of European Politics, the innovation of the form of government of the Union, the measures introduced in order to improve and strengthen the role of the institutions of the Union, the consequences of the expansion of the Union, consolidation of the democratic nature of the Union, the diverse share of competences of the Union and of Member States, the reform of legal sources and the simplification of legislation, and finally the introduction of mechanisms for the respect of the principle of support and assistance from the State (subsidiary).

26 G. Liut, op. cit.

27 We ought to underline that, in this area, included in the ones in which EU has shared competence with the one of the Member States, has been deeply reformed with the Treaty of Lisbon, since it took place the abolition of the third pillar and the extension of the community method also to the judicial cooperation in criminal matters and police cooperation. See also P. Bilancia, Lo spazio di libertà, sicurezza e giustizia tra realtà intergovernativa e prospettiva comunitaria, in Rivista italiana di diritto pubblico comunitario 2004.

28 M.P. Maduro, L'importanza di chiamarsi costituzione: autorità costituzionale ed autorità del costituzionalismo 2004; G. Liut, op. cit.

29 EU Council, 113/2004 (CNS) COM (2004) p. 328.

belonging to vulnerable categories (handicapped, deaf-dumb, etc.), the consular assistance for foreigners, whether they have been arrested or stopped by the police. If you look carefully, "more than guarantees, they seem to be conditions of the effectiveness of the procedural guarantees, and so, as such, are pre-guarantees which are unlikely to be used effectively for the protection of the defendant or those under investigation".[30] Besides the proposal of decision on the procedural rights, we can note that there are other important issues on this subject: in particular as regards judiciary cooperation in legal matters, we are reminded of the adoption of specific measures, which the establishment of Eurojust – a judiciary organization which has the task of strengthening the fight against serious forms of criminality, in particular organized crime, by means of a higher level of judiciary cooperation between Member States, and where each member elects a representative who has the power of attorney, judge or law enforcement officer with the same privileges[31]; The Treaty of Lisbon furthermore increased its operational competences. As well as adopting the policy on arrest warrants in Europe – regarding any judiciary decision made in an EU country where an individual is arrested and handed over to another Member State, already in force in Italy[32] – consider also search warrants[33] and the Public Prosecutor's Office in Europe.[34]

Now, as we all know, at the beginning, the European ambition was to create a "commercial space". This would be space that was to stand out from the free movement of capitals, services, goods and persons, it really meant the power of work in order to create an internal, integrated market, where in all the Member States citizens could do business and grow in economic terms without compromising the

30 The inadequacy of the proposal seems to be even more apparent when reading the opinion expressed by the Juridical Commission of the European Parliament (European Parliament, Juridical Commission 2004/0113 – CNS – O3/02/2005. You only have to read the text of the amendment. 1, Art. 2, paragraph 1, in reference to the right of the suspect to legal assistance. The Commission of the Parliament proposes to modify the term "as soon as possible and during all" to "at every step and degree" of the proceedings. The term "when he expresses the intention to want to benefit from it" remains unchanged and states that "the technical defence of defendants … Is compulsory and must not be renounced". However, the text was not modified as afore mentioned. G. LUIT, op. cit.

31 Decision of the 28th of February 2002 no. 2002/187/Gai.

32 Law 22/04/2005, no.69 "Dispositions to adapt domestic law to the decision outlined in 2002/584/gai of the Council on the 13th June 2002, relating to arrest warrants and to the procedures for handing over suspects between member states", official legal no. 98 of journal 20/04/2005

33 Proposal of decision (COM 2003/688) of the European Council, in relation to the creation of a European mandate on the search for evidence of objects, documents and data to be used for probative purposes during penal proceedings (not published in the official legal journal).

34 On the 11th of December 2001 the Commission of the Union wrote the Green Book on the penal protection of financial EC interests and on the creation of Power of Attorney in Europe (com. 2001-715, not published in the official legal journal). The Treaty that founds a constitution for Europe, in title III dedicated to regulate the competences of the Union, provided for the realisation of the Space of Freedom, Security and Justice in art. III/175, the creation of Power of Attorney in Europe to fight serious criminality, introducing a trans-national dimension and the crimes that harm the interests of the Union. The new Treaty of Lisbon states that the Council, by means of regulations adopted in accordance with a special legislative procedure, may establish a European Public Prosecutor's Office from Eurojust. The Council shall act unanimously after obtaining the consent of the European Parliament (Art. 86 TFUE).

individual interests of the Member States themselves. Having satisfied this first goal, the projection of Europe started to grow and reached broader areas; as a consequence, European Law has progressively begun to expand into other areas: European Labor Law, European Environmental Law and European Criminal Law. In doing so, aspects of European life, over and above the initial limits imposed by business and finance, started to be of interest. It is understandable therefore that as the ambition of European Law has gradually reached a higher level in democratic terms, the intervention of the EU in the lives of its citizens is and representative legitimate, particularly in view of the probable founding of a Constitution.

It is clear that justice, in the broadest sense of the term, must be considered a fundamental aspect in the process of European Constitutionalism by means of Law. This means subjecting the excesses of the market to protect citizens' rights. No longer "justice-for-the-market",[35] but justice which is intended to mean the constitutional factor in Europe, and in practical terms refers to the space of freedom, security and justice of the EU, factors which were given attention in the closing speech by the President of Finland at the Council of Europe held in Tampere (15–16 October 1999). The agenda of Tampere was ambitious, addressing all areas in the search for a more converging type of law, increasingly inspired by common models and as such emphasizing the need for reciprocal trust and the abolition of mechanisms which traditionally prevented the recognition the actions of judicial powers and the institutions of the administration of justice, creating a higher degree of harmonization between Member States.

Indeed, the main problem as regards legal proceedings in a united Europe is not the fact that it is impossible to transfer models from one country to another, also because in Europe there does not appear to be a legal system, which can act as a point of reference or as a model. In terms of the legal order in Europe, the clear heterogeneous nature of the judiciary organization highlights the need, particularly in the penal sector, to establish a reasonable level of compatibility between different systems in order to make the utterances of judges more easily recognizable between one system and another.

With regard to criminal law, there is essentially a higher level of harmonization, particularly in terms of individuals' rights, which would correspond to a higher level of reciprocal trust between State systems and a more efficient working of the instruments of penal cooperation. And it is for this reason that the reconciliation of State legislation is fundamental with regard to the guarantees in terms of the proceedings and procedures.

This process of harmonization, however, is not costless. "The error we can fall into is that of putting at stake the idea of 'Europe always, however and at any cost' to create a judicial space in Europe, above all if centered on security and common defense, the fundamental values of law and of justice of a Nation, of a State".[36] There is no real "space" without the respect for the fundamental rights; there is no effective jurisdictional protection without a justice, which may be able to guarantee the inviolable right of defense in all circumstances. It appears then, of special importance to study standards of the protection of the rights in the national constitutions.

35 J.F. Lopez Aguilar, Giustizia e Costituzione europea, in S. Gambino (ed.), op. cit.
36 G. Liut, op. cit., translation of the author.

Such a study permits, through the legal comparison, to find an ideal type of the protection of the person, articulated in the different rights. From the interaction between European law and national law, the fundamental question becomes the balancing of such an ideal type with the standard of protection of the person in EU law, that seems somehow functional to the characteristics of the process through which European integration took place. When we are facing the question of the protection of essential aspects for the protection of the life of the person in the community, such as the right to defense, we ought to consider the ideal type that emerges from the comparison of the standards of the national protection as prevailing, and namely requiring its full application. The standards characterizing the protection granted by the European Charters ought instead to integrate the former.[37]

Our wish is that within the development of the constitutional integration in Europe, together with the revision of the national constitutions, there could be underlined first of all the issues related to the growth of the system, especially for what concerns the constitutional protection of the individuals. It seems to us that the European legislator proceeded in the same direction along with the modifications of the Lisbon Treaty. The explicit reference to the Charter of the Fundamental rights of European Union, by means of article 6 TEU, appears to stress the central role of the protection of human rights. The analysis developed in this paper however, induce us to be cautious in claiming new conquers, which may be truly reached only with the time and on the base of the above said confrontation of the European parameter with the standards of protection guaranteed in the internal legislation.

4 The Right of Defence and the European Court of Justice (ECJ). A Practical Case: Lawyers, Money Laundering, Fair Trial, Professional Secrecy

The directive of the Council of Europe 91/308/CEE in relation to the prevention of the use of the financial system for the purpose of money laundering constitutes one of the major international instruments in the fight against money laundering. In 2001 it was modified with reference to the conclusions of the Commission and the wishes expressed by the European Parliament and by the Member States (directive of the European Parliament and the Council 2001/97/CE). From that moment, notaries and independent legal professionals, as they were defined by the Member States, are subjected to the dispositions of the directive, when they take part in some financial or real estate operations or they act on behalf of a company in any financial or real estate operations.

With two appeals set on the 22nd of July 2004 by different Councils of the order of lawyers, the Court d'arbitrage (Constitutional Court in Belgium) was asked to eliminate some articles of the Belgian law.[38]

37 For what concerns the use and the implications of the concept of protection of the existential manifestations of the human person see P. Policastro, Interdipendenze costituzionali e protezione della persona in Scritti in onore di Luigi Arcidiacono, Torino 2010.

38 Appeals brought before the judge respectively, from the "Ordre des barreaux francophones et germaphones", from the "Ordre français des avocats du barreau de Bruxelles", from the "Ordre des barreaux flamands", and from the "Ordre néerlandais des avocats du barreau de Bruxelles",

Those who presented the appeal maintain, in particular, that the extension to lawyers of the obligations to inform the competent authorities when they observe some facts that they think or know to be connected with money laundering and to provide the authorities with some useful supplementary information, brings unjustified prejudice to the principles of the professional secrecy and the independence of the lawyers; these principles constitute a primary element of the fundamental right of every individual to a fair trial and to the respect for the right of defense.

In such a context, the Court d'arbitrage asked the Court of Justice of the European Community if the imposition for lawyers to inform and collaborate with the authorities responsible in the fight against money laundering violates the right to a fair trial.[39]

Art. 6 of ECHR states that everyone, with regard to the controversies on civil rights and duties, or in the context of a civil or penal proceeding, has the right for his case to be examined fairly. According to the Law of the European Court of Human Rights, the notion of a "fair trial" is made up of different elements, in particular: the rights of defense, the principle of equality of both parties, the right to the access to justice, the right to a lawyer in civil as well as penal cases. The lawyer would not be able to adequately carry out his role of advice, defense and representation of his client and the client, consequently, would not have the rights included in art. 6 of ECHR, if the lawyer during the judicial proceedings should decide to collaborate with the prosecution giving them some information obtained during the juridical counsel.

The Court, in the other hand, is reminded that the duties of information and collaboration are to be applied to lawyers only in cases in which they advise their clients in operations of a strictly financial and real estate nature, or if they represent their clients in any the financial or real estate operation. As a general rule, these activities by their very nature are not connected to a judicial proceeding and, for this reason, do not apply in terms of the right to a fair trial.

From the moment the assistance of a lawyer is requested for the defense or legal representation of a client or to obtain some advice for a judicial proceeding, this lawyer is exempt from the duty to inform and collaborate as any information before, during or after the proceedings is considered to be this is irrelevant. Such exemption is intended to guarantee the right of the client to a fair trial.[40]

with the intention to obtain the annulment of some articles of the Law of the 12th of January 2004 which modified the Law of the 11th of January 1993, regarding the prevention of the use of the financial system for the purpose of money laundering, the Law of the 22nd of March 1993 regarding the status and the control of banks, and the Law of the 6th of April 1995 regarding the status of investment companies and under their control, the financial consultants (Moniteur Belge 23rd of January 2004, page 4352, and subsequently the Law of the 12th of January 2004)

39 As guaranteed by art. 6 of the Convention for the protection of Human Rights and of the Fundamental Freedoms (ECHR) and of art. 6 TEU.

40 "Les articles 2 bis, point 5, et 6 de la directive 91/308/CEE du Conseil, du 10 juin 1991, relative à la prévention de l'utilisation du système financier aux fins du blanchiment de capitaux, telle que modifiée par la directive 2001/97/CE du Parlement européen et du Conseil, du 4 décembre 2001, sont valides pour autant qu'ils sont interprétés, conformément au dix septième considérant de ladite directive et dans le respect des droits fondamentaux à la protection du secret professionnel de l'avocat, en ce sens qu'il y a lieu d'exonérer de toute obligation de

Thus, the Court declares that the duties of the lawyers to inform and collaborate with the authorities responsible in the fight against money laundering when assisting in financial operations does not violate the right to a fair trial since in such cases there is no connection with judicial proceedings.[41]

déclaration les informations obtenues avant, pendant ou après une procédure judiciaire ou lors de la fourniture de conseils juridiques": conclusions of the advocate general Poiares Maduro in the case C-305/05, which took place in the Court of Justice of the European Union owing to the committal for trial in the Belgian Constitutional Court regarding the Directive II on money laundering.

41 Such duties are justified by the real need to fight against money laundering which exerts a clear influence in the development of organised crime, which constitutes a particular threat in the societies of the member states.

Teresa Freixes / Mercè Sales

Multilevel Constitutionalism, Equality and Non-Discrimination

Abstract:
Les instruments juridiques du "multilevel" concernant l'égalité dans les systèmes juridiques complexes se structurent selon différents niveaux. En droit international il faut signaler les Pactes et les Conventions au sein des Nations Unies et la Convention Européenne des Droits Humains et autres du Conseil de l'Europe. En droit de l'Union européenne il faut distinguer entre les normes de *Hard law* (Traités, règlements, directives, décisions, jurisprudence ...) et celles de *Soft law* (Chartes, recommandations, programmes). En droit interne, il faut différencier entre les systèmes unitaires et les systèmes composés ou complexes. Si on applique ce "multilevel" aux droits fondamentaux, l'égalité par exemple, le Droit international offre des instruments universels, le Droit communautaire renforce juridiquement l'égalité en Europe, les Constitutions internes règlent de différentes façons l'égalité, la non-discrimination ou les actions positives et elles ont besoin des lois de développement (nationales et régionales) qui concrétisent dans chaque domaine (famille, entreprise, fonction publique, représentation politique) sa protection. La clause du standard le plus élevé, avec la réception interne d'instruments juridiques internationaux et européens, tels que le "mainstreaming" et l'évaluation de l'impact sur le genre, nous offre des possibilités pertinentes d'interprétation et application du "multilevel" constitutionnel concernant l'égalité et la non discrimination.

1 Introduction

The increasing interaction between EU law and the Member States' legislation (including regional law) has given rise to new paradoxes related to multilevel legal systems that connect different normative levels. Traditional national identities feel threatened by supranational structures and the advance of decentralization, leading to organizational crises. The legislative harmonization in Europe, more much extended than often suspected, has not been accepted without reluctance in all Member States due to a communication crisis. Moreover, new paradigms have confronted traditional doctrine with autonomous concepts generated by the process of European integration. Legal doctrine, therefore, is also in crisis.

For this reason, it is necessary to carry out a closer investigation into these multilevel tendencies in order to discover the true consequences of the complexity inherent to the interdependent legal systems of the European Union and its Member States.

For this purpose and as a first step, multilevel constitutionalism can be conceived as an "autonomous" paradigm aiming to explain this legal complexity. It is discussed using classical doctrine, related to systematic interpretation and federalism. It is applicable to systems made up of subsystems (competences, legal sources ...) and, above all, it is based on the supremacy of EU law and the incorporation of international law into internal law, at which level one should also take into account the distribution of competences between the State, regions and local communities. Thus, multilevel constitutionalism is all-pervasive, as it is present in both vertical (hierarchy), horizontal (competences) and network relations (cooperation and subsidiarity).

2 Multilevel Constitutionalism as Paradigm of the New Europe

Ingolf Pernice introduced the concept when, with regard to the activities of the Convention on the Future of Europe, he discussed with Dieter Grimm and Jürgen Habermas whether or not Europe needed a Constitution. For Pernice a formal Constitution was not necessary as Europe already possessed a "multilevel constitution" consisting of the Member States' constitutions and the constitutional *corpus* formed by the European Treaties.

However, the Amsterdam Treaty already included the Protocol on the principles of proportionality and subsidiarity where the multilevel system is said to include the European Union, the Member States, the regions (*Länder*, Autonomous Communities ...) and local communities. Also, investigations had already been done on multilevel constitutionalism[1] based on the reality of federal, regional or – in the case of Spain[2] – autonomous States, that is, when regions have legislative competences derived from the State's Constitution and basic institutional regulations belonging to the regional legal system (Constitutions of the *Bundesländer*, Statutes of Autonomy).

In addition, it should be noted that, in order to outline the multilevel debate, the White Paper on European Governance started by saying: "Today, political leaders throughout Europe are facing a real paradox. On the one hand, Europeans want them to find solutions to the major problems confronting our societies. On the other hand, people increasingly distrust institutions and politics or are simply not interested in them".[3] Consequently, the White Paper presents new proposals regarding Europe which essentially aim to accomplish better policies, better regulations and better delivery, clarify the functioning of the European Union, establish a European partnership at different levels and create mechanisms of participation for territories with specific characteristics and local communities. In this way multilevel constitutionalism entered fully into the European legal debate.

2.1 Reasons for Further Developing 'Multilevel Constitutionalism'

There are therefore several reasons for further developing 'multilevel constitutionalism'. Doctrinal reasons, stemming from the need to reinforce by legal means the legitimacy of decision making and policy implementation. Functional reasons, so as to achieve an increased effectiveness of the regulatory process, decision making and practical delivery ("democracy and proximity"). Added value is created by the insertion into protocols of the legally binding principles of subsidiarity and proportionality and finally the formal recognition of good practices such as those emanating from contracts with territorial objectives (for example, when carrying out projects

1 One example is the book edited by BILANCIA, P. and DE MARCO, E. La tutela multilevello dei Diritti, Giuffrè Editore, Milano 2004 (with the participation of, among others, T. Freixes, G. Zagrebelsjy, A. Barbera, V. Onida, F. Pizzetti). See also POLICASTRO, P. Challenges of Multi-Level Constitutionalism (ed. with J. Nergelius and K. Urata), Polpress, Cracow 2004.

2 FREIXES, T. "Multilevel constitutionalism y principios fundacionales de los ordenamentos supranacionales: el caso de España", in: P. Bilancia (ed.), Federalismi e integrazioni sopranazionali nell'arena della globalizzazione: Unione Europea e Mercosur. Giuffrè Editore, Milan 2006.

3 First lines of the White Paper on Governance. (COM [2001] 428 final, Brussels 25-07-2001).

financed by the European structural funds) or the establishment of new interinstitutional relations (as done by the European Parliament through the Directorate on the relations with national parliaments).

2.2 Provisions of the New "Reform Treaty"

According to the provisions of the new "Reform Treaty" agreed by the Council of the European Union on 21 and 22 June 2007, the Protocol on subsidiarity and proportionality, as well as the Protocol on the National Parliaments will be maintained, preserving their legally binding character, with two relevant modifications: the extension of the time limit for providing a reasoned opinion in case of early warning procedures from 6 to 8 days and the creation of a new procedure for the reinforced control of subsidiarity.

In this context, different systems are envisaged that reinforce the relationship between the European Union and national parliaments:

- In the first place, we should point out the consultation of the Member States by the Commission before proposing a European legislative act, taking into account, where necessary, the regional and local aspects (although in case of emergency this can be passed over with a motivated decision). The project must include an evaluation of the financial and legal impact on the Member States, sub-State bodies included.
- In the second place, an early warning system with the participation of national and regional parliaments is provided for, ensuring that national parliaments are kept informed on the state of legislative procedures. Every national parliament, once it receives the Commission's communication regarding a legislative project, has eight weeks to draw up a report contrary to the project. Each parliament has two votes: if 1/3 of all votes are contrary to the project, it should be reconsidered (veto). Every national parliament must consult, if need be, the regional parliaments with legislative powers.

Moreover, a new subsidiarity control procedure has been added. Even if no veto is pronounced, Council and Parliament will study the compatibility of the proposal with the subsidiarity principle, taking into account the allegations of the national parliaments and the Commission; if 55 % of the Council members or a majority of the votes cast by the European Parliament consider that the proposal is incompatible, it will be rejected.

Finally, we should point out the subsidiarity review procedure before the European Court of Justice, which can be presented by Member States or the Committee of the Regions (in cases where the procedure requires their opinion). In case it is presented by the Member States, these will determine the way in which sub-State bodies will be consulted on the review procedure.

3 A Practical Example of Multilevel Constitutionalism: Complex Legal Systems and the Legal Foundation of Multilevel Equality

In order to illustrate the reality of the phenomenon of multilevel constitutionalism, of which we have just outlined the main aspects, we will present a practical case: equality in the multilevel system. To be sure, the legal foundations of multilevel equality in complex legal systems are to be found on different levels. In international law we should refer to the Covenants and Conventions of the United Nations, as well as the European Convention of Human Rights and other agreements of the Council of Europe. As for EU law, one should distinguish between 'hard law' regulation (Treaties, regulations, directives, decisions, case law …) and 'soft law' regulation (Charters, recommendations, programs). Regarding internal law, one should distinguish between unitary systems and composed or complex systems. Within the latter, the Constitution, constitutional case law and the central state's laws that develop the constitution, coexist with statutes of autonomy or regional constitutions and the laws that develop them. All these interrelated levels constitute a system of multilevel constitutionalism, which we will now apply to the regulations regarding equality.

3.1 Multilevel Equality in International Law

In international law, equality is regulated both by the Covenants and Conventions of the United Nations and by the rules of the Council of Europe, sometimes with regard to all areas (in a general fashion), sometimes with regard to specific areas. Keeping this in mind, we will now briefly examine, first of all, the principal regulations that deal with equality in specific areas (political, civil, labor, family and gender equality), after which we will analyze those of a general nature that apply the principle to all existing areas based on a transversal perspective of equality ("mainstreaming").

In the political domain, the 1952 Convention on the Political Rights of Women stipulates in article 2 that "Women shall be eligible for election to all publicly elected bodies, established by national law, on equal terms with men, without any discrimination" and in article 3 that "Women shall be entitled to hold public office and to exercise all public functions, established by national law, on equal terms with men, without any discrimination". These "equal terms" do not presuppose a formal equality of treatment, but a contextual equality in exercising the right to equal access to public offices and functions, intended to create a new legal reality.

In the civil and political domain, the International Covenant on Civil and Political Rights, adopted in 1966, establishes the equal rights of men and women to marry, their rights during marriage and in case of separation or divorce, as well as to take part in the conduct of public affairs, by means of active and passive suffrage, and to have access, on general terms of equality, to public service in their country.[4]

In the field of labor relations and the family, the International Covenant on Economic, Social and Cultural Rights, also adopted in 1966, includes in article 7

4 Article 23 and 25 of the International Covenant on Civil and Political Rights, adopted in 1966.

several forms of equality, among which the obligation to ensure that women enjoy working conditions not inferior to those enjoyed by men, equal opportunities for all with regard to the right to professional education and training, as well as the obligation of the signatory States to provide a special protection to mothers.

Furthermore, as regards all domains concerning women we should point out the Convention on the Elimination of All Forms of Discrimination against Women (CEDAW), adopted in 1979, that defines discrimination as "any distinction, exclusion or restriction made on the basis of sex which has the effect or purpose of impairing or nullifying the recognition, enjoyment or exercise by women, irrespective of their marital status, on a basis of equality of men and women, of human rights and fundamental freedoms in the political, economic, social, cultural, civil or any other field."[5] This Convention obliges the signatory States to take appropriate measures, including legislation, to ensure the full development and advancement of women in all fields.[6] It considers that the adoption by States Parties of special measures aimed at accelerating *de facto* equality between men and women are not to be considered discrimination, as long as they are discontinued once the objectives of equality of opportunity and treatment have been achieved.[7] And it establishes a Committee on the Elimination of Discrimination against Women with which victims can directly file a complaint as soon as the Optional Protocol has been adopted.

It would however take until 1995 for the Declaration and the Platform of Beijing to refer to equality in all spheres of life and introduce the transversal perspective on equality ("mainstreaming"). Based on this perspective, it reinforces the introduction of affirmative action in order to promote the access and permanence of women in political life, the evaluation of the differential impact of electoral systems on female representation, the balance between professional and family life, as well as measures for the elimination of violence against women.

With regard to the European Convention on Human Rights (ECHR), adopted in 1950, it should be pointed out that the principle of gender equality is protected by means of article 14,[8] which prohibits all discrimination and establishes that the rights of the Convention shall be secured "without discrimination" according to the English version, and "sans distinction aucune", according to the French version, both versions having the same validity. Ever since its first judgments, the European Court of Human Rights has had to analyze the meaning of this article, as it is not the same ensuring the enjoyment of the rights of the Convention by means of an equal treatment that prohibits "toute distinction" as ensuring it "without discrimination", leading the Court to follow the English version. In addition, it has created, based on the idea that article 14 does not impede a difference in treatment, the praetorian figure of an equality and non-discrimination "test".[9]

5 Article 1 of Part I, Convention on the Elimination of All Forms of Discrimination against Women (CEDAW), adopted in 1979.

6 Ibid., art. 3.

7 Ibid., art. 4.

8 Article 14 ECHR states: "The enjoyment of the rights and freedoms set forth in this Convention shall be secured without discrimination on any ground such as sex, race, colour, language, religion, political or other opinion, national or social origin, association with a national minority, property, birth or other status".

9 This "test" implies the systematic analysis of three concrete aspects in all cases examined by

Finally, Protocol N° 12 to the ECHR (already in force) establishes the protection of equality in all fields, even if they are not expressly regulated by the articles of the Convention.[10]

3.2 Multilevel Equality in Community Law

EU law has in its turn created a general interpretative figure regarding equality, as well as regulations concerning its specific manifestations in accordance with its desire to construct an integrated legal order and to regulate the policies affecting the citizens of the Member States.

With regard to its general dimension, the equal treatment of men and women constitutes a fundamental principle of the European Union, which comprises a veritable fundamental right. The objectives of the European Union in this area are twofold, seeking at the same time the incorporation of the "gender perspective" into all EU policies and actions (*gender mainstreaming*) and the performance of specific actions in favor of women in order to eliminate persisting structural inequalities.[11] The European Commission indicates that "gender mainstreaming involves not restricting efforts to promote equality to the implementation of specific measures to help women, but mobilizing all general policies and measures specifically for the purpose of achieving equality by actively and openly taking into account at the planning stage their possible effects on the respective situation of men and women".[12]

Thus, from its beginnings, the principles of equal treatment and equal opportunities have been applied in a general way within the community legal order and presently constitute the foundations of an extensive community *acquis* affecting numerous areas.

The Treaty of Amsterdam considerably reinforced the legal foundation of community action in the field of equality between men and women introducing into

the Court in relation to article 14. In the first place, it should be established whether there exist comparable situations showing indications of the need for a certain differential treatment (in identical situations equal treatment is obvious and in situations which are not comparable treatment should be different); in the second place, the pertinence of differential treatment should be established, which must be justified with objective reasons and be compatible with the generally recognized principles in a democratic society; finally, the principle of proportionality should be considered: the differences in treatment must be proportional to the original causes and to the goals pursued, in content and in means. If the three aspects evaluated by the "test" are positive, the differential treatment is not considered discriminatory and compatible with the requisites of article 14 ECHR. As we shall see further on, the same "test" is used by the European Court of Justice, and also by several constitutional Courts of the Member States.

10 Protocol n° 12 entered into force on 01-04-2005.

11 See the Communication of the Commission to the Council, the European Parliament, the Economic and Social Committee and to the Committee of the Regions of 7 June 2000, Towards a Community framework strategy on gender equality (2001–2005), COM (2000) 335 final. The Framework-strategy presented by the Commission for the period 2001–2005 establishes an action framework providing for gender mainstreaming in all Community activities in such a way that they help to attain the goal of removing inequalities and promoting gender equality.

12 Extracts from the Communication of the European Commission of 21 February 1996, Incorporating equal opportunities for women and men into all Community policies and activities, COM(96) 67 final.

community law the recommendations of the Beijing Declaration and the Platform for Action of the Fourth World Conference on Women of 1995. The provisions of the Amsterdam Treaty on equality reflect the Community's commitment to the adoption of the "gender perspective", turning the accomplishment of gender equality into a specific task of the Community and a horizontal, across-the board objective for all community activities. As mentioned earlier, the principle of *gender mainstreaming* or transversal equality implies taking into account systematically the different conditions, situations and needs of men and women in the elaboration, interpretation and application of all community rules and policies, fundamental rights included.[13] Moreover, as the principle of gender equality constitutes one of the tasks of the Community, it can also take measures on the basis of article 13 EC to fight discrimination in this area.[14]

Article 2 of the present EC Treaty stipulates that "the Community shall have as its task [...] to promote throughout the Community [...] equality between men and women" and article 3 EC states that in all the activities referred to in this article, "the Community shall aim to eliminate inequalities, and to promote equality, between men and women". In addition, the Charter on Fundamental Rights of the European Union provides in article 23 that "equality between men and women must be ensured in all areas, including employment, work and pay" and authorizes derogations to the principle of equality by the "the maintenance or adoption of measures providing for specific advantages in favor of the under-represented sex". This article should be read in conjunction with articles 20 and 21 of the Charter which respectively establish the principles of non-discrimination and equality before the law. The promotion of equality between men and women constitutes therefore both a general task of the European Community and a fundamental right.

The Court of Justice of the European Communities (CJEC) as guardian of this general objective and the rights deriving from the community legal order, has emphasized that the principle prohibiting gender discrimination is also to be applied to situations of indirect discrimination. It is generally admitted that indirect discrimination can be said to exist when an apparently neutral provision, standard or practice affects a considerably larger proportion of one of the sexes, unless the application of this provision, standard or practice is objectively justified and the means used to attain it are appropriate and necessary. It should be reminded that the "test" of the European Court of Human Rights, referred to earlier, is also applied by the European Court of Justice with regard to non-discrimination. The consideration of facts that allow to assume the existence of a direct or indirect discrimination is a competence of the national judicial organ or other competent organs, in accordance with national law or practices. To determine indirect gender discrimination in labor relations, the CJEC states that "a separate assessment [should] be made of each of the key conditions governing the exercise of a professional activity laid down in

13 This comprehensive approach marks an important change in the community approach to gender equality. It was confirmed by the Community framework-strategy on gender equality (2001–2005).

14 In this regard it should be noted that Council Directive 2000/78/EC of 27 November 2000 establishing a general framework for equal treatment in employment and occupation (see Commentary on article 21 of the Charter) does not deal explicitly with situations of gender discrimination, but rather discrimination based on sexual orientation, among others.

specified provisions, in so far as those key elements constitute in themselves specific measures based on their own criteria of application and affecting a significant number of persons belonging to a determined category".[15] Moreover, the Court of Justice has introduced the reversal of the burden of proof in case of complaints about gender discrimination. This praetorian figure has been included in Council Directive 97/80/EC, of 15 December 1997,[16] which imposes the burden of proof on the defending party in all legal procedures concerning gender discrimination within the social, administrative or civil jurisdiction of the Courts.

This general dimension of equality finds direct application in specific areas, such as: equality of pay, equal treatment at work, equal treatment in social security and social assistance, equal treatment of self-employed workers, equal rights in marriage, pregnancy protection, maternity leave, parental leave, the balance of work and family life, part-time work, dignity at work and the prohibition of sexual harassment at work, affirmative action at the work place, balanced participation in political, economic and social decision making, the use of images of both sexes in the media and publicity, development cooperation, science, education and life-long-learning, violence against women and children, and the gender perspective with regard to structural funds and budgetary and financial plans.

The principle of gender equality was recognized from the beginning with regard to pay and employment. The first implies guaranteeing equal pay for equal work or for work of the same value, on which the Court elaborated by stating that the principle of equal pay should be applied to all elements of pay awarded to men and women, and not globally to the total sum of advantages granted to one or the other.[17] The other principle supposes the absence of all direct or indirect gender discrimination regarding, for example, the conditions of access to employment, the access to all types and all levels of professional guidance and education, employment and labor conditions, conditions of dismissal and pay, as well as membership of, and participation in workers' or employers' organizations.[18]

In a later stage, the principle of equal treatment is applied to social security and social assistance, in which case the principle implies the absence of all discrimination based on gender with regard to, particularly, the scope of application of social security schemes, the conditions of access to schemes, the obligation and calculation of contributions, the calculation of benefits and the conditions of the duration and maintenance of the right to benefits. However, the application of the principle

15 CJEC 6 April 2000, Jørgensen, C-226/98, Rec., p. I-2447. See also CJEC 15 December 1994, Stadt Lengerich and a.c. Helmig e.a., C-399/92, Rec., p. I-5727 and CJEC 9 February 1999, Seymour Smith and Pérez v. United Kingdom, C-167/97, Rec., p. I-623. Thus, the Court for example qualified as indirect gender discrimination the clause of a collective labour agreement which established that full-time work predetermined professional promotion. CJEC 7 February 1991, H. Nimz v. Freie und Hansestadt Hamburg, C-184/89, Rec., p. I-297.

16 Council Directive 97/80/EC, of 15 December 1997 on the burden of proof in cases of discrimination based on sex (Official Journal L 014, 20/01/1998 p. 0006–0008).

17 CJEC 17 May 1999, Barber v. Guardian Royal Exchange Assurance Group, Case 262/88, Rec., p. I-1889.

18 New article 3 of Council Directive 76/207/EC on the implementation of the principle of equal treatment for men and women as regards access to employment, vocational training and promotion, and working conditions, as modified by Directive 2002/73/EC of the European Parliament and the Council of 23 September 2002, Official Journal L 269 of 05.10.2002, p. 15.

in these cases cannot go against the provisions regarding the protection of women in case of maternity. Furthermore, women are entitled, without discrimination, to retirement pensions, unemployment benefits, sick leave, pensions for permanent disability, old age or any other loss of work capacity, as well as paid holidays.[19] Women are further entitled to dignity at work, which is also reflected in the prohibition of harassment, which is defined for the first time in article 2 of Directive 2002/73/EC[20] as: "where any form of unwanted verbal, non-verbal or physical conduct of a sexual nature occurs, with the purpose or effect of violating the dignity of a person, in particular when creating an intimidating, hostile, degrading, humiliating or offensive environment". With that in mind, it should be pointed out that these kinds of discrimination do not only happen at the work place, but also concerning the access to employment and professional education. Council Directive 2004/113/EC of 13 December 2004 introduces the principle of gender equality in the access to, and supply of goods and services[21] which prohibits, for example, the use of gender as a criterion for the calculation of premiums and benefits for the purpose of insurance and other financial services, and in general condemns any discrimination based on gender outside the labor market. In addition, Council Regulation (EC) no 1260/1999 of 21 June 1999 laying down general provisions on the Structural Funds[22] obliges States to take into account the necessity of promoting the equality between men and women when using and evaluating the use of structural funds. Regulation (EC) 1784/1999 of 12 July 1999 on the European Social Fund[23] requires the Member States and the Commission, when planning and implementing the projects financed by the ESF, to take into account whether they contribute to the promotion of the equality of opportunity between men and women, as well as the promotion of the integration and retention of disadvantaged groups and individuals in the labor market.[24] This regulation also promotes a balanced participa-

19 Council Directive 79/7/EEC of 19 December 1978 on the progressive implementation of the principle of equal treatment for men and women in matters of social security (Official Journal L 6, 10.01.1979) and Council Directive 86/378/EEC of 24 July 1986 on the implementation of the principle of equal treatment for men and women in occupational social security schemes (Official Journal L 225, 12/08/1986 p. 0040–0042), modified by Council Directive 96/97/EC of 20 December 1996 (OJ L 46, 17.2.1997, p. 20–24) regulate the implementation of equal treatment between men and women in matters of social security and in occupational social security schemes.

20 Directive 2002/73/EC of the European Parliament and of the Council of 23 September 2002 (Official Journal L 269 of 5.10.2002), p. 15.

21 Council Directive 2004/113/EC of 13 December 2004 implementing the principle of equal treatment between women and men in the access to and supply of goods and services (Official Journal L 373 of 21/12/2004, p. 0037–0043).

22 Council Regulation (EC) No 1260/1999 of 21 June 1999 laying down general provisions on the Structural Funds (Official Journal L 161, 26.6.1999, p. 1–42), p. 1.

23 Regulation 1784/1999 of the European Parliament and the Council of 12 July 1999 on the European Social Fund (Official Journal L 213 of 13.08.1999), p. 5.

24 On this subject, see also Council Regulation 1257/1999/EC on support for rural development from the European Agricultural Guidance and Guarantee Fund, modifying and abrogating certain regulations (Official Journal L 160, 26.06.1999, p. 80); Regulation (EC) No 1783/1999 of the European Parliament and of the Council of 12 June 1999 on the European Regional Development Fund (OJ L 213 13.08.1999, p. 0001–0004), p. 1; Council Regulation 2369/2002/EC amending Regulation 2792/1999/EC laying down the detailed rules and arrangements re-

tion in political, economic and social decision-making, which is also included in several Council Resolutions and Recommendations which deem it necessary to adopt a comprehensive strategy for the promotion of the balanced participation of men and women in decision making processes, in order to accomplish a better balance between men and women at all levels of government, to further equality in both public service and the private sector, as well as to reinforce the presence of women at all levels of decision making by adopting equality plans and affirmative action programs.[25]

3.3 Multilevel Equality in National Constitutional Law

In the national constitutions of the Member States the principle of gender equality is regulated in different ways. In some cases, the principle is not recognized explicitly, but can be derived from general constitutional principles. In other cases, we find a general recognition of equality and the right to non-discrimination or even a specific recognition of the equality of men and women and non-discrimination. Finally, constitutions that have recently been modified may include both the principle of gender equality, non-discrimination and affirmative action.

Among the Member States who have carried out constitutional reforms on this subject, we may refer to France, where article 3 of the Constitution states that "the Law will promote equal access of men and women to electoral mandates and eligible positions"; Law 493/2000 of 6 June 2000 therefore proceeded to regulate the presentation of balanced candidate lists as well as economic sanctions for parties which do not comply with this obligation. In turn, the reformed Italian constitution establishes in article 51 that "all citizens of both sexes will be allowed to hold public positions and eligible positions on equal terms in accordance with the law. To this end, the Republic shall promote by means of affirmative action the equality of opportunities between men and women". The Belgian constitution stipulates in article 11 bis that "laws, decrees and regional laws shall guarantee equality for men and women when exercising their rights and freedoms and shall particularly promote equal access to public and eligible positions". This article was further developed in the Law of 3 May 2003.

garding Community structural assistance in the fisheries sector (Official Journal L 358/49 of 31.12.2002) p. 49.

25 See Council Resolution of 27 March 1995 on the balanced participation of men and women in decision-making (OJ C 168, 4.7.1995, p. 3–4), p. 11 and Council Recommendation of 2 December 1996 on the balanced participation of women and men in the decision-making process (Official Journal L 319, 10/12/1996, p. 0011–0015), p. 11.

4 The Inclusion of Multilevel Equality into the Spanish Legal Order

4.1 The Inclusion of Multilevel Equality through the Doctrine of the Spanish Constitutional Court

The international and European regulations and case law are incorporated into the Spanish legal system through the doctrine of the Constitutional Court.

Regarding the effects of the judgments of the European Court of Human Rights, it should be pointed out that the Constitutional Court has stated, on several occasions, that if one of the rights included in the European Convention on Human Rights, which is also recognized by the Spanish Constitution, is violated according to a judgment of the Court in Strasbourg, this will also constitute a violation of the Constitution, which the competent national bodies are obliged to remedy.[26] In this way, the system of the Council of Europe is incorporated into national law.

The effects of the judgments of the European Court of Justice, according to the Constitutional Court, are diverse:

First of all, the effect of interpretation should be taken into account. The entire case law of the European Court is considered to be a source of law, the integration of which into internal law is obligatory. However, this integration is realized in a particular way, as according to the Constitutional Court community law does not constitute a constitutional canon for the purpose of interpretation, but directly applicable internal law, because of which transgressions are to be considered simple problems of legality to be elucidated by ordinary judges.

Furthermore, community law has a direct effect in cases involving Spain or a Spanish citizen, in case of judgments of compulsory compliance and sanction procedures in case of non-compliance (condemnation, economic sanctions and possible withdrawal of structural funds). In this case, the threat of economic sanctions facilitates the integration of community case law into the internal legal order.

The case law of the Spanish Constitutional Court also applies the multilevel system. Just one example we would like to mention, one that we indicated earlier, is the "test" introduced by the Court of Strasbourg, which led the Spanish Constitutional Court to declare that not every differential treatment which benefits a group or a certain category of people necessarily implies the existence of discrimination (STC 128/1987). It also applies the CEDAW Convention, as in the case regarding female mine workers (STC 229/1992) where the Spanish Court invalidated outdated "protection measures" appealing to the case law of the European Court of Justice. It also applies community law related to indirect discrimination, as in the case regarding hospital cleaning personnel (STC 145/1991) and the case *Galletas Fontaneda* (STC 286/1994), where it ruled that female workers are entitled to the same pay for the same work, regardless of the professional category.

26 Bultó Case, STC 245/1991.

4.2 The Integration of Multilevel Equality Through Legislative Action on Equality and Non-Discrimination

The sources of law of the different legal systems that make up the multilevel system in many cases constitute the basis for internal legislative action. It should however be noted that in the case of decentralized States that comprise regions with legislative competences, these regions sometimes take the lead creating innovative legislation that does not use as a benchmark the national legal system, but other systems that make up the multilevel constitutional system. This is the case of Spain, where on the subject of equality national legislation coexists with the legislation of the autonomous communities.

As the Spanish Constitution is concerned, it considers equality as a principle of constitutional value, and declares it to belong to the highest values of the Spanish legal system, together with freedom, justice and political plurality (article 1.1). At the same time, it is considered to be a subjective public right contained in the equality of all Spaniards before the law (article 14, paragraph 1), as well as a subjective right derived from the prohibition of all discrimination on account of gender (article 14, paragraph 2). Moreover, the Constitution contains several examples of specific rights regarding equality: the right to accede under conditions of equality to public functions and positions (article 23.2); equality regarding fiscal obligations (article 31.1); the right to marry with full legal equality (article 32.1); the prohibition of gender discrimination at the work place or with regard to pay (article 35.1); the equality of children before the law, regardless of their parentage (article 39.2). Equality is also considered to imply the obligation of the public authorities to promote equality and remove obstacles that impede or impair their full enjoyment (article 9.2).

As for general legislation concerning equality, it is worth noting, on a national level, the Law LO 3/2007 for the effective equality of men and women, as well as the laws adopted by several autonomous communities (Basque Country, Galicia, Valencia, Castille-Leon). As for more specific laws, some autonomous communities (Balearic Islands, Castille-La Mancha and Basque Country) have established electoral equality by law, just as the Law 3/2007 has done on a national level; the reversal of the burden of proof has been included in the Workers Statute in case of discrimination complaints, which has been made generally extensive in the field of criminal law by Law 3/2007; in 2003 the Law on the balance between work and family life was adopted (also in several autonomous communities); a compulsory gender impact evaluation for legislative proposals was introduced in 2003 (in Catalonia as of 2001, since then also in Andalusia, Basque Country and Navarra); and on a national level the Organic Law 1/2004 was approved on measures for the comprehensive protection against gender-based violence.

4.3 The Integration of Multilevel Equality Through Legislative Action on Equality and Non-Discrimination in the Autonomous Community of Catalonia

The Autonomous Community of Catalonia has progressively incorporated, since the adoption of its first Statute of Autonomy (the basic law of the Community and internal source of law) and the Statute's reform in 2006, values derived from the multilevel constitutional system. The Preamble of the Statute considers equality to rank among the highest values of its legal order, together with freedom and justice. The Statute also promotes rights and freedoms recognized by the Spanish Constitution, the European Union, the Universal Declaration of Human Rights, the ECHR and other international treaties and conventions that recognize and guarantee fundamental rights and freedoms (article 4), thus explicitly recognizing multilevel constitutionalism. It specifically recognizes the right of women to participate on equal terms as men in all areas of public and private life (article 19), obligates public authorities to guarantee gender mainstreaming (article 41) and establishes specific competences for gender policies (article 153), that among others include the establishment of affirmative action in order to eradicate gender discrimination and the establishment of equality and non-discrimination policies.

As for laws in Catalonia further developing equality, we should note the Law 10/1998 on non-marital partnerships, the Law 18/2003 on family support, the Law 8/2006 on measures promoting the balance between private, family and professional life of Catalan civil servants, and Law 4/2001, which is the first law in Spain that obliges to perform a gender impact evaluation when preparing draft laws and regulations.

4.4 The Interpretation and Application of the Rules on Equality in the Multilevel Constitutional System

The existing multilevel constitutional system shows, on the one hand, the connections between different legal levels and, on the other hand, that different legal institutions are regulated in a similar, yet not identical manner on different levels. This rapidly presents us with the problem of which standard is to be applied in each particular case. To be sure, the classical system of interpretation already offers us valuable methods helping us to apply the rules in a consistent way based on the connection between legal systems derived from the integration of international treaties into the internal legal system (where treaties represent the minimal standard of protection) and the primacy of EU law over the law of the Member States, in accordance with the case law of the European Court of Justice.

But we can also find normative elements that help us to determine the applicable level of protection within the multilevel constitutional system, such as the transversal clause of the highest standard, reflected in article 53 of the Charter on Fundamental Rights. This article permits us to apply the legal system that best protects the fundamental right concerned, thus making it necessary to know all legal instruments offering protection, determine their different levels of protection and subsequently apply the highest standard.

5 Conclusion

By way of conclusion, we can state that there exists a multilevel constitutional system that comprises international Law, EU Law, national constitutions, regional statutes or constitutions (as the case may be), which must be interpreted and applied in a legally adequate and consistent way. If one applies the multilevel system to fundamental rights, for example equality, international law offers universal instruments, EU law reinforces equality in Europe, the national constitutions regulate in different ways equality, non-discrimination and affirmative action, and in turn need to be developed on a national and regional level, creating specific rules for protection in specific areas (family, business, public service, political representation).

The clause on the highest standard of application, together with the internal implementation of international and European legal instruments, as well as "mainstreaming" and gender impact evaluation, offers us useful means of interpreting and applying multilevel constitutionalism to the principles of equality and non-discrimination.

Markku Kiikeri

Legal-cultural Approach to European Law

Abstract:
La point de départ de cet article est dans la littérature juridique; dans les concepts de la cohérence et de l'exactitude et dans les idées de l'intégration par droit. On étudie le thème à travers de la naissance de droit européenne et la jurisprudence actuelle. On utilise comme matériel les cas constitutionnels Costa, Van Gend, Köbler, Omega entre autres, pour comprendre comment on représent dans ces cas constitutionnels l'ordre juridique, le système juridique, droit dynamique et progressive; l'autonomie, la tradition juridique, la certitude juridique, droit international et le principe de proportionnalité. Dans cet article on affirme, que dans le centre de l'approche juridique-culturelle on trouve l'interaction dynamique des ordres juridiques nationales et surtout la nature et les limites de ces ordres juridiques nationales. On analyse cet interaction a travers de la coopération organique des tribunaux nationaux et surtout à travers des cas qui traitent le principe de proportionnalité "délégué". La question fondamentale de l'approche juridique-culturelle est d'expliquer, quel décideur juridique est l'acteur institutionnel principal et quand est ce-qu'on peut considérer que la système soit cohérente. La conclusion est que droit européenne est fondée sur la constitutionnalité juridique-culturelle et qu'on doit l'examiner comme un phénomène juridique-culturel. La base de cette approche se trouve l'héritage juridique européen d'un individu, et on le doit remarquer en appliquant la justice européenne.

1 Introduction

European law did not appear out of nowhere. For example, the similarity of structure and content between articles 96 and 97 in *Summa Theologiae* and the European legal system in general is remarkable. *Thomas Aquinas* writes:[1]

> "If law is just, it orders the conscience ... law can be unjust, if it has a wrong maker, it does not aim at common good or it gives disproportional benefits or burdens to citizens. Such laws are not right laws, and they do not command conscience. However, one must obey them, if avoiding of moral corruption or general disorder so determines. However, if the law is against the divine law, one does not have to obey it on any grounds ...
>
> Virtuous nation makes its own laws ...
>
> The customary law ... is based on the fact that the repetition expresses the practical reason of the nation ... this custom can change the law, if the nation is free and morally autonomous taking responsibility of its own government.
>
> Laws must be changed, when ... circumstances change. Laws must be proportional to circumstances ... in the change of laws cautiousness must be applied, because the stability is necessary for their function of habituation."

Modern European law uses more modest conceptualization and is structured in a more dynamic way. The analysis of the relationship between conscience and law reminds the modern legal philosophical discussion regarding law, morality and values and the questions regarding conscience have been conceptualized with the "cognitive" approach ("consciousness") rather than by stressing affective elements of the phenomenon. A law is, furthermore, "valid" and "acceptable" more than

1 Summation of the content of Thomas Aquinas' Summa Theologiae, by J-P. Rentto. In Summa Theologiae, translated to Finnish by J-P. Rentto, Turku 2002 (trans. here to English by author of this article.

"right". Furthermore, a modern law must be obeyed unconditionally except in the case of disproportionality or/and discrimination, excluding the case, where the morality or public order so determine. Arbitrary discrimination or abuse of law excludes the obligation categorically. In a modern European legal order, the decisions regarding this are made within an institutional system by aiming at a comprehensive and coherence-oriented justification.

"Present" European legal culture was not, consequently, born from "ashes", even if created in rather unexceptional circumstances and in a peculiar way.[2] It was derived from as a strange mixture from the legal heritage and cultural consciousness of the lawyers, not based on a direct socio-political interest discussion. The innovation was a creative process and continues to be so.[3] The creators had to approach the existing Europe and its law *legal-culturally*. They were "prisoners" of their legal heritage (of coherence and language game[4]), which gave them, however, space for their legal imagination. The system rose from traditional elements appearing necessary at that stage. It was based on their ideas about European legal history and legal theory. Understandably, the legal system was called *"own"*, *"special"*, and autonomous in realm of international law.[5]

In order to understand and explain the phenomenon of European legal system we must take the "legal-cultural approach" and the theory of European legal system seriously[6] instead of the institutional, legal "orderic" and pragmatic point of view. Taking this approach we ask what were and are the basic legal philosophical and comparative approaches within the system and how does the court thought and thinks now itself as a social actor? What would be the basic concepts we must consider and why? The answers derive, in my opinion, from the discussion on *Van Gend* and *Costa v. Enel* including the discussion between the two Advocate Generals, Mr. Roemer and Mr. Lagrange.[7] The last mentioned represent very different perspectives to the European law.[8]

This paper does not aim to a very coherent and comprehensive argument. It basically tries to establish background for further research. The argument here is not directly "idea-historical", even if some features of the "amalgam" of European law may be reached.

2 See, Monnet, J. 1997, p. 151.
3 See, Monnet 1997, p. 151, Lagrange, M. 1961, Koopmans, T. 1991.
4 As Aarnio, A. 1998, p. 35.
5 Judgment of the Court of 5 February 1963, NV Algemene Transport- en Expeditie Onderneming van Gend & Loos v Netherlands Inland Revenue Administration, Reference for a preliminary ruling: Tariefcommissie – Pays-Bas, Case 26-62, European Court reports, English special edition Page 00001 (and Opinion of Mr Advocate General Roemer delivered on 12 December 1962). Judgment of the Court of 15 July 1964, Flaminio Costa v E.N.E.L., Reference for a preliminary ruling: Giudice conciliatore di Milano – Italy, Case 6/64, European Court reports, English special edition Page 00585 (and Opinion of Mr Advocate General Lagrange delivered on 25 June 1964).
6 Walker, N. 2005.
7 See Lagrange, M. 1979.
8 See Weiler, J. 1999, p. 286.

2 European Legal System as a Legal-Cultural System

This paper departs from two dimensions: formality and effectiveness. Indeed, legal system should be coherent, all-related and comprehensive ideal system of norms[9] or at least systematically associated cultural construction.[10] Justification is a functional means of effective systematization and coherence creation. Also the claim of correctness is built into the idea of legal system. The concept of legal order, on the other hand, represents different variations of effectiveness and weighing. Weighing is an active exercise,[11] part of making the legal system effective and the dynamic side of legal system. Legal order is the pragmatic and institutional side of the legal system.

In the cultural systems theory, distinctions, norms or propositions are related by "associative" connections.[12] Within the legal theory they are related by coherence (consistency, comprehensiveness and connectivity) and correctness and weighing of legal propositions.[13] The basic ingredients of (legal) culture are common values. Law in the cultural theory is considered important integrative instrument. Within the European social order, law could be considered the main cultural-integrative instrument.[14]

In the European *legal*-cultural system itself, it is the legal environment which determines and has determined the development and evolution of the European law. Unlike the traditional interest-discussion and social discourse in traditional modern democratic state legal "systems", the "environment" of European legal system is essentially legal. This results in particular mechanisms within the evolution of the European legal system. This idea is decisive in considering the idea of coherence of the European legal system.

The legal cultural quality of the European legal system is undoubtedly based on such doctrines[15] as European legal system as "*outline law*", European legal system as a "*evolutionary system*", "*legal heritage*" (of the system of individuals' rights), "*rule/conceptual/spiritual integration*", "*systemic coherence*", "*autonomy*" of the community legal system (order), European substantive "*legal certainty*", legal subjectivity of individuals (with direct effect and "*self-executive nature*" of international rules), "*organic cooperation*" between the courts, legal "*globalism*" and distance from the traditional international law ("*own legal system*"), validity and legitimacy based on the national legal orders, and the dynamism of law in general, all found in the two basic cases of the Community law, in one form or another. "Internationalism" was thus far superseded by the globalism in the *Costa* and *Van Gend*. Lagrange also spoke about the

9 Alexy, R. 1998, p. 42.
10 Luhmann, N. 2006, Aarnio, A. 1998, p. 38.
11 Alexy, R. 1998, p. 47.
12 Luhmann, N. 2006.
13 Alexy, R. 1998, p. 42.
14 On this, Integration through law: Europe and the American federal experience. Edited by Mauro Capelletti, Monica Seccombe and Joseph Weiler. Vol 1: Methods, tools and institutions, Berlin 1985.
15 See, Annex to this paper.

pre-federal nature of the Community based on the Member States as a group as whole ensuring the respect of the system.[16]

The Court speaks in its first constitutional case law about European legal system, even if a bit eccentric way – especially considering different language-translations. The Court maintains in *Van Gend* that ECC constitutes a "*new legal order of the international law*". This concept of "*order*" is repeated in all language versions of that case. However, in *Costa* the English version speaks about "*own legal system*" and repeats it consistently in that particular translation. The French version is "*un ordre juridique*". The French version qualifies it also "*propre*" legal order. Italian one maintains "*ordinamento juridico*" and the German, Dutch and Finnish are the same ("*eigene Rechtsordnung*", "*eigen rechtsorde*", "*oikeusjärjestys*"). The Swedish version sustains, first, the "*särskild rättsordning*" (special legal order), but, in mentioning the national ones, about "*legal system*" ("*rättssystem*"). It upholds that the national entities are systems, but the European one an order. Later in the translation, however, the Swedish version speaks about national legal orders ("… *Den överföring som staterna företagit från sin nationella rättsordning till förmån för gemenskapsrättsordningen av rättigheter och skyldigheter* …"), which would suggest that the translation is only inconsistent. Consequently, it seems that within the international law the European order is a *new legal order*, whereas its positive "internally" derived and interpreted sense it is "*own legal system*". The concepts of legal order and legal system are quite inconsistently used.

Furthermore, when speaking about "autonomy" of the system many legal scholars use interchangeably these two different concepts. The situation is perplexed. Or, is it? Is there behind this something, perhaps, legal cultural or systematic preferences? Some seem to indicate this.[17] Similar questions could be asked in connection to the "*spirit of the Treaty*" (translated as "aim" in Finnish version, for example) and regarding the legal "*heritage of rights*" of individuals, translated in Finnish, for example, as "*legal status*" of the individual (on this see below).

The legal order and legal systems can be assimilated. There may be even an explanation to this type of approach.[18] Both approaches are philosophically defendable. However, theoretically speaking, the legal system is an aim. When equating order and system, on the other hand, one usually argues pragmatically about justice and "good results" of law. In the context of European and national law, however, the distinction between system and order should be made for better understanding[19] of the construction and in order to conceive how the European system differs from the traditional idea of legal system. Coherence seems to play a role in defining the relationship between the European and national legal orders. The question is also about the nature of the "differentiation" of the national legal orders.

16 Lagrange, M. 1966, p. 711.
17 Weiler 1999, p. 286.
18 See also, Raz, J. 1992, p. 297, Alexy, R. 1998, p. 44.
19 "To make sense", Alexy, R. 1998, p. 47.

3 The Argument: Legal Cultural Constitutionalism

My claim is that the European legal system comprises a plurality of legal orders. National legal "systems" can be described in the context of European law as organizationally and legislatively differentiated orders, with some qualifications (see below, weighing and justification). If we accept, which we should, that the European legal norms and system of treaties have become the integral part of the national legal orders, and it is very difficult to describe the national legal sphere systematically differentiated. As far as we maintain the acceptability of the national legal rules ultimately mirrored (weighed, balanced, interpreted) against the norms and principles of the European community law – whether this takes place in the European legal order or in national legal orders – this superiority and primacy of the Community law creates the common systematic sphere, which is to be described as the European system of law.

Even if one claims that the European legal system is based on some kind of value pluralism, the superiority and primacy of the Community system and the lack of systematic coherence of the national legal orders because of the autonomous and coherent nature of the European legal system makes them legal orders. So, in the end, we should not anymore define national legal orders within the European legal system legally or functionally differentiated systems, but rather as organizationally differentiated systems. This has constitutional significance.

It must also be remembered that with the "plurality of national legal orders" we may mean also that the orders are different. They do not have to be similar, for the aims, objectives and values prevailing in the European legal system may be achieved in many different ways. The apparent difference does not lead to systemic differentiation. This type of "plurality" is part of the European legal systematic coherence. Furthermore, the existence of a control mechanism in one state – even if different – may be even a justification for the creation of control mechanism of different kind in another order. This all shows the very complexity of what we may mean about the coherence from the point of view European legal system as a whole.

Consequently, it is difficult to define national legal systems as culturally differentiated legal systems. The values are in principle and legally the same and any derogation from the principles must be explicitly authorized and restrictively interpreted, ultimately in the European coherence. National legal "systems" are differentiated in the instrumentalist-organizatorial sphere, which makes me to say that they are legal-orderly differentiated.

National legal systems are, however, in many ways, "sources" of European law. The use of this "legality" is, however, many ways restricted by the interests to qualify them as basic principles and philosophy of the European legal system.[20] We may think in this connection also about the distinction between chaining (legally "strong") and accumulation (legally "weak").[21] "National" legal norms are more like "evidence" of law (cumulative arguments) or socio-political interests rather than part of the chain in European justification of the norm. They are part of the European legal system "comparatively" and as their "adhesion" to each other, but, as

20 See, Kiikeri, M. 2002, p. 147.
21 Peczenik, A. 1998, pp. 59–60.

such, part of the coherence within the European legal system. The process is not, consequently, only a process of European law becoming part of the national legal orders, but the direction is also reversed, a metamorphosis of the national legal systems to a European legal system.

Many fundamental conceptions and institutional ideas are derived from the legal-cultural heritage with the help of national judges, for example. This way the birth of the European legal system was and is comparatively *legal-cultural*. The interaction between the national legal orders and the European legal order has been decisive for the development of the system as a whole, as we may see especially in *Van Gend*. Without the existence of the "*self-executiveness*", the formulation of the *direct effect* could not have been possible.[22] In this sense, we may even say, that the loci, source of law, of the European law was a national legal system more or less directly.

This systematic development has been based on the idea of "outline law" with "evolutionary nature". Without this type of basic idea the interactive creation could not have been possible. The teleology is there as a legal-cultural principle, not only as a Treaty-structural construction. This idea seems to be the connecting factor for all the influences and the building of a coherent legal system. The comparative influences derive from national legal orders and influence them back via the reasoning of the European system. The interpretation of these influences remains autonomously a European matter (with qualifications). So, the outline law is written together with the national legal judges in cooperation with the European ones. The coherence, in this way, is not determined by the formal structure of different formal sources of law, but it is the result of the various norms and norm propositions situated in the European legal system as a whole. One could also speak about some kind of "opportune" of law, legally something that Mr. Roemer just did not accept in *Van Gend*. This way, as Mr. Lagrange maintained,[23] the national legal orders give the legitimacy to the European legal system, both as traditions as well as regarding the effectiveness.

Accordingly, the European legal system seems to have a "legal-cultural constitution". Sources of European law (human rights, general principles, treaties, secondary legislation, interpretative principles, cooperative application and the Courts case law related to that etc.) are in many ways related to the legal traditions of the national legal systems and their history. This relates not only to the interpretation of the basic statutory law but also to deciding the most difficult cases of constitutional law. This is why it is very difficult to make the distinction between the European law and the national constitutional law in this sense, even if some try still to make it, even from the cultural point of view[24] and the point of view of human rights (constitutional basic rights approach). The challenging of the legal-cultural identity and the self-descriptively constructed comparative or other type of systemic nature of the national legal systems is contested within the European *legal* system. This is not made, however, in the "traditional "comparative" and comprehensive way taking into account the whole political and social interest building mechanisms.

22 Weiler, J. 1999, p. 4.
23 Lagrange, M. 1966.
24 Häberle, p. 1998.

4 Evolution and Dynamics as Part of the Legal Culturalism

The dynamics and the evolution can be seen as one of the legal systematic "meta"concepts and fundamentally constitutive aspect of the European law, system and the legal orders. European legal systematic development "follows" the development within the economic and social system. European law maintains system of hierarchies, even if different from the traditional idea. It seems to be in practice a discussion regarding values rather than their coherent systematic interpretation. The evolutionary nature is based on the aim to create a consistent European legal system. Ideas regarding the "stage" of European law are moments for evaluating the evolution. The teleological nature of the Treaty and the methods of interpretation are part of the idea.

How much this was conceptualization formulated originally and how much it was determined by perspectives for the progress is unclear. The idea was perhaps not so clear during the first years of the functioning of the order. Soon the actors seemed to understand, however, the need for the evolutionary dynamics and conceptual of "outline law" to enable the system to develop. The evolution in 70's and 80's confirmed the need for this type of conceptualization.

The idea of evolution has been maintained as the basic principle of the Community legal system in 60's by Mr. Lagrange in *Costa*. He related it to the efficacy of law maintaining that system is evolutionary whenever the development betters individual's possibilities to seek legal protection.[25] Evolution is "continuous creation" of the system.[26] Dynamics and evolution are maintained by the Court by encouraging the political side to govern and develop the system and take part of the achievement of the basic aims, when this evolutionary process in other fields of regulation is clogged. The Court's role is to maintain the dynamics with its judicial politics by law.[27] In this sense, any action or inaction impeding the effectiveness of achieving common aims, are always suspicious from the point view of the European system.

The aim-oriented philosophy and the evolutionary dynamics can be seen also in the system of legal processes; annulment, inactivity and preliminary ruling. It gives possibility for the legal order to regulate effectively dynamics of the system. The dynamics is, consequently, very much related to the way the different legal actors in the European legal institutional system interact with each other ("*organic interaction*"). The national court in 234 processes begs the question regarding the European chain of the final justification and the European court gives preliminary ruling so that the models contained in it are dynamic enough for the national court. If the model would be too strict the national court would not be able to really consider and justify itself the solution to the problem. Furthermore, the solution would be limitedly considered. The Court, understanding this, appears as a profound cultural actor. It must conceive the evolutionary potentialities. The evolutionary and dynamic nature is, thus, maintained by feeding the value-questions (legal irritants[28]) into the institutional system and problematizing them in the interactive legal insti-

25 Lagrange 1961, p. 5.
26 Lagrange 1966, p. 710.
27 Lagrange 1966, p. 712.
28 See, Teubner, G. 1998.

tutional discourse. This is interestingly related to the legal predictability and legal certainty. These and other constitutional themes can be understood only in the context of evolution.

The dynamics is, consequently, based on the idea of equality of the different legal-institutional actors within the system. All actors must be in the service of this evolution. It is the task of the European legal institutional community. The real challenge for the European lawyer is especially the process of justification in realm of the hard cases (see below). The "culturality" comes up in this basic premise of interaction between different legal actors within the European process. However, the "autonomy" given to the national legal orders is given for the sake of efficacy, not from the value-constitutional point of view. The European legal system is in a constant "emergency" or "crisis" situation, but within the legal limits and realm of the interests to develop the system as such. The crisis is, however, in control as long as the modern "emancipatory" legislation is in the basic juridical control.

The idea of evolution makes the European legal system aim-oriented, value-based and effectiveness seeking system. This is related to be its strong legal institutional character. The values are contained in each national legal sphere as a European systematic legal presumption. This means that in the European legal system one makes not only the illegal/legal distinctions, but within the system one may bring also "non-legal" (within the national legal system) to the sphere of legal. This way European legal order may fundamentally break the cultural self-descriptions within the national legal discourse. Some theories regarding the unpredictability of the European law can be associated with this.[29] We must remember, however, that the legal certainty is evaluated from the European legal substantive point of view. Even extensive national interest discussions may be re-examined within the European system. This takes place especially in connection to principle of proportionality (see below).

5 Legal Coherence, Cohesion and Adhesion as Part of the Legal Culturalism

The deconstruction and questioning of the legal systematic coherence of the national legal orders lead lawyers to the basic balancing between different aims and values. Ultimately in the legal orderic decision-making this shows the way to the re-systematization, justification of this systematization. The European level systematization is "re-associative" and "re-systematory" function of law. Thus, we could claim to have the idea of coherent legal system as a European legal-cultural system. The coherence of the national legal systems is deconstructable only in the context of European law. Can a legal-cultural system, however, really be coherent? Two concepts may be useful in explaining this: cohesion and adhesion of the legal systems, legal orders and their norms. These ideas serve also as the theoretical tool for analyzing the development and evolution of the case law. They bring some light to the inter-connections between seemingly autonomous parts of legal orders. They suit to analysis of the European legal system based on the interactive organic coop-

29 Wilhelmsson, T. 1997, p. 357.

eration between different legal orders in establishing, creating, developing and maintaining the system.

Cohesion may be defined as the systemic association between two or more aims, principles or values. Cohesion is examined in the context of the principle of proportionality. If the norm of a national legal order does not have this (proportional) connection – taking into account all its ingredients (including alternativeless necessity) – with the basic value it is supposed to assist or enforce, cohesion does not exist. This is related to the idea of "outline" law and the idea of coherence of the European legal system.

Legal systematic "adhesion", on the other hand, appears in the context of several legal orders within the European legal system. It may be described as value interdependence between different legal orders despite the lack of real coherence within the European legal system as such. Thus, one may describe the European legal system consisting also of the national legal orders which are seemingly and legal "comparatively" different, but which belong together and could can be evaluated on the basis of the common values or aims within the European law, which form the constitutional limits of the particular legal orders within the Community law. This explains, for example, the processes of including certain "nationally autonomous" fields of law (like direct taxation in late 80's, for example) to the normative supervision of the Court. Adhesive fields of law are potentially cohesive.

Consequently, the adhesion could be applied to analysis of such fields of law, where only partial or no integration of legal orders has taken place and where common community interests have not been explicated (direct taxes, private law, etc). The question is about adhesive interdependence of the national legal order in the absence of Community rules, norms or explicitly applied general principles of law. This is related to the "international dimension" of the European law; national legal systems, from the point of view of the international law, may appear autonomous and culturally independent. However, there is the "cultural existence" of the non-explicated Community law.

This idea suits as well to the analysis "European comparative law" and historical research. From the European systematic perspective the national legal information has qualities of legal knowledge, but being relative this information is not really "legal knowledge". It is to be qualified within the European legal system. The European legal system is, consequently, traditional "functional comparative legal system" (cultural legal system) not being directly restricted to the European legal orders. The adhesion of the national legal orders, consequently, creates the comparative-cultural sphere with all the possibilities for the basic legitimacy and the reciprocal influences. In this sense the European comparative law is comparative *law* in its very meaning and escapes many problems of the traditional problems of the concept of law within the comparative law in general.[30]

The idea has application also within the field of legislative and socio-discursive dimension (dimension of interest discussion). The European constitutionalism has quite completely breached the limits of national and European interest discussion. The moves from the "national level" to the "European level" discussion are reflected in the evolution of the European legislation, even in the sphere of so called "exclu-

30 See, Kiikeri, M. 2002.

sive" autonomy of national systems to regulate the issue (for example, direct taxation) or complementary European competences (health, consumer protection). The adhesion of the social discourse is increasingly determined by the overlaps between the European and national interests. And even if the institutional legal and political order would maintain some kind of autonomy in this regard, the cross-border European social sphere is an element – even if in an incoherent way – of the adhesion of different socio-legal orders.

This way the "unofficial" integration takes place within the overlapping interest discussion keeping the socio-legal systems together without or despite the official integrative development. The increasing integration in the field of environment is a very good example of this type of evolution within the European legal system. This is also one of the aspects of the "culturally" determined evolution of the European legal system.

6 Weighing and Justification as Part of the Legal Culturalism

The systematic interpretation in European law is comprehensive exercise. Law is interpreted as its wording, aims, systematic connections etc.[31] It is aiming at the coherence of the European law relating also to the allocation of the mechanisms of the legal justification and its effectiveness. This feature comes definitely up in the hard cases of European law. The dynamics and the evolutionary nature of the system as whole are also at stake.[32] This feature can be explained in the following way.

The "systematization" process in the European law seems to be based on the evaluation of the various interest discussions from the point of view of values. The traditional proportionality mechanism is functioning as a relativizing the "democratic" interest-formations in the form of law with the basic values of the European Community. The main value of this system is, of course, the equality (nationalities, sex, etc.). Through it are established new connections and more comprehensive and coherent system, stage by stage. The effectiveness of these values within the traditional legislative framework is questioned. One could maintain that the task of the European court is to question, on the basis of the European values, the coherence of the national legal orders (systems?) and this way create in a dynamic way the European legal system.

This feature is, however, strongly tight to need to justify value-judgments. The judgments have to be justified the best and most comprehensive way by aiming at the coherence with all particular and supporting connections. This seems to be why the European court may refer the justification of the proportionality to the legal environment of a particular national system[33]; the forceful justification established by the changing of the all features of the legal system may be known best by the

31 See, Opinion of the Advocate general Léger delivered on 27 February 2003, case C-423/01 Färber GmbH & Co. v Stadt Neustadt an der Weinstraße.

32 Lagrange 1961, p. 7.

33 Judgment of the Court (Third Chamber) of 28 September 2006, Criminal proceedings against Jan-Erik Anders Ahokainen and Mati Leppik, Reference for a preliminary ruling: Korkein oikeus – Finland, Case C-434/04, European Court reports 2006 Page I-09171 (and Opinion of Mr Advocate General Poiares Maduro delivered on 13 July 2006).

national judge. This indication about the social context refers to the need to examine the various interests behind the particular system under scrutiny. Fundamentally the question is about who gives the justification in situations where the decision is related directly to the interest discussions, social and economic contexts and ultimately the fundamental values within the European system as a whole. This is why the principle of proportionality is evaluated in the context of social and economic particularities within that order.[34]

This mechanism is confirmed by the latest case law of the court. Sometimes the principle is seen best evaluated by the Community judge, sometimes the court maintains that it is for the national judge to establish, whether the proportional actions have been taken. The national judge is instructed to take into account all the legal and social particularities within that particular system.[35] This recent case law indicates for me also a peculiar, kind of a reverse, "comparative" approach within the European system. The European judge does not play "*Montesquieuan* comparativist" and pretend to understand institutional, legal, social and cultural particularities of each national environment. Rather, understanding the particular ways of the social-interest discussion, legal complexities and connections, the alternative mechanism within the socio-legal order, and even the peculiarities of the legal sources in the doctrine, it respects this partial autonomy of the socio-legal order and delegate institutionally the decision-making to the "*national judge in a better situation*".[36]

The effectiveness the European principles and general principles of law cannot be compromised, but certain type of "autonomy" seems to exist. We could call this "justificatory autonomy". These "delegations" seem to aim at substantively correct decision by the best possible justification of the issue. Some would perhaps speak about aiming at "more weighing",[37] and some would perhaps suggest that the European level decision-makers understand to be "prisoners" of their own coherence and language game,[38] which leads to some kind need to delegated justificatory process in hard cases.

The application of this "delegative principle of proportionality" or "functional-legal subsidiarity"[39] could also be considered as an indication for the legislator to re-think alternative ways of organizing the legal question. Indeed, the interactivity may not be related only to the axis of legal orders, but may extent to the European particular socio-legal discourse within the particular order. This, consequently, increases the role of the European court and the European legal order as a part of the general discourse within the European socio-cultural system and stresses its role as a constitutional actor.

34 Tridimas, T. 1999, p. 38.
35 Case 434/04 (note 33).
36 Note the similarities between the European Human rights system and the European system in this sense, see also cases 434/04, 470/03 (A.G.M.-COS.MET Srr) of the Court of Justice. See also, Opinion of Mr Advocate General Poiares Maduro delivered on 13 July 2006 in case 434/04 and Opinion of Advocate General Kokott delivered on 17 November 2005 1(1) in that case C-470/03.
37 Peczenik, A. 1998, p. 12.
38 Aarnio, A. 1998, p. 35.
39 See Kiikeri, M. 2002, pp. 67, 73, 148, 253, 299.

As indicated, these types of "delegations" also invite the national legal actors to see themselves as autonomous in that particular political-administrative order. This can be associated, consequently, to the stressing of the constitutional role of the courts in general. The mechanism seems to bring legitimacy towards the national *legal* order, emphasizing its autonomy and encouraging the application of the legal system within the doctrine of separation of powers, formerly very confused in many modern national legal orders. This way the European legal system is based on the principle of "internal" interaction within the socio-legal order itself and it could be seen legal-culturally oriented.

The principle of proportionality is of course interesting in such fields of law mainly in the competence of Member States and at same time scrutinized from the point of view of the discrimination-principle. Tax law is a good example. Tax measures are related quite directly to the particular social-cohesion and they are complicated as to the burden transferred to various members of the community. It is also such a field of law, where the maintenance of the fiscal interests and balance is extremely complicated and needs to be evaluated from different perspective than other rules of law, where the general principles are easier to associate with the aims and intentions of the legislation. The European values, in this context, mainly relate to the general efficacy of the legal order and general legal protection. This is why the exceptions to the national discrimination or discrimination on the basis of the residence have been accepted only on the basis of fiscal supervision. The Community interest seems to lie mainly in the strict application of the general discrimination principle.[40] Namely, if the law is applied in a non-discriminatory way to all residents within the jurisdiction, there do not, in general, seem to be problems. However, any unbalanced increase of economic burdens results directly in discrimination and exceptions are hard to justify just on the basis of pure public interest. The conflict is seen mainly between the general principle of discrimination and the public interest, which latter cannot prevail without further supporting arguments related to the basic efficacy of the legal order or loss of general order resulting from destruction of the coherence of the fiscal system in more profound way.

Nevertheless, the point is that in such highly instrumental fields of law, where the reasonable margins of discrimination are accepted, discrimination from the European perspective is difficult to conceive. The coherence of the national tax system functions in these margins. The "fiscal discrimination" is embedded in that resource-political and instrumental quality and the measures are strictly disproportional and cause extra burden to certain individuals. Without a general Community level interest-discussion and common Community wide objectives the European order may regulate "national tax-coherence" only from the strict application of the equality principle and disproportional. The "proportionality" of the division of burdens is very much in the hands of the Member States. Fiscal interests as such cannot be examined and maintained as the basis of the exceptions due to their socio-political interest-connectivity. The "European" legal systemic coherence in this regard is

40 See Judgment of the Court (Grand Chamber) of 14 November 2006, Mark Kerckhaert and Bernadette Morres v Belgische Staat, Reference for a preliminary ruling: Rechtbank van eerste aanleg te Gent – Belgium, Case C-513/04, European Court reports 2006 Page I-10967, also Kiikeri, M. 2007.

highly dynamic, based on the interference by the fundamental legal principles in order to make the legislator to think over the coherence of the tax system anew from the European point of view. Any exceptions have to be strict substantive reasons creating the circumstances for the effective application of Community law in general.[41]

Consequently, we may see how the European legal system contains a very complex idea of weighing. The question is many times about the weighing between the European legal principles and common interests vis-à-vis national or European legal-orderic interest-based norms. This activity takes ultimately place in the European legal institution. Moreover, and this is implied, in the weighing sure reflected considerations regarding who really does this weighing in the first place and especially who justifies and is able to justify the issue most coherent way within the overall European legal system.[42] This phenomenon seems to be very much based on the idea that values, even if common in the European sense, can be considered in different institutional systems. Furthermore, the idea seems to be that different values get different weight depending on how other values are presented in that particular legal-political order and its law. We have a margin of European systematic coherence considered within the "national sphere". This could be called, for many reasons, European legal-orderic coherence. Here I refer to the idea of legal adhesion as a way to understand this mechanism.

The "invitation to justification" is aiming at the best possible justification. The justifications are not necessarily achieved in the best way by the actors of European legal order, but may be so also by the national judges. The "claim of correctness" is tightly bound to the consideration of the "best possible justification". In this justificatory process possible counter-arguments are and must be tested and mapped in this way and this type of process and possibly answered in the course of the development of the case law. This last feature refers definitely also to the justificatory autonomy for the sake of efficacy of the legal system as a whole. The whole process produces in its evolutionary development various types of justifications aiming, in the end, to the coherent European legal system. The consideration of the principle of proportionality within the national legal order opens up the restricted interest-based discussion to more European oriented way and invites the national judge to aim at the European legal coherence.

The evolution in this context seems to be, at the moment, two directional. On one hand, the "delegated proportionality" guarantees the extensive and comprehensive justification of the case, whereas the *Köbler*[43]-type of case law on institutional responsibility guarantees that the national courts take their task seriously.

The system is based also on the idea of "equalizing" the participants of the system within the discourse and organizatorial systems. The legal system delimits itself from the general cultural system. This is an important point of view of the European law and the "organic cooperation" between the legal orders. The question is about

41 See, on these types of substantive reasons, Peczenik 1998, p. 13.

42 See, case 434/04 and Opinion of Advoc ate general.

43 Judgment of the Court of 30 September 2003, Gerhard Köbler v Republik Österreich, Reference for a preliminary ruling: Landesgericht für Zivilrechtssachen Wien – Austria, Case C-224/01, European Court reports 2003 Page I-10239

the way different organizational players consider themselves within the European legal discourse, i.e., in this "organic cooperation".

In another context I have called this interactive process and search for the best justification as "discursive integrity". It seems to be the prevailing principle in the realm of the European legal system.[44] Within this theory the question is about different auditories of the justification and about who wants to get convinced and by what means. The national judge is sometimes obliged to think more than the national auditory, especially in the case where the question is about the conflict between socio-politically discussed balance of interests and legal principles.

This is a feature of the European legal system as a legal-cultural system. The aiming at the most comprehensive and convincing justification and establishment of the connections between various interests and particular norms may result the need to transfer the work of justification to the national judge, even if the case is clearly a hard-case of the European law. The national judge is asked and invited to interpret the national law in the context of European law as instructed by the European court.

In the end, because the interpretation of law in the light of general principles of European law is a matter of balancing the European legal principles with the national or European legal legislative regulation, even if determined by the principle of best possible justification, the autonomy and primacy of the European legal system demands ultimately the constitutionality and the effectiveness of the European law. If the European principles do not achieve the necessary effectiveness, the constitutionality of the whole system is in danger. However, the requests put for the national court to aim at some kind of idea of European legal system and European coherence creates dynamics towards the European legal system and gives, on the other hand, if followed by the Court of Justice, more perspectives on what the European legal-cultural system is all about.

7 Conclusion: European Legal Consciousness

Consciousness is about remembering something.[45] Here the whole project has been, ultimately about how European legal tradition is remembered. A beautiful example in the Court's case law is *Costa* (Lagrange) maintaining that the rights based on the responsibility of the State – and not on the explicit form in the Treaty – become and are part of the "*legal heritage of the individual*". In some language versions, unfortunately, this sublime idea of heritage does not come up. The term "*legal status*" refers merely to the modern conception of rights and looses the "legal-cultural" dimension. There the individual has been "given" subjectivity, but on the basis of his modern status. This makes clear that it must be the European lawyer who remembers the cultural heritage. Rights must be part of the legal consciousness of the European lawyer, which must also describe this phenomenon as a European legal agent. When taking the European perspective, one sees oneself as a European lawyer and European legal actor.

44 Kiikeri, M. 2002.
45 Ricoeur 2004, p. 3.

In this context, it may be asked how much the European legal community is a value community more than a modern legal community? This must have come up some way in the discussions between those six judges sitting in the *Villa Vauban* in Luxembourg trying to figure out what the European legal system is all about and where it comes from. Its sources are not formally restricted; it deals with the questions about ultimate evaluation of the law. It is very much concerned with establishing the agency of all its legal actors and promoting their idea about the purposive nature of their European legal activity. It may discuss and contest even societal (and "democratic") interest discussions and their outcomes. This European legal consciousness cannot be, consequently, only "cognitive", but it has to lead to effective application of the European legal system, how complicated it may be.

The efficacy is the basic idea of European law. The efficacy in enforcing the European rights and freedoms has been the main concern of the European court since the beginning. The doctrines of direct applicability and effect, *effet utile*, primacy, etc. are the derivations of this principle. In fact, when the court requests the national courts to the cooperation within the European legal system it invites them to be European legal agents. The European legal consciousness is based on the understanding of oneself as a purpose-oriented European lawyer and a European legal agent giving efficiently force to the European rights in an equal way to all persons within the realm of the European jurisdiction. This is the European legal enterprise. This is what the "national" lawyers and especially the judges must take seriously, especially at times when the European rights and freedoms are under the "constitutional" attack. Justifications of all purpose-oriented value-statements must be made coherently from the point of view of the European legal system.

The legal-cultural concept, the European legal system, and the effectiveness of the order are related to the interactive qualities of the system. The maintenance of the legal traditions within different legal spheres must be associated with the effective application of law in a coherent and justificatory way. The considerations regarding an effective justification are particular from the traditional systematic point of view. Effectiveness is related also to the requirement for effective processes for the individual, who seeks his rights to be given applied.

The successes of the European legal system have been based on its dynamic qualities related to the justification and institutional interaction. This must be kept in mind also in the future. The "economic constitution" concentrating more on the activity than the pure status of the individual is part of the flexibility. All democratic and legislative actions must be constantly justified, re-considered and weighted according to the changes in the cultural environment. If understanding his role in the process of channeling the European aims and values in the current legal discussion and processes, the lawyer is a European lawyer. Only this type of legal ideological understanding creates the European legal system. The process is, in other words, cultural rather than legal integrative, also in the modern sense of the word. This has to do with the "spiritual" integration, established by the Court in *Costa*.

Literature

Aarnio, A. (1998): Why Coherence – A Philosophical Point of View. In: On Coherence Theory of Law (Lund; Aarnio, A., Alexy, R., Peczenik. A., Rabinowicz, W., Wolenski, J.).
Alexy, R. (1998): Coherence and argumentation or the Genuine Twin Criterialess Super Criterion. In: On Coherence Theory of Law (Lund) 1998 (Aarnio, A., Alexy, R., Peczenik. A., Rabinowicz, W., Wolenski, J.).
Häberle, P. (1998): Verfassungslehre als Kulturwissenschaft, Baden-Baden.
Kelsen, H. (1968): Puhdas oikeusoppi [Pure Theory of Law], Helsinki.
Kiikeri, M. (2002): Comparative legal reasoning and European law (Dortrecht).
Kiikeri, M. (2007): (Eurooppalainen välitön verotus Fide-kongressissa 2006) Takaisin ikuisuusongelmaan [(EC Direct taxation in Fide 2006) Back to the eternal problem]. In: Lakimies, 3/2007.
Koopmans, T. (1991): The Birth Of European Law At the Crossroads of Legal Traditions. In: The American Journal of Comparative Law, Vol. 39, No. 3 (Summer, 1991).
Lagrange, M. (1961): Le role de la Cour de justice des Communautés européennes tel qu'il se dégage de sa jurisprudence. In: revue Droit social, no 1, janvier 1961.
Lagrange, M. (1966): The Court of Justice as a Factor in European Integration. The American Journal of Comparative Law, Vol. 15, No. 4 (1966–1967) 15.
Lagrange, M. (1964): Speech delivered by Advocate General Maurice Lagrange at the formal sitting of the Court on 8 October 1964.
Lagrange, M. (1979): The Court of Justice of the European Communities from the Schuman Plan to the European Union. In: Mélanges Fernand Dehousse, 2: La construction européenne. Paris, Nathan, 1979.
Luhmann, N. (2006): System as Difference. In: Organization, London: Jan 2006. Vol. 13.
Monnet, J. (1997): Muistelmat, Helsinki.
Peczenik, A. (1998): A Coherence Theory of Juristic Knowledge. In: On Coherence Theory of Law (Lund; Aarnio, A., Alexy, R., Peczenik. A., Rabinowicz, W., Wolenski, J.).
Peczenik, A. (1998): Second Thoughts on Coherence and Juristic Knowledge. In: On Coherence Theory of Law (Lund; Aarnio, A., Alexy, R., Peczenik. A., Rabinowicz, W., Wolenski, J.).
Raz, J. (1992): The relevance of coherence. In: Boston University Law Review 72.
Ricoeur, Paul (2004): Memory, History, Forgetting, trans. K. Blamey and D. Pellauer (Chicago).
Rueff, J. (1948): L'Ordre social, Paris.
Teubner, G. (1998): Legal Irritants: Good Faith in British Law or How Unifying Law Ends Up in New Differences. In Modern Law Review, Vol. 61.
Tridimas, T. (1999): The General Principles of EC Law, Oxford.
Weiler, J.H.H. (1999): The constitution of Europe, 'Do the New Clothes Have an Emperor?', Cambridge.
Walker, N. (2005): The Elusive Novelty of EU Legal Theory. Oxford Journal of Legal Studies.
Wilhelmsson, T. (1997): Vieteriukkoteoria EY-oikeudesta [Jack-in-the-box-theory of EC law]. In: Oikeustiede Jurisprudentia XXX.

Authors

Prof. Dr. Anne van Aaken
St. Gallen, Switzerland. Max Schmidheiny Foundation Tenure-Track-Professor for Law and Economics, Public, International and European Law, University of St. Gallen Law School. For the academic year 2010/11 Fellow at the Institute for Advanced Study Berlin. Guisanstr. 36, CH-9010 St. Gallen, Tel: ++41-71-242 20 20, Fax: ++41-71-242 20 21, Email: anne.vanaaken@unisg.ch. Fields of interest: International Law and its theories, (Behavioral) Law and Economics, German and Comparative State Liability Law and International Investment Law, Political Corruption.

Jelena von Achenbach
Berlin, Germany. Researcher at the Chair for Public Law and Legal Philosophy, Humboldt University, Unter den Linden 6, D-10099 Berlin, jelena.von.achenbach@rewi.hu-berlin.de. Former Research Fellow at Max Planck Institute for Comparative Public Law and International Law. Fields of interest: Constitutional Law, especially of the European Union, Theory of Democracy.

Prof. Dr. Michael Anderheiden
Heidelberg, Germany. Universität Heidelberg, Juristisches Seminar, Friedrich-Ebert-Anlage 6–10, 69117 Heidelberg, Tel.: +49 (0) 6221/ 54 74 97, Fax: +49 (0) 6221/ 54 74 63, anderheidenm@jurs.uni-heidelberg.de, Fields of interest: Law and its relation to Social and Human Sciences, Methodology of Public Law, Philosophy of Law.

Dr. Vasiliki Christou
Athens, Greece. Law Faculty, Assistant for Public Law, 186 Thessalias Str., 13231 Petroupolis Athen, Tel. +302107264630, Fax +30 2107264510, vasilikichristou@yahoo.gr, fields of interest: Public Law (Constitutional and Human Rights Law), Administrative Law, Legal Philosophy, European Law, Environmental Law, Planning Law.

Dr. Péter Cserne
Tilburg, Netherlands/Budapest, Hungary. Assistant professor Tilburg Law School, senior research fellow Tilburg Law and Economics Center, assistant professor Pázmány Péter Catholic University Faculty of Law. PO Box 90153 5000 LE Tilburg, The Netherlands. Tel. +31.13.466.3645, Fax: +31.13.466.8047. peter.cserne@uvt.nl http://works.bepress.com/peter_cserne. Fields of interest: Legal Theory, Law and Economics, Contract Law and Theory, History of Political and Legal Thought.

Prof. Dr. Teresa Freixes
Barcelona, Spain. Professor of Constitutional Law Autonomous University of Barcelona, Jean Monnet Chair ad personam, President of the Fundació Universitària Martí l'Humà Senior Expert EU Fundamental Rights Agency, Director of the Joint European Master in Law and Policies of the European Integration. Universitat Autònoma de Barcelona. Facultat de Dret. Edifici B Departament de Ciència Política i Dret Públic, E 08193 Bellaterra; tfreixes@telefonica.net; Tel.: +34935812243; Fax: +34935812988. Fields of interest: European Constitutional Law, Comparative Constitutional Law, Multilevel Constitutionalism, Human Rights, Gender Equality.

Prof. Miodrag A. Jovanović, Ph.D., LL.M.
Belgrade, Serbia. Miodrag A. Jovanović is an associate Professor in the Introduction to Jurisprudence at the Faculty of Law, University of Belgrade (Bulevar Kralja Aleksandra 67, 11000, Belgrade, Serbia, e-mail: miodrag@ius.bg.ac.rs) Fields of interest: legal theory, political philosophy, philosophy of international law.

Dr. iur. Markku Kiikeri
Rovaniemi, Finland. Docent, senior lecturer, University of Lapland, Postal Address, P.O.Box 122, FI-96101 Rovaniemi, Finland, Tel. +358 40 4844010, Fax. +358 50 85148898, markku.kiikeri@ulapland.fi. Fields of interest: Legal philosophy (ontology of legal world), European law, Comparative law, Philosophy, Pedagogy.

Prof. Dr. Stephan Kirste
Budapest, Hungary/Heidelberg, Germany. Dean of the Faculty for Comparative Studies of State and Legal Sciences of the German Speaking Andrássy University Budapest. Adjunct Professor for Public Law and Legal Philosophy at the University of Heidelberg. H 1088 Budapest, Pollack Mihály tér 3. Tel. +36 1 266 3101-137; Fax +36 1 266 3099. kirste@jurs.uni-heidelberg.de. Fields of interest: History of Legal Thought, Legal Philosophy (Human Dignity, Paternalism in Law, Time and Law), European Administrative Law, Comparative Public Law.

Prof. Dr. Bart van Klink
Amsterdam, The Netherlands. Professor of Legal Methodology at the Department of Legal Theory and Legal History, Faculty of Law, VU University Amsterdam, De Boelelaan 1105, 1081 HV Amsterdam, The Netherlands. Tel.: +31 20 59 86327; Fax +31 20 59 86211; E-mail: b.van.klink@vu.nl. Fields of interest: Methodology of Law (Research Methods, Interdisciplinarity, Legal Interpretation), Legal and Political Philosophy (Positivism, Decisionism, Hermeneutics) and the Rule of Law.

Raffaele Lapenta, LL.M.
Naples, Italy. Master's Degree in Law; Post-Graduate Specialization in Legal Professions – both conferred by Federico II University of Naples. Tel. +393493546398. raffaele.lapenta@hotmail.it. Fields of interest: Comparative Public Law; European Administrative Law, International Law.

Dr. Oliver W. Lembcke
Leipzig/Jena, Germany. Senior researcher of political science at Jena University and Visiting Professor of Comparative Politics at Leipzig University. FSU Jena, Legal Faculty, Public Law and Legal Philosophy, 07737 Jena, phone +49 3641 942228, fax +49 3641 942222. mail@oliver-lembcke.de. Fields of interest: Political Theory; History of Political Ideas; Comparative Politics in Europe; Constitutionalism and Constitutional Courts.

Prof. Dr. iur. Klaus Mathis, MA in Economics
Lucerne, Switzerland. Professor of Public Law and Law of the Sustainable Economy. Frohburgstrasse 3, Postfach 4466, CH-6002 Luzern, Tel. + 41 (0)41 229 53 80, Fax + 41 (0)41 229 53 01, klaus.mathis@unilu.ch. Fields of interest: Public Law, Philosophy of Law, Economic Analysis of Law.

Prof. Juliana Neuenschwander-Magalhães, Ph.D., LL.M.
Rio de Janeiro, Brazil. Professor at Universidade Federal do Rio de Janeiro. Graduate at Law from Universidade Federal de Minas Gerais (1991), master's at Law from Universidade Federal de Santa Catarina (1994), ph.d. at Law from Universidade Federal de Minas Gerais (2000) and ph.d. at Sociology of Law from Università degli Studi di Lecce (2003). Universidade Federal do Rio de Janeiro, Rua Moncorvo Filho, 08, Centro, 20211-340 Rio de Janeiro, RJ-Brazil, jneue-wander@yahoo.com.br.

Prof. US Dr. hab. Pasquale Policastro
Szczecin, Poland. Professor of Constitutional Law and European Integration, Faculty of Law and Administration University of Szczecin; Institute of Administration and Public Security, State University of Applied Science, Gorzów Wielkopolski. PL 70-240 Szczecin, Al. Narutowicza 17A, tel. +48914441153, +48914442861 (tel&fax), pasquale@mec.univ.szczecin.pl. Fields of interest: Comparative Constitutional Law, European Constitutional Law, Theory of the Constitution, Philosophy of Law.

Dr. Mercè Sales
Barcelona, Spain. Lecturer of Constitucional Law, Autonomous University of Barcelona, Universitat Autònoma de Barcelona. Facultat de Dret. Edifici B Departament de Ciència Política i Dret Públic, E 08193 Bellaterra; tfreixes@telefonica.net; Tel.: +34935812243; Fax: +34935812988. Fields of interests: European Constitutional Law, Area of Freedom Security and Justice, Human Rights, Gender Equality.

Prof. Dr. Sanne Taekema
Rotterdam, The Netherlands. Professor of Jurisprudence at the Erasmus School of Law, Erasmus University Rotterdam, PO Box 1738, 3000 DR Rotterdam, The Netherlands. Tel. +31 10 408 1580; Fax +31 10 408 9191; E-mail: taekema@law.eur.nl. Fields of interest: Legal Philosophy (Pragmatism, Values in Law), Methodology of Law (Interdisciplinarity, Law and Humanities) and the Rule of Law.

ARCHIV FÜR RECHTS- UND SOZIALPHILOSOPHIE – BEIHEFTE

Herausgeben von der Internationalen Vereinigung für Rechts- und Sozialphilosophie (IVR). Die Bände 1–4 sind im Luchterhand-Fachverlag erschienen.

Franz Steiner Verlag ISSN 0341–079X

81. Kurt Seelmann (Hg.)
Wirtschaftsethik und Recht
Vorträge der Tagung der Schweizer Sektion der Internationalen Vereinigung für Rechts- und Sozialphilosophie im Oktober 2000 in Fribourg/Schweiz
2001. 123 S., kt.
ISBN 978-3-515-07899-3

82. Michel Troper / Annalisa Verza (Hg.)
Legal Philosophy: General Aspects
Concepts, Rights and Doctrines. Proceedings of the 19th World Congress of the International Association for Philosophy of Law and Social Philosophy in New York, 24th–30th June 1999
2002. 208 S., kt.
ISBN 978-3-515-08026-2

83. Gralf-Peter Calliess / Matthias Mahlmann (Hg.)
Der Staat der Zukunft
Vorträge der 9. Tagung des Jungen Forum Rechtsphilosophie in der Internationalen Vereinigung für Rechts- und Sozialphilosophie vom 27.–29. April 2001 an der Freien Universität Berlin
2002. 226 S., kt.
ISBN 978-3-515-08048-4

84. Winfried Brugger / Görg Haverkate (Hg.)
Grenzen als Thema der Rechts- und Sozialphilosophie
Referate der Tagung der Deutschen Sektion der Internationalen Vereinigung für Rechts- und Sozialphilosophie vom 22.–23. September 2000 in Heidelberg
2002. 218 S., kt.
ISBN 978-3-515-08042-2

85. Paricia Smith / Paolo Comanducci (Hg.)
Legal Philosophy: General Aspects
Theoretical Examinations and Practical Application. Proceedings of the 19th World Congress of the International Association for Philosophy of Law and Social Philosophy in New York, 24th–30th June 1999
2002. 176 S., kt.
ISBN 978-3-515-08100-9

86. Hirokazu Kawaguchi / Kurt Seelmann (Hg.)
Rechtliche und ethische Fragen der Transplantationstechnologie in einem interkulturellen Vergleich
2003. 180 S., kt.
ISBN 978-3-515-08132-0

87. Rolf Gröschner / Gerhard Haney (Hg.)
Die Bedeutung P. J. A. Feuerbachs (1755–1833) für die Gegenwart
Tagung der Deutschen Sektion der Internationalen Vereinigung für Rechts- und Sozialphilosophie vom 15.–16. März 2002 in Jena
2003. 240 S., kt.
ISBN 978-3-515-08193-1

88. Arend Soeteman (Hg.)
Pluralism and Law I
Justice. Proceedings of the 20th World Congress of the International Association for Philosophy of Law and Social Philosophy in Amsterdam, 2001
2003. 203 S., kt.
ISBN 978-3-515-08327-0

89. Arend Soeteman (Hg.)
Pluralism and Law II
State, Nation, Community, Civil Society. Proceedings of the 20th World Congress of the International Association for Philosophy of Law and Social Philosophy in Amsterdam, 2001
2003. 193 S., kt.
ISBN 978-3-515-08362-1

90. Arend Soeteman (Hg.)
Pluralism and Law III
Global Problems. Proceedings of the 20th World Congress of the International Association for Philosophy of Law and Social Philosophy in Amsterdam, 2001
2004. 217 S., kt.
ISBN 978-3-515-08446-8

91. Arend Soeteman (Hg.)
Pluralism and Law IV
Legal Reasoning. Proceedings of the 20th World Congress of the International Association for Philosophy of Law and Social Philosophy in Amsterdam, 2001

2004. 195 S., kt.
ISBN 978-3-515-08503-8

92. Christian Hiebaum / Peter Koller (Hg.)
Politische Ziele und juristische Argumentation
Symposium der Internationalen Vereinigung für Rechts- und Sozialphilosophie vom 11.–12. Oktober 2002 in Graz
2003. 142 S., kt.
ISBN 978-3-515-08284-6

93. Jan C. Joerden / Roland Wittmann (Hg.)
Recht und Politik
Jahrestagung der Deutschen Sektion der Internationalen Vereinigung für Rechts- und Sozialphilosophie vom 26.–29. September 2002 in Frankfurt an der Oder
2004. 184 S., kt.
ISBN 978-3-515-08458-1

94. Philippe Mastronardi (Hg.)
Das Recht im Spannungsfeld utilitaristischer und deontologischer Ehtik
Vorträge der Tagung der Schweizer Sektion der Internationalen Vereinigung für Rechts- und Sozialphilosophie vom 15.–16. November 2002 in Luzern
2004. 170 S., kt.
ISBN 978-3-515-08366-9

95. Aleksander Peczenik (Hg.)
Justice
Proceedings of the 21st World Congress of the International Association for Philosophy of Law and Social Philosophy in Lund (Sweden), 12th–18th August 2003
Volume 1
2004. 218 S., kt.
ISBN 978-3-515-08483-3

96. Yasutomo Morigiwa / Fumihiko Ishiyama / Tetsu Sakurai (Hg.)
Universal Minority Rights?
A Transnatioal Approach. Proceedings of the 5th Kobe Lectures. Tokyo and Kyoto, December 1998
2004. 126 S., kt.
ISBN 978-3-515-08504-5

97. Svein Eng (Hg.)
Law and Practice
Proceedings of the 21st World Congress of the International Association for Philosophy of Law and Social Philosophy in Lund (Sweden), 12th–18th August 2003
Volume 2
2005. 213 S., kt.
ISBN 978-3-515-08524-3

98. Kenneth Einar Himma (Hg.)
Law, Morality, and Legal Positivism
Proceedings of the 21st World Congress of the International Association for Philosophy of Law and Social Philosophy in Lund (Sweden), 12th–18th August 2003
Volume 3
2004. 183 S., kt.
ISBN 978-3-515-08513-7

99. Günther Kreuzbauer / Silvia Augeneder (Hg.)
Der Juristische Streit
Recht zwischen Rhetorik, Argumentation und Dogmatik
2004. 166 S., kt.
ISBN 978-3-515-08480-2

100. Ulfrid Neumann / Winfried Hassemer / Ulrich Schroth (Hg.)
Verantwortetes Recht
Die Rechtsphilosophie Arthur Kaufmanns. Tagung vom 10.–11. Mai 2003 in München
2005. 188 S., kt.
ISBN 978-3-515-08580-9

101. Kurt Seelmann (Hg.)
Menschenwürde als Rechtsbegriff
Tagung der Schweizer Sektion der Internationalen Vereinigung für Rechts- und Sozialphilosophie vom 25.–28. Juni 2003 in Basel
2004. 175 S., kt.
ISBN 978-3-515-08591-5

102. Zenon Bankowski (Hg.)
Epistemology and Ontology
Proceedings of the 21st World Congress of the International Association for Philosophy of Law and Social Philosophy in Lund (Sweden), 12th–18th August 2003
Volume 4
2005. 195 S., kt.
ISBN 978-3-515-08707-0

103. Carsten Bäcker / Stefan Baufeld (Hg.)
Objektivität und Flexibilität im Recht
Tagungen des Jungen Forums Rechtsphilosophie in der Internationalen Vereinigung für Rechts- und Sozialphilosophie im September 2004 in Kiel und im April 2005 in Hagen
2005. 213 S., kt.
ISBN 978-3-515-08743-8

104. Robert Alexy (Hg.)
Juristische Grundlagenforschung
Tagung der Deutschen Sektion der Internationalen Vereinigung für Rechts- und Sozialphilosophie vom 23.–25. September 2004 in Kiel

2005. 251 S., kt.
ISBN 978-3-515-08640-0

105. Philippe Mastronardi / Denis Taubert (Hg.)
Staats- und Verfassungstheorie im Spannungsfeld der Disziplinen
Tagung der Schweizerischen Vereinigung für Rechts- und Sozialphilosophie vom 12.–13. November 2004 an der Universität St. Gallen
2006. 255 S., kt.
ISBN 978-3-515-08851-0

106. José Juan Moreso (Hg.)
Legal Theory / Teoría del derecho
Legal Positivism and Conceptual Analysis / Positivismo juridico y análisis conceptual. Proceedings of the 22nd World Congress of the International Association for Philosophy of Law and Social Philosophy in Granada, 2005
Volume 1
2007. 263 S., kt.
ISBN 978-3-515-08910-4

107. José Rubio Carrecedo (Hg.)
Political Philosophy / Filosofía política
New Proposals for New Questions / Nuevas propuestas para nuevas cuestiones. Proceedings of the 22nd World Congress of the International Association for Philosophy of Law and Social Philosophy in Granada, 2005
Volume 2
2007. 239 S., kt.
ISBN 978-3-515-08911-1

108. Andrés Ollero (Hg.)
Human Rights and Ethics / Derechos humanos y Ética
Proceedings of the 22nd World Congress of the International Association for Philosophy of Law and Social Philosophy in Granada, 2005
Volume 3
2007. 323 S., kt.
ISBN 978-3-515-08912-8

109. Nicolás López Calera (Hg.)
Globalization, Law and Economy / Globalización, Derecho y Economía
Proceedings of the 22nd World Congress of the International Association for Philosophy of Law and Social Philosophy in Granada, 2005
Volume 4
2007. 321 S., kt
ISBN 978-3-515-08913-5

110. Josep Aguiló-Regla (Hg.)
Logic, Argumentation and Interpretation / Lógica, Argumentación e Interpretación
Proceedings of the 22nd World Congress of the International Association for Philosophy of Law and Social Philosophy in Granada, 2005
Volume 5
2007. 206 S., kt.
ISBN 978-3-515-08914-2

111. Marcel Senn / Dániel Puskás (Hg.)
Gehirnforschung und rechtliche Verantwortung
Fachtagung der Scheizerischen Vereinigung für Rechts- und Sozialphilosophie vom 19.–20. Mai 2006 an der Universität Bern
2006. 171 S., kt.
ISBN 978-3-515-08963-0

112. Annette Brockmöller (Hg.)
Hundert Jahre Archiv für Rechts- und Sozialphilosophie (1907–2007)
Auswahl 14 bedeutender Aufsätze von Kelsen, Radbruch, Luhmann u. a.
2007. 330 S., kt.
ISBN 978-3-515-09100-8

113. Horst Dreier / Eric Hilgendorf (Hg.)
Kulturelle Identität als Grund und Grenze des Rechts
Akten der Tagung der Internationalen Vereinigung für Rechts- und Sozialphilosophie vom 28.–30. September 2006 in Würzburg
2008. 374 S., geb.
ISBN 978-3-515-09101-5

114. Jochen Bung / Brian Valerius / Sascha Ziemann (Hg.)
Normativität und Rechtskritik
Tagungen des Jungen Forums Rechtsphilosophie in der Internationalen Vereinigung für Rechts- und Sozialphilosophie im September 2006 in Würzburg und im März 2007 in Frankfurt am Main
2007. 269 S., kt.
ISBN 978-3-515-09130-5

115. Marcel Senn / Dániel Puskás (Hg.)
Rechtswissenschaft als Kulturwissenschaft?
Kongress der Schweizerischen Vereinigung für Rechts- und Sozialphilosophie vom 15.–16. Juni 2007 an der Universität Zürich
2007. 220 S., kt.
ISBN 978-3-515-09149-7

116. Annette Brockmöller / Eric Hilgendorf (Hg.)
Rechtsphilosophie im 20. Jahrhundert

100 Jahre Archiv für Rechts- und Sozialphilosophie
2009. 207 S., kt.
ISBN 978-3-515-09285-2

117. Marcel Senn / Barbara Fritschi (Hg.)
Rechtswissenschaft und Hermeneutik
Kongress der Schweizerischen Vereinigung für Rechts- und Sozialphilosophie vom 16.–17. Mai 2008 an der Universität Zürich
2009. 258 S., kt.
ISBN 978-3-515-09155-8

118. Bart C. Labuschagne / Ari M. Solon (Hg.)
Religion and State
From separation to cooperation? Proceedings of the Special Workshop "Legal-philosophical reflections for a de-secularized world" held at the 23rd World Congress of the International Association for Philosophy of Law and Social Philosophy in Kraków, 2007
2009. 209 S., kt.
ISBN 978-3-515-09368-2

119. Martin Borowski (Hg.)
On the Nature of Legal Principles
Proceedings of the Special Workshop "The Principles Theory" held at the 23rd World Congress of the International Association for Philosophy of Law and Social Philosophy in Kraków, 2007
2010. 182 S., kt.
ISBN 978-3-515-09608-9

120. Friedrich Toepel (Hg.)
Free Will in Criminal Law and Procedure
Proceedings of the 23rd and 24th World Congress of the International Association for Philosophy of Law and Social Philosophy in Kraków, 2007, and in Beijing, 2009
2010. 122 S., kt.
ISBN 978-3-515-09320-0

121. Marcel Senn / Bénédict Winiger / Barbara Fritschi / Philippe Avramov (Hg.)
Recht und Globalisierung / Droit et Mondialisation
Kongress der Schweizerischen Vereinigung für Rechts- und Sozialphilosophie, 15.–16. Mai 2009, Universität Genf / Congrès de l'Association Suisse de Philosophie du Droit et de Philosophie Sociale, 15–16 mai 2009, Université de Genève
2010. 196 S., kt.
ISBN 978-3-515-09673-7

122. Imer B. Flores / Uygur Gülriz (Hg.)
Alternative Methods in the Education of Philosophy of Law and the Importance of Legal Philosophy in the Legal Education
Proceedings of the 23rd World Congress of the International Associaction for Philosophy of Law and Social Philosophy "Law and Legal Cultures in the 21st Century: Diversity and Unity" in Kraków, 2007
2010. 114 S., kt.
ISBN 978-3-515-09695-9

123. Sascha Ziemann
Archiv für Rechts- und Sozialphilosophie: Bibliographie und Dokumentation (1907–2009)
2010. 434 S., kt.
ISBN 978-3-515-09719-2

124. Jan-Reinard Sieckmann (Hg.)
Legal Reasoning: The Methods of Balancing
Proceedings of the Special Workshop "Legal Reasoning: The Methods of Balancing" held at the 24th World Congress of the International Association for Philosophy of Law and Social Philosophy (IVR), Beijing, 2009
2010. 205 S., kt.
ISBN 978-3-515-09723-9

125. Edward Schramm / Wibke Frey / Lorenz Kähler / Sabine Müller-Mall / Friederike Wapler (Hg.)
Konflikte im Recht – Recht der Konflikte
Tagungen des Jungen Forums Rechtsphilosophie in der Internationalen Vereinigung für Rechts- und Sozialphilosophie in Tübingen und Göttingen
2010. 308 S., kt.
ISBN 978-3-515-09729-1

126. Kristian Kühl (Hg.)
Zur Kompetenz der Rechtsphilosophie in Rechtsfragen
Tagung der Deutschen Sektion der Internationalen Vereinigung für Rechts- und Sozialphilosophie vom 24.–26. September 2008 in Tübingen
2011. 140 S., kt.
ISBN 978-3-515-09816-8

127. Stephan Kirste / Anne van Aaken / Michael Anderheiden / Pasquale Policastro (Hg.)
Interdisciplinary Research in Jurisprudence and Constitutionalism
2012. 267 S. mit 2 Abb. und 2 Tab., kt.
ISBN 978-3-515-09941-7